CW00541298

A Genealogy of Tropical Architecture

A Genealogy of Tropical Architecture traces the origins of tropical architecture to nineteenth-century British colonial architectural knowledge and practices. It uncovers how systematic knowledge and practices on building and environmental technologies in the tropics were linked to military technologies, medical theories and sanitary practices, and were manifested in colonial building types such as military barracks, hospitals and housing. It also explores the various ways in which these colonial knowledge and practices shaped postwar technoscientific research and education in climatic design and modern tropical architecture.

Drawing on the interdisciplinary scholarships on postcolonial studies, science studies and environmental history, Jiat-Hwee Chang argues that tropical architecture was inextricably entangled with the socio-cultural constructions of tropical nature, and the politics of colonial governance and post-colonial development in the British colonial and post-colonial networks.

By bringing to light new historical materials through formidable research and tracing the history of tropical architecture beyond what is widely considered today as its "founding moment" in the mid-twentieth century, this important and original book revises our understanding of the colonial built environment. It also provides a new historical framework that significantly bears upon contemporary concerns with climatic design and sustainable architecture.

This book is an essential resource for understanding tropical architecture and its various contemporary manifestations. Its in-depth discussion and path-breaking insights will be invaluable to specialists, academics, students and practitioners.

Jiat-Hwee Chang is Assistant Professor in the Department of Architecture, School of Design and Environment, National University of Singapore.

THE ARCHI*TEXT* SERIES

Edited by Thomas A. Markus and Anthony D. King

Architectural discourse has traditionally represented buildings as art objects or technical objects. Yet buildings are also social objects in that they are invested with social meaning and shape social relations. Recognizing these assumptions, the Architext series aims to bring together recent debates in social and cultural theory and the study and practice of architecture and urban design. Critical, comparative and interdisciplinary, the books in the series, by theorizing architecture, bring the space of the built environment centrally into the social sciences and humanities, as well as bringing the theoretical insights of the latter into the discourses of architecture and urban design. Particular attention is paid to issues of gender, race, sexuality and the body, to questions of identity and place, to the cultural politics of representation and language, and to the global and postcolonial contexts in which these are addressed.

Framing Places
Kim Dovey

Gender Space Architecture
by Jane Rendell, Barbara Penner & Iain Borden

Behind the Postcolonial
Abidin Kusno

The Architecture of Oppression
Paul Jaskot

Words Between the Spaces
Thomas A. Markus and Deborah Cameron

Embodied Utopias
Gender, social change and the modern metropolis
Rebeccah Zorach, Lise Sanders, Amy Bingaman

Writing Spaces
Discourses of architecture, urbanism, and the built environment
C. Greig Crysler

Drifting – Migrancy and Architecture
Edited by Stephen Cairns

Beyond Description
Space Historicity Singapore
Edited by Ryan Bishop, John Phillips & Wei-Wei Yeo

Spaces of Global Cultures
Architecture Urbanism Identity
Anthony D. King

Indigenous Modernities
Negotiating architecture and urbanism
Jyoti Hosagrahar

Moderns Abroad
Architecture, cities and Italian imperialism
Mia Fuller

Colonial Modernities
Building, dwelling and architecture in British India and Ceylon
Edited by Peter Scriver & Vikram Prakash

Desire Lines
Space, memory and identity in the post-apartheid City
Edited by Noëleen Murray, Nick Shepherd & Martin Hall

Visualizing the City
Edited by Alan Marcus & Dietrich Neumann

Framing Places 2nd edition
Kim Dovey

Re-Shaping Cities
How Global Mobility Transforms Architecture and Urban Form
Edited by Michael Guggenheim & Ola Söderström

Bauhaus Dream-house
Modernity and Globalization
Katerina Rüedi-Ray

Stadium Worlds
Football, Space and the Built Environment
Edited by Sybille Frank & Silke Steets

Building the State
Architecture, Politics, and State Formation in Postwar Central Europe
Virag Molner

City Halls and Civic Materialism
Towards a Global History of Urban Public Space
Edited by Swati Chattopadhyay & Jeremy White

Ethno-Architecture and the Politics of Migration
Edited by Mirjana Lozanovska

Writing the Global City
Anthony D. King

"In this masterly account of the evolution of tropical architecture, Jiat-Hwee Chang combines the insights of Foucauldian governmentality with in-depth historical research and a keen understanding of colonial exceptionality. Focussing on four building types – the home, the barracks, the hospital and 'native' housing – he uncovers the colonial lineage of modern architectural forms and offers a radical reinterpretation of the ancestry of architectural tropicality. While centring on Singapore, Chang's theoretically informed and richly empirical study opens up a wider critical perspective on architectural history across the entire region of South and Southeast Asia."

David Arnold, Professor Emeritus, University of Warwick, UK,
author of *Colonizing the Body* and *The Problem of Nature*

"Meticulous and rigorous, Jiat-Hwee Chang brings us the first major study convincingly to span Victorian and modern colonial architecture. From colonial bungalows, through barracks, hospitals, public housing, court buildings and shophouses, covering technoscientific research and architectural education, and drawing from rich visual and scientific material, the book provocatively re-draws our understanding of tropical architecture. This is a true 'genealogy', a history of an idea as much as an account of its technologies and architectural manifestations."

Mark Crinson, Professor of Architectural History,
Birkbeck College (London), UK,
author of *Modern Architecture and the End of Empire*

"Jiat-Hwee Chang gives us a masterful history of 'tropical architecture' way before that term was invented. He shows us how this architecture is entangled with social constructions of nature, the politics of colonialism, and the development of post-colonial discourses. It is a substantive and fascinating account that will be of significance to the architecture practitioners and academics in the region and beyond."

Nezar AlSayyad, Professor of Architecture, Planning,
Urban Design, and Urban History,
University of California, Berkeley, USA

"In this important and timely book, Jiat-Hwee Chang argues that tropical architecture – often understood as a localized response to climatic conditions in the global south – was conceived and produced through (post)colonial networks of knowledge and power. Drawing upon the case of Singapore, Chang's meticulous and carefully theorized account reveals how the tropical and its architectural variants are at once a mode of governing, a framework for biopolitics, and a historical struggle over technoscience."

C. Greig Crysler, Associate Professor of Architecture and
Arcus Chair for Gender, Sexuality and the Built Environment,
College of Environmental Design, University of California, Berkeley, USA

Jiat-Hwee Chang

A Genealogy of Tropical Architecture

Colonial networks, nature and technoscience

Routledge
Taylor & Francis Group
LONDON AND NEW YORK

First published 2016
by Routledge
2 Park Square, Milton Park, Abingdon, Oxon OX14 4RN

and by Routledge
711 Third Avenue, New York, NY 10017

Routledge is an imprint of the Taylor & Francis Group, an informa business

British Library Cataloguing-in-Publication Data
A catalogue record for this book is available from the British Library

Library of Congress Cataloging-in-Publication Data
Names: Chang, Jiat-Hwee, author.
Title: A genealogy of tropical architecture : colonial networks, nature and technoscience / By Jiat-Hwee Chang.
Description: New York : Routledge, 2016. | Series: The architext series | Includes bibliographical references and index.
Identifiers: LCCN 2015044456| ISBN 9780415840774 (hb : alk. paper) | ISBN 9780415840781 (pb : alk. paper) | ISBN 9781315712680 (ebook)
Subjects: LCSH: Architecture, Tropical--British influences. | Architecture, British colonial. | Architecture and society--Tropics. | Architecture and society--Singapore.
Classification: LCC NA2542.T7 C48 2016 | DDC 720.1/03--dc23
LC record available at http://lccn.loc.gov/2015044456

ISBN: 978-0-415-84077-4 (hbk)
ISBN: 978-0-415-84078-1 (pbk)
ISBN: 978-1-315-71268-0 (ebk)

Typeset in Frutiger
by Saxon Graphics Ltd, Derby

MIX
Paper from responsible sources
FSC® C013056

Printed and bound in Great Britain by
TJ International Ltd, Padstow, Cornwall

To Pei Ling

Contents

Figures

Preface

Since I was an architecture student at the Department of Architecture, National University of Singapore (NUS), in the early 1990s, I have encountered various discourses and practices of tropical architecture. It began as early as my first-year field trip to Bali, to learn from "Balinese" tropical resorts.[1] The trip was designed by my studio tutor to allow us to immerse ourselves in the delightful sensory environment of the resorts and experience "tropical living." At that time, tropical living was understood as living at the interface between indoor spaces and outdoor landscape, enjoying the thermal delight of shade and breezes amidst the heat and humidity. Implicit in the celebration of the open-to-nature, thermally varying, multi-sensorial environment of "tropical living" in the "Balinese" tropical resorts was its imagined opposite – the hermetically sealed, thermally constant and purportedly impoverished sensorial environment of the air-conditioned spaces ubiquitous in the "air-conditioned nation" of Singapore which we, the students, inhabited.[2] The intended escape from the air-conditioned spaces was, however, only partial. As poor students who could not afford to stay at the exclusive tropical resorts, we stayed in the air-conditioned rooms of a budget hotel instead and visited the different resorts during the day. Upon returning from the trip, we were tasked to design a tropical house as our final project, drawing inspirations from our brief experience of "tropical living," in our over-cooled air-conditioned design studio. Our studio group's field trip and design brief were not atypical. Other first-year students in the Department were likewise involved in similar initiation rites of "tropicalization."[3]

Later in my education, my course mates and I were exposed to other types of discourses and practices on tropical architecture. These included a body of works by local architects Tay Kheng Soon and Ken Yeang that engaged with larger issues of urban environmental sustainability in the rapidly developing tropical cities in Asia. Extending the climatic design approach of modern tropical architecture from the mid-twentieth century, they proposed tropical skyscrapers and high-density urban forms that were covered with vertical greenery, well-shaded and, sometimes, naturally ventilated.[4] At the same time, we also became aware of another body of works that sought to engage with environmental sustainability by drawing from the region's vernacular architectural traditions. Instead of deploying the latest technologies and constructing large-scale buildings, this body of works, as exemplified by the architecture of Malaysian architect Jimmy C. S. Lim, utilized simple traditional techniques in construction and environmental control, and involved primarily small-scale residential projects. I later found out that these two bodies of works were not just environmental discourses but also cultural discourses inextricably intertwined with the identity politics of the post-colonial globalized world. Concerned with how tropical architecture could be used to assert "local" and "regional" differences and thus, identities, these works emerged in the mid-1980s through the Aga Khan Award for Architecture (AKAA), the regional seminars it organized and *Mimar*, the periodical it published.[5]

Tropical architecture was, however, not just produced by architects in private practice and engaged with the project of architectural regionalism. It even entered official discourse when the state planning agency of Singapore, Urban Redevelopment Authority, called its vision of the 1991 Concept Plan, "towards a tropical city of excellence."[6] By the mid-1990s, the various discourses and the attendant works of tropical architecture were all grouped under the label of "Asian Tropical Style" or one of its interchangeable variants, and celebrated in pictorial books and lifestyle magazines. "Asian Tropical Style" was a vague label used in a loose manner. It referred to not just different types of contemporary architecture in the region, it was also used in connection to diverse architecture from Southeast Asia's past, such as vernacular architecture, colonial architecture, and post-independence modernist architecture. Due to the popularity of the pictorial books and lifestyle magazines featuring "Asian Tropical Style," the stylistic label became a stand-in for tropical architecture. By the time I graduated in the late 1990s, tropical architecture had become this taken-for-granted and seldom interrogated entity nebulously associated with an array of keywords like climate, culture and sustainability. When probed further, these associations appeared to be contradictory. For example, tropical architecture was said to be responsive to the climate but it was frequently air-conditioned, tropical houses were supposedly closely connected to the culture of a place but tended to be inhabited by highly mobile and wealthy expatriates, and tropical designs were purportedly about the sustainable use of limited natural resources but they were often about luxurious houses characterized by energy and resource profligacy.

When I joined academia in 2001, I was fascinated but also concerned by both the proliferation of the discourses of tropical architecture and the various underlying contradictions, and I began to research it seriously. As an architectural historian, I believed, and still believe, that the present carries sedimented meanings of the past and I decided to research the longer history and deeper structure of tropical architecture. By longer history, I am referring to the history before the phrase "tropical architecture" was first institutionalized and named as such in the mid-twentieth century. By deeper structure, I am referring to the socio-cultural assumptions and sociotechnical foundations behind the nomenclature of tropical architecture that privileges nature as the prime determinant of architectural form. This book is the outcome of that research. As will become clear in the following pages, this longer history and deeper structure, which I call genealogy, is primarily a narrative of how the knowledges and practices, and their underlying epistemological foundations, of tropical architecture were constructed in the British colonial and post-colonial eras. My interest is in how the different British colonial institutions and actors systematically constructed these knowledges and practices that buttressed the production of buildings in the tropics. In other words, this is a historical project about *the building of building*, as understood along the line of "the conduct of conduct" for Foucauldian governmentality (see Introduction). To write this account, I carried out research at the archives of metropolitan and local institutions, using predominantly colonial records. Such records obviously present certain limits and two caveats are perhaps necessary at this point to explain what is included and excluded in this account, and why.

While this is primarily a colonial history, it is emphatically not a Eurocentric account. Although I have included quite a wide array of different actors, readers will notice that there are very few local/indigenous actors and their voices in this account.[7] I have written quite extensively about local actors related to the built environment in various colonial and post-colonial contexts elsewhere but I have not included many of them in this account for a few reasons.[8] My account focuses on the nineteenth century to the mid-twentieth century, a period where there were very few local architects in Singapore and the other British colonies in the tropics that I study. Although there were many local builders involved, their voices were typically not recorded in the archival materials that I consulted. I went to great lengths to locate historical materials, including those in vernacular languages, on the local contractors in colonial Singapore but could only uncover very few relevant materials. My interests in these local builders are, however, unlike those of scholars like Brenda Yeoh and James Francis Warren, who wrote histories from below and sought to give agency to the colonized population.[9] While I agree that it is important to account for how the colonized population resisted and contested the dominant colonial power structure, this book is primarily about understanding the hegemonic colonial structure and its underlying epistemological foundation, because these have not been historicized in the context of tropical architecture. Therefore, my interest in the local builders is more about how they were accounted for and addressed in colonial knowledges and practices of tropical architecture. I am aware of the dangers of overemphasizing colonial successes and overstating colonial power. I consciously read between the lines and look at the cracks of the colonial edifice, attending to scandals and failures of the colonial institutions and actors, and contingencies and uncertainties of colonial knowledges and practices.

Any history of tropical architecture would necessarily be a global, or at least extra-local, history in that it would involve actors, knowledges and practices from many sites. This book is no different, but it approaches the global history of tropical architecture from a particular site, Singapore, and traces the British colonial and post-colonial networks, and the circulations of people, ideas and practices from it.

Such an approach obviously has its omissions. For example, in focusing on the British colonial networks, the important histories and significant contributions to tropical architecture of other European and American colonial powers are not included. Likewise, this book is also silent on the influences of institutions and actors from the socialist countries, Scandinavia and Israel in shaping tropical architecture in the so-called Third World during the Cold War through international aid or technical assistance programs. Even within the British Empire, this book focuses on networks and connections that passed through Singapore, and, in the view of some, might not be sufficiently attentive to other British colonial territories like those in the West Indies, India and Africa. For readers interested in the above omitted topics, I would urge them to refer to a small but growing body of scholarship on them as they are beyond the scope of this book.[10] In scripting a global history of tropical architecture in this book, I have chosen a situated but limited point of view rather than multiple floating but all-encompassing viewpoints.

NOTES

1 The Balinese tropical resort has in recent years proliferated beyond the geographical confines of Bali and Southeast Asia to places like Mauritius. See Dejan Sudjic, "Is That Room Service? Where Am I?," *Observer*, 20 August 2000. For a history of Balinese resort "tropical architecture," see Philip Goad, *Architecture Bali: Architectures of Welcome* (Sydney: Pesaro Publishing, 2000).

2 Cherian George, *Singapore, the Air-Conditioned Nation: Essays on the Politics of Comfort and Control, 1990-2000* (Singapore: Landmark Books, 2000).

3 For architectural education as a series of rites, see Dana Cuff, *Architecture: The Story of Practice* (Cambridge, MA: MIT Press, 1991).

4 Robert Powell and Kheng Soon Tay, *Line, Edge and Shade: The Search for a Design Language in Tropical Asia* (Singapore: Page One Pub., 1997); Robert Powell, *Ken Yeang: Rethinking the Environmental Filter* (Singapore: Landmark Books, 1989).

5 Robert Powell, ed., *Regionalism in Architecture: Proceedings of the Regional Seminar in the Series Exploring Architecture in Islamic Cultures* (Singapore: Concept Media, 1985); Robert Powell, ed., *Architecture and Identity: Proceedings of the Regional Seminar in the Series Exploring Architecture in Islamic Cultures* (Singapore: Concept Media, 1983). For the organization and activities of AKAA, see its official website: http://www.akdn.org/akaa. For a critical discussion of AKAA, see Sibel Bozdoğan, "The Aga Khan Award for Architecture: A Philosophy of Reconciliation," *JAE* 45, no. 3 (1992). I have written about AKAA and tropical architecture elsewhere, see Jiat-Hwee Chang, ""Natural" Traditions: Constructing Tropical Architecture in Transnational Malaysia and Singapore," *Explorations* 7, no. 1 (2007).

6 URA, *Living the Next Lap: Towards a Tropical City of Excellence* (Singapore: URA, 1991).

7 My use of "indigenous" population in this book includes the migrant population. As J. S. Furnivall noted in his classic study, many colonial societies were also plural societies in that migrant communities like the Indian and Chinese mixed and intermingled with the Europeans and the "natives" in the colonial marketplace. Colonial Singapore, the focus of this book, was a typical plural society in that it was a multiethnic colonial city with a majority of Chinese and Indian migrants. As many of these migrants stayed in Singapore for a long period, they have been indigenized to various degrees. Therefore, I include them as part of the "indigenous" population even though the indigenous population in Singapore refers specifically to the Malays. In this book, I use "indigenous

population" interchangeably with "local population." Essentially, the indigenous population here refers to the non-European population in a colonial society. I use it as a substitute for the pejorative expression "natives." See J. S. Furnivall, *Colonial Policy and Practice* (New York: New York University Press, 1956).

8 For my writings on local actors, see for example, William S. W. Lim and Jiat-Hwee Chang, eds., *Non West Modernist Past: On Architecture and Modernities* (Singapore: World Scientific, 2011); Jiat-Hwee Chang, "Deviating Discourse: Tay Kheng Soon and the Architecture of Postcolonial Development in Tropical Asia," *JAE* 63, no. 3 (2010); Jiat-Hwee Chang,"An Other Modern Architecture: Postcolonial Spectacles, Cambodian Nationalism and Khmer Traditions," *Singapore Architect* 250 (2009).

9 Brenda S. A. Yeoh, *Contesting Space: Power Relations and the Urban Built Environment in Colonial Singapore* (Kuala Lumpur: Oxford University Press, 1996); James Francis Warren, *Rickshaw Coolie: A People's History of Singapore, 1880-1940* (Singapore: Oxford University Press, 1986).

10 See Mia Fuller, *Moderns Abroad: Architecture, Cities, and Italian Imperialism* (London: Routledge, 2010); Mark Crinson, *Modern Architecture and the End of Empire* (Aldershot: Ashgate, 2003); Łukasz Stanek, "Introduction: The 'Second World's' Architecture and Planning in the 'Third World'," *JoA* 17, no. 3 (2012); Johan Lagae and Kim De Raedt, "Editorial," *ABE* 4 (2013); Setiadi Sopandi and Avianti Armand, *Tropicality Revisited* (Frankfurt: The German Architecture Museum, 2015); Duanfang Lu, "Introduction: Architecture, Modernity and Identity in the Third World," in Duanfang Lu, ed., *Third World Modernism: Architecture, Development and Identity* (London: Routledge, 2010).

Acknowledgements

My journey in writing this book is a long one and I have left an equally long trail of debts. I wrote my first conference paper on this topic in 2002 and later it was formalized as my doctoral research topic at UC Berkeley. The book is based on my doctoral dissertation and it would not have been written without the careful guidance, encouragement and trust of my dissertation advisors Nezar AlSayyad, C. Greig Crysler and Aihwa Ong. At Berkeley, I also benefited from the knowledge and insights of other Professors, particularly my examination committee members, Cris Benton and Nathan Sayre.

Special gratitude also goes to Tony King, whose path-breaking work on "tropical architecture" opens up an important avenue of inquiry for me to follow. Tony encouraged my research, and generously shared with me his book proposal and related historical materials on "tropical architecture." He later suggested that I submit my manuscript to the Architext series and expertly guided it through the review and publication process. I am also grateful to Tom Markus, the other editor of the series, for his review of my book proposal and manuscript, and his detailed comments.

Tim Winter, Lee Kah Wee and Anooradha Siddique read the whole manuscript. As usual, Tim gave me incisive comments and helpful suggestions for revising the manuscript. Kah Wee and Anoo held me to very high standards and asked me great probing questions that helped me refine my arguments. Chris Cowell, Imran bin Tajudeen, Rachel Lee and Patrick Wakely read drafts of specific chapters and gave me valuable feedbacks. Cecilia Chu and Lynne Horiuchi read drafts of my dissertation chapters and gave me encouraging comments when I was struggling to complete my dissertation. I hope they all see evidence of their contributions in the book. Of course any failings that remain are entirely mine.

Research related to this book has been presented at various conferences and lectures internationally, and published in different journals and edited volumes. I sincerely thank the following individuals for their invitations, helpful comments and encouragements: Daniel Barber, Tim Bunnell, Stephen Cairns, Tiago Castela, Lilian Chee, Mark Crinson, Michael Guggenheim, Simon Guy, Hilde Heynen,

Jessica Holland, Iain Jackson, Nirmal Kishnani, Izumi Kuroishi, Abidin Kusno, Johan Lagae, Hannah Le Roux, William Lim, Duanfang Lu, Pyla Panayiota, Robert Peckham, Anoma Pieris, David Promfret, Paulo Providência, Peter Scriver, Ola Söderström, Łukasz Stanek, Mark Swenarton, and Ola Uduku.

In Singapore, and particularly at the Department of Architecture, National University of Singapore, where I have been based since 2001, I have learned much from my teachers, colleagues and friends there, particularly Tan Hock Beng, Tay Kheng Soon, Cheah Kok Ming, T. K. Sabapathy, Ho Weng Hin and Lai Chee Kien. My doctoral studies at Berkeley were supported by an Overseas Government Scholarship from the National University of Singapore. My former teachers and current senior colleagues at the Department of Architecture – Professor Heng Chye Kiang, Associate Professor Joseph Lim and Associate Professor Bobby Wong – supported my scholarship application. I am also appreciative that Associate Professor Wong Yunn Chii, the Head of Department of Architecture, gave me time off from teaching to work on this book. The research for this book is supported by a start-up grant "A Genealogy of Tropical Architecture: Singapore in the British Colonial Networks 1820–1960" (WBS No.: R-295-000-079-133) from the National University of Singapore.

My research was carried out at the following libraries and archives, and I am grateful for the assistance of librarians and archivists at these institutions: the Architectural Association Library (particularly Edward Bottoms of the Archives), Arkib Negara Malaysia, British Library, Cambridge University Library (particularly Rachel Rowe of the Royal Commonwealth Society's Collection), Library of Congress, National Archives at Kew, National Archives of Singapore, National Library of Australia, National Library of Singapore, the National University of Singapore Libraries (particularly Winnifred Wong), Royal Engineers Library at Chatham (particularly Charlotte Hughes), Royal Institute of British Architects Library and Archives (particularly Alison Chew), University of California at Berkeley Libraries, Special Collections and Archives at the University of Liverpool Library, and Wellcome Library. Besides the collections in the above libraries and archives, I also have access to the private papers of Professors Otto Koenigsberger and Patrick Wakely, for which I am indebted to the late Renate Koenigsberger and Patrick Wakely.

I am also grateful to Francesca Ford and Trudy Varcianna, who both supported and guided the project at Routledge. Thanks also go to Nigel Hope, the copy editor, and Dave Wright, the production manager at Saxon Graphics. Earlier and shorter versions of three chapters in book have been published elsewhere: Chapter 3 as "Tropicalising Technologies of Environment and Government: The Singapore General Hospital and the Circulation of the Pavilion Plan Hospital in the British Empire, 1860-1930" in Michael Guggenheim and Ola Söderström eds, *Re-Shaping Cities: How Global Mobility Transforms Architecture and Urban Form* (London: Routledge, 2009); Chapter 4 as "'Tropicalizing' Planning: Sanitation, Housing and Technologies of Improvement in Colonial Singapore, 1907-42" in Robert Peckham and David Promfret eds, *Imperial Contagions: Medicine and Culture of Planning in Asia, 1880–1949* (Hong Kong: Hong Kong University Press,

2012); and Chapter 5 as "Building a Colonial Technoscientific Network: Tropical Architecture, Building Science and the Power-Knowledge of Decolonization" in Duanfang Lu, ed., *Third World Modernism: Architecture, Development and Identity* (London: Routledge, 2010).

Finally, and most importantly, I owe a heartfelt sense of gratitude to my family, who provides the emotional support that nourishes me and my work. My father Chang Seng Kiang, my mother Lim Kee Hiok and my sister Chang Jiat Khee have been most understanding and supportive. My beloved aunt Lim Moey Kia, who made it possible for me to pursue my doctoral studies, passed away prematurely in 2006 and did not live to see the publication of this book. Above all, I am most grateful to Lim Pei Ling, my wife and soul-mate, who is always there for me. It is to her that this book is dedicated.

Abbreviations

AA	Architectural Association
AAA	Architectural Association Archives
ABE	*ABE Journal: European Architecture beyond Europe* [Online]
AJ	*The Architects' Journal*
AKAA	Aga Khan Award for Architecture
ANMKL	Arkib Negara Malaysia (National Archives of Malaysia), Kuala Lumpur
ANT	Actor Network Theory
ARCASIA	Architects Regional Council for Asia
ARSM	Administration Report of the Singapore Municipality for the Year
ASG	Architectural Science Group
ASHRAE	American Society of Heating, Refrigerating and Air-conditioning Engineers
BAE	Board of Architectural Education
BHIC	Barrack and Hospital Improvement Commission
BRS	Building Research Station
CAA	Commonwealth Association of Architects
CBAE	Commonwealth Board of Architectural Education
CBN	*Colonial Building Notes*
CDWA	Colonial Development and Welfare Act
CLU	Colonial Liaison Unit
DDTS	Department of Development and Tropical Studies
DPU	Development Planning Unit
DSIR	Department of Science and Industrial Research
DTA	Department of Tropical Architecture
DTS	Department of Tropical Studies
HI	*Habitat International*
JAE	*Journal of Architectural Education*
JIAES	*The Journal of the Indian Archipelago and Eastern Sea*
JIAM	*Journal of the Institute of Architects of Malaya*

JMBRAS	*Journal of the Malaysian Branch of the Royal Asiatic Society*
JoA	*The Journal of Architecture*
JRIBA	*Journal of the Royal Institute of British Architects*
JSAH	*Journal of the Society of Architectural Historians*
JSSAI	*Journal of the Singapore Society of Architects Incorporated*
JTPI	*Journal of the Town Planning Institute*
NAS	National Archives of Singapore
NAUK	National Archives of United Kingdom
PCRE	*Papers on Subjects Connected with the Duties of the Corps of Royal Engineers*
PLCSS	*Proceedings of the Legislative Council of the Straits Settlements for the Year*
PP	*Planning Perspectives*
PPCRE	*Professional Papers of the Corps of Royal Engineers, Occasional Papers*
PRO	Public Record Office, National Archives of United Kingdom
PWD	Public Works Department
QJIAM	*The Quarterly Journal of the Institute of Architects of Malaya*
RCSSAI	Royal Commission on the Sanitary State of the Army in India
REL	Royal Engineers Library
REJ	*The Royal Engineers Journal*
RIBA	Royal Institute of British Architects
RIBAJ	*Royal Institute of British Architects Journal*
SFP	*The Singapore Free Press*
SFPMA	*The Singapore Free Press and Mercantile Advertiser*
SGH	Singapore General Hospital
SIA	Singapore Institute of Architects
SIAJ	*Singapore Institute of Architects' Journal*
SIT	Singapore Improvement Trust
SP	Singapore Polytechnic
ST	*The Straits Times*
TBD	Tropical Building Division
TMMJ	*The Malayan Medical Journal*
TPR	*Town Planning Review*
TTSH	Tan Tock Seng Hospital
UN	United Nations
WO	War Office

Introduction

Framing Tropical Architecture

What is tropical architecture? According to contemporary discourses, tropical architecture refers to buildings as diverse as bioclimatic skyscrapers, modernist "climate-responsive" buildings, vernacular houses, neo-vernacular resorts and colonial bungalows.[1] Why is this wide array of different building types and design approaches situated in heterogeneous social, cultural, historical and political contexts subsumed under the label of tropical architecture? Is it because the designers of these buildings "start[ed] by looking at nature" to understand its ecosystems?[2] Or that "[t]he point of departure for most tropical architecture is climate," as some of the advocates and practitioners of tropical architecture claimed?[3] If that is the case, these discourses are privileging the "natural" forces of the tropics – particularly ecology and climate – as the prime determinants of architectural form and space. By privileging tropical ecology and climate, these discourses are also appealing to the purportedly timeless and unchanging essence of designing in the tropics. According to some writers, this essence of designing in the tropics, evident in the vernacular "architecture without architects," was purportedly grasped by both "modern masters" – Le Corbusier and Oscar Niemeyer, for example – and regionalist architects – such as Lina Bo Bardi, Minette de Silva, Jane Drew, Maxwell Fry, Otto Koenigsberger, Paul Rudolph, Richard Neutra, the Olgyay brothers, and Tay Kheng Soon – and transmitted between generations of architects.[4] Yet, in doing this, aren't these discourses wittingly or unwittingly glossing over the various historical and political forces that shaped these tropical architectures across different time-spaces, flattening them out and rendering them both ahistorical and apolitical?

In the Singapore context, this discourse that shrouded tropical architecture in a fog of climatic or ecological determinism was destabilized by a minor controversy in 2001. Tay Kheng Soon, an eminent local architect in his sixties at that time, wrote a critique of a tropical workshop led by Chan Soo Khian, a younger American-trained, Singapore-based architect.[5] Chan titled the workshop held at the National University of Singapore "Neo-tropicality" and framed the design exercise as a search for a new architectural expression for the tropics. Tay was critical of the exercise. He wrote:

> I was disturbed [by the exercise] because of the unconscious underlying formalistics in the way the exercise was framed for the students.
>
> To understand my being disturbed, I have to go back to 1959 when our school of architecture first started. The issue then was tropicality. It still is. This is how elusive the subject is. The difference is that then, we were in the throes of decolonisation. The issue of tropicality in architectural design was therefore part of the context of freeing oneself from the political and taste-dictates of our masters. Today, it seems that tropicality is more of a fashion statement.

Tay felt that, in formulating the design brief based on a cube and extolling the aesthetics of "interlocking rectilinear cubic forms," Chan had "unwittingly legitimised the primacy of the cube and the surface plane as the language of form and space applied to the problem of tropical aesthetics notwithstanding the physics of tropical design ..." Tay argued that this architectural aesthetics has its "derivative origins" in the 'Neo-Plastic' movement of the 1920s Netherlands, and to term it as a *new* form of tropicality, i.e. "Neo-tropicality," is to disguise its enslavement by the Western architectural hegemony, which Tay sees as an extension of colonial hegemony. Hence, according to Tay, 'Neo-tropicality' "defers and deflects ... [the] quest for a contemporary architectural aesthetic of tropicality in our terms and none other."[6]

Although the above controversy took place in Singapore, I argue that it reflects some of the broader issues in the contemporary ahistorical and apolitical discourses of tropical architecture. In particular, it foregrounds two aspects of tropical architecture. First, in Tay's association of the architectural aesthetics of tropicality with decolonization and independence from colonial/Western hegemony, he emphasizes that tropical architecture was indissolubly bound up with colonial and post-colonial power relations. In other words, despite the appeal to tropical nature, tropical architecture is political through and through. Second, in contrasting mid-twentieth-century tropical architecture as a search for an emancipatory architectural aesthetics with tropical architecture as a fashion statement pandering to the taste of the West at the turn of the twenty-first century, Tay argues that tropical architecture is not an immutable construct derived from timeless nature but a shifting, context-dependent concept shaped by historical forces.

This book interrogates the ahistorical and apolitical discourses of tropical architecture that have not only persisted but have in fact proliferated since the 2000s. Today, however, sustainability is the new hegemonic paradigm.[7] The book constructs a genealogy – a concept that I will elaborate below – from the beginning of the nineteenth to the mid-twentieth century that historicizes tropical architecture, and aims to understand its production and circulation in the situated and power-laden social, cultural and political contexts of British colonialism. An existing body of scholarship by Mark Crinson, Hannah Le Roux, Łukasz Stanek,

Anoma Pieris and others examines the work of European expatriate and indigenous architects in the tropics, and attends closely to the politics of tropical architecture in the contexts of decolonization and the cold war.[8] The focus of this scholarship is, however, largely confined to the history of tropical architecture after its institutionalization and naming-as-such in the 1950s. It overlooks the formative influences of colonial knowledge and practices of building in the tropics from the nineteenth and early twentieth centuries which scholars such as John Weiler, Peter Scriver and, most notably, Anthony D. King, have traced by exploring the work of primarily non-architects like engineers, medical and sanitary experts.[9] By taking a longer historical view from around 1800 to the 1960s, this book connects these two distinct bodies of scholarship, building in part on their insights but also substantially reframing and adding to them.

The use of genealogy here refers to the historiographical approach developed by Michel Foucault.[10] This genealogy is, in a way, what Foucault calls a "history of the present," one that seeks to understand the current condition by historicizing how we got here.[11] In tracing back in time the current discourses of tropical architecture, my main concern is to understand how and why tropical nature was privileged among the different variables shaping the production of architecture as the prime determinant. This genealogy attends to actors, knowledges, practices and buildings that are peripheral to, if not entirely overlooked by, most architect-centric histories of tropical architecture. Besides architects, the main actors in this genealogy are what Foucault calls, "specialists of space" like military engineers (Chapters 1 and 2), medical and sanitary experts (Chapters 3 and 4) who were more closely involved than architects in the planning and building of British colonial cities up until the early twentieth century.[12] This genealogy also examines the work of building scientists and technologists (Chapters 5 and 6), who were central to the production of tropical architecture in the mid-twentieth century because of the technoscientific turn at that time. The foci of this genealogy are on environmental technologies of architecture – sun-shading, ventilation, cooling, etc. – and the technoscientific knowledges and practices of building in the tropics – including not just those from engineering and building science but also aspects of tropical medicine and sanitation related to the built environment. These foci are again marginal to the concerns of most architectural histories of North America and Europe, let alone the tropics.[13]

In foregrounding these previously peripheral discourses, this genealogy follows the "insurrection of subjugated knowledges" which are systematically overlooked or disqualified that Foucault advances in his approach.[14] Through these subjugated knowledges, this genealogy interrogates the ahistorical and apolitical discourses of tropical architecture. Instead of a timeless and unchanging relationship between tropical nature and the built environment based on some deep underlying law, tropical nature was privileged as the prime determinant of architectural form for different reasons at distinct historical moments, and contingent upon broader colonial and post-colonial contextual forces. Furthermore, implicit in the genealogical approach is the assumption that power is indissolubly linked to the knowledges and practices constructed by unitary discourses. Foucault argues that the genealogy "wage[s] its struggle" primarily against the power effects of unitary discourses. As our genealogy covers the period of colonial rule in tropical territories – mainly in the British colonies as we shall see – it addresses the inextricable entanglements of tropical architecture with the asymmetrical power relations of colonialism. These are the very entanglements typically obfuscated by the discourses of tropical architecture. In King's words,

> The anodyne phrase 'tropical architecture' masks a cluster of controversial facts. Its emergence as a sphere of (European) knowledge marks the expansion of Europe into areas where Europeans had not previously lived. It elides or skims over the fact that 'tropical architecture' was for people of alien cultures exercising colonial power. The application of its principles, whether concerning design, construction, materials, sanitation, lay-out or technology, first to colonial and then to 'native' populations was inseparable from the total economic, social and political restructuring of the culture being controlled.[15]

Building on the above insights, this genealogy aims to reframe and expand on the ways we understand power in relation to colonial and post-colonial architecture.

Geographically, this genealogy covers the British Empire by following how people, knowledge, practices and things related to the built environment circulated through the imperial networks. This book does that from a nodal point – namely, Singapore – within the larger British imperial networks in which various forms of circulation took place. Just as I began this introductory chapter, in each of the later ones – apart from Chapter 5 – my account opens with a discussion of a building, discourse or practice in Singapore where I trace the connecting routes and their attendant social, cultural and/or political forces that led to it and/or followed from it. In the process, I explore the links to various sites in the British Empire, including the West Indies, British India, West Africa, South Africa, Australia and, of course, Britain itself. I choose Singapore because it was an important nodal point in the various networks linking the building types and knowledges this book covers. The movements of the building, discourse or practice depend on the people, institutions and underlying networks that facilitate the connections. In the subsequent chapters, I explore the roles played by an array of different types of highly mobile experts who travelled through different parts of the British Empire, contributing to the circulation of knowledge and practices of tropical architecture. These experts include well-known figures such as metropolitan sanitary expert William J. Simpson, pioneer town planner Edwin P. Richards, and modernist architect/planner/educator Otto Koenigsberger. This genealogy also covers the contributions of important but lesser-known traveling figures such as Irish surveyor/architect George D. Coleman, military engineer and colonial administrator Henry E. McCallum, and architect/technical expert George A. Atkinson. While their contributions are significant, these figures are not seen as autonomous agents. Their works are situated within broader social, cultural, political and institutional contexts.

This book also attends to the roles that Empire-wide organizations played in building the networks and facilitating the circulations. Most prominent among these organizations was the Colonial Office, which was in charge of most of the British colonies and the policies that shaped the built environment in these colonies. In the nineteenth century, the Colonial Office intervened in the planning and design of colonial hospitals and military barracks after the outbreak of major scandals (Chapters 2 and 3). At the turn of the twentieth century, with the formalization of colonial development and the institutionalization of tropical medicine, the Colonial Office became actively involved in advising the colonies on medical and sanitary matters, including the dispatch of metropolitan experts to the colonies to advise on housing and town planning matters (Chapter 4). Later in the 1940s, the passing of the Colonial Development and Welfare Act led the Colonial Office to actively interfere in even more spheres of colonial governance. More metropolitan technical experts were involved in shaping the colonial built environment either directly, as architects and planners, or indirectly as researchers/advisors and educators (Chapters 5 and 6). Besides the Colonial Office, this book also explores other Empire-wide organizations such as the War Office and the Corps of Royal Engineers, both of which were involved in the planning of cantonments and design of military barracks in the Empire. As the genealogy ends in the mid-twentieth century, during the dismantling of the British Empire and transition to the Commonwealth, this book explores how the geopolitical transition influenced organizational transformations. My foci include the Building Research Station at Garston, Watford, and its technoscientific networks in the British Empire/Commonwealth (Chapter 5), the Royal Institute of British Architects and its allied societies in the dominions and the colonies (Chapter 6). The genealogy also includes an examination of the Department of Tropical Studies at the Architectural Association, a London-based transnational institution that overlapped with the British geopolitical interests in the tropics and was involved in the teaching of climatic design in the tropics (Chapter 6). Other colonial organizations dealt with – namely the Public Works Department (PWD) and the Improvement Trust (IT) – though smaller in that they were either restricted to the colony (for the PWDs) or the city (for the ITs) in which they were based. They were nonetheless organizational and operational models replicated throughout the Empire.[16]

Having described the objectives and the temporal and geographical scope of the book, in the next three sections, we will look at three overlapping sets of interdisciplinary theories that frame this study and shape the interpretations and analyses of tropical architecture in this book.

TROPICALITY AND COLONIAL NATURE

Tropical architecture is a taxonomic peculiarity. Implied in any construction of tropical architecture is its unspoken opposite, i.e. temperate architecture. But temperate architecture as an architectural category does not exist. Architecture in the temperate world was, and still is, categorized according to either smaller geographical units based on nations or regions – such as English and French architecture or Scandinavian architecture – or styles – such as Classical, Baroque or Modern architecture. In other words, unlike the privileging of nature as the prime determinant for architecture in the tropical world, culture – be it national/regional culture or culture in connection with aesthetics – was implicitly assumed to be the more significant factor in shaping the architecture of the temperate world. This taxonomic peculiarity implies that since tropical architecture is determined by an external and immutable nature, it is a homogeneous and static entity, whereas temperate architecture is heterogeneous and dynamic because it is shaped by evolving cultural forces.

How can we understand this taxonomic peculiarity, particularly the asymmetry in representing tropical and "temperate" architecture? The insight from Edward Said's seminal work *Orientalism*, and the subsequent scholarship on the postcolonial critique, is instructive here.[17] Drawing on the Foucauldian concept of power-knowledge, Said puts forward an understanding of colonial dominance beyond overt forms of power, i.e. those associated with military might, economic wealth and political dominance. He specifically directs our attention to cultural and epistemic power through the production of culture and knowledge, and their corresponding effects, especially those produced through the articulation of self–other categories and the maintenance of difference to underwrite colonial structures of dominance. And precisely because colonial power was ingrained in the formation of knowledge and not merely restricted to those aspects commonly associated with formal colonization, it was much more pervasive and deep-seated, so much so that Partha Chatterjee calls it an "epistemic conquest," the effects of which persisted well beyond the end of formal colonization.[18]

Postcolonial criticism has had profound repercussions for different disciplines and fields, including the scholarship on colonial architectural and urban history. Like scholars in disciplines such as history, geography and anthropology, scholars in architectural and urban history have become increasingly aware of its recent colonial disciplinary formation.[19] As such, the foundations of these bodies of knowledge – for example, the classificatory categories and their underlying assumptions in colonial architectural and urban historiography – are no longer seen as value-free scholarly discourses but are understood to be inextricably linked to asymmetrical power relations of colonialism. In the past two decades, a wide-ranging body of scholarship has emerged to interrogate some of these persistent binary conceptions in architectural and urban history – such as historical versus non-historical, modern versus traditional, and core versus periphery – and colonial classificatory categories with purportedly indubitable essences such as "Indian architecture," "Indo-Saracenic architecture" and "Islamic cities."[20] Questions such as who constructed these binary conceptions and classificatory categories, where, how and why were they constructed, and to what material effects were posed. One of the key strategies of interrogation was to complicate and destabilize, if not displace, these Eurocentric conceptions, and to show that these normative categories are not only historically contingent socio-cultural constructions with no fixed essences, but are also inadequate in understanding "other" cultures.

I argue that tropical architecture should be understood as an example of such classificatory categories even though it is based on what is purportedly a "natural" and not a cultural classification. But as Raymond Williams famously notes, "the idea of nature contains, though often unnoticed, an extraordinary amount of human history ... both complicated and changing, as other ideas and experiences change," tropical nature should accordingly also be understood as inextricably linked to the constant changes of human history even though it was assumed to be an external and immutable entity in the discourses of tropical architecture.[21] The privileging of nature in the discourses of tropical architecture took place under specific historical circumstances. The tropics are not just a physical geography defined as the zone bounded by the Tropic of Cancer and the Tropic of Capricorn, or characterized by hot climatic conditions, they are also an "imaginative geography" that was, in the mode of Saidian Orientalism, constructed as an otherness to European civilization.[22] David Arnold notes that the tropics generated a powerful array of associations that "existed only in mental juxtaposition to something else – the perceived normality of the temperate lands."[23] He calls this complex of Western ideas and attitudes towards the tropics, "tropicality" – an environmental otherness deeply entwined with other social, cultural, political, racial and gender alterities – and he argues that they were deeply ambivalent, oscillating between the affirmative and the negative.[24]

Behind these characterizations of the tropics was the archetypal text of Hippocrates's *Airs, Waters, Places*, which put forward one of the earliest and most influential environmental formulations that humans are shaped by their geographical location, climate and topography. Hippocrates' environmental determinist theories were revived from the mid-seventeenth to the late-nineteenth century and were central to European constructions of the tropics.[25] On the one hand, the tropics were characterized as the "torrid zone," or the pestilential other that has detrimental effects on the physical and mental well-being of Europeans.[26] Neo-Hippocratic theories supported the idea that the hot and humid tropical climate was producing enormous amounts of poisonous miasma that caused the prevalence of tropical diseases and led to extremely high mortality rates among Europeans in the tropics.[27] On the other hand, the tropics were also constructed as the Edenic other. European travelers, explorers and naturalists to the tropics, especially those from Northern Europe, from the eighteenth century onwards, such as Alexander von Humboldt and Charles Darwin, were struck by the different ecologies and bountiful nature. They portrayed them as an exotic and paradisiacal landscape of "wealth, fecundity and plenitude."[28] However, lurking behind the affirmative characterization of the tropics as an earthly paradise was a recurring sense of repugnance and disdain. Old Hippocratic assertions that the equable climates and fertile soils in the tropics produce lazy inhabitants incapable of physical toil and not disposed to mental exertion were often evoked alongside the admiration for bountiful tropical nature. While paradisiacal, the tropics were also irredeemably backward and lacking in civilization.

Tropicality and these deeply ambivalent constructions of the tropics had important implications for British colonialism and its built environment in the tropics. The perception of the tropics as the pestilential other and, more significantly, the awareness of the economic costs of the high mortality and morbidity rates among Europeans led to the development of tropical medicine and sanitation – institutionalized as specialized fields in the 1890s and early 1900s – to enhance the health and well-being of Europeans and, subsequently, the local/indigenous population living in the tropical territories.[29] Tropical medicine and sanitation had far-reaching influences and impacts on tropical architecture. Some of these topics are explored in this genealogy through three building types in Chapters 2 to 4 – military barracks, hospitals and mass housing. Furthermore, the articulation of the tropics as a backward but Edenic other served to legitimize European colonial rule, particularly its civilizing mission, and justify the colonial exploitation of rich tropical resources. Colonial technoscientific research in botany, forestry and agriculture was also established by the Europeans and systematically expanded to assist in the extraction and commodification of tropical resources.[30] In Chapters 5 and 6, I show how these pioneer colonial technoscientific fields provided the model for organizing technoscientific research in tropical building science and climatic design in the decolonizing British Empire during the mid-twentieth century.[31] In fact, theories on climate and civilization, particularly the hot climate and the lack of civilization, continued to be influential in the mid-twentieth century and underpinned the dissemination of climatic design for the tropics at that time.

COLONIAL TECHNOSCIENTIFIC NETWORKS AND CIRCULATIONS

As noted earlier, this book explores tropical architecture in relation to the colonial circulation of people, knowledge, practices and things in the British imperial networks. But how should one go about studying these circulations and under what framework should these circulations be understood? Traditional architectural historiography tends to rely on a diffusionist narrative that sees metropole–colony relations as one-way flows, i.e. ideas and practices originating from the metropolitan center being transferred unidirectionally to the peripheral colony, with the colony passively receiving and faithfully reproducing those metropolitan ideas and practices, albeit in inferior ways.[32] Colonial architectural and urban history was thus frequently reduced to what Dell Upton calls, "source search," i.e. tracing colonial "derivations" to the metropolitan "origin."[33] This diffusionist narrative and its underlying assumptions have rightly been much critiqued and challenged. Among other things, scholars have argued that instead of passively accepting metropolitan ideas and practices, the indigenous population negotiated, resisted, appropriated and translated these ideas and practices according to their own needs and circumstances, in the process transforming these ideas and practices, producing hybrid transcultural forms.[34] Scholars have also interrogated the hierarchical binaries used to characterize metropole–colony relations that undergirded these diffusionist narratives. Instead of seeing the metropolitan center as the sole source of modernity and the only site of innovation, and consigning the peripheral colony to the repository of tradition and the site of passive reception, scholars have shown that the colonies were laboratories of modernity and sites of innovation that helped to constitute metropolitan modernity.[35]

This book extends but also reframes the insights of the above scholarship to understand the circulation of people, ideas and practices related to tropical architecture. I attend specifically to how these ideas and practices were transformed when they circulated and were thus translated and "tropicalized" in order to adapt to the different sociotechnical and socio-environmental contexts. By "tropicalized," I am not suggesting that the transformations were due to climatic differences. Rather, as suggested in the notion of tropicality, the changes could be caused by the various forms of colonial social, cultural and political differences that were entwined with climatic differences. Among the differences that this book explores are the distinct building cultures of the local/indigenous builders (in Chapter 1) and the notion of colonial governmentality – as I shall elaborate in the next section – with its prioritization of the health and well-being of the Europeans by colonial governments, leading to the neglect and under-investment in the health and welfare of the colonized population (in Chapters 2, 3 and 4).

As the book's focus is on the circulation of technoscientific knowledge, practices and things – including buildings – I argue that their circulation has to be understood differently from the circulations of cultural knowledge and social practices. I share Latour's concern about socio-cultural relativism in the constructivist approach to understanding the circulation of "universals." Latour argues that relativism

> forgets that measuring instruments have to be set up … neglect[s] even more thoroughly the enormous efforts Westerners have made to "take the measure" of other [societies, natures and cultures], to "size them up" by rendering them commensurable and by creating measuring standards that did not exist before.[36]

In their study of the circulation of global form, Aihwa Ong and Stephen Collier similarly note that understanding the 'universal' quality of global form "involves neither a sociological … nor a cultural reduction or relativization of such 'universal' phenomena. Rather, it suggests a careful technical analysis – a technical criticism." They argue instead that "[g]lobal forms are limited or delimited by specific technical infrastructures, administrative apparatuses, or value regimes, not by the vagaries of a social or cultural field."[37] Combining what the critics of the diffusionist narrative put forward and the arguments of Latour, Ong and Collier, this book explores how the various forms of circulating entities were constructed to remain fairly stable and immutable even while acknowledging that they were often also transformed as they encountered contingencies and uncertainties during the crossing of boundaries. In this book, I show that the stability and relative immutability were achieved through the prescription of common type plans and space standards, the dissemination of standardized practices and regulatory methods, and the deployment of various "technologies of distance" – such as prefabrication and quantification.

Scholars in Science and Technology Studies, particularly those who deploy Actor Network Theory (ANT), see the network as central to the stable circulation of knowledges, practices and objects. This book draws on such a conception of the network to understand the various circulations. One should, however, also note that these scholars use network to interrogate *a priori* geographical conceptions, particularly binary conceptions like center versus periphery, and global versus local. They argue that all knowledge is local; even global knowledge is local knowledge made "global" by turning it into an immutable mobile, i.e. an entity that could circulate to other sites and conditions without distortion because of the prior network-building and translations done.[38] With insights gleaned from ANT, historians of the British Empire have recently also deployed the network concept to understand how ideas, things and knowledge circulated in the British Empire. They emphasize that colonial/imperial networks were provisional and even ephemeral, requiring much work to maintain. These networks stretched in contingent manners, in a multiplicity of directions, remaking the spaces – whether metropolitan or colonial – that they connected.[39] I draw on these insights to explore how colonial/Commonwealth technoscientific and professional networks – of building research stations and the Commonwealth Association of Architects respectively – were built in the decolonizing days along with the promotion of tropical architecture to maintain colonial hegemony in the post-colonial world in Chapters 5 and 6. I also argue that, together with the discourse of tropical architecture, these colonial networks were contested and appropriated by former colonial subjects to build their own networks and institutions.

GOVERNMENTALITY AND COLONIAL POWER

One of the main purposes of this genealogy is to challenge the apolitical discourses of tropical architecture and explore how tropical architecture was inextricably linked to colonial power relations. Part of that exploration entails understanding tropical architecture in relation to Foucauldian power-knowledge and the postcolonial critique, as discussed earlier. Besides this approach, current scholarship on colonial architectural and urban histories also puts forward another common approach of analyzing power in relation to architecture that relies primarily on formal analysis, with the tendency to correlate social, cultural and political effects with formal qualities. The focus tends to be on buildings as, what Sibel Bozdoğan calls in another context, "visible politics," i.e. a highly visible and politicized image of power.[40] As a consequence, this approach directs its attention toward the more visible, spectacular and monumental public buildings – the train stations, town halls, banking headquarters and exhibition pavilions – and it tends to fall into what Arindam Dutta describes as, "the linear theme of power-display-knowledge …

[which] is patently inadequate to understanding the *informal* skeins of power."[41] This book endeavors to go beyond the approach that sees architecture as "visible politics" by attending to the neglected ordinary colonial built environment and understanding the capillary power in such spaces through Foucauldian governmentality.

Governmentality, a neologism Foucault first coined in a 1978 lecture at Collège de France, is also known variously as "governmental rationality" or "the art of government."[42] Using governmentality, Foucault reframes our understanding of the exercise of governmental power. He argues that the state governs not only through coercion but through the "conduct of conduct" or the calculated and rational exercise of power on the governed to direct their behaviors and structure their actions towards particular ends.[43] Under governmentality, multiple authorities and agencies are grouped together, and a variety of techniques and forms of knowledge are employed in what Paul Rabinow and Nikolas Rose call a "strategic bricolage" to first define and specify targets of government, and then to regulate and control them.[44] The analytical focus of governmentality is on the "how" of government, particularly how specific technologies of government in the strategic bricolage render problems of government visible, facilitate political calculations and constitute the rationality of government. In this context, architecture and the built environment can be seen alongside statistics, maps, medical knowledges and sanitary practices as part of the larger strategic bricolage of governmentality.[45]

In Foucault's earlier works, he distinguishes governmentality and the related concepts of disciplinary and biopolitical power from what he sees as the old regime of power – sovereign power. For example, in *Discipline and Punish*, Foucault uses the shift in the systems of punishment – from the public spectacle of the criminal body on the scaffold to the private surveillance of the reformed body in the Panopticon – to illustrate the transition from the regime of sovereign power to the regime of disciplinary power.[46] In *History of Sexuality: An Introduction*, Foucault traces the shift from sovereign power that *takes* life to biopower that *gives* (or invests in) life.[47] Even in his lecture on governmentality, Foucault argues that, unlike sovereignty that was preoccupied with the control of territory, governmentality focused on population, particularly "the welfare of the population, the improvement of its condition, the increase of its wealth, longevity, health, etc."[48] However, Foucault later conceptualizes governmentality as a triangle of sovereignty–discipline–government, in which different modalities of power coexist. Thus, under governmentality, the liberal modes of government associated with life-giving biopower coexist with the coercive and violent sovereign power that takes life. By extension, the architecture of the panopticon that allows the inspection of a great multitude by an individual is also supplemented by the architectural spectacle of temples, theaters and other highly visible monuments that rendered accessible the inspection of a small number of objects by a multitude of men and women.[49] In this book, I complement and extend the scholarship on "visible politics" and the projection of sovereign power of the monumental buildings to the masses with a study of ordinary colonial barracks, hospitals and housing (Chapters 2 to 4) that were built to instill discipline and invest in the healthy lives of the population.

As governmentality was primarily developed to understand the "liberal modes of government" in Europe, scholars of colonialism argue that metropolitan governmental rationality was dislocated and translated in the colonial contexts of illiberal and coercive rule in racialized, deficient, excessive and fragmented ways.[50] As shaped by what Partha Chatterjee calls the "colonial rule of difference," colonial governmentality violated its metropolitan liberal conception and created a built environment that reflected the contradictions of such violations.[51] This book documents a few examples of such a built environment – the military cantonment as an enclaved space of exception for European soldiers in the contaminated landscape of the colonial city (Chapter 2), the modern colonial hospital as not a "curing machine" that invested biopolitical power in the indigenous population but a compensatory colonial monument that projected sovereign power (Chapter 3), and the piecemeal and belated nature of colonial public housing provision and sanitary improvement (Chapter 4).

PLAN OF THE BOOK

This book is divided into two parts. The first part consists of the first four chapters while the second part has two chapters. The first part explores the early, i.e. pre-institutionalization, history of "tropical architecture" from the eighteenth century to the mid-twentieth century through four different broad building types – bungalow, military barracks, pavilion plan hospital, and public housing. Although these chapters are primarily arranged thematically, they are also loosely chronological. They start with the earliest tropicalized building type and trace the socio-spatial expansion of "tropical architecture" from specific colonial socio-spatial enclaves for the Europeans, such as the military barracks in the cantonments, to the spaces beyond those European enclaves, to include, for example, the pavilion plan hospitals in the medical enclaves and the public housing in sections of the "native" town. These chapters also examine how "tropical architecture" transformed from being improvisational practical knowledge influenced by indigenous practices to become a systematic body of abstract, technoscientific knowledge.

The second, and shorter, part of the book shifts our attention from tropical building types to knowledge production concerning building in the tropics. Underpinning this study of knowledge production is the Foucauldian notion of power-knowledge, or that "power and knowledge directly imply one another, that there is no power relation without the correlative constitution of a field of knowledge, nor any knowledge that does not presuppose and constitute at the same time power relations."[52] Chronologically, the two chapters in this part continue from a pre-1942 discussion in the first part and cover the period between the 1940s and the late 1960s, focusing on the history of tropical architecture during and after its institutionalization and naming-as-such in the mid-twentieth century. Instead of looking at key buildings and architects that other scholars have already explored, these two chapters attend to the much less researched aspects of mid-twentieth-century tropical architecture, specifically issues of knowledge production and circulation through research and education. Chapter 5 attends to the work of the Tropical Building Division of the Building Research Station, Garston, and Chapter 6 examines the work of the Department of Tropical Studies at the Architectural Association, London. While Part II deals with more abstract notions than Part I, the knowledge examined in Part II was arguably more pervasive as it was broadly applicable to all building types.

Finally, I end the book with a short reflection on the afterlives of tropical architecture after the early 1970s, focusing particularly on tropical architecture in the contemporary world. I argue that tropical architecture today carries historically sedimented meanings. Key themes and concepts that appeared in the genealogy – such as nature, technoscience, governmentality and network – recur, albeit in mutated forms, in today's tropical architecture. Climate change and the reconstruction of tropical nature, technological optimism, if not determinism, of the recent paradigm of sustainable development, new networks of circulation and the neoliberal governmental rationality are some of these (mutated) themes that continue to shape tropical architecture in the contemporary world.[53] Indeed, the genealogy is a history of the present. It helps us understand why many of the problems with tropical architecture today are deeply rooted historically. Without a rigorous interrogation of the past, we cannot possibly have a better understanding of the present.

NOTES

1 See, for example, Joo-Hwa Bay and Boon-Lay Ong, eds., *Tropical Sustainable Architecture: Social and Environmental Dimensions* (Oxford: Architectural Press, 2006); Alexander Tzonis, Liane Lefaivre, and Bruno Stagno, eds., *Tropical Architecture: Critical Regionalism in the Age of Globalization* (Chichester: Wiley-Academic, 2001); Wolfgang Lauber et al., *Tropical Architecture: Sustainable and Humane Building in Africa, Latin America, and South-East Asia* (New York: Prestel, 2005).

2 Ken Yeang, "Green Design in the Hot Humid Tropical Zone," in *Tropical Sustainable Architecture: Social and Environmental Dimensions*, ed. Joo-Hwa Bay and Boon-Lay Ong (Oxford: Architectural Press, 2006), 49.

3 Joo-Hwa Bay and Boon-Lay Ong, "Social and Environmental Dimension in Tropical Sustainable Architecture: Introductory Comments," in *Tropical Sustainable Architecture: Social and Environmental Dimensions*, ed. Joo-Hwa Bay and Boon-Lay Ong (Oxford: Architectural Press, 2006), 3.

4 Bay and Ong,"Social and Environmental Dimensions in Tropical Sustainable Architecture," 2; Alexander Tzonis and Liane Lefaivre, "The Suppression and Rethinking of Regionalism and Tropicalism after 1945," in *Tropical Architecture: Critical Regionalism in the Age of Globalization*, ed. Alexander Tzonis, Bruno Stagno, and Liane Lefaivre (Chichester: Wiley-Academic, 2001).

5 For the work of Tay Kheng Soon, see Jiat-Hwee Chang, "Deviating Discourse: Tay Kheng Soon and the Architecture of Postcolonial Development in Tropical Asia," *JAE* 63, no. 3 (2010).

6 Kheng Soon Tay, "Neo-Tropicality or Neo-Colonialism?," *Singapore Architect* 211 (2001): 21. For Chan's reply, see Soo Khian Chan and Kheng Soon Tay, "Who Is Afraid of the Neo-Tropical?," *Singapore Architect* 212.

7 For a critical review of the proliferation of tropical architecture in the age of sustainability, see Jiat-Hwee Chang, "Tropical Variants of Sustainable Architecture: A Postcolonial Perspective," in *Handbook of Architectural Theory*, ed. Greig Crysler, Stephen Cairns and Hilde Heynen (London: Sage, 2012).

8 See, for example, Hannah Le Roux, "The Networks of Tropical Architecture," *JoA* 8 (2003); Mark Crinson, *Modern Architecture and the End of Empire* (Aldershot: Ashgate, 2003); Łukasz Stanek, "Introduction: The 'Second World's' Architecture and Planning in the 'Third World'," *JoA* 17, no. 3 (2012); Anoma Pieris, *Imagining Modernity: The Architecture of Valentine Gunasekara* (Colombo: Stamford Lake & Social Scientists' Association, 2007). See Chapter 5 for a more extensive discussion of this scholarship.

9 John Weiler, "Army Architects: The Royal Engineers and the Development of Building Technology in the Nineteenth Century" (PhD thesis, University of York, 1987); Anthony D. King, *The Bungalow: The Production of a Global Culture*, 2nd ed. (New York: Oxford University Press, 1995 [1984]); Peter Scriver, *Rationalization, Standardization, and Control in Design: A Cognitive Historical Study of Architectural Design and Planning in the Public Works Department of British India, 1855–1901* (Delft: Publikatieburo Bouwkunde, Technische Universiteit Delft, 1994).

10 It was an approach based on Foucault's reading of Nietzsche's work. See Michel Foucault, "Nietzsche, Genealogy, History," in *The Essential Foucault: Selections from the Essential Works of Foucault 1954–1984*, ed. Paul Rabinow and Nikolas S. Rose (New York: The New Press, 2005 [1971]). The approach was first used in Michel Foucault, *Discipline and Punish: The Birth of the Prison*, trans. Alan Sheridan, 2nd ed. (New York: Vintage Books, 1995 [1977]). For an overview of the genealogical approach, see Hubert L. Dreyfus and Paul Rabinow, *Michel Foucault: Beyond Structuralism and Hermeneutics*, 2nd ed. (Chicago: University of Chicago Press, 1983), 118–25.

11 Foucault, *Discipline and Punish*, 31. History of the present should be differentiated from both "presentism" and "finalism." See Dreyfus and Rabinow, *Michel Foucault*, 118–20.

12 Michel Foucault, "The Eye of the Power," in *Power/Knowledge: Selected Interviews and Other Writings*, ed. Colin Gordon (New York: Pantheon, 1980).

13 There are a few architectural historians who currently work on the environmental technologies of architecture. Their works include Daniel A. Barber, "Tomorrow's House: Architecture and the Future of Energy in the 1940s," *Technology and Culture* 55, no. 1 (2014); Alistair Fair, "'A Laboratory of Heating and Ventilation': The Johns Hopkins Hospital as Experimental Architecture, 1870–90," *JoA* 19, no. 3 (2014).

14 Michel Foucault, "Two Lectures," trans. Alessandro Fortana and Pasquale Pasquino, in *Power/Knowledge: Selected Interviews and Other Writings, 1972–1977*, ed. Colin Gordon (New York: Pantheon Books, 1980), 81.

15 King, *The Bungalow*, 259.

16 For the Improvement Trusts, see Chapter 4. For the Public Works Departments, see Peter Scriver, "Empire-Building and Thinking in the Public Works Department of British India," in *Colonial Modernities: Building, Dwelling and Architecture in British India and Ceylon*, ed. Peter Scriver and Vikramaditya Prakash (London and New York: Routledge, 2007); Yunn Chii Wong, "Public Works Department Singapore in the Inter-War Years (1919–1941): From Monumental to Instrumental Modernism" (Unpublished Research Report, National University of Singapore, 2003). See also Chapter 3.

17 Edward W. Said, *Culture and Imperialism* (New York: Vintage Books, 1994 [1993]); Edward W. Said, *Orientalism* (New York: Vintage Books, 1994 [1978]).

18 Partha Chatterjee, *Nationalist Thought and the Colonial World: A Derivative Discourse* (Minneapolis: University of Minnesota Press, 2001 [1986]).

19 See, for example, James Ferguson, "Anthropology and Its Evil Twin: 'Development' in the Constitution of a Discipline," in *International Development and the Social Sciences: Essays on the History and Politics of Knowledge*, ed. Frederick Cooper and Randall M. Packard (Berkeley: University of California Press, 1997); Anne Godlewska and Neil Smith, *Geography and Empire* (Cambridge, MA: Blackwell, 1994); Dipesh Chakrabarty, *Provincializing Europe: Postcolonial Thought and Historical Difference* (Princeton: Princeton University Press, 2000).

20 Zeynep Çelik, "New Approaches to the 'Non-Western' City," *JSAH* 58, no. 3 (1999); Gülsüm Baydar Nalbantoğlu, "Toward Postcolonial Openings: Rereading Sir Banister Fletcher's 'History of Architecture'," *Assemblage* 35 (1998); Jyoti Hosagrahar, *Indigenous Modernities: Negotiating Architecture and Urbanism* (London; New York: Routledge, 2005); Jyoti Hosagrahar, "South Asia: Looking Back, Moving Ahead – History and Modernization," *JSAH* 61, no. 3 (2002); Jane M. Jacobs, *Edge of Empire: Postcolonialism and the City* (London: Routledge, 1996); Thomas R. Metcalf, *An Imperial Vision: Indian Architecture and Britain's Raj* (New Delhi: Oxford University Press, 2002 [1989]); Nezar AlSayyad, ed. *Forms of Dominance: On the Architecture and Urbanism of the Colonial Enterprise* (Aldershot: Avebury, 1992).

21 Raymond Williams, "Ideas of Nature," in *Problems in Materialism and Culture: Selected Essays* (London: Verso, 1980), 67.

22 The term 'imaginative geography' first came into prominence in Edward Said's *Orientalism*. It refers to the imaginative or figurative quality that one endows an objective space with. Imaginative geography demarcates social, ethnic and cultural boundaries and "help[s] the mind to intensify its own sense of itself by dramatizing the distance and difference between what is close to it and what is far away" and that "all kinds of suppositions, associations, and fictions appear to crowd the unfamiliar space outside one's own." Said, *Orientalism*, 54.

23 David Arnold, *The Problem of Nature: Environment, Culture and European Expansion* (Oxford: Blackwell, 1996), 143.

24 Ibid., 141–68. See also Felix Driver and Brenda S. A. Yeoh, "Constructing the Tropics: Introduction," *Singapore Journal of Tropical Geography* 21, no. 1 (2000); Nancy Leys Stepan, *Picturing Tropical Nature* (Ithaca, NY: Cornell University Press, 2001); Felix Driver, "Imagining the Tropics: Views and Visions of the Tropical World," *Singapore Journal of Tropical Geography* 25, no. 1 (2004).

25 Arnold, *The Problem of Nature*, 14–19. Here, Arnold is drawing from the seminal work of Clarence Glacken. See Clarence J. Glacken, *Traces on the Rhodian Shore: Nature and Culture in Western Thought from Ancient Times to the End of the Eighteenth Century* (Berkeley: University of California Press, 1967).

26 Victor Savage, *Western Impressions of Nature and Landscape in Southeast Asia* (Singapore: Singapore University Press, 1984), 141–187.

27 See Philip D. Curtin, *Death by Migration: Europe's Encounter with the Tropical World in the Nineteenth Century* (Cambridge: Cambridge University Press, 1989). I further explicate the miasmatic theories of disease transmission later in the book.

28 Savage, *Western Impressions*, 67–140; Bernard Smith, *European Vision and the South Pacific*, 2nd ed. (New Haven: Yale University Press, 1985), 41–50.

29 Mark Harrison, *Public Health in British India: Anglo-Indian Preventive Medicine 1859–1914* (Cambridge: Cambridge University Press, 1994); Lenore Manderson, *Sickness and the State: Health and Illness in Colonial Malaya, 1870–1940* (Cambridge: Cambridge University Press, 1996); David Arnold, ed., *Imperial Medicine and Indigenous Societies* (Manchester: Manchester University Press, 1988); David Arnold,

Colonizing the Body: State Medicine and Epidemic Disease in Nineteenth-Century India (Berkeley: University of California Press, 1993).

30 Lucile H. Brockway, *Science and Colonial Expansion: The Role of the British Royal Botanic Gardens* (New Haven: Yale University Press, 2002 [1979]); Richard Drayton, *Nature's Government: Science, Imperial Britain, and the "Improvement" of the World* (New Haven: Yale University Press, 2000); Joseph M. Hodge, "Science, Development, and Empire: The Colonial Advisory Council on Agriculture and Animal Health, 1929–43," *The Journal of Imperial and Commonwealth History* 30, no. 1 (2002).

31 See also Sir Charles Joseph Jeffries, ed. *A Review of Colonial Research, 1940–1960* (London: HMSO, 1964).

32 Jiat-Hwee Chang and William S. W. Lim, "Non West Modernist Past: Rethinking Modernisms and Modernities Beyond the West," in *Non West Modernist Past: On Architecture and Modernities*, ed. William S. W. Lim and Jiat-Hwee Chang (Singapore: World Scientific, 2011).

33 Dell Upton, *Holy Things and Profane: Anglican Parish Churches in Colonial Virginia* (New York; Cambridge, MA: Architectural History Foundation, MIT Press, 1986), xxi.

34 William Glover, *Making Lahore Modern: Constructing and Imagining a Colonial City* (Minneapolis: University of Minnesota Press, 2008); Tom Avermaete, Serhat Karakayali, and Marion von Osten, eds., *Colonial Modern: Aesthetics of the Past – Rebellions for the Future* (London: Black Dog Publishing, 2010); Hosagrahar, *Indigenous Modernities*; Swati Chattopadhyay, *Representing Calcutta: Modernity, Nationalism, and the Colonial Uncanny* (London: Routledge, 2005); Preeti Chopra, *A Joint Enterprise: Indian Elites and the Making of British Bombay* (Minneapolis: University of Minnesota Press, 2011).

35 Sidney W. Mintz, *Sweetness and Power: The Place of Sugar in Modern History* (New York: Penguin, 1986); Timothy Mitchell, *Colonising Egypt* (Berkeley: University of California Press, 1991); Paul Rabinow, *French Modern: Norms and Forms of the Social Environment* (Chicago: University of Chicago Press, 1989); Gwendolyn Wright, *The Politics of Design in French Colonial Urbanism* (Chicago: University of Chicago Press, 1991); Mary Louise Pratt, *Imperial Eyes: Travel Writing and Transculturation* (London: Routledge, 1992).

36 Bruno Latour, *We Have Never Been Modern* (Cambridge, MA: Harvard University Press, 1993), 113.

37 Stephen J. Collier and Aihwa Ong, "Global Assemblages, Anthropological Problems," in *Global Assemblages: Technology, Politics, and Ethics as Anthropological Problems*, ed. Aihwa Ong and Stephen J. Collier (Malden: Blackwell Publishing, 2005), 10, 11.

38 See Chapter 5 and John Law and John Hassard, eds., *Actor Network Theory and After* (Malden: Blackwell, 1999).

39 Alan Lester, "Imperial Circuits and Networks: Geographies of the British Empire," *History Compass* 4, no. 1 (2006); Simon J. Potter, "Webs, Networks, and Systems: Globalization and the Mass Media in the Nineteenth- and Twentieth-Century British Empire," *Journal of British Studies* 46, no. 3 (2007).

40 Sibel Bozdoğan, *Modernism and Nation Building: Turkish Architectural Culture in the Early Republic* (Seattle: University of Washington Press, 2001).

41 Arindam Dutta, "Review of Mark Crinson, *Modern Architecture and the End of Empire* (Aldershot: Ashgate, 2003)," *JSAH* 67, no. 2 (2008). This is probably an unfair generalization. See Mark Crinson, "The Powers That Be: Architectural Potency and Spatialized Power," *ABE* 4 (2013); Jiat-Hwee Chang, "Multiple Power in Colonial Spaces," *ABE* 5 (2014).

42 The lecture series was recently published as Michel Foucault et al., *Security, Territory, Population: Lectures at the Collège De France, 1977–78* (Basingstoke: Palgrave Macmillan, 2007). The specific lecture in the series on governmentality was first

published in 1979 in English in the journal *Ideology and Consciousness*, and subsequently reprinted in the well-known collection Michel Foucault et al., eds., *The Foucault Effect: Studies in Governmentality* (Chicago: University of Chicago Press, 1991).

43 Mitchell Dean, *Governmentality: Power and Rule in Modern Society* (London: Sage, 1999); Nikolas S. Rose, *Powers of Freedom: Reframing Political Thought* (Cambridge: Cambridge University Press, 1999); Michel Foucault, *Society Must Be Defended: Lectures at the College de France, 1975–76*, trans. David Macey (New York: Picador, 2003).

44 Paul Rabinow and Nikolas S. Rose, "Introduction," in *The Essential Foucault: Selections from Essential Works of Foucault, 1954–1984*, ed. Paul Rabinow and Nikolas S. Rose (New York: New Press, 2003), xv–xvii.

45 Margo Huxley, "Geographies of Governmentality," in *Space, Knowledge and Power: Foucault and Geography*, ed. Jeremy W. Crampton and Stuart Elden (Aldershot: Ashgate, 2007), 194.

46 Michel Foucault, *Discipline and Punish*.

47 Michel Foucault, *The History of Sexuality: An Introduction, Volume 1*, trans. Robert Hurley (New York: Vintage, 1990 [1978]), 135–59.

48 Michel Foucault, "Governmentality," in *The Foucault Effect: Studies in Governmentality*, ed. Michel Foucault et al. (Chicago: University of Chicago Press, 1991), 100.

49 Michel Foucault, *Discipline and Punish*, 216.

50 See, for example, Gyan Prakash, *Another Reason: Science and the Imagination of Modern India* (Princeton: Princeton University Press, 1999); David Scott, "Colonial Governmentality," in *Anthropologies of Modernity*, ed. Jonathan Xavier Inda (Malden: Blackwell, 2005 [1999]); James S. Duncan, *In the Shadows of the Tropics: Climate, Race and Biopower in Nineteenth Century Ceylon* (Aldershot: Ashgate, 2007); Peter Redfield, *Space in the Tropics: From Convicts to Rockets in French Guiana* (Berkeley: University of California Press, 2000); Stephen Legg, *Spaces of Colonialism: Delhi's Urban Governmentalities* (Malden: Blackwell, 2007); Ann Laura Stoler, *Race and the Education of Desire: Foucault's History of Sexuality and the Colonial Order of Things* (Durham, NC: Duke University Press, 1995).

51 Partha Chatterjee, *The Nation and Its Fragments: Colonial and Postcolonial Histories* (Princeton: Princeton University Press, 1993).

52 Michel Foucault, *Discipline and Punish*, 27.

53 See also Chang, "Tropical Variants of Sustainable Architecture."

Part I
Building Types

Chapter 1: The Emergence of the Tropicalized House

Comfort in the Heteronomous and Heterogeneous Conditions of Colonial Architectural Production

The earliest architectural historical accounts of colonial architecture in Singapore are those written by T. H. H. Hancock, a Senior Architect with the colonial Public Works Department (PWD), during the 1950s on the early nineteenth-century buildings erected by George Doumgold Coleman, purportedly the first architect of Singapore.[1] Hancock was involved in the mid-twentieth-century remodeling of the Legislative Assembly building, which was previously Maxwell House designed by Coleman.[2] That undertaking might have led him to research on Coleman and his works. With the research, Hancock argued that Coleman was central to the creation of a "tropical Colonial style."[3] In an exhibition catalogue on what was probably the first architectural exhibition in Singapore, Hancock summarizes the "tropical Colonial style" in the following manner:

> Coleman and his immediate successors skillfully adapted the Palladian manner to suit the tropics. These early architects, skilled in classical proportions, developed a Colonial classic idiom with the solidity of the Doric order, with deep and wide verandas and hooded openings for shade, single room thickness for through ventilation and louvred windows to give light, yet reducing glare, and for protection from sudden heavy rain storms.[4]

This "tropical Colonial style" was seen essentially as an outcome of Coleman's adapting Palladianism to the climatic conditions of the tropics so as "to provide conditions of maximum comfort for [Coleman's] clients and their families."[5] Perhaps because little was written about Coleman and early colonial architecture in Singapore until Hancock started doing so in the 1950s, Hancock's trailblazing accounts became very influential. Many architectural historians writing about Singapore's colonial architecture subsequently repeat – sometimes without attribution – Hancock's argument that Coleman was solely responsible for adapting Palladianism to the tropical climate of Singapore. For example, local historian Marjorie Doggett writes that Coleman "developed a colonial classical idiom with wide verandahs for shade, and louvred windows to reduce glare, give protection against torrential rains and provide adequate through ventilation."[6]

Likewise Eu-Jin Seow, prominent local architect and Professor of Architecture, notes that Coleman "had adapted the Palladian theme to tropical architecture" in his doctoral dissertation and Gretchen Mahbubani argues that "Coleman's genius lay in skillfully adapting the Palladian manner to suit the tropical climate."[7]

Hancock's accounts are not unusual in that other architectural historians have also written about the "acclimatization" of classical architecture from the temperate metropole to the tropical colonies in their studies of the architectural history of other former colonies. In fact, Sten Nilsson, the pioneer architectural historian of colonial architecture in British India, even argues in *European Architecture in India 1750–1850* that India's tropical climate was in fact more congenial to classical architecture, which originated in the warm Mediterranean climate of Greece and Rome, than Britain's northerly climes. Designed to exclude the powerful sun rays, rain, and provide shade in the Mediterranean climate, classical architectural devices such as shaded porticos, loggias and colonnades were, according to Nilsson, easily adapted to the Indian context.[8] Hancock's accounts are instead distinguished by his presentism and his insistence on seeing Coleman as a professional architect, as we shall see below.

In this chapter, Hancock's accounts of Coleman are used as an entry point to foreground some of the historiographical problems of colonial architecture in Singapore and, more broadly, tropical architecture. Like Hancock, I am interested in origins, specifically, the origins of acclimatized or tropicalized colonial houses. This chapter focuses on the architectural history of early houses in Singapore built before 1870. Most of these were built for the Europeans, but wealthy locals also lived in such houses. Even though the processes described in this chapter did not end in 1870, it was chosen as an endpoint for a number of interconnected reasons. First of all, 1870 marks the end of the prevalence of an early type of colonial house that local architectural historian Lee Kip Lin characterized as square and compact, plain and unadorned, and largely symmetrical.[9] The year 1870 was also shortly after two momentous events that accelerated colonial Singapore's socio-economic development – Singapore, as a part of the Straits Settlements, became a crown colony and came under the direct rule of the Colonial Office in London in 1867, and the opening of the Suez Canal in 1869 which shortened the distance between Singapore and Europe. The year 1870 also roughly marked the arrival of professional architects and military engineers who were systematically trained in building construction. Most importantly, for the purpose of this genealogy, it was around 1870 that a systematic and explicit body of knowledge on how to build in the tropics emerged, as we shall see in Chapters 2 and 3. Unlike Hancock, however, I do not consider a building to be solely the outcome of the genius of the designer and trace the origins of early colonial architecture in Singapore to the metropole. Instead I explore what I call the heteronomous and heterogeneous conditions of architectural production. I end the chapter by exploring the types of early colonial house produced by multicultural influences and in relation to the preoccupation with comfort.

PRESENTISM AND HISTORIOGRAPHICAL PROBLEMS

A few years before Hancock published his first account on Coleman, his colleague at the PWD, Kenneth A. Brundle, published an important article on the change in climatic design principles from the prewar era to the postwar era. As an illustration of the change, Brundle criticizes the prewar Bungalow. He notes,

> [T]here have been changes in planning technique, and post-war designs reveal a different approach to the problem of keeping the houses cool. The pre-war doctrine of "High Ceilings" preached by Health Officers and others appears to have influenced pre-war planners and never produced a really cool house. In this [prewar] example the height of the ceiling above first floor is sixteen feet, whereas the top of the highest ventilator is only eight feet. The trapping of enormous quantities of hot air is further assisted by the general shape and interior planning of the building, and one might be pardoned for wondering why the building has not "taken off" in the manner of Montgolfiers' balloon which it so closely resemble in elevation.[10]

After dismissing the design of the prewar colonial bungalow (Figure 1.1), Brundle presents a few PWD postwar house designs (such as Figures 1.2 and 1.3) and argues that the postwar designs were based on better design strategies to facilitate cross-ventilation and sun-shading, and to provide for the comfort of their inhabitants. These strategies include the "one room thick" principle, i.e. the cross section of the building is only one room wide, the positioning of large windows and ventilators so that there would be no "dead air pockets", and the proper orientation of the building with regard to the sun's paths and prevailing wind directions. The strategies that Brundle proposes were based on the latest findings from building research carried out by the Colonial Liaison Unit (CLU), later the Tropical Building Division (TBD), of the Building Research Station (BRS) discussed in Chapter 5.

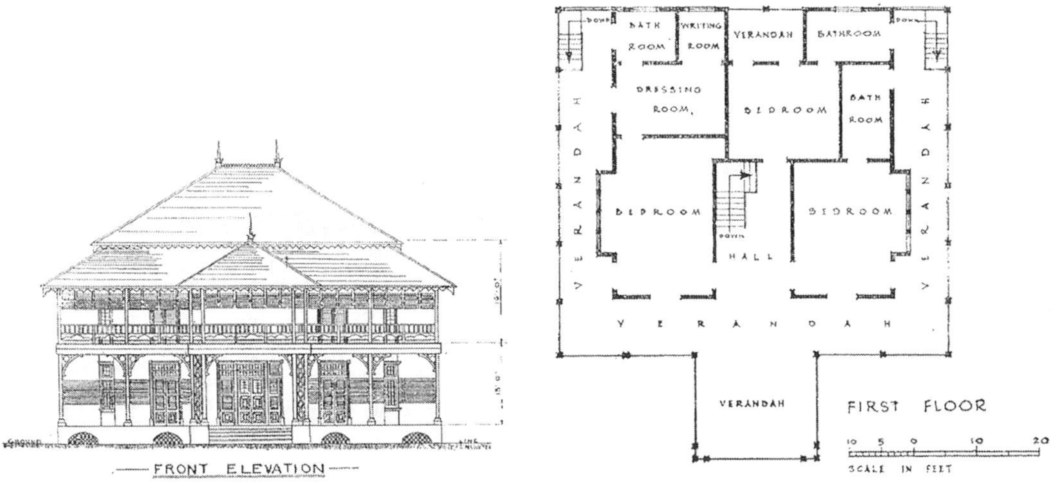

Figure 1.1
Elevation and first floor plan of a prewar colonial bungalow for senior officers, Goodwood Hill. Source: *QJIAM* 1 (2), 1951.

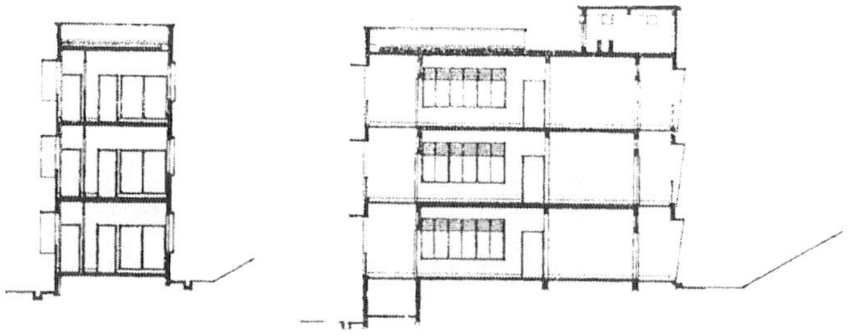

Figure 1.2
Sections of Nassim Hill Flats, an example of postwar apartments for senior officers. Source: *QJIAM* 1 (2), 1951.

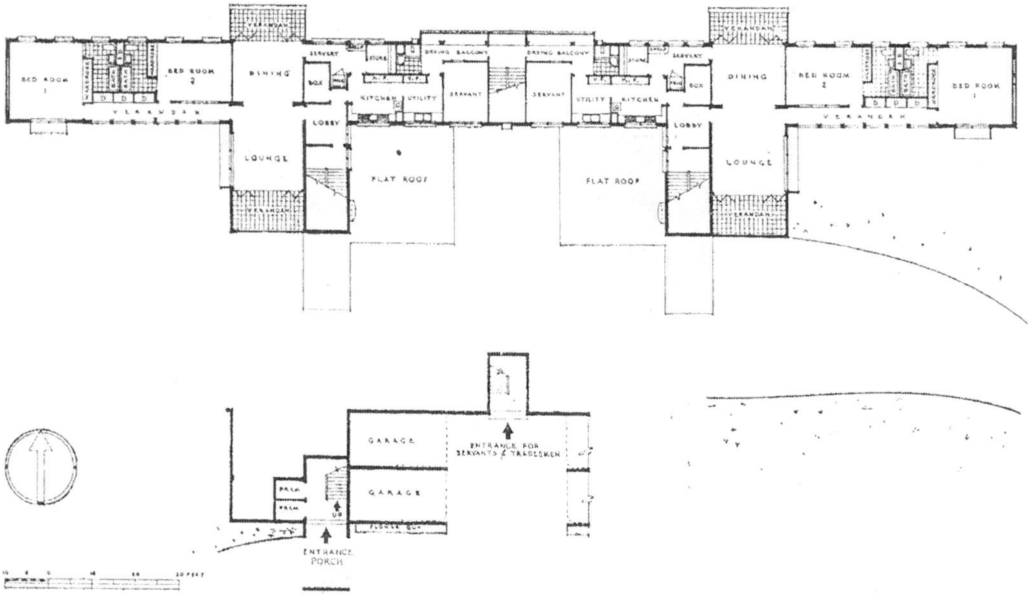

Figure 1.3
Plans of Nassim Hill Flats, an example of postwar apartments for senior officers. Source: *QJIAM* 1 (2), 1951.

Although Brundle was referring to the typical colonial bungalow planned and designed by the Colonial PWD as an example of the prewar climatic design doctrine, he could very well be referring to the houses designed by Coleman. If we study two of Coleman's best-known buildings – Maxwell House, completed in 1827 (Figure 1.4), and the house he built for himself, completed in 1829 (Figures 1.5–1.7) – we can notice the similarities with the colonial bungalow. Both the colonial bungalow and Coleman's houses are compact with deep plans, which are certainly not "one room thick." Furthermore, they are lofty and have "high ceilings" but definitely do not have openings or ventilators positioned just below their ceilings. Thus, they are bound to have "dead air pockets." As a colleague of Brundle, Hancock would have been aware of the new climatic design doctrine. Moreover, Hancock singled out the senior government officers' flats at Nassim Hill, used by Brundle to illustrate the new doctrine in the article, as an example of the outstanding modern buildings in the exhibition on "Architecture in Singapore" he co-curated.[11] Despite Hancock's familiarity with the new doctrine and the obvious incompatibility between the new doctrine and Coleman's designs, Hancock chose

Figure 1.4
Exterior view of Maxwell House, painting by John Turnbull Thomson, 1846. Reprinted, by permission, from Hocken Collections, Uare Taoka o Hākena, University of Otago.

Figure 1.5
Panoramic view of Singapore from St Andrew's Church spire, 1863. Coleman's House is on the left, fronting a street. Reprinted, by permission, from the NAUK.

to apply the design strategies of the new doctrine retrospectively to describe Coleman's houses. In misreading Coleman's houses as having "single room thickness planning" and wrongly asserting that "[p]ermanent openings were found by Coleman to be necessary at ceiling and floor level," Hancock appears to be engaging in a peculiar form of presentism by uncritically interpreting the past according to present-day attitudes and values.[12]

Hancock's presentism could be situated in relation to the end of the colonial rule in the mid-twentieth century. That end was implied in Brundle's discussion of the shift in climatic design principles and techniques, and through its connection to the reorganization of the classes of accommodation for the colonial civil service. The more than ten categories of accommodation in the prewar period were reduced to

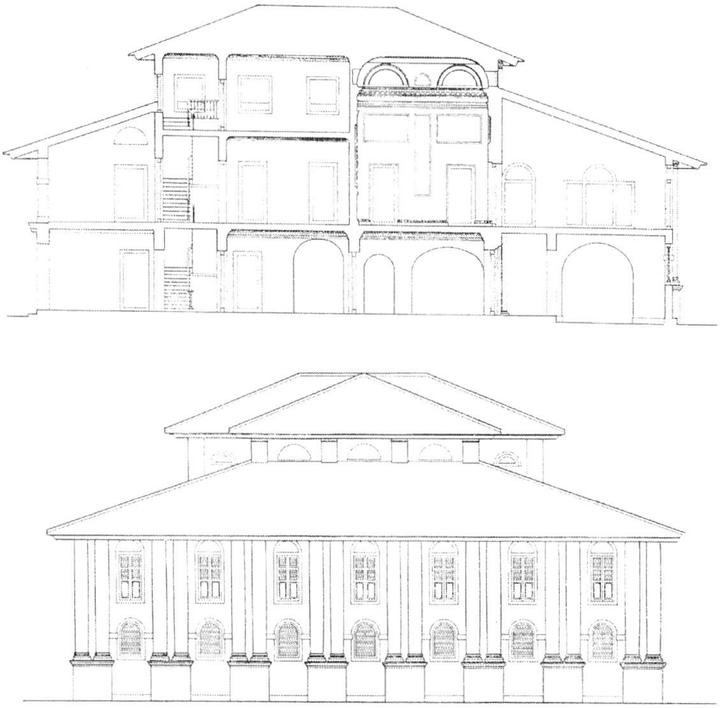

Figure 1.6
Front elevation and cross section of Coleman's house. "Conjectural restoration" made in 1955 by T. H. H. Hancock. Source: The Friends of Singapore, ed., *The House in Coleman Street* (Singapore: The Friends of Singapore, 1958).

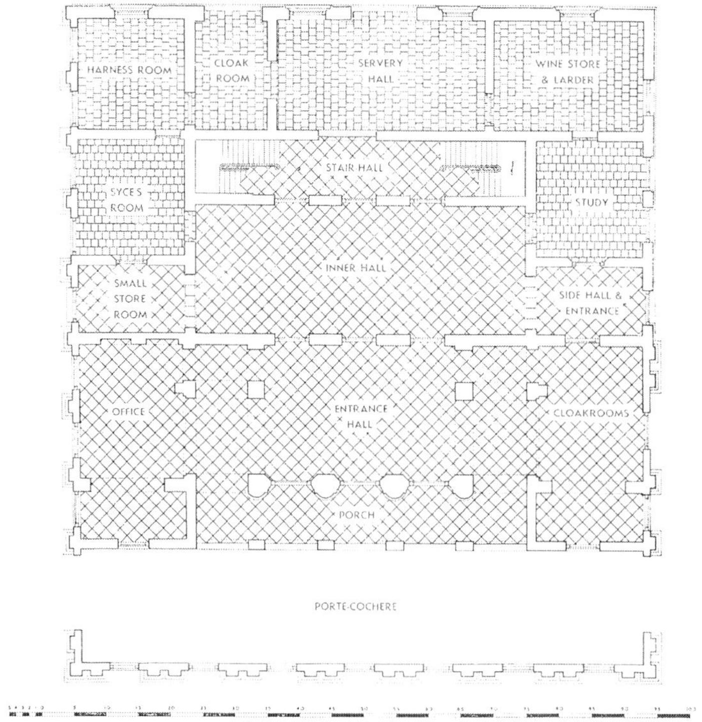

Figure 1.7
Ground floor plan of Coleman's house. "Conjectural restoration" made in 1955 by T. H. H. Hancock. Source: The Friends of Singapore, ed., *The House in Coleman Street* (Singapore: The Friends of Singapore, 1958).

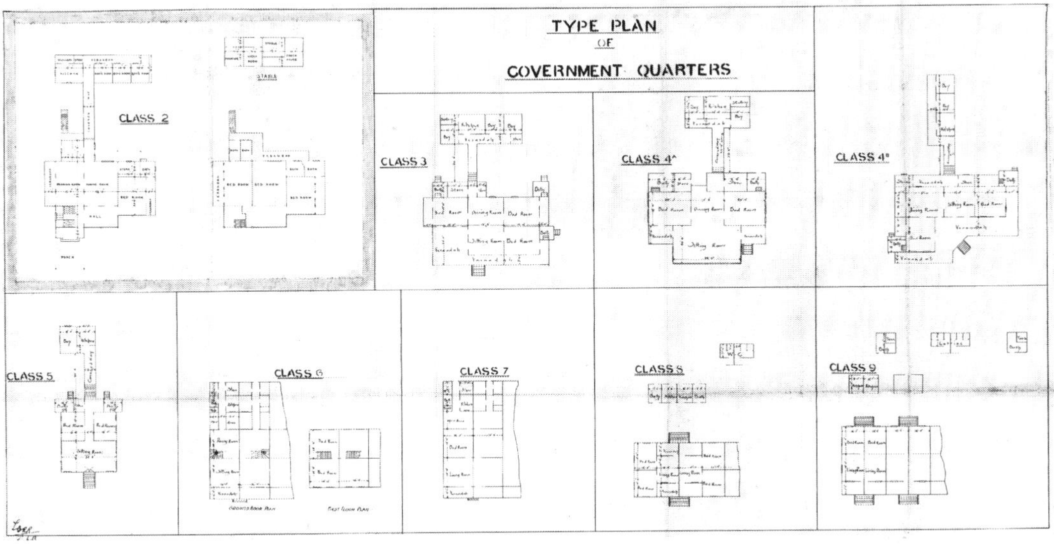

Figure 1.8
Type plans of Class 2 to Class 9 government quarters planned and designed by PWD Federated Malay States for the Federated Malay States government. The type plans for the Straits Settlements government would have been similar. Reprinted, by permission, from Arkib Negara Malaysia.

three categories of the postwar era and the differences between the standards of accommodation for senior and junior officers were greatly reduced (Figure 1.8). While the "palatial" bungalows for the senior (typically British) officers were discontinued and replaced with smaller flats, the accommodation standard for the (typically local) artisans and laborers was improved. These new and more equitable standards reflected two broader changes. The first change covered the new egalitarian norms of colonial governance that followed the passing of the Colonial Development and Welfare Act (CDWA) in 1940, the architectural implications of which I discuss in greater depth in Chapters 5 and 6. The second was postwar economic austerity. Brundle characterized the architectural changes as a shift from "Colonial Monumental to an Architecture of Economy."[13] The new climatic design principles and housing standards meant savings in construction costs and were seen as "economic answers to the many tropical building problems."[14]

In this new socio-political context of egalitarianism and austerity, Coleman's grand houses would appear in the official discourse as an antiquated architecture of excess. At that time, the house Coleman built for himself at No. 3 Coleman Street was threatened with demolition and redevelopment. Hancock was actively involved with the "Friends of Singapore" Society to save it. He researched and wrote about Coleman and celebrated the houses he designed; he also led a group of students to prepare measured drawings of the house and proposed turning it into an art gallery.[15] On the one hand, the presentism in Hancock's writings on Coleman could be seen as a counter-discourse to redeem the value and assert the relevance of Coleman's architecture. On the other hand, they could also be read as a form of nostalgia for the good ol' colonial days at the end of colonialism, especially when they are read in conjunction with what others involved in saving Coleman's House wrote. For example, C. Northcote Parkinson, the Vice-President of "The Friends of Singapore," saw Coleman's House as encapsulating the "very essence of Singapore ... [,] a fine Georgian intolerance of the second-rate [and] a lesson of civilization."[16]

Our interest here is not so much to uncover the hidden motivations behind Hancock's writings. Rather, it is to discuss the historiographical problems with his influential writings and to address these problems in our study of early colonial houses in Singapore. The first historiographical problem concerns the way we understand these early acclimatized houses. As I have argued above, Hancock chose to claim that Coleman's houses followed the latest climatic design principles despite the material evidences indicating otherwise. In doing so, Hancock was not only committing a presentist argument, he was also implying that the way architects responded to the hot and humid climate was both timeless and immutable, independent of shifting social, cultural and technoscientific constructions of the tropics. The first historiographical problem is compounded by the second one of architect-centricity and the unwarranted autonomy attributed to the architectural profession in Hancock's writings.

According to Hancock, Coleman was an exception to the general rule of having military engineers designing and erecting buildings in the British tropical colonies during the early nineteenth century. As engineer-designed buildings were, according to Hancock, "of the simplest kind, and often coarse and crude," Colonial Singapore was fortunate in having secured the services of an architect and "accomplished designer" like Coleman, who left behind elegant Classical buildings that have "simple, yet vigorous, detailing."[17] There was, however, scarcely any evidence to support Coleman's status as an architect. Little is known of Coleman's life before he came to Singapore. Almost nothing was known about his early life in his Irish hometown Drogheda (1795–1815), his early career at Calcutta (1815–20) and also Batavia (1820–24). Unable to locate any evidence, Hancock made a series of conjectures about Coleman's educational background and architectural training without anything more than circumstantial evidence. He then asked his readers to "accept [the] sequence of probabilities" he conjured up in order to resolve "the mystery of George Coleman's meteoric entry into the architectural scene in Calcutta, Batavia and Singapore."[18] It is perhaps not surprising that Coleman's status as an architect rests on such flimsy foundations given the state of the architectural profession in the early nineteenth century.

Even if we disregard the colonial context and turn our attention to the metropole, the notion of the architect as a member of a profession with a clearly defined role only developed in late eighteenth-century England.[19] It emerged when the architect was no longer an artificer, when design was separated from the execution of the design. The architect's role was to design houses and supervise their erection. The execution of the design was left to the highly skilled building craftsmen.[20] Before the eighteenth century, there were very few architects and they were mostly "gentleman-architects" from the aristocracy who had had no special training beyond their own readings and travels.[21] Most buildings were erected by builders with "no pretensions to being designers." They were mainly surveyors or master masons trained through pupillage and apprenticeship but not systematically so.[22] It was only in 1834 that the Institute of British Architects was established with the designation of "Royal" conferred in 1866.

In mid-eighteenth century England, the architect and the surveyor were virtually synonymous.[23] A similar state of affairs existed in eighteenth-century North America, except that architects there practiced engineering too – they surveyed land, built roads, bridges and other utilitarian structures.[24] Until the mid-nineteenth century, the designers of buildings in colonial India were likewise engineers, primarily military engineers. Their practice was often eclectic too, combining surveying, engineering, architecture and mechanical works.[25] If we look at the career of Coleman in Singapore, we will notice that he had a similarly diversified practice. He was employed first as a Government Surveyor and then as a Superintendent of Public Works, and his work involved surveying the town and its coastal environ, building roads into the interior of the island and bridges over rivers, and the clearing and draining of marshes to lay out the town of Singapore. Of course Coleman also designed and supervised the construction of many buildings in early nineteenth-century Singapore, primarily in private practice. He was also a contractor offering to build his designs for his clients at a fixed sum. As such, Coleman defied the division of labor between design and the execution of design that characterized the late eighteenth-century emergence of the professional architect in England.

In terms of the diverse type of work straddling surveying, engineering and architecture, Coleman was not very different from his successors, such as John Turnbull Thomson, the Surveyor and Engineer of Singapore between 1841 and 1853, and Major John Frederick Adolphus McNair, Executive Engineer between 1857 and 1865 and Colonial Engineer between 1867 and 1873. Both Thomson and McNair were not formally trained as architects or even engineers.[26] The absence of formally trained engineers was not unique to colonial Singapore. Most of the military engineers in British India involved in the design and construction of buildings during the early nineteenth century were likewise not formally trained but were self-taught and learnt "on the job."[27] Professional architects and engineers formally trained in "practical architecture" only started arriving in colonial Singapore and elsewhere in the British Empire in the later part of the nineteenth century, as we shall see in Chapter 2.

Hancock's account of Coleman as an architect was very much based on projecting back into history the architectural profession's self-image of autonomy in the mid-twentieth century. In the mid-twentieth century, architecture was a well-established profession with its own legislated status, associated professional and educational institutions, and its own specialized body of knowledge. Traditional architectural historiography was, and still is, a constituent part of the specialized body of knowledge used to reinforce the fallacy of what sociologist Magali Larson calls "the ideological syllogism of [the] architecture [profession]" that only architects produce architecture.[28] Hancock's architect-centric accounts of Coleman belonged to this traditional historiography which relies on what Greig Crysler describes as the narrative genre of the "life-and-work."[29] For scholars who take this approach, identifying the architect behind a particular building is crucial for their understanding of the building. Thus, these scholars are always in search of the architect. In the absence of a veritable architect, common for buildings built in nineteenth-century Singapore, these scholars might accept those who could be described as "surrogate architects." In Hancock's case, Coleman was such a surrogate architect. In the architectural history of Singapore, Hancock's "life-and-work" narrative genre was later canonized by two doctoral theses that expanded on the colonial buildings identified and attributed them to more architects and surrogate architects discovered.[30]

The problem with the "life-and-work" narrative genre is its overemphasis on the roles and agencies of architects in the production of the built environment. This overemphasis came at the expense of other social actors and more nuanced understandings of how social, political and technoscientific contexts shaped architectural production. In the various accounts of the architectural history of colonial Singapore, the focus is invariably on European architects and surrogate architects. The local builders, craftsmen and contractors were wittingly or unwittingly left out of these accounts. Furthermore, these accounts tend to emphasize aesthetics or, more specifically, style and the external appearance of buildings. This focus on aesthetics inevitably entails what Dell Upton calls, "source search," tracing all colonial architecture in Singapore to models and precedents in metropolitan England as if the multicultural builders and users of Singapore exert negligible, if any, influence on these colonial buildings.

To address the above historiographical problems, I propose to approach the acclimatized Palladian villas attributed to Coleman in particular, and early colonial houses in general, differently. I see Singapore's early colonial houses as contingent upon the heteronomous and heterogeneous conditions of early colonial architectural production. By heteronomous, I am drawing on Larson's use of heteronomy to describe architects' reliance on other social actors, such as clients, builders, craftsmen and advisors, to realize (build) their architectural design.[31] In contrast to England, where there were highly skilled craftsmen for the architects to depend on, the local builders of the colonial context presented an entirely different set of challenges that colonial engineers/surveyors had to overcome. By heterogeneous, I am drawing on what John Law calls "heterogeneous engineering" to describe the necessity of a stable artifact to have diverse, i.e. heterogeneous, elements aligned in a contingent assembly.[32]

HETERONOMY AND THE DEPENDENCE ON LOCAL BUILDERS

One way to acknowledge the heteronomy of colonial architectural production is to attend to its dependence on local builders. By local builders in colonial Singapore, we are not referring primarily to builders – both skilled artisans or craftsmen and unskilled laborers – from the indigenous population, i.e. the Malay, but to the migrant populations. There were various reasons for this peculiarity, the most important being the socio-economic organization of the Malays. According to J. M. Gullick, house building in traditional Malay society was a village cooperative effort that relied on the help of relatives and villagers of the house owner. Even a sultan's *istana* (palace) depended on the labor of villagers, only at a larger scale of manpower mobilization.[33] Malays in a traditional society had enough for subsistence through either agriculture or fishing; most of them chose not to participate in the monetized colonial capitalist economy of British Malaya, including that of the colonial building industry, in the nineteenth century.[34] Although Gullick claimed that there was neither a building industry nor professional builders in a traditional Malay society, there was evidence of Malay builders and craftsmen involved in the building trade in the nineteenth century.[35] There were probably not many of them and therefore most accounts suggest that colonial building relied mainly on immigrant Chinese and Indian builders.

Although Chinese were reported to have "practically monopolized the building and skilled artisan trades," there is a paucity of historical accounts describing Chinese builders in colonial Singapore.[36] I know of only two extant accounts from the nineteenth century – both in English and from European colonial perspectives: Thomson's 1852 description of the building of Horsburgh Lighthouse at Pedra Branca between 1849 and 1851 and Henry Edward McCallum's 1881 discussion of the construction of the defense work at Pulau Blakang Mati.[37] In Thomson's description, he notes that "[o]n this [Chinese population] … we were entirely dependent for the carrying on and completion of the works."[38] The contract for building the lighthouse was awarded to a Chinese contractor from the Hakka dialect group by the name of "Choa-ah-Lam … who had executed satisfactorily several Government buildings under (Thomson's) supervision."[39] Choa, however, absconded halfway through the construction, leaving Thomson to take over the direct instruction of the Chinese stone-cutters, carpenters, bricklayers, plumbers and coolies hired. Although Thomson claimed that he was "entirely dependent" on the Chinese builders, "who [were] almost the only artificers in the Straits,"[40] he also relied on builders of other ethnicities, such as Javanese and Malay brass founders and Indian convict laborers. In fact Thomson counted twelve languages being spoken by all those involved in the building of the Horsburgh Lighthouse. Besides Malay, English and the three dialects among the Chinese, there were the languages spoken by the "Javanese, Indo-Portuguese, Boyans, Klings, Bengalese, Papua from New Guinea and Rawas from the interior of Sumatra."[41] The multiple languages spoken presented Thomson with a huge challenge in communicating his ideas to them, especially when the only local language that Thomson could speak was Malay but almost all the Chinese laborers were new arrivals who could not understand Malay.

Besides the linguistic barrier, Thomson also encountered other challenges pertaining to the labor he had at his command. Chief among his complaints was "the lack of energy and *vis animae* combined with the rudeness and unskillfulness" of these people.[42] Thomson described the Chinese artisans' skills deficiency in the following manner:

> while they will finish smoothly and neatly, in a manner to satisfy the unpractised eye, yet their work will not bear the test of the plummet, level or straight edge,

> and until well drilled, the Chinese have a great distaste to the use of these instruments. In all their constructive operations, from the building of a temple to the making of a door-latch, this absence of correctness will be found to pervade the whole, their joinings and fittings are made close, less by geometrical rule and correct workmanship, than by patient trials.[43]

Not unlike Thomson, H. E. McCallum also noted three decades later that the Chinese coolies he was supervising in the various constructions of defense work at Pulau Blakang Mati were of "a very indifferent subject from Amoy and Swatow" and he had to take special measures to deal with their "carelessness."[44] Despite these supposed inadequacies, Thomson was confident that "the Chinese under tuition and training may be made quite equal to the less educated of their western brethren."[45] These complaints by Thomson and McCallum were undoubtedly tainted by their cultural bias. If British craftsmen were asked to build Chinese architecture, their culturally specific training and skills would likewise have been found to be wanting. But putting aside the colonial tropes of representing the "natives" and legitimizing colonial rule in these observations, such perceptions meant that the British colonial engineers/architects were obliged to train the local builders. Part of that training entailed observing and understanding how these local builders work. It was in this context that Thomson provided detailed descriptions, accompanied by sketches, of how the Chinese artisans – stone-cutters, carpenters and bricklayers – and Malay and Javanese brass founders performed their various tasks and the tools they used (Figures 1.9–1.10).

On top of the problems with resources and labor, building in the colonial context also meant "the absence of mechanical appliances by which in Europe all difficulties in construction are so easily and quietly overcome."[46] English architect and later Professor of architecture, T. Roger Smith remarked in 1868 that "in designing for the tropics, the architect should suppose that his work is going to be carried out much as medieval work was done."[47] Although Smith was specifically referring to British India, his remark could also be seen as a reference to how engineers and architects in the mid-nineteenth-century British colonial contexts had to cope with the challenges of unreliable builders, their purportedly backward building techniques and the primitive technologies in place. How did colonial engineers and architects deal with such problems associated with the heteronomy of architectural production?

Experience of the place and attendant local knowledge acquired seem central to addressing the problems of heteronomy. In his 1833 letter to the Resident Councillor, Coleman complained about the failings of a certain Captain Lake, the Inspector General of Works of Colonial Singapore at that time. Coleman argued that as

> a perfect stranger, unacquainted with the languages and customs of the people, it is almost impossible that [Captain Lake] can be able to conduct the works that are required so successfully as [he] who has actually laid out and built a considerable portion of the town and has had the advantage of seven years of residence in it.[48]

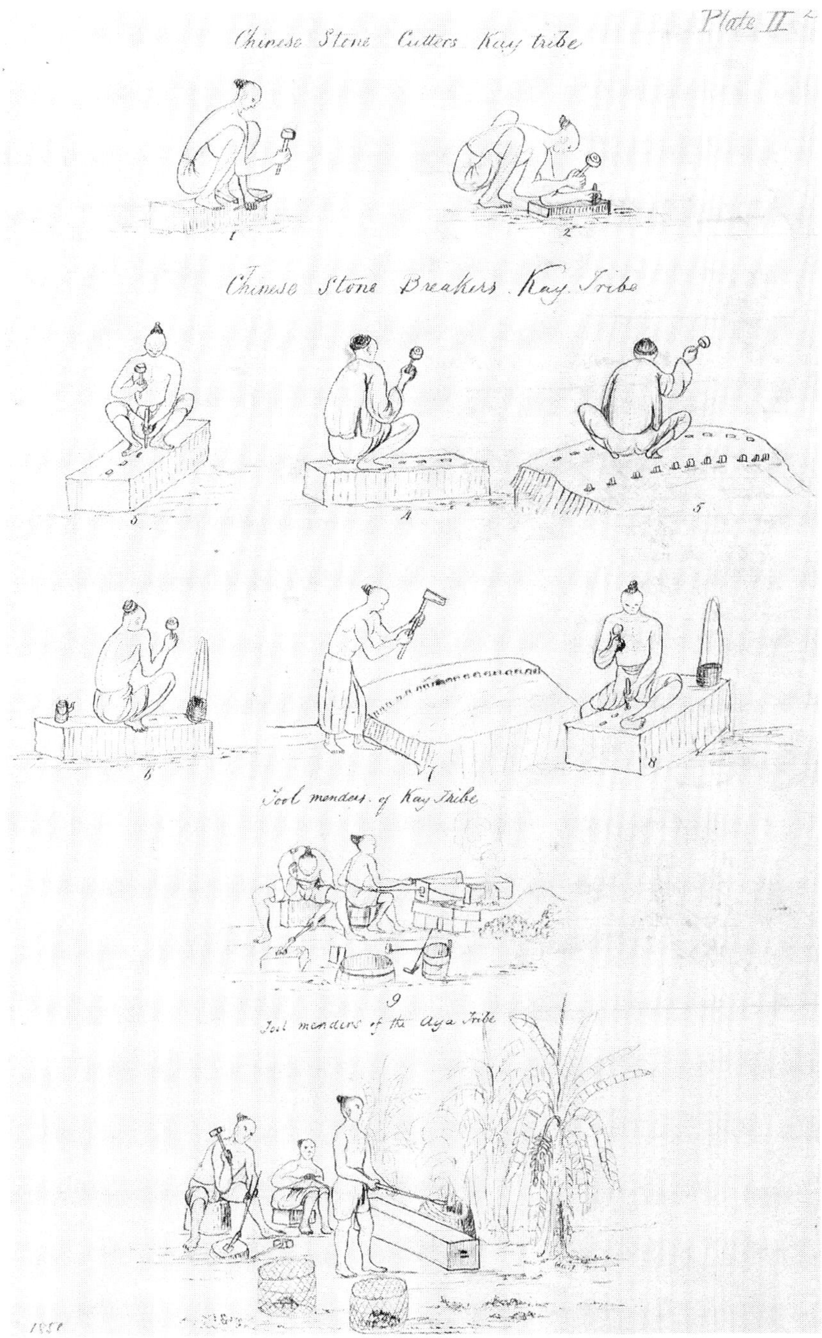

Figure 1.9
Sketches by John Turnbull Thomson titled "Chinese stone cutters, Kay [*sic*] tribe" and "Chinese stone breakers, Kay [*sic*] tribe," 1851. Reprinted, by permission, from Hocken Collections, Uare Taoka o Hākena, University of Otago.

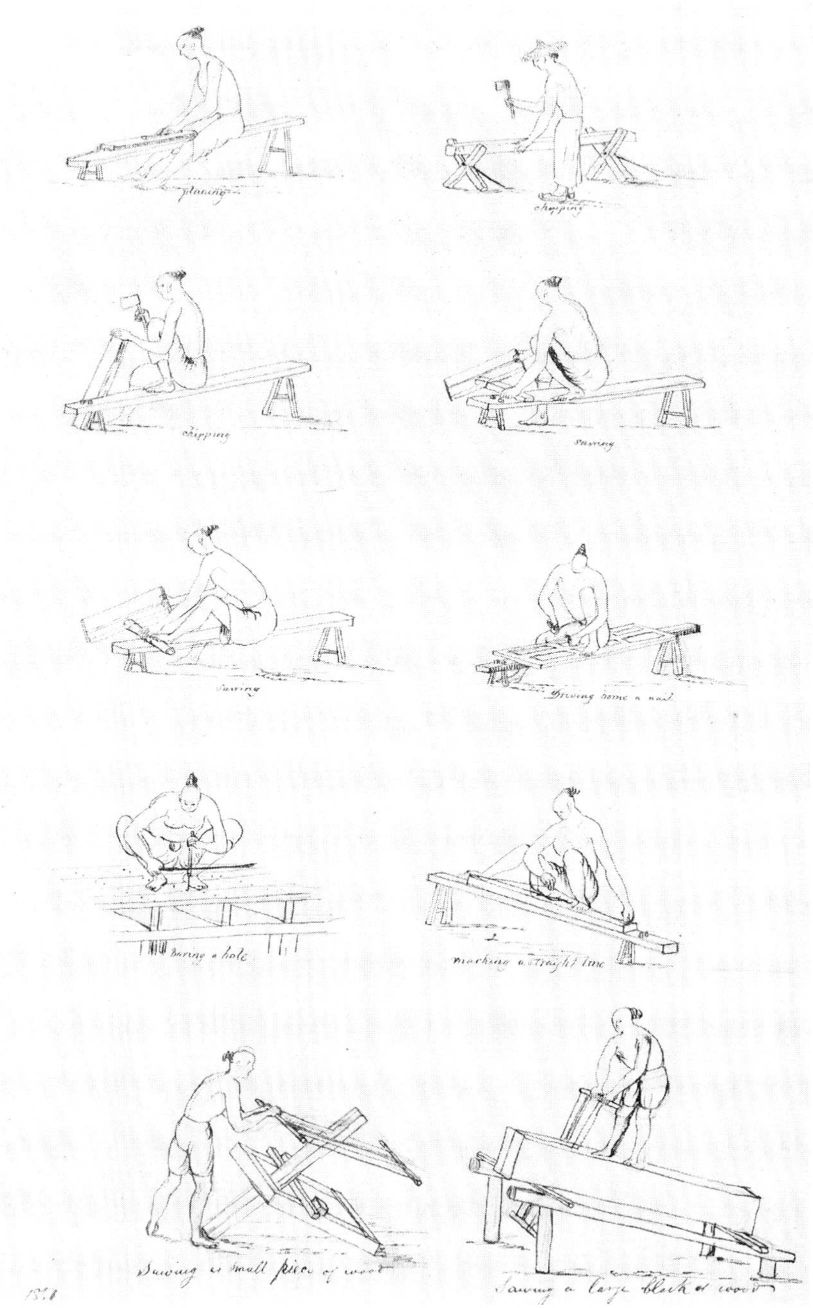

Figure 1.10
Sketches by John Turnbull Thomson titled "Chinese artificers," 1851. Reprinted, by permission, from Hocken Collections, Uare Taoka o Hākena, University of Otago.

Coleman was implying that his years of residing in Singapore and his command of Hindustani, Tamil and Malay, gave him local knowledge that enabled him to execute the building work successfully. Despite our earlier discussion of the linguistic problem Thomson faced, he was also recognized for his in-depth local knowledge. Not only was he able to identify the most suitable local materials for the building of the Horsburgh lighthouse – such as granite from Pulau Ubin and durable *tempinis* ironwood – he also translated *Hikayat Abdullah* in 1873, eighteen years after he left Singapore, because of the "ever recurring interest" he had in Singapore.[49]

Besides local knowledge, another important attribute of a successful colonial engineer/builder was to tailor the architectural design to the limitations of the labor. One of the strategies was to keep the architectural form, particularly ornament, simple. An example was Colonel Ronald MacPherson's design of St. Andrew's Cathedral during its rebuilding in 1856, for which he chose "as simple and easy a form of architecture as he could, and with as little ornament as possible, and therefore within the capacity of his workpeople." For his builders, consisting primarily of Indian convict laborers, MacPherson devised a stripped-down version of Neo-Gothic architecture for the Cathedral, using "simple columns, with plain mouldings only."[50] The same considerations might also account for what Lee saw as the "comparative plainness" of the classical architecture erected in Singapore in the first half of the nineteenth century. Lee noted the prevalence of the Roman Doric and Tuscan orders, "the simplest and the easiest to construct of the Classical Orders," among the early houses. Extending the same reasoning, Lee argued that the "austere subtlety of Greek Doric" was only employed once because it was "difficult to construct: the triglyphs and fluting of the columns, both essential, could not be omitted, and the fluting required skill to render in *chunam*."[51]

Training the local builders and effectively organizing the construction process were the other strategies for coping with heteronomy in nineteenth-century colonial Singapore. The most systematic and celebrated case of these practices was MacPherson and McNair's work with the convict laborers, which was lauded as "a most remarkable example of the successful industrial training of convicts."[52] The convicts, transported to Singapore and largely from India and Ceylon, were organized into different racial/labor categories and trained as "artificers in various trades" at Singapore Prison.[53] Brick kilns and industrial workshops for fabricating different building materials were also established within the prison complex. Between 1825 and 1873, when the scheme ceased, the convict laborers were involved in the construction of many public work projects – clearing jungles, filling swamps, building roads, and constructing public buildings, most notably St. Andrew's Cathedral and the Government House.[54] Special arrangements were also made during the construction process to ensure that the convict laborers could fabricate what was required. McNair, who took over the supervision of the building of St. Andrew's Cathedral from MacPherson, described one such arrangement made for the convict laborers to accurately produce the Gothic pointed arches during the building of St. Andrew's Cathedral:

> As a pattern for the convicts to follow, we built two arches on the ground, the exact counterpart of those in the building; and, indeed, at any time when they wanted a guide, we had a model made; and the natives of India are such wonderful imitators, as we all know, that they soon were able to follow the copy we had given them.[55]

Although they employed not convict laborers but Chinese builders, similar arrangements were made by Thomson during the building of Horsburgh Lighthouse in order to compensate for the local builders' "carelessness" and "unskillfulness." In determining the exterior geometry of the shaft of the lighthouse, Thomson adopted a

> curve, whose elements could be accurately calculated … [which] would also be of the greatest service to the works in setting off the dimensions of the courses to the stone-cutters and in constructing the models for their guidance.[56]

These constructed models were then used by the stone masons as guides for producing their granite pieces off-site near the Pulau Ubin quarry, before the finished pieces were shipped to Pedra Branca, the site of the Horsburgh lighthouse.

HETEROGENEITY AND BUILDING ARTIFACTS

We tend to view buildings as stable artifacts because of their imposing physical presence and perceived permanence. Scholars in Science and Technology Studies, such as Ken Alder, however, argue that "[s]haping the material world is a laborious process. Physical matter is lumpy and recalcitrant. Even apparently well-made artifacts often prove fragile in actual use."[57] This observation might apply to colonial buildings in early Singapore not only because their realization depended on purportedly unreliable and unskillful labor as we have seen earlier but also because their stability is contingent upon the alignment of various heterogeneous elements, such as the material properties of the construction materials, and the site and climatic conditions. In the early days of colonial Singapore, when a systematic knowledge of local resources and conditions was not yet developed, the alignment of these various heterogeneous elements hinged on various forms of improvisation, on-the-job-learning and other strategies of coping on the part of the engineers and surveyors involved. The tenuous nature of the alignments in many colonial buildings was perhaps most glaringly illustrated in the various types and extents of failures that plagued them, especially in the first half of the nineteenth century.

For example, some of the buildings and fortifications designed and built under the supervision of Captain Lake in the 1830s were fraught with all kinds of problems. Coleman noted that the "embrazures [*sic*] of the Battery [Lake designed and supervised] were blown away in firing the first salute" and the jail Lake designed was located on a site so poorly drained that it was "inundated at every high tide."[58] Even Coleman was not spared from the curse of building failure. The roof of his Armenian Church, completed in 1835, was originally a high dome but it became unsafe and was altered to a pitched roof.[59] The first St. Andrew's Cathedral, completed in 1837 and based on Coleman's design, likewise ran into problems. It was badly damaged in 1852 by lightning because no lightning conductor had been installed. Unused for a number of years after the incident, the Cathedral degenerated into a "ruinous state" and was regarded as "a disgrace to the Settlement."[60]

The Colonial Engineer most notoriously associated with building failures, however, was Captain Charles Edward Faber, the Colonial Engineer of Singapore between 1844 and 1850.[61] In November 1846, a major accident took place at a construction site under his supervision. The roof gave way when the builders were working on it, injuring several of them. The accident was attributed to undersized structural elements – the roof beams and the columns – that were too weak to support the roof.[62] One of the newspaper reports further noted other failures connected to Faber:

> First Faber's Bridge could not be made to maintain its proper position after several attempts; next, the walls of the new [Ellenborough] market, after it was finished, were found to be cracking most alarmingly in several places, owing to the ends of the building proving too heavy in comparison to the sides, and, from the treacherous nature of the soil which had not been sufficiently guarded against, beginning to sink very fast.[63]

Although we do not know the exact reasons behind the above cases of building failures in colonial Singapore, they foreground the challenges of aligning the heterogeneous elements required to construct a stable artifact and, in the case of Faber, his sheer incompetency. Before the emergence of systematic and explicit colonial knowledge on building in the tropics, which we shall discuss in Chapter 2, colonial administrators, engineers and surveyors relied heavily on locally available building resources and knowledge. Their reliance is perhaps best illustrated by the similarities – perhaps not in the typological sense but certainly in appearance and construction materials used – between the early houses erected in colonial Singapore and indigenous architecture of the region.[64] As Lee notes in his book *The Singapore House*: "The first houses erected by the new arrivals were timber with *attap* roofs and walls lined with *kajang*, waterproof matting of *pandanus* or *mengkuang*. These were similar to the houses of the original inhabitants."[65] Even the Government House, completed within a fortnight after the arrival of the British, for Stamford Raffles – the "founder" of modern Singapore – was a not very substantial house with *attap* roof, walls of "rough planks and venetian windows." Even as it was subsequently modified and extended with the addition of more rooms and verandahs, the Government House remained until 1859 as a timber house with a thatched roof.

As Singapore's long-term future as a British colony was secured around 1824 after the Dutch relinquished all claims to the Malay Peninsula and more land was ceded to the British by the indigenous ruler, more brick buildings were erected. These buildings appear to use bricks produced locally as suggested by the presence of many brick kilns in the Kallang area in a 1836 map based on Coleman's first topographical survey of Singapore conducted in 1829. Later, around the 1840s, the colonial government ordered the PWD to set up a brick kiln at Serangoon

Road, staffed by convict laborers, to produce more bricks.[66] Besides locally supplied bricks, many of these new brick buildings also used a locally manufactured plaster called "Madras *chunam*." As suggested by its name, the plaster made from shell lime, egg white, sugar and coconut husk had its origin in Madras. Probably brought to Singapore by engineers like MacPherson and McNair, who were both with the Madras Artillery before being posted to Singapore, Madras *chunam* could be polished to produce "a remarkably smooth and glossy surface" and was regarded as a critical component for classical architecture in colonial Singapore.[67]

These locally produced building materials hinted at the processes of local adaptation and improvisation that had taken place in order to produce the classical masonry buildings that British engineers and surveyors tended to design in the nineteenth century. Erecting these new masonry buildings, however, did not just entail the use of different building materials. It also required a different constructional method with its own structural logic, which in turn depends on variables such as the type of brick bond used, the strength of the type of bricks and mortar used, and environmental considerations such as soil conditions and wind. All these might appear to be straightforward today but in early colonial Singapore, when systematic knowledge and standards on construction and structure were not yet established, the confluence of these various uncertainties meant that some degree of trial-and-error was unavoidable. Unfortunately, these improvised experiments were seldom recorded in colonial accounts. A rare exception was Thomson's discussion of how he tested the structure required for the Horsburgh lighthouse by putting up brick pillars on various parts of Pedra Branca to test the force of the waves for nine months.[68]

We have thus far discussed the heterogeneity of architectural production in relation to building construction, material and structure. But since we are examining pre-1870 colonial houses when there were many classical villas, we should not ignore the fact that classicism is an aesthetic code with its own rules, i.e. different classical orders and proportion systems. It thus called for not just practical knowledge of building construction and structure but also some knowledge of stylistic conventions. Many architectural historians claimed that architects, engineers and other builders in the different colonies of the British Empire and also North America relied on pattern books to produce the classical designs for their buildings, especially during the eighteenth and nineteenth centuries.[69] The general perception is that a pattern book is purely an illustrated volume that presents a variety of plans and perspectives of exemplary designs for the reader to select. In other words, it is seen as a source book with different designs of various styles but it has no clear instructive purpose. But a pattern book is more than that. The term itself is a broad overarching one that describes different types of illustrated books. Source books of style constitute only a minority of the pattern books published.[70] Most of the illustrated architectural books published in the eighteenth and nineteenth centuries were in fact either books on classical orders or builders' manuals.

Books on classical orders helped to make the aesthetic rules plain and easy for the reader, typically a builder, to understand and apply. While early architectural treatises by famous figures such as Andrea Palladio and Vicenzo Scamozzi popularized classicism, they do not instruct a builder how to proportion a building or determine the dimensions of the various architectural components. The books on classical orders helped to bridge the gap by offering builders various simple methods of determining, for example, the diameters of a column and the dimensions of a decorative detail. William Halfpenny's *Practical Architecture* (1724) and James Gibbs' *Rules for Drawing the Five Orders* (1732) are examples of such (pattern) books on classical orders.

Besides proportioning and measuring, the variety of novel building forms introduced by the popularization of classicism in the eighteenth and nineteenth centuries also exceeded the practical knowledge of many local builders in the metropole, thus creating a demand for builders' manuals.[71] These builders' manuals, which provided practical instructions for carpenters, joiners, masons and bricklayers to execute all kinds of basic building works in classical architecture, formed the other common subcategory of pattern books. A prominent example, William Pain's *The Builder's Pocket-Treasure*, identified by Lee and Seow as an example of a pattern book that was used in colonial Singapore, was written as a manual of instruction that offered the "uninstructed" builder simple methods of determining the measurements of the different architectural elements and "put his Design in Practice."[72] As Pain explains in his Preface,

> In the Course of the following Sheets Plainness and Perspicuity have been principally considered. Elegance of Style would be no Advantage to the Subject; but, on the contrary, would be repugnant to the End and Design of the present Publication, which is to obviate and remove the many Difficulties which common Mechanics usually meet with in perusing Books of Architecture; who, after having been at great Pains to improve themselves in their Professions, meet with so many Discouragements that they are oftentimes obliged to desist from their Undertaking ...[73]

The generous number of engraved plates in Pain's book was central to its ambition to instruct and was considered as "the *raison d'être* of his books."[74] In a place like colonial Singapore, a thorough mastery of such builders' manuals, alongside textbooks on proportional systems, allowed the colonial engineers and surveyors who did not receive formal architectural training to gain at least some level of competence to build proportionately correct albeit simplified versions of classical buildings.

MULTICULTURAL INFLUENCES, COMFORT AND HOUSE TYPOLOGIES

In our discussion in this chapter thus far, we have only shown how British engineers and surveyors like Thomson, McNair and McCallum dealt with the heteronomous and heterogeneous conditions of architectural production in early colonial

Singapore. In noting how they managed and "civilized" the local builders, experimented with local materials, and gained competence through manuals and textbooks, we might have unwittingly treated the local builders as mere subordinate workers devoid of agency, who did not contribute to the early colonial built environment in a constructive manner. This neglect of the contribution of local builders is common to all the key accounts of early colonial architecture in Singapore, including those of Hancock discussed at the beginning of this chapter.[75] Given that these accounts, besides Lee's *The Singapore House*, are architect-centric architectural histories, this inattention is perhaps not surprising. In fact these accounts do not even mention the local builders, let alone their contribution. The silence in the official records of the roles played by local builders, and the absence of textual records of their work perhaps make this neglect understandable. Other than relying on textual records, are there other avenues of locating the necessary historical evidence to acknowledge the contribution of local builders? An avenue of exploration is through typological study and how we can discern the influence of not just the local builder but also the indigenous building norms on colonial architecture.[76] In the final section of this chapter, I will briefly explore the pre-1870 typologies of colonial houses in Singapore to discern a few plausible local and extra-local influences. I end by situating these typologies and their multicultural influences in the context of material comfort.

The classical houses from the pre-1870 era in colonial Singapore were seen by some architectural historians as derived from metropolitan models such as the Georgian House or the Palladian Villa. This tendency to see colonial architecture as largely derivative is one that is not restricted to the case of Singapore but it has been challenged in the recent histories of colonial architecture.[77] In the case of houses in the Straits Settlements, which consisted of Singapore alongside Penang and Malacca, Northcote Parkinson has argued as early as 1955 that "[t]hese Penang houses ... were not a tropical variant of something seen in England. It was the English houses that were an Europeanised variant of something seen in India."[78] Not only did Parkinson question England as the source, he also pointed to the local multicultural influences behind the colonial houses: "the early European house in Malaya was basically of a Malay pattern, raised off the ground with a roof of Chinese tiles, to replace a still earlier roof of attap."[79] Among the multicultural influences on the colonial houses for the Europeans, local historians tend to single out particularly the influences of the Malay indigenous architecture. For example, Seow sees the colonial bungalows and villas in Singapore as following the "lessons and the theme of the Malay prototype."[80] Peter and Waveney Jenkins go as far as to characterize the four stages in the evolution of the planter's bungalow in Malaya with reference to the Malay house, naming them as "The Malay House," "The Malay Transitional House," "Developed Malay House" and "Corporate Mansion" respectively. In their descriptions, the Jenkins associate the porch, or *porte-cochère*, and the verandah of the planter's bungalow with the *anjung* and *serambi* respectively of the indigenous Malay house.[81]

Although there are typological similarities among the indigenous houses across lowland Malay-speaking communities from Sumatra's coast, the Malay Peninsula, and coastal Borneo, in terms of their layout and structural-formal characteristics, the Malay house is not a monolithic entity. There are variations in regional models, many of which were shaped by multicultural influences. For example, the Melaka's version of the Malay house called *Rumah Serambi Melaka* incorporated architectural elements thought to be derived from Chinese and Portuguese architecture. Another version, *Rumah Limas*, or the Hip-Roof House found in Perak and Riau, has adaptations thought to be based on Dutch Colonial antecedents.[82] The Malay House is therefore not a static and immutable indigenous architecture that was implied by Seow and the Jenkins. As with other types of indigenous architecture, the Malay House was a dynamic and evolving type that absorbed the cultural influences around it, including those of the Europeans. The relationship between the Malay house and the colonial house was probably not as unidirectional, with the Malay house exerting a one-way influence on the colonial house.

Furthermore, it would be prudent to not make too direct an association between these features of the colonial house in Singapore and Malaya with specific characteristics of the Malay indigenous house. By the time the British came to Malaya in the late eighteenth century, when Penang was ceded to the English East India Company in 1786, they already had a long history and extensive experience of building in their tropical colonies, most notably, India and the West Indies. The bungalow and the verandah were both Anglo-Indian terms that referred respectively to a well-defined typology and an established building feature by the late eighteenth century. Features similar to the verandah – such as the loggia, piazza and gallery – and timber-framed buildings being elevated off the ground on brick piers or timber columns could also be found in the creole vernacular houses of the Caribbean and the American Southeast before the late eighteenth century. In his study of creole vernacular houses, Jay Edwards argues that these features had complex histories and were outcomes that synthesized influences from a multitude of sources linked to the waves of European colonization and movements of people to the West Indies from Africa and Europe, and between the West Indies and the American Southwest. Among the plausible influences on these features, Edwards identifies the Spanish, English and French Antillean creole vernacular architecture, the African vernacular architecture on the coast of the Gulf of Guinea between Liberia and Angola, where the slaves in the Antilles came from since the sixteenth century, and European classicism, especially the Palladian variant.[83] For Edwards, creole architecture is a "synthesized tropical colonial form" produced through cultural exchanges and adaptations in contact zones where different groups of people intermingled. He further elaborates: "Profound cultural amalgamations, referred to as cultural syncretism, often occur under pioneering circumstances as a result of interethnic communication. Roughly analogous traditions from several cultures, blend to form an entirely new and adaptive pattern."[84]

From the above discussion, we could argue that "profound cultural amalgamations" of Anglo-Indian, Malay, Chinese and even Creole influences shaped the early colonial architecture in Singapore, resulting in two main types of pre-1870 houses. As early as 1840, Major Low, who was the Magistrate and head of Police at Singapore, distinguished in his journals between the "Garden houses ... in a handsome style of architecture and are almost invariably of two stories" and the "bungalow style" preferred by "old Indians."[85] The houses designed by Coleman mentioned at the beginning of the chapter – Maxwell House and his own house – were what Low called "garden houses." They were characterized by classical style and tended to be more compact with a square-shouldered silhouette. Most of the pre-1870s built houses in the area next to the esplanade and around St. Andrew's Cathedral belong to this type (see Figure 1.5). As for the bungalow style, John Cameron provided us with a detailed description from his 1865 book:

> Bungalows, a term so often applied to any style of dwelling-house in the East, are, properly speaking, only of one story, elevated some five or six feet from the ground upon arched masonry. A moderate-sized building of this description might be 90 feet long, 60 or 70 deep, usually a parallelogram in form ... The walls from the flooring to the roof are seldom less than fifteen feet high, which gives a lofty ceiling to the apartments, and the roof is covered with tiles. The most striking feature of these buildings, however, is the broad verandah which runs right round the house about eight or ten feet in width, resting on the plinths of the pillars that, extending upwards in round columns with neatly moulded capitals, support the continuation of the roof which projects some four feet beyond the pillars, forming deep overhanging eaves. On to the verandah, which is surrounded by a neat railing, all the doors of the bungalow open, and as these also serve the purpose of the windows, they are pretty numerous; they are in two halves, opening down the centre like cottage doors at home, with the lower panels plain and the two upper ones fitted with venetians to open or close at pleasure. From the centre of the building in front a portico projects some twenty-five or thirty feet, and generally about twenty-five broad, covering the carriage way and a broad flight of stone steps leading from the ground to the verandah.[86]

An example of the bungalow was Panglima Prang (Figures 1.11–1.13) owned by Tan Kim Seng, a wealthy Peranakan merchant and philanthropist, and his descendants. First built at around 1860, Panglima Prang was then extended with a formal dining room and a pair of two-storey blocks, but it was demolished in 1982. In many ways, Panglima Prang fitted Cameron's description. The original building was a single-storey rectangular structure with the main floor elevated on arched masonry; the lofty interior was encircled with a wide verandah to which the doors opened; the plastered columns supported deep overhanging eaves and there was a front *porte-cochère.*[87]

Although the garden houses were different formally, they appeared to be designed based on similar considerations of comfort in a hot and humid climate, as

Figure 1.11
Exterior view of Panglima Prang. Courtesy of the Lee Kip Lin Collection. Lee Kip Lin and National Library Board, Singapore 2009.

Figure 1.12
View of the front verandah of Panglima Prang. Courtesy of the Lee Kip Lin Collection. Lee Kip Lin and National Library Board, Singapore 2009.

Figure 1.13
Interior view of the dining room of Panglima Prang. Courtesy of the Lee Kip Lin Collection. All rights reserved. Lee Kip Lin and National Library Board, Singapore 2009.

were the bungalows. The interiors were similarly lofty and, according to Cameron, "[t]he wooden doors leading from room to room are usually thrown open, there being silk screens on hinges attached to each doorway, which, while they maintain a sufficient privacy, admit of a free ventilation throughout the house."[88] They were very different from the climatically inappropriate earlier colonial houses the British built in, for example, India, which Thomas Williamson noted had very small windows and doors that prevented proper ventilation and resulted in "very, very warm air" in the interior.[89] The difference suggests that, by the time the British came to Singapore and the Straits Settlements, they already had, through centuries of trial-and-error and adaptation in other parts of the British Empire found a method, though yet uncodified, of building comfortable houses in the hot and humid tropics.

Comfort, however, did not just rely on building features. Comfort was also secured by the lifestyle of the Europeans and the very wealthy locals who followed the Europeans' way, which included the use of the "luxurious addition" of "American ice," i.e. ice harvested in North America during the winter and shipped to Asia, and the services provided by a retinue of servants, which for a "moderate" European family included "a butler, two under-servants, a maid (or *Ayah*) or nurse, tailor, an assistant, washerman, two grooms, grass-cutter, lamp-lighter, sweeper, scavenger, waterman."[90] The preoccupation with comfort in the early colonial houses and the lifestyles of the inhabitants distinguish them from the subsequent obsession with health and sanitation that drove the design and planning of the built environment, as we shall see in Chapters 2 and 3. In the early nineteenth century, the tropics were only beginning to be constructed as a pathological "other" through statistics and medical discourses. The pathologization of the tropics was not yet very common.[91] While concerns with comfort preceded the obsession with health as the main driver of early colonial architecture in the tropics, we should not make naturalistic assumptions about comfort. In his historical study of comfort in the Anglo-American context, John E. Crowley characterizes physical comfort as the "self-conscious satisfaction with the relationship between one's body and its immediate physical environment" and he argues that physical comfort was an Anglo-American invention in the eighteenth century.[92] Prior to that, comfort was a "moral term" and "[p]hysical comfort lacked priority as a value or a problem in medieval material culture."[93] Crowley notes that the new understanding of comfort brought about a disposition to criticize traditional material culture and improve upon it. The emergence of comfortable houses in the British colonies that were suited to the hot and humid tropical climate might be understood in the context of the new understanding of comfort in the eighteenth century. This also distinguishes the relationship between comfort and material culture in the early colonial houses from the preoccupation with technoscientific notions of thermal comfort in the mid-twentieth century tropical architecture that Hancock tried to conflate, as we saw at the beginning of this chapter.

In this chapter, we have challenged the conventional narrative of the origin of tropical architecture. I argued that the conventional narrative was shaped by presentism, which is the practice of interpreting the past in accordance to present-day attitudes and values. If we are instead to write a history of the present and construct a genealogy of tropical architecture, we will critically historicize the past and find that early colonial architecture is very different from mid-twentieth century tropical architecture. We will also discover that we cannot attribute the origin of tropical architecture to the genius of any European architect in the tropics – in our case George Doumgold Coleman – and a few early nineteenth-century buildings that he designed. In fact, we saw that the architecture profession, as we know it from the mid-twentieth century, was not yet established in the metropole, let alone in the colonies. Instead of a professional architect in full control of the design and building process, we saw that the colonial "architect" in the early nineteenth century was more likely to be an engineer-surveyor who happened to be also an amateur builder. As an amateur builder, he (they were invariably all men) improvised, learnt on the job from the local builders, and absorbed the multicultural influences from indigenous architecture to cope with the constraints posed by the heteronomous and heterogeneous conditions of colonial architectural production. Although we stopped at 1870 because systematic knowledge of building in the tropics emerged at around that time and professional builders, both architects and engineers, began to appear in many British colonies, improvisations and adaptations continued long after 1870. Houses were built in Singapore and Malaya by the local population without the involvement of architects and engineers until the mid-twentieth century at the earliest.

Even after professional architects and engineers were involved, and systematic knowledge and standardized typologies emerged, improvisation did not stop. Neither did the reliance on local builders and crafts cease. It was the degree and extent of improvisation and adaptation that changed. As this genealogy is primarily concerned with systematic knowledge and standardized typologies of tropical architecture, exploring the processes and outcomes of improvisation and adaptation in further detail is beyond the scope of this book. But it is still useful to note that one does not displace the other. Instead they form parallel universes, coexisting side by side. Building manuals and pattern books were not supplanted but supplemented by barrack synopses and type plans, just as local crafts and trial-and-errors were complemented by systematic training and experimentations in building and environmental technologies. Systematic training, technoscientific knowledge and new building regulations that we shall see in the next three chapters did not totally eradicate building failures. Standardized tropical types for military barracks, hospitals and housing were developed from around 1870 to the mid-twentieth century and many of these antecedents to modern tropical architecture were built. During the same period, buildings produced through adaptations and multicultural amalgamations led to a proliferation of residential buildings of different hybrid typologies, such as Straits Chinese Bungalow, Black and White House and Compound House.[94]

NOTES

1 The accounts are T. H. H. Hancock, "George Doumgold Coleman, Architect and Planning Advisor to Sir Stamford Raffles, Designer of the Armenian Church, Singapore," *QJIAM* 1, no. 3 (1951); T. H. H. Hancock, *Coleman of Singapore* (Singapore: Antiques of the Orient, 1985 [1955]); T. H. H. Hancock, *Coleman's Singapore* (Singapore: The Malaysian Branch of the Royal Asiatic Society, 1986 [1955]); T. H. H. Hancock and C. A. Gibson-Hill, *Architecture in Singapore* (Singapore: Singapore Art Institute and Institute of Architects of Malaya, 1954).
2 Maxwell House was completed in 1827 according to Coleman's design, but it was subsequently altered and enlarged a few times as its use changed from that of a house to a courthouse and government offices.
3 Hancock, *Coleman of Singapore*, u.p.
4 Hancock and Gibson-Hill, *Architecture in Singapore*, u.p.
5 Hancock, *Coleman's Singapore*, 28.
6 Marjorie Doggett, *Characters of Light*, 2nd ed. (Singapore: Times Books International, 1985 [1957]), 79.
7 Eu-jin Seow, "Architectural Development in Singapore" (PhD thesis, University of Melbourne, 1973), 123; Gretchen Mahbubani, *Pastel Portraits* (Singapore: Singapore Coordinating Committee, 1984), 16.
8 Sten Nilsson, *European Architecture in India 1750–1850*, trans. Agnes George and Eleonore Zettersten (London: Faber and Faber, 1968).
9 Kip Lin Lee, *The Singapore House, 1819–1942* (Singapore: Times Editions, Preservation of Monuments Board, 1988), 42.
10 K. A. Brundle, "P.W.D. Housing: Some Comparative Notes and Diagrams on the Planning of Pre-War and Post-War Quarters Built by the Public Works Department, Singapore," *QJIAM* 1, no. 2 (1951).
11 Hancock also singled out that building in his interview with the press. See "Architects to Hold Their First Show: How Singapore Has Grown," *ST*, 19 March 1954.
12 Hancock, *Coleman's Singapore*, 26 and 28.
13 K. A. Brundle, "Economy in Architecture," *QJIAM* 4, no. 4 (1955): 3.

14 Brundle, "P.W.D. Housing."
15 "Wanted: Law to Save Our History – Friends May Appeal to Colony Govt.," *ST*, 22 July 1955; The Friends of Singapore, ed., *The House in Coleman Street* (Singapore: The Friends of Singapore, 1958). The "Friends of Singapore" Society was founded in 1937 by Roland Braddell. Their main mission was the "[p]romotion and encouragement of the historical, artistic and cultural movements in Singapore." See "Appeal to All Races …", *SFP*, 7 February 1957. See also "S'pore 'Friends' Want Members," *SFP*, 10 September 1947.
16 C. Northcote Parkinson, "Foreword," in *The House in Coleman Street*, ed. The Friends of Singapore (Singapore: The Friends of Singapore, 1958), 3.
17 Hancock, *Coleman of Singapore*, u.p.
18 Ibid., 7.
19 John Wilton-Ely, "The Rise of the Professional Architect in England," in *The Architect: Chapters in the History of the Profession*, ed. Spiro Kostof (New York: Oxford University Press, 1977).
20 Barrington Kaye, *The Development of the Architectural Profession in Britain: A Sociological Study* (London: Allen & Unwin, 1962), 47.
21 Ibid., 40.
22 Mark Crinson and Jules Lubbock, *Architecture – Art or Profession? Three Hundred Years of Architectural Education in Britain* (Manchester: Manchester University Press, 1994), 2.
23 Wilton-Ely, "The Rise of the Professional Architect in England," 188.
24 Dell Upton, "Defining the Profession," in *Architecture School: Three Centuries of Educating Architects in North America*, ed. Joan Ockman (Washington, D.C. and Cambridge, MA: ACSA and MIT Press, 2012).
25 Nilsson, *European Architecture in India*; Shanti Jayewardene-Pillai, *Imperial Conversations: Indo-Britons and the Architecture of South India* (New Delhi: Yoda Press, 2007).
26 John Hall-Jones and Christopher Hooi, *An Early Surveyor in Singapore: John Turnbull Thomson in Singapore 1841–1853* (Singapore: National Museum of Singapore, 1979); C. M. Turnbull, "McNair, (John) Frederick Adolphus," in *Oxford Dictionary of National Biography*, ed. H. C. G. Matthew and Brian Harrison (Oxford: Oxford University Press, 2005), online edition, Jan 2008, accessed 5 January 2016, http://www.oxforddnb.com/view/article/34804; Jon Sun Hock Lim, *The Penang House and the Straits Architect 1887–1941* (Penang: Areca Books, 2015), 12–13.
27 Jayewardene-Pillai, *Imperial Conversations*, 109. Captain Charles Pasley, the founder of the Royal Engineers training establishment at Chatham, made a similar observation. See Chapter 2.
28 Magali Sarfatti Larson, *Behind the Postmodern Facade: Architectural Change in Late Twentieth-Century America* (Berkeley: University of California Press, 1993).
29 C. Greig Crysler, *Writing Spaces: Discourses of Architecture, Urbanism, and the Built Environment, 1960–2000* (New York: Routledge, 2003), 37.
30 Jon Sun Hock Lim, "Colonial Architecture and Architects of Georgetown (Penang) and Singapore, between 1786 and 1942" (PhD thesis, National University of Singapore, 1990); Seow, "Architectural Development in Singapore."
31 Larson, *Behind the Postmodern Facade*.
32 John Law, "Technology and Heterogeneous Engineering: The Case of Portuguese Expansion," in *The Social Construction of Technological Systems: New Directions in the Sociology and History of Technology*, ed. Wiebe E. Bijker, Thomas P. Hughes and T. J. Pinch (Cambridge, MA: MIT Press, 1987).
33 J. M. Gullick, "The Builders," *JMBRAS* 85, no. 2 (2012).

34 Syed Hussein Alatas, *The Myth of the Lazy Native: A Study of the Image of the Malays, Filipinos and Javanese from the 16th to the 20th Century and Its Function in the Ideology of Colonial Capitalism* (London: F. Cass, 1977).

35 Baron H. G. Nahuijs van Burgst, "A Dutch Account of Singapore," in *Travellers' Singapore: An Anthology*, ed. John Bastin (Kuala Lumpur: Oxford University Press, 1994 [1823]), 15; Munshi Abdullah and A. H. Hill, "The Hikayat Abdullah," *JMBRAS* 42, no. 1 (215) (1969).

36 Victor Purcell, *The Chinese in Modern Malaya* (Singapore: Eastern Universities Press, 1960), 25. A 1932 survey lists nine major Chinese contractor firms. See Xingnong Pan, ed., *Xinjiapo Zhinan* [*Singapore Directory*] (Singapore: Nanyang Chubanshe [Nanyang Publisher], 1932), 36–37.

37 McCallum was the Colonial Engineer of the Straits Settlements between 1884 and 1897. More about the work of McCallum will be covered in Chapter 2.

38 John Turnbull Thomson, "Account of the Horsburgh Light-House," *JIAES* 4, no. 1 (1852): 378.

39 Ibid., 401.

40 Ibid., 395.

41 Ibid., 407. The Chinese builders were divided into different building trades based on their dialect groups in the nineteenth century. In 1848, Seah Eu Chin estimated that 3,250 or more than half of the population from the Cantonese dialect group were employed as "carpenters, wood cutters, lime burners, brick makers and coolies employed in assisting masons." A quarter or 1,000 of the Hakka population was employed as "house builders" whereas a comparatively smaller number of the Chinese from the Teochew and Hokkien dialect groups was involved in the building trades. U Chin Siah, "The Chinese in Singapore No. II: General Sketch of the Numbers, Tribes, and Avocations of the Chinese in Singapore," *JIAES* 2 (1848).

42 Thomson, "Account of the Horsburgh Light-House," 377–78.

43 Ibid., 378.

44 H. E. McCallum, "Report on Blasting Operations at Mount Siloso, Singapore," *PPCRE* IV (1881): 56. Amoy is the old name of Xiamen, a coastal city in Fujian province where most of the Hokkien population in Singapore came from. Swatow is the historic name of Shantou, a coastal city in Guangdong province, where most of the Teochew population in Singapore boarded the ships for Singapore.

45 Thomson, "Account of the Horsburgh Light-House," 395.

46 Ibid., 377–78.

47 T. Roger Smith, "On Buildings for European Occupation in Tropical Climates, Especially India," in *Papers Read at the Royal Institute of British Architects 1867–68* (1868), 203.

48 Coleman's letter to S. G. Bonham, the Resident Councilor of Singapore, dated 23 January 1833. Quoted in Hancock, *Coleman's Singapore*, 36–37.

49 Thomson called tempinis "tampeny" and described it as "the best and most durable wood grown in Singapore." Thomson, "Account of the Horsburgh Light-House," 445–6. For his translation of Hikayat Abdullah, see Charles Burton Buckley, *An Anecdotal History of Old Times in Singapore*, vol. 2 (Singapore: Fraser & Neave, 1902), 571.

50 John Frederick Adolphus McNair, *Prisoners Their Own Warders* (Westminster: A. Constable, 1899), 97, 99.

51 Lee, *The Singapore House, 1819–1942*, 45.

52 Cited in Buckley, *An Anecdotal History of Old Times in Singapore*, vol. 1, 294.

53 Ibid., 2: 642.

54 See Anoma Pieris, *Hidden Hands and Divided Landscapes: A Penal History of Singapore's Plural Society* (Honolulu: University of Hawaii Press, 2009).

55 McNair, *Prisoners Their Own Warders*, 99–100.

56 Thomson, "Account of the Horsburgh Light-House," 393.
57 Ken Alder, *Engineering the Revolution: Arms and Enlightenment in France, 1763–1815* (Princeton, NJ: Princeton University Press, 1997), 12–13.
58 Coleman's letter to S. G. Bonham, the Resident Councilor of Singapore, dated 23 January 1833. Quoted in Hancock, *Coleman of Singapore*, 37; Buckley, *An Anecdotal History of Old Times in Singapore*, 1, 228.
59 Seow, "Architectural Development in Singapore."
60 Buckley, *An Anecdotal History of Old Times in Singapore*, 1, 292.
61 "Untitled," *ST*, 19 February 1850; Seow, "Architectural Development in Singapore."
62 "Untitled," *ST*, 4 November 1846; "Untitled," *SFPMA*, 5 November 1846.
63 "Untitled," *SFPMA*, 5 November 1846.
64 The prevalence of houses that resembled indigenous architecture in early Colonial Singapore is evident in Philip Jackson's "View of the Town" dated June 5, 1823, one of the earliest surviving sketches of Singapore. This was not unique to colonial Singapore. It was also the case in colonial India, Hong Kong and Africa.
65 *Attap* roof is a type of thatched roof and *kajang* walls is a type of mat stitched from palm leaves. Lee, *The Singapore House, 1819–1942*, 20.
66 McNair, *Prisoners Their Own Warders*, 57–58.
67 Ibid., 100.
68 Thomson, "Account of the Horsburgh Light-House," 390–91.
69 Daniel Drake Reiff, *Houses from Books: Treatises, Pattern Books, and Catalogs in American Architecture 1738–1950* (University Park, PA: Penn State University Press, 2000); Dell Upton, "Pattern Books and Professionalism: Aspects of the Transformation of Domestic Architecture in America, 1800–1860," *Winterthur Portfolio* 19, no. 2/3 (1984).
70 Eileen Harris, *British Architectural Books and Writers, 1556–1785* (Cambridge: Cambridge University Press, 1990).
71 Ibid., 39.
72 William Pain, *The Builder's Pocket-Treasure; or, Palladio Delineated and Explained* (London: W. Owen, 1763), iv.
73 Ibid., iii–iv.
74 Harris, *British Architectural Books and Writers, 1556–1785*, 339.
75 These accounts include Seow, "Architectural Development in Singapore"; Lim, "Colonial Architecture and Architects of Georgetown (Penang) and Singapore, between 1786 and 1942"; Lee, *The Singapore House, 1819–1942*.
76 Another approach in discerning the influence of the local builder was that taken in Shanti Jayawardene-Pillai's fascinating study of British colonial engineers' work in Madras, British India, during the eighteenth and nineteenth centuries. She argued that the colonial engineers engaged in "ethnoscientific ventures" to learn from the indigenous Indian knowledge of building construction. Although the Indian contributions to colonial buildings were suppressed in the official records, Jayawardene-Pillai was able to demonstrate the knowledge sharing through her studies of material evidence. See Jayewardene-Pillai, *Imperial Conversations*, 77–80.
77 For a British Indian case, see Swati Chattopadhyay, "Blurring Boundaries: The Limits of 'White Town' in Colonial Calcutta," *JSAH* 59, no. 2 (2000). For the case of colonial America, see Dell Upton, *Holy Things and Profane: Anglican Parish Churches in Colonial Virginia* (New York; Cambridge, MA: Architectural History Foundation, MIT Press, 1986).
78 C. Northcote Parkinson, "The Homes of Malaya," *The Malayan Historical Journal* 2, no. 2 (1955). Parkinson's argument was of course later substantiated by Anthony D. King's seminal study of the global history of the bungalow that first emerged in British India.

See Anthony D. King, *The Bungalow: The Production of a Global Culture*, 2nd ed. (New York: Oxford University Press, 1995 [1984]).

79 Parkinson, "The Homes of Malaya," 125.

80 Seow, "Architectural Development in Singapore," 237.

81 Peter Jenkins and Waveney Jenkins, *The Planter's Bungalow: A Journey Down the Malay Peninsula* (Singapore: Editions Didier Millet, 2007), 17–19. The *anjung* was seen as "the prolongation of the *serambi*" and the *serambi* was described as "a gallery running the length of the house" and "vestibule just within the front door." R. N. Hilton, "The Basic Malay House," *JMBRAS* 29, no. 3 (175) (1956): 145, 36, 43.

82 Imran bin Tajudeen, "Beyond Racialized Representations: Architectural Linguae Francae and Urban Histories in the Kampung Houses and Shophouses of Melaka and Singapore," in *Colonial Frames, Nationalist Histories: Imperial Legacies, Architecture and Modernity*, ed. Mrinalini Rajagopalan and Madhuri Desai (Burlington: Ashgate, 2012), 215–20; Jee Yuan Lim, *The Malay House: Rediscovering Malaysia's Indigenous Shelter System* (Pulau Pinang: Institut Masyarakat, 1987).

83 Jay D. Edwards, "The Origins of Creole Architecture," *Winterthur Portfolio* 29, nos. 2/3 (1994); Jay D. Edwards, "The Complex Origins of the American Domestic Piazza-Veranda-Gallery," *Material Culture* 21, no. 2 (1989).

84 Edwards, "The Origins of Creole Architecture," 157, 76.

85 Buckley, *An Anecdotal History of Old Times in Singapore*, 1, 356.

86 John Cameron, *Our Tropical Possessions in Malayan India* (London: Smith, Elder and Co., 1865), 75–76.

87 See Lee, *The Singapore House, 1819–1942*, 154–57.

88 Cameron, *Our Tropical Possessions in Malayan India*, 76.

89 Thomas Williamson, *The East India Vade Mecum*, vols. 1 and 2 (London: Black, Parry, 1810), 6–7.

90 Buckley, *An Anecdotal History of Old Times in Singapore*, 2, 357.

91 See for example, Mark Harrison, *Climates and Constitutions: Health, Race, Environment and British Imperialism in India 1600–1850* (Oxford: Oxford University Press, 1999).

92 John E. Crowley, *The Invention of Comfort: Sensibility and Design in Early Modern Britain and Early America* (Baltimore: Johns Hopkins University Press, 2001), 141.

93 Ibid., 3.

94 See Lee, *The Singapore House, 1819–1942*; Imran bin Tajudeen, "Kampung/Compound Houses." *Singapura Stories* website, accessed 31 October 2015, http://singapurastories.com/2012/06/1267/"

Chapter 2: Engineering Military Barracks

Experimentation, Systematization and Colonial Spaces of Exception

In the military landscape of pre-World War II Singapore, Changi Cantonment, completed in 1941 after one and a half decades of on-off construction, was the largest and perhaps the most significant. It was first planned in 1926 and the planning principle was investigated and set out in a report by the Gillman Commission, a high level commission from Britain dispatched by the Army Council to study "on the spot" the details of the proposed defenses of the new Imperial Naval Base.[1] Changi Cantonment was a key component of the interwar effort to turn Singapore into Britain's major defensive stronghold east of Suez to counter the growing Japanese threat in the 1920s and 1930s. Together with the completion of the Imperial Naval Base at Sembawang, and the air bases at Seletar and Tengah in the late 1930s, Changi Cantonment was key to making Singapore the "Gibraltar of the East," the major British imperial defensive bulwark in the Far East, simultaneously protecting British territories and trade interests, specifically Hong Kong and the China trade route, and the British dominions to the south, i.e. Australia and New Zealand.[2]

Occupying an area of approximately 2,000 acres, Changi consisted of three main groups of barracks – Kitchener Barracks housing the largest Royal Engineers Station outside Britain, Robert Barracks housing the Royal Artillery Regiment, and Selarang Barracks housing the Gordon Highlanders Infantry Battalion.[3] Changi was in many ways a model cantonment. The design of the buildings was based on a combination of the latest type plans from the War Office and the improvement of local military buildings erected at the other sites, such as Pulau Blakang Mati, Tanglin and Fort Canning.[4] The buildings had the latest equipment and installations. The siting of the buildings was carefully planned "in one of the finest natural settings of any military base anywhere in the world." The result "became almost a garden city"[5] (Figure 2.1). Other than the buildings and landscaping, Changi Cantonment had a vast array of recreational amenities catering to various sporting activities. It even had an air-conditioned cinema and a golf course was in the midst of construction when the Japanese invaded and occupied Singapore in early 1942.[6] With such an environment, it is unsurprising that the Changi Cantonment would frequently be recalled by its former residents variously as "a beautiful paradise" and "a delightful setting complete in itself" with "palatial mess[es]."[7]

Figure 2.1
Changi as "almost a Garden City." View of a barrack block in Changi with the Johor Straits in the background. Courtesy of the REL.

Taking the construction of the Changi Cantonment and its barracks in Colonial Singapore during the 1920s and 1930s as a culmination point, this chapter traces the history of the design and planning of military barracks in colonial Singapore from the early nineteenth century to the 1940s. During this period, the military barracks was transformed from a poorly equipped building converted from a Palladian villa type to a specialized building meticulously designed and planned to ensure the health and well-being of the British soldier. As Singapore was an important military outpost in the British Empire, the history of the military barracks in Singapore overlaps with and reflects the broader history of the design and planning of military barracks across the British Empire.

This chapter shows that the military barracks was the earliest British colonial building type to be formally "tropicalized." By that I mean that a systematic body of explicit knowledge was first developed and implemented to regulate the planning and design of British military barracks in the tropics. In contrast to the tacit knowledge and improvisations behind the tropicalization of houses that led to different hybridized variations discussed in Chapter 1, this systematic knowledge was able to ensure a high degree of uniformity between the military barracks built in the different parts of the British tropical colonies through the clear stipulation of the space standards, planning principles and environmental technologies. We shall examine how the body of systematic knowledge first emerged in the British West Indies in the 1820s and was further developed and formalized in the recommendations of the various Royal Commissions and Barrack and Hospital Improvement Commissions (BHIC) established to improve the sanitary state of the British Army in the British Empire in the mid-nineteenth century. These reforms were subsequently institutionalized and disseminated throughout the Empire as a series of barrack synopses and type plans to ensure uniformity and replicability.

The main actors involved in producing the body of systematic knowledge were the military engineers, i.e. the Royal Engineers. As various scholars have noted, military engineers were among the first to be systematically trained in building construction and they were also pioneers that experimented and innovated in various aspects of building construction. This chapter focuses on the work of the Royal Engineers, especially their "experimental tradition," in relation to the production of tropical barracks in the colonies. Drawing on the notion of "heterogeneous engineering" elaborated in Chapter 1, this chapter discusses how the Royal Engineers methodically built up a body of knowledge and practices that succeeded in addressing the various socio-ecological difficulties of building in far-flung British tropical colonies. The planning and design of Changi Cantonment and barracks in the 1920s and 1930s could be considered as the culmination of more than a century of heterogeneous engineering.

In the last section, I argue that the cantonments that housed tropicalized military barracks were spaces of exception in the discrepant urbanism of colonial cities. They were sanitized enclaves designed to optimize the health and well-being of the British soldiers amidst larger landscapes of contamination where the local population dwelled in conditions of biopolitical neglect. The cantonments also served as enclaves that provided grids of intelligibility that permitted the carrying out of carefully regulated socio-spatial experiments.

MILITARY BARRACKS AS TROPICALIZED "GLOBAL FORM"

When the Gillman Commission submitted its report on the defense of Singapore in 1927, it also prepared a masterplan of the Changi Cantonment (Figure 2.2). What was subsequently built (Figure 2.3), however, deviated slightly from this masterplan. In the Gillman Commission's masterplan, all buildings, except for the officers' quarters, were rectangular in shape and were almost all oriented along the east–west axis such that the longer sides faced the north and south. This orientation has the advantage of minimizing the buildings' exposure to the hot morning and afternoon sun. While such an ideal orientation makes sense in the abstract, it could be awkward when rigidly applied to a hilly site such as Changi. In the Gillman Commission's masterplan, many of the buildings appeared to be positioned without taking into consideration the contours of the hilly site. A few of the proposed buildings were in fact placed perpendicularly to the contour lines, which suggests that quite a bit of cutting and filling of the site would be necessary had the buildings been built in those positions. When the buildings were built later, the rigid orientation along the east–west axis gave way to buildings offset to various extents from the east–west axis to follow the contours of the hilly terrain or to be sited along the ridges of the hills. I suggest that this departure of the buildings from what was planned could be understood on at least two levels.

At one level, the departure of the buildings from what was planned could be attributed to pragmatic considerations such as the adjustment of the position of buildings to preserve existing trees, or the acceptance of the need for improvisations and adjustments given that the fast pace of "construction went hand in hand with planning."[8] The departure, however, seemed to be already taken into account at the initial planning stage and was not unanticipated. For example, while certain principles such as the siting of the buildings along the

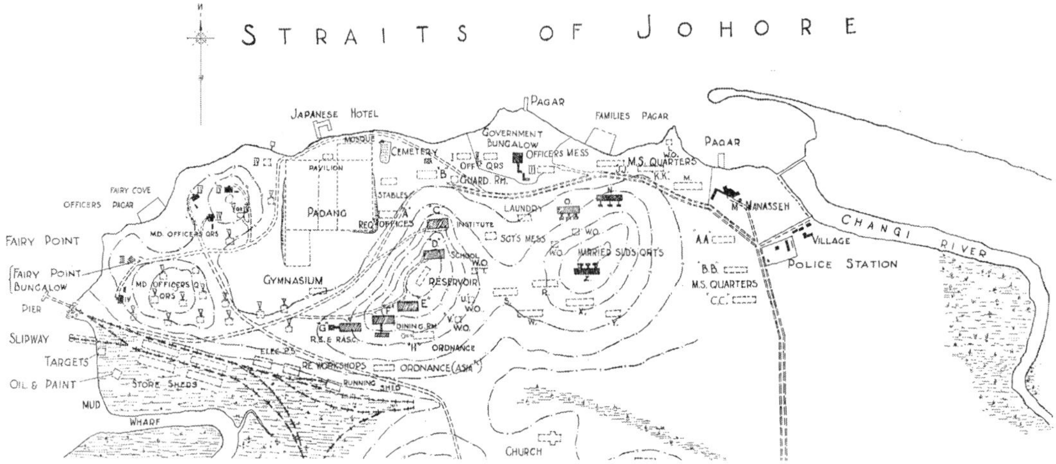

Figure 2.2
Masterplan of Changi Cantonment prepared by the Gillman Commission in 1927. Reprinted, by permission, from the *REJ* 52, 1938.

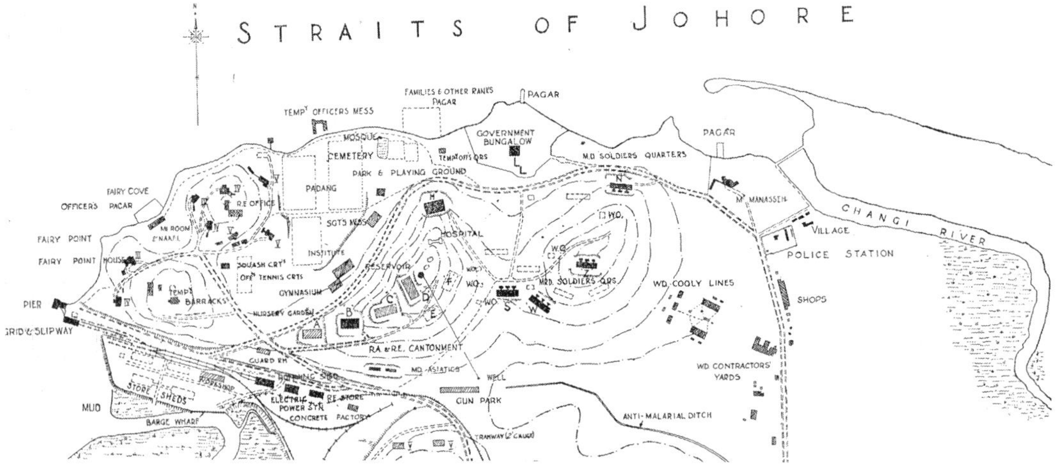

Figure 2.3
Masterplan of Changi Cantonment as completed in 1930. Reprinted, by permission, from the *REJ* 52, 1938.

ridges to ensure the maximum circulation of air were regarded as the key criteria in selecting building sites in the masterplan, the Gillman Commission also emphasized that "until a considerable quantity of jungle has been cleared and further survey made, it is not practicable at present [planning] stage to gauge the full possibilities of the site in this respect."[9]

Similar leeway for local adjustment was also apparent in the design of the different types of buildings in the cantonment. On the one hand, the designs of the buildings adhered to the standards and type plans approved by the War Office in Britain. In the case of the design of the barrack blocks (Figures 2.4–2.5), the enveloping of the barracks with wide verandahs, the placement of beds between openings and the use of the ground floor for dining rooms, offices, stores, study rooms or any purposes other than sleeping quarters, were all norms that have been systematically developed for military buildings in the British tropical colonies

Figure 2.4
View of a Changi barrack block, circa 1930s. Courtesy of the REL.

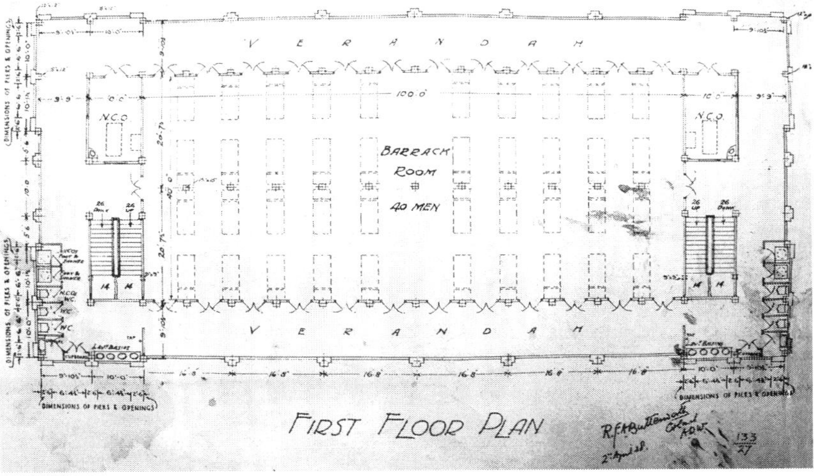

Figure 2.5
First floor plan of the barrack block. Reprinted, by permission, from the NAUK.

since the mid-nineteenth century, as we shall see. Furthermore, for these barrack blocks, the floor to ceiling height of approximately 14 feet, verandah of 10 feet width, floor space per head of 100 square feet, "air space" of approximately 1,400 cubic feet per head, were exactly the same as the ideal figures recommended for "Category IV" of military stations in the British Empire in the 1923 edition of *Barrack Synopsis* issued by the War Office (Figure 2.6). Like the previous norms, these quantifiable standards and their climatic variations have a long history. Even what was regarded by Colonel L. N. Malan, the Chief Engineer and the officer in charge of the design of the Changi Cantonment, as the "unusual feature"[10] of using the end verandahs as sanitary annexes, was specifically allowed in *Barrack Synopsis* as long as "two opposite corners out of the four [were] being left free."[11]

6 PART I.

Table showing Minimum Height and Floor and Cubic Space per Bed to be provided in Barrack Rooms for British Troops—*continued.*

Stations.	Height to Wall Plate or Ceiling (ft.).	Floor Space (sq. ft.).	Cubic Space (cub. ft.).	Verandahs if provided (width in ft.)
North China (special case)	11	70	770	8
CATEGORY III.				
Egypt ... ... Ceylon (Coast) ... ... South China (except Hong Kong Peak) ... Mauritius ... ... West African Hill Stations ... ... West Indies	13	80	1,040	10
CATEGORY IV.				
Soudan ... ... West Africa (Plains) ... Straits Settlements ...	14	100	1,400	10

Figure 2.6
Table on the space standards for housing British soldiers in the 1931 edition of *Barracks Synopsis*. Source: WO, *Barrack Synopsis*, 1931.

At another level, the type plans were not meant as rigid prescriptions. The type plans were typically conceived in a sufficiently flexible manner to accommodate some degree of change. For example, the type plan for the officers' quarters could "be arranged in different ways to suit different sites ... [so long as it] always have its verandah east and west."[12] Similarly, for the barrack block, a design was prepared and left at the War Office in order for the steel reinforcement of the concrete structure to be worked out there while "[t]he architectural completion of this skeleton framework was subsequently designed in Singapore to suit the local conditions of the site and surroundings."[13] Part of the "architectural completion" included the design and testing of different window systems.[14] Besides infill and windows, two different roof systems, flat concrete slab roof and tiled pitched roof, were also tested on buildings with similar plans and structural systems (Figure 2.7). Opinions were divided regarding the relative merits of the two systems and both were implemented. Such local experimentations and variations from the type plans and prescribed standards were not unusual. In fact the introductory note of the various editions of *Barrack Synopsis* explicitly announces that while

> [t]his Synopsis contains statements of particulars, based upon decisions which have, from time to time, been laid down by authority, as regards the military buildings authorized for various units, and the standard of accommodation and fittings in connection therewith ... [c]ases may occur where the circumstances render justifiable a departure from the scales herein contained, and in the case of Foreign Stations, the climatic and other conditions may necessitate some deviation from these standards.[15]

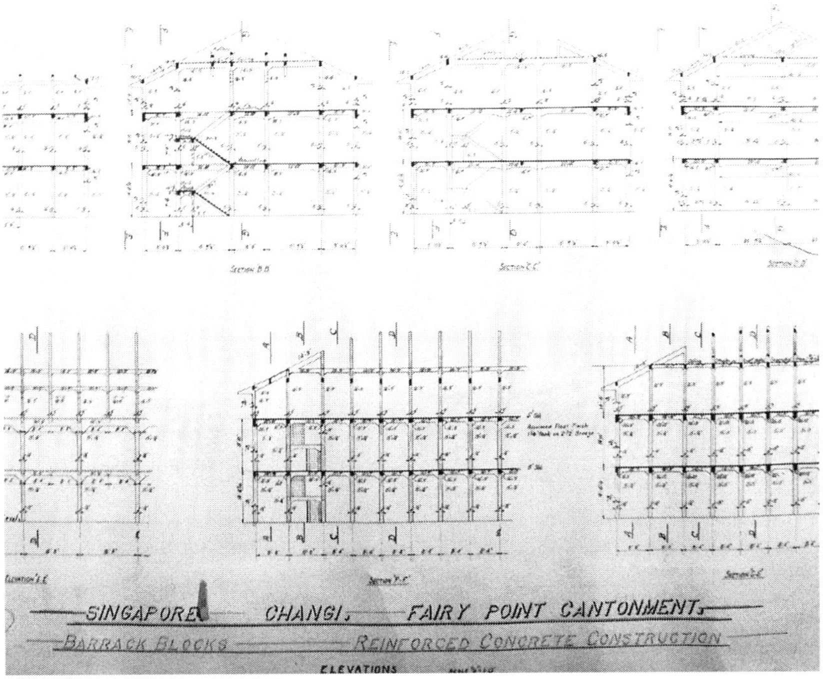

Figure 2.7
Sectional drawings of the barrack block showing reinforced concrete structural frame. Reprinted, by permission, from the NAUK.

The accommodation, both conceptually and in practice, of local deviations from and variations of the prescribed standards and norms spelt out in the type plans and barrack synopses was arrived at only after many years of trials. Local *in situ* translations and adaptations of abstract standards and norms formulated in the metropolitan administrative center into specific buildings did not always go as smoothly as presented in the case of Changi Cantonment. In fact, differences between the demands of the abstract metropolitan standards and norms on the one hand, and the specificities of the local available resources and local needs on the other hand, and the ensuing tensions and disagreements on how to negotiate between the two, has been a recurring theme in the execution of military engineering works in the colonies.[16] The tension here was not so much between the global and the local but between "universal" abstract simplified knowledge and "local" practical knowledge or, what James Scott calls, episteme and mētis.[17] The distinction here is between the localized, quotidian and embodied nature of mētis versus the codified, standardized and technical nature of episteme which is meant to be applicable across diverse territories and heterogeneous contexts. Notwithstanding the problems of such a formulation, this distinction serves as a useful departure point for attending to the difficulties of translating "universal" standards and norms of building a cantonment and barrack in a particular site, to which I will now turn.[18]

The building of Pulau Brani and Pulau Blakang Mati Cantonments in the 1890s is one example that will provide interesting insights into the universal–local, episteme–mētis tensions. These two cantonments were built as part of an 1880s military plan devised to protect the New Harbor at Tanjong Pagar. The 1882 report of the Royal Commission for the Defence of Colonial Possessions and Garrisons Abroad had earlier ascertained that Singapore was the second most important coaling station in the British Empire. The opening of the Suez Canal in 1869 and the substitution of steam ships for sail ships at around the same time turned Singapore into a key coaling station for all commercial steamers going to and coming from China and Japan, and a strategic coaling station and maintenance base for the British Royal Navy in the Eastern Seas. As the construction of the Pulau Brani and Pulau Blakang Mati cantonments was perceived locally as serving imperial interests, there were disagreements between the Straits Government and the imperial government over how much the colony should contribute towards the defenses. These disagreements extended into a dispute between the Straits Government, as represented by the Colonial Engineer, Major Henry Edward McCallum, the War Office and the locally based British military commanders over how and to what standard the cantonments should be built.

McCallum, who epitomized the military engineer well versed in both the episteme and mētis of building technologies, played a decisive role in the dispute.[19] During his military training, McCallum was awarded two medals for his proficiency in building- constructional technologies.[20] Besides his technical know-how, McCallum was also highly commended by both the Straits Governor William Jervois and his successor as Acting-Governor, A. E. H. Anson, for his knowledge of the local language, "his tact and good management in overcoming no light difficulties in connection with the [local Chinese] contractors and labourers he employed."[21] McCallum's much-valued knowledge of local practices was deployed to his advantage in his exchanges with the War Office on matters relating to barracks construction at Pulau Brani.

Early in the exchanges, McCallum and the General Officer Commanding of the Straits Settlements Charles Warren came to an agreement that, in lieu of the type plans sent by the War Office, which were based on St. Lucia precedents, they would use a set of plans designed locally. The St. Lucia type plans were considered unsuitable as the Commanding Royal Engineer John Chard explained in a letter to the War Office:

> The conditions of climate, &c, in St. Lucia are not similar to Singapore; glazed windows are not required, and deep overhanging eaves are required to outbuildings. The hurricanes and earthquakes, which occur in St. Lucia, do not occur in Singapore, so that as open and light a construction as possible should be adopted, especially underneath the building.[22]

Based on the locally designed plans, most of the buildings were to be two storied and of half-brick and half-timber construction. The main structures were to be of brick piers and arches, while the roof structure and the upper floor were to be of hard timber. Portland cement concrete was to be used for the ground floors and for rendering the walls (Figures 2.8 and 2.9). Besides the basic construction, Chard

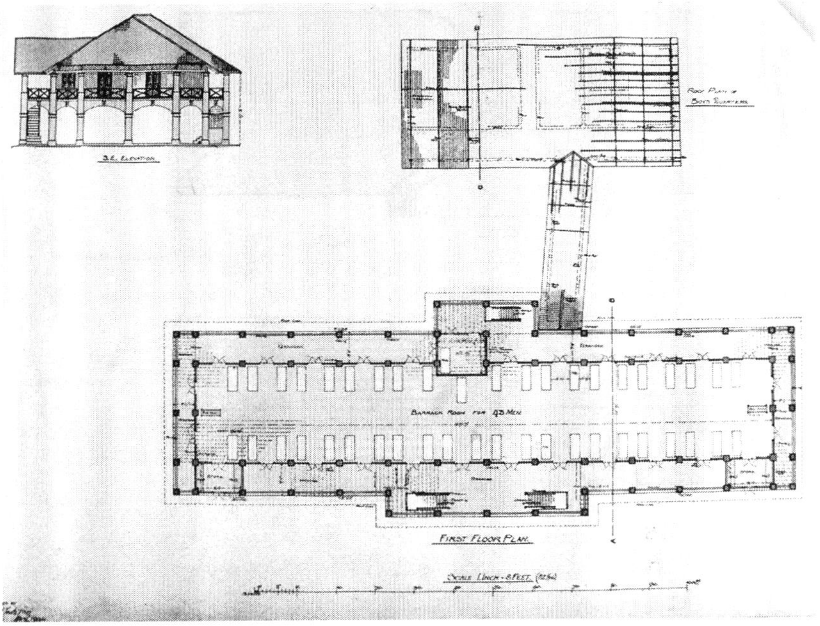

Figure 2.8
Side elevation and first floor plan of the barrack block at Pulau Blakang Mati, which was built only a few years after those in Pulau Brani and was similar to those at Brani. Reprinted, by permission, from the NAUK.

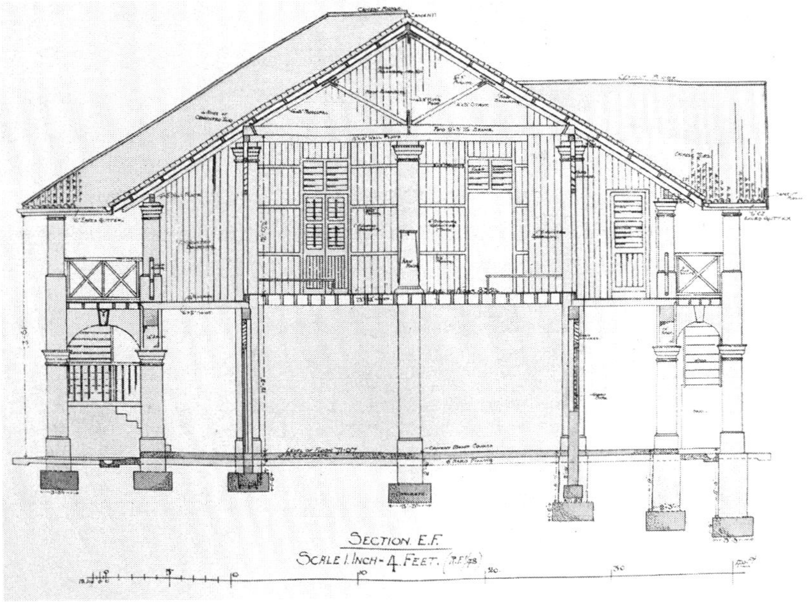

Figure 2.9
Cross section of the barrack block at Pulau Blakang Mati. Reprinted, by permission, from the NAUK.

also provided a long list of both rough and detailed specifications addressing the different aspects of the barrack design and constructions, from sanitation, to floor spaces, to means of ventilation, to materials, to colors of paint. In explaining these specifications, Chard tended to substantiate his claims based on metropolitan norms and the standards spelt out in *Barrack Synopsis*.[23]

McCallum, however, objected to many of Chard's detailed specifications. His objections were mainly targeted at what he perceived to be the excesses in the proposal so as to keep the construction costs low, costs which the Straits Government had to foot. For example, McCallum noted that the proposed drill sheds were not provided for in a copy of Indian Synopsis which he owned, and that the proposed stables were also not necessary for the small hilly island of Pulau Brani. The main portion of McCallum's objections was based on the incompatibility of the proposed specifications with local practices. For example, he noted that flat plain roof tiles requested were not manufactured in Singapore and he proposed instead that the colonial practice of using pantiles be followed instead. McCallum also objected to the proposed use of gable ventilation as ridge ventilation was "universally employed in the Colony." He further argued that since verandah piers would not be carrying the roof, they should be in wood as in "general Colonial construction."[24] The gist of McCallum's objection was based on his "opinion that we should follow Colonial custom."[25] The War Office ended up agreeing in general to most of McCallum's views on specifications.[26]

It was perhaps easy for McCallum to assert that local "Colonial custom" be followed because metropolitan standards for barrack construction, and how these standards should be varied in accordance to the local conditions of the colonies, were still in a state of flux and inconsistency at that time. For instance, the recommended floor area per soldier of a barrack room fluctuated significantly between the different editions of barracks synopses published between the 1860s and 1890s.

Even though Brani differed from Changi in some ways, they also shared many similarities, especially when compared to the earlier barrack buildings at Tanglin in Singapore. Tanglin Barracks (Figure 2.10), one of earliest purpose-built barracks in Singapore, was designed by Captain George Collyer originally of the Madras Engineers.[27] Tanglin Barracks were built between 1860 and 1862; each barrack building consisted primarily of an airy timber structure with the floor raised four feet off the ground, surrounded on all sides by verandahs and covered by a thatched roof with deep overhang.[28] The use of materials such as timber and thatch contrasted with more permanent materials, such as reinforced concrete or masonry structures and the flat concrete or tiled pitched roofs, used at Brani and Changi. Furthermore, unlike both Brani and Changi where the soldiers were provided with an array of recreational and sporting facilities, the soldiers at Tanglin Barracks were not provided with any facilities initially, and they had to clear the dense surrounding jungle and build their own cricket ground.[29] Yet, if the Tanglin Barracks are in turn compared to those barracks at Pearl's Hill converted from hospitals in 1857, they were better off in that they were at least purpose-built as barracks. Besides, the buildings at Pearl's Hill, designed by John Turnbull Thomson and built in the 1840s, have very deficient sanitary provisions in spite of the rather impressive classical exterior, as we shall see in Chapter 3. The examples of the Pearl's Hill Barracks and the Tanglin Barracks indicate that the "tropical" barracks of Changi and Brani, which were built with reference to metropolitan standards, were relatively recent developments.

ure 2.10
nglin Barracks
dergoing rebuilding
th the old thatch roof
rrack in front, c. 1917.
urtesy of the REL.

We could perhaps discern two key themes from the above overview of the shifts in architectural knowledge and practices between the different phases of barrack building in Singapore – from Tanglin, to Pulau Brani, to Changi. One, the metropolitan standards and norms in the design of barracks, whether they were prescribed by barrack synopses and/or guided by type plans, became more *mobile*, i.e. they were more successfully translated in the colonial sites and contexts. While the type plans sent by the War Office were considered as irrelevant and substantially altered in the case of Pulau Brani Barracks, the War Office's type plans were implemented smoothly in the case of Changi Barracks. The increasing mobility that we have witnessed was not just about the imposition of "universal" metropolitan standards on "local" colonial sites. Rather, it was about the coming together of the "universal" and "local", the episteme and mētis, in which metropolitan standards were formulated with knowledge of the local conditions – such as climate, resources and labor practices – and fine-tuned to accommodate some level of variation necessitated by the local contexts. The intrinsic flexibility of these standards made them suitable for various colonial conditions and allowed them to circulate much more successfully than earlier context-insensitive specifications.

The second theme was the emergence of an increasingly stable artifact, specifically a progressively well-defined and minutely specified barrack building type. From the rough timber and thatch shed at Tanglin in the 1860s to the double story masonry and timber barrack at Brani to the reinforced concrete barrack block at Changi, the barrack building type not only became more modern in the use of construction materials but also more specific and less dependent on local "customs" in terms of space standards, constructional specifications, functional definitions and sanitary requirements.

To be sure, I am not suggesting a dichotomy of local versus metropole or variation versus standardization. Neither am I suggesting a narrative with a teleological sense of finality or inevitability proceeding from a state of ignorance to a state of knowledge. Rather, I am providing an account of how the military barracks in the British Empire were systematically tropicalized and became *mobile* and *stable* between the nineteenth and the twentieth centuries despite the heteronomous and the heterogeneous conditions of colonial architectural production discussed earlier. While these conditions had led to the types of building failures discussed in Chapter 1, they were successfully dealt with in the case of military barracks through what Science and Technology Studies scholar John Law calls "heterogeneous engineering" in which diverse social, cultural, political and technical elements were aligned and assembled into a contingent network that enabled metropolitan norms and forms to be replicated.[30]

In the next few sections of this chapter, we will situate the emergence of tropicalized barracks with a few different related aspects of heterogeneous engineering in the British Empire – the training of the Royal Engineers and their experimental tradition, the early nineteenth century prefabrication of tropicalized barracks in the West Indies, and military sanitary reforms and the introduction of barrack synopses and type plans.

ROYAL ENGINEERS, CONSTRUCTIONAL TRAINING AND EXPERIMENTAL TRADITION

As in France and the United States of America, the earliest systematic and concerted training in building construction in Britain began with the military engineers.[31] The early training of the Royal Engineers took place at the Royal Military Academy at Woolwich (founded in 1741), and those military engineers bound for India were trained at the military college established by the East India Company at Addiscombe in 1809. The training military engineers received at Woolwich and Addiscombe was mainly in theoretical courses heavy on mathematics and physics, with no specific training related to construction and building.[32] The deficiencies of the officers trained at Woolwich, especially their lack of field knowledge in fortification and building bridges, were later criticized by Captain Charles Pasley, and that led to the founding of the Royal Engineers Establishment at Chatham in 1812 (known as the School of Military Engineering after 1869).[33] In 1825, a course in practical architecture was established at Chatham, and a year later, Pasley published an influential textbook, *An Outline of a Course of Practical Architecture, compiled for the use of Junior Officers of the Royal Engineers* based on the course. Pasley foregrounded in the book the deficiencies in the existing literature on building construction that he aimed to rectify. In the preface, he writes:

> My object has been to endeavor to fill up these deficiencies, an attempt which, if successful, may be useful to the junior officers of the Corps, who are often sent to the British Colonies soon after they enter His Majesty's Service, and are there

> required to perform duties analogous to those of architects or civil engineers, without having had any previous opportunity of acquiring a practical knowledge of the details of those duties; and where, although they will derive considerable assistance from a good collection of the books before alluded to, they will still find themselves at a loss in respect to many particulars of considerable importance, which are not sufficiently explained.[34]

Pasley's book addressed these deficiencies by including the latest materials on topics as varied as a review of limes and cements, the methods of constructing concrete foundations, the types of fireproof construction, and heating and ventilating arrangements. As noted, among the main groups of readers targeted by Pasley's book were the military engineers in the colonies, who were involved in the building not only of military works but also of public works. Indeed, as in British India, most of the public works in the Straits Settlements during the nineteenth century were designed and built by military engineers, as we saw in Chapter 1. The theoretical and practical knowledge taught in Pasley's course and textbook was intended to equip the Royal Engineers with as comprehensive as possible an education to deal with the potential problems of designing and supervising the building of barracks and other works in a far-flung colony with unfamiliar labor conditions and limited resources. The course in construction was thus a way of consolidating the network of heterogeneous elements by sending well-trained personnel to supervise and guide the local building projects.

The training of Royal Engineers in building and construction was further reformed in the mid-nineteenth century following two major Parliamentary investigations, the 1857 *Report of the Commissioners Appointed to consider the Best Mode of Re-organizing the System for Training Officers* and the 1862 *Report of the Barrack Works Committee*.[35] These investigations came about because of the sanitary scandal in the Crimean War and the related criticisms of the design and construction of barracks. Many of the prominent Royal Engineers officers interviewed in these investigations placed great emphasis on the importance of practical knowledge and noted that there was inadequate practical training for the officers during their time at Chatham. As a consequence, these investigations concluded with the recommendations that learning by doing or practical training, along the lines of the apprenticeship system in the civil realm, should be included in the Royal Engineers officers' study program at Chatham.

Following the investigations, the building and construction courses at Chatham were reformed. Instead of just emphasizing practical training, the director of the Royal Engineers Establishment between 1860 and 1865, Lieutenant Colonel Henry Drury Harness, who believed that all officers should be acquainted with the principles of physical sciences, lengthened the duration of the architectural course and appointed new instructors to teach new areas, such as the application of mechanics to construction and the provision of information on building materials.[36] Harness' reform was perhaps best demonstrated in the work of Major Henry Wray, who was appointed as an instructor in construction at

Chatham in 1866. Wray taught applied mechanics and the properties of different building materials, enabling the engineer officers to calculate structural strength, prepare detailed working drawings, specifications and cost estimates. Wray's approach appears to be not so much about dealing with either theoretical or practical knowledge or opposing episteme to mētis, but about combining the two, i.e. the teaching of theoretical knowledge informed by practice and with important practical implications.[37]

Besides pioneering methodical training in building construction, the Royal Engineers were also involved in some of the earliest systematic researches into the different aspects of building, from the performances of building materials to environmental technologies and building practices. What John Weiler describes as the "experimental science in building" was from the beginning an important component of Pasley's overall effort to improve the Royal Engineers' abilities in building and construction.[38] Many of these experiments and researches were published as either technical manuals or in the technical periodicals founded by the Royal Engineers.[39] My descriptions below draw from the literature published in these manuals and journals, which were themselves means of network building through documenting and disseminating knowledge and information to the different parts of the British Empire and beyond.[40]

Pasley himself experimented with different limes and cement mixtures, and he played an important role in the development of new artificial cements in nineteenth-century Britain. Besides cement, Pasley also experimented with novel construction methods, such as concrete foundation and hoop iron reinforced brickwork. Pasley's "experimental tradition" was continued by other Royal Engineers afterwards. [41] As many Royal Engineers worked in the colonies, the experimental tradition was not restricted to the metropole, but extended to the colonies. In fact, researches from the colonies formed a significant proportion of the works published in the journals. This should not be surprising given that one of the recurring themes in Royal Engineers literature was the need to gather information on the colonies, to know them so as to overcome the various aforementioned forms of building difficulties. In an 1876 article describing engineering operations in the Gold Coast, Lieutenant Colonel Home even noted that at the "root of all successful military engineering" was the idea that "the engineering must be adapted to the country, not the country to the engineering." Home, thus, argued that it was important to gather as much information as possible on "the nature of the country and the resources available to overcome the material difficulties."[42] Captain John Smyth, who spent six years in the West Indies and was behind some of the earliest tropical barracks, which we shall see later, went even further. He advocated an even more systematic approach, encouraging his fellow Royal Engineers to prepare "memoranda on the nature, quality, price of materials, with tables and short descriptions of the timber, etc of the places in which they may be stationed."[43] Later in the early twentieth century, another Royal Engineer, Captain E. H. Harvey, suggested that short notes on the "work conditions" of the different colonial stations be compiled as a "compact and easily accessible source of information," like *Barrack Synopsis* or *Drainage Manual*, for the reference of Royal Engineers posted there.[44]

Different types of experiments were also performed as part of this gathering of information on the colonies. The most common type of experiments involved the testing of local materials. For example, partly inspired by Pasley's work on cement, Captain John Thomas Smith of the Madras Engineers used locally available materials to create different mortars and cements in the 1820s, which he experimented with and came up with a new type of cement, the magnesia cement.[45] It was, however, not always a case of the experiments in the metropole inspiring those in the colonies. Sometimes, innovations first took place in the colonies. For example, Portland cement was extensively used in fortifications in Bermuda during the 1860s before it was used in Britain.[46]

Local timber found in the colonies such as Bermuda, India and Singapore was also widely tested. Common to these different experiments was the use of a standard formula as the basis for testing the strength of timber so that different timbers from diverse localities and otherwise unconnected contexts could be put on a common basis for comparing their performances under structural stress. Through such a comparison, what was a local resource could be made global, in the sense that the knowledge of its comparative performance in relation to other timbers elsewhere would facilitate its use elsewhere and its export to these sites.[47] Just as the differences between local and global resources were not absolute, the boundary between local practical knowledge, i.e. mētis, and global or universal scientific knowledge, i.e. episteme, was also an indistinct one. That was because the very scientific knowledge that produced these colonial experiments was often dependent upon the local practical knowledge of informants.

Other than building materials, local labor – another heterogeneous component in the colonial production of architecture – was also attended to, carefully described, and in some cases, tabulated and put on a comparative basis. Not unlike the manner of describing local building laborers in colonial Singapore we saw earlier in Chapter 1, some of the literature described the peculiarities of local laborers and their building practices. There were also detailed calculations and comparisons of the relative cost and efficiency of employing different forms of labor for building work in the colonies.[48]

In addition to building materials and labor, the experimental tradition of the Royal Engineers was also extended into many other miscellaneous areas such as meteorological observations, to arrive at a systematic and accurate method of obtaining climatic data of a locality;[49] environmental technologies, particularly the thickness of walls on coolness in the tropics;[50] and the design of "sun-screens".[51] The Royal Engineers were also quick to keep up to date with the earliest developments in fields that influenced the planning of the built environment, such as sanitary research and medical research.[52] Much of this research, which was carried out in a rather *ad hoc* manner early in the nineteenth century, was to anticipate the large-scale, state-sponsored building science research, especially pertaining to the tropics, to be carried out by institutions such as the Building Research Stations in the mid-twentieth century, as we shall see in Chapter 5.

THE PREFABRICATED TROPICALIZED BARRACKS

It was under the conditions in which the Royal Engineers were systematically reforming their training in construction and experimenting with different aspects of building that some of earliest "tropicalized" barracks were produced in the West Indies. By tropicalized, I refer to those buildings designed with the heterogeneous conditions of architectural production in the British tropical colonies, with not just climatic but also the labor and resources in mind. As early as 1838, Captain Smyth had argued that the Royal Engineers had to introduce "a system of building for barracks, or cantonments, adapted to and varying with the localities in which they may be situated."[53] Smyth was responding to the prevailing system of uniformity and the lack of adaptation in barrack design to the "varying circumstances of climate and situation." Smyth, who had lived in the West Indies for almost six years, was especially concerned that the design of barracks failed to account for the particularities of the tropical climate, a climate where "marsh miasma [was] prevalent."[54] His central concern was with the preservation of soldiers' health and the manner in which the tropical climate affected the soldiers' health through miasma.

Smyth's focus on the health of soldiers is not surprising. In 1835, a medical crisis at an army hospital in the Bahamas led Lord Howick, the Secretary of War, to appoint a special board of inquiry to look into the crisis.[55] The inquiry subsequently expanded into a more general investigation into the health of troops in the British Empire.[56] The first report they produced was the book-length *Statistical Report on Sickness, Invaliding, and Mortality among troops in the West Indies* in 1838.[57] In the report, detailed medical statistics on the different stations in the West Indies were collated and analyzed. The report confirmed the abnormally high mortality and illness rates of British soldiers in many West Indian stations, and led to important reforms to improve the situation. These included reduction in the length of service, improvement in the diet of the soldiers, provision of improved barracks and hospitals, and the healthier location of military stations.[58]

Smyth's concern with the health of soldiers and the design of barracks in the West Indies was part of much broader concerns regarding the high mortality and illness rates of British soldiers, an issue further elaborated in Chapter 3. To preserve the health of soldiers, Smyth suggested that the interior of the barracks should be as spacious as possible, with at least 300–500 cubic feet per person. Louvered ventilators should be installed for the roofs and the partitions in the rooms should be kept low to facilitate "through ventilation." However, Smyth also cautioned that windows on the sides of the building exposed to marsh miasma should be closed by glazed window sashes; even those on the sides of the building open to the sea should be covered with moveable jalousies in order to prevent soldiers from being exposed to "violent currents of air" and getting sudden chills bringing about dysentery, fever and rheumatism. Furthermore, Smyth recommended that galleries or verandahs of 10 to 11 feet should be provided on all sides of the building to shelter it from the heat and rain. Finally, he emphasized the importance of barracks being located away from miasmatic marshes, especially to the leeward of a marsh.[59]

Smyth's suggestions were, however, not exactly path-breaking. Much of what he suggested had already been implemented in the earlier design of barracks in the West Indies. In 1824, Colonel Charles Smith, the Commanding Royal Engineer in the West Indies, submitted to the Board of Ordinance a proposal for a "new system of barracks that should, as far as practicable, insure uniformity of design."[60] The barrack building proposed by Smith (Figures 2.11 and 2.12) was designed to cope with the "extremes of heat and moisture," and the miasmatic marshes in the West Indies. Smith proposed a two-storey barrack building elevated on a half-story ventilated basement. Similar to Smyth's recommendations, it had galleries, or verandahs, on both sides shielding the barrack rooms from rain and sun. It was also quite spacious, providing approximately 440 cubic feet of air space per person in the barrack rooms.[61] Smith was also concerned with miasma and, on the recommendation of Dr. Arthur, an army medical staff member, the windows were designed to incorporate copper gauze screens "to prevent or mitigate the effect of the marsh malaria."[62] The gauze screens, moreover, had the further advantage of securing a "more moderate and equable diffusion of wind through the building," thus avoiding drafts.[63]

The barrack proposed by Smith was not only designed with the tropical climate and health concerns in mind, it was also a constructional "system" that could be replicated at different sites in the tropics. The barrack consisted of many cast iron components, such as the columns, girders, floor joists, windows, and even the cornices and jalousie, which could be prefabricated in Britain and shipped

Figure 2.11
Elevation of the barrack proposed by Smith.
Source: *PCRE*, II (1838).

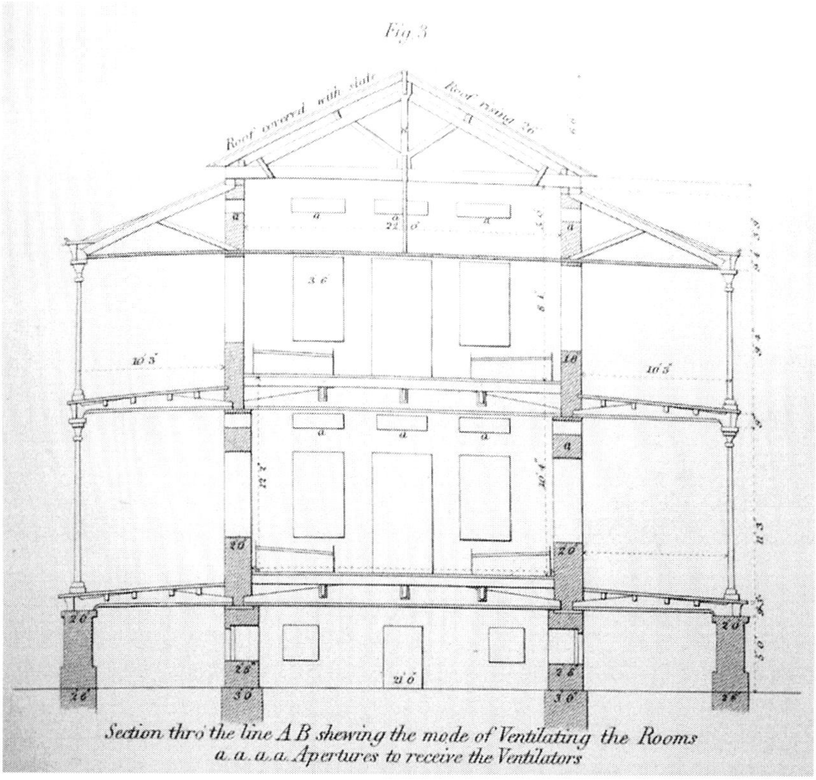

Figure 2.12
Sections of the barrack proposed by Smith.
Source: *PCRE*, II, 1838.

to the West Indies. Joineries between the cast iron components were specially designed to facilitate easier assembly. Instead of regular bolts and flange joints, dovetails and pivot joints, further secured with lead, were used. The simpler dovetails and pivot joints had the advantages of avoiding bolts and bolt-holes, and any danger of irregular pressure on the flanges (Figure 2.13). The use of prefabricated components not only enabled these barrack buildings to be built quickly and be easily replicated in different parts of the West Indies, it also helped to ameliorate two of the main problems Smith faced – the shortage of Royal Engineers under his command to build and maintain military establishments and the lack of skilled building tradesmen in the West Indies. Moreover, prefabricated cast iron building parts had been used in the West Indies, especially for the verandahs, before 1820, and had proven to be suitable. In the context of the West Indies, cast iron, unlike timber, had the further advantages of being resistant to termite attack, and also structurally strong to withstand hurricanes.[64] And significantly for Smith, unlike many local materials in the West Indies, cast iron had been tested extensively in the metropole and its structural performance was known. Thus, the use of prefabricated cast iron components allowed Smith to minimize his dependence on the uncertainties of the heterogeneous elements involved in colonial architectural production in the West Indies.

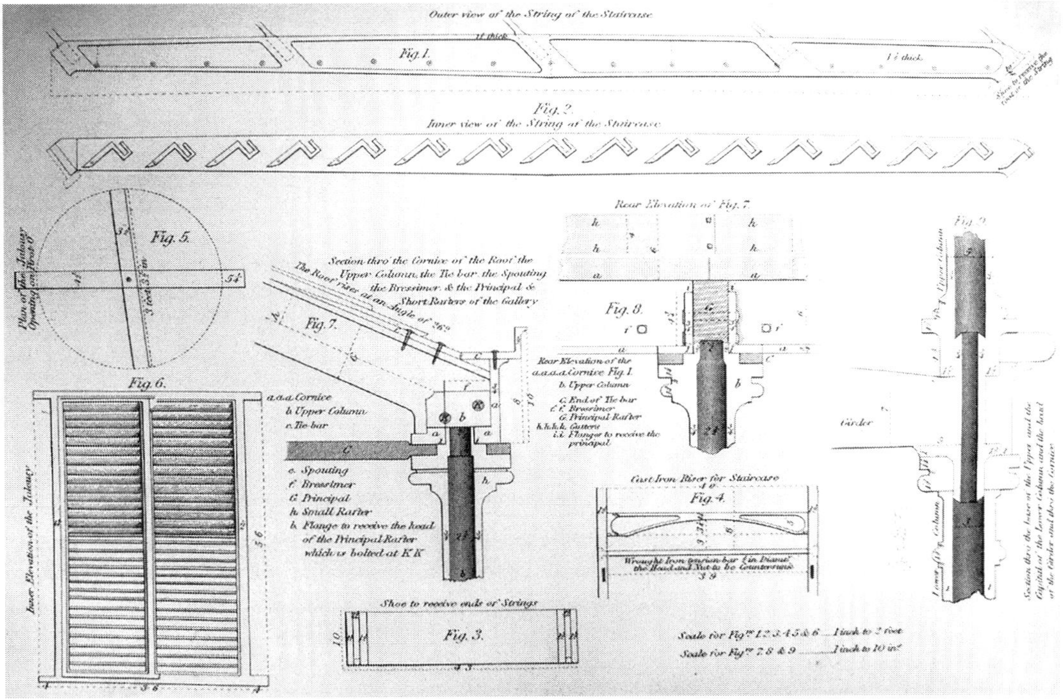

Figure 2.13
Drawings of cast iron components, such as staircase and jalousies, and the joineries. Source: *PCRE*, II, 1838.

The use of prefabricated components also allowed him to strengthen one of the nodes in the network by assigning Captain Brandreth, previously based in the West Indies and who had experience in superintending the castings of a building for the Bahamas, to be based in Birmingham for three years to supervise the casting of the building parts at the foundry. While he was there, Brandreth carried out some experiments to test Smith's designs. Using the results of these experiments, he managed to improve the strength and mode of connection of some of the cast iron components designed by Smith. Brandreth was also able to reduce the sections of the floor joists in the original plan.[65] Barracks and hospitals based on Smith's proposal were subsequently erected by different Royal Engineers Units in the various stations of the West Indies, such as Antigua, Barbados and St. Lucia. Smith's designs continued to be used well into the 1840s, although they were still a minority amongst the military buildings built and appeared to have been discontinued afterwards.[66] Despite the important innovations of Smith's design, the tropicalized barrack would only become further systematized and more widespread in the mid-nineteenth century during the army's sanitary reform in the post-Crimean War and post-Indian Rebellion period.

BARRACK SYNOPSES, CLIMATES AND TYPE PLANS

The design of barracks was already under review in the 1850s, with many of the changes under consideration included in the 1855 *Report of the Committee on the Barrack Accommodation for the Army*. However, at this point it was put under the spotlight after Florence Nightingale's revelation about the medical mismanagement and appalling sanitary conditions in Scutari hospital in the Crimean War. After the War in 1857, a Royal Commission on the Health of the Army was appointed to look into all health and sanitary matters related to the British Army. A report was produced in 1858 that revealed the high mortality rates in the British Army, as compared to the civilian population, and the squalid conditions in which these soldiers lived. Soldiers lived in dark, gloomy, damp, overcrowded, ill-ventilated and inadequately heated barracks; conditions that were, according to the miasmatic theories of disease transmission, the most conducive for the spread of disease.[67] The squalid living conditions shocked the press and the public, and brought about widespread outrage.[68]

The outbreak and suppression of the Indian Rebellion in 1857–58 and the subsequent transfer of the governance of India from the British East India Company to the British Crown, with the attendant stationing of greater numbers of British soldiers in India, turned the sanitary reformers' attention to the sanitary conditions in India's military stations.[69] A Royal Commission on the Sanitary State of the Army in India (RCSSAI) was appointed to study the Army in India along the lines of the 1857 Royal Commission. The RCSSAI was to reveal even more unusually high mortality rates and appalling living conditions among the British soldiers in Indian stations (Figure 2.14).

Following the recommendations of the Royal Commission on the Health of the Army, a Barrack and Hospital Improvement Commission (BHIC), chaired by Sidney Herbert, and consisting of Dr. John Sutherland, Royal Engineer Captain Douglas Galton and Dr. W. H. Burrell, was appointed "for the purpose of examining the sanitary condition of barracks and hospitals, and of devising means for removing any

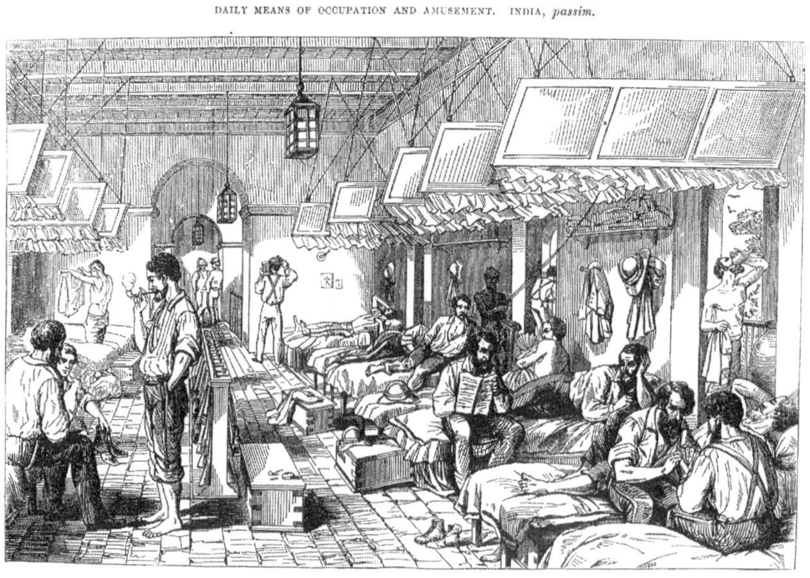

Figure 2.14
An overcrowded barrack room in India, labeled as "Daily Means of Occupation and Amusement." Source: Nightingale, *Observations on the Evidence Contained in Stational Reports Submitted to Her by the RCSSAI*, 1863.

defects injurious to health."[70] The Commission inspected 162 barracks and 112 military hospitals in Britain between 1858 and 1861, and produced a report in 1861 that provided specific recommendations for the sanitary improvements of barracks. Besides inspecting the barracks in the "home" stations, i.e. Britain, Sutherland and Galton were later appointed to another BHIC to inspect and report on the sanitary conditions of the barracks and hospitals in the Mediterranean stations – specifically Malta, Gibraltar and the Ionian Islands – following which a report was published in 1863.[71] Another BHIC was appointed to provide suggestions to improve the sanitary conditions of the Indian stations after the RCSSAI issued its report and recommendations in 1863, and the BHIC for Indian stations published its report in 1864.[72] Unlike the other two BHICs, this one did not inspect the barracks and hospitals in the country under investigation. Instead, its recommendations relied on the report of the RCSSAI and also Nightingale's comments on the station reports submitted to the RCSSAI.[73] Furthermore, many members of this BHIC were either members of the RCSSAI or had lived and worked in India.

The main concern for the BHIC for home stations was that "no intelligent uniform plan of constructing barracks [had] been arrived at; no fundamental principles [were] recognized as absolutely necessary for health."[74] Hence, one of the main aims of the BHIC was to arrive at a "uniform plan" based on "fundamental principles" of sanitation. Different commissions were appointed primarily because of climatic differences, which were thought to have different effects on the health of the soldiers. The climate of the Mediterranean stations was considered

> as occupying an intermediate position between [that of] England and those of the tropics: generally warm, at times depressing and variable, but not necessarily unhealthy to healthy people, although of such a nature as to add intensity to any local causes of unhealthiness existing at the stations.[75]

The tropical climate was of course assumed, as the Royal Commission noted, to be "hostile to human life, and to be especially deadly to the English race."[76]

The perceived effect of climate on health was inextricably linked to the prevailing miasmatic theory of disease transmission as discussed earlier. It was reasoned that the hotter and more humid the climate, the rate of putrefaction of organic matters in the marshes would correspondingly increase and more poisonous miasma would be emitted. Hence, the differences between the three BHICs were premised on the same medical theories and sanitary principles. As such, while there was acknowledgement in the reports that "the points in which improvements for barracks and hospitals in these [Mediterranean and tropical] climates necessarily differ from those recommended by use for barracks and hospitals at home,"[77] it was also noted that "the general principles and forms and procedures which have been found useful at home, ..., it is hoped, with required modifications, may be useful in India and in tropical stations generally."[78] This idea of variations based on a common set of principles was especially evident in the model plans for the different stations proposed by the three BHICs (Figures 2.15–2.18).

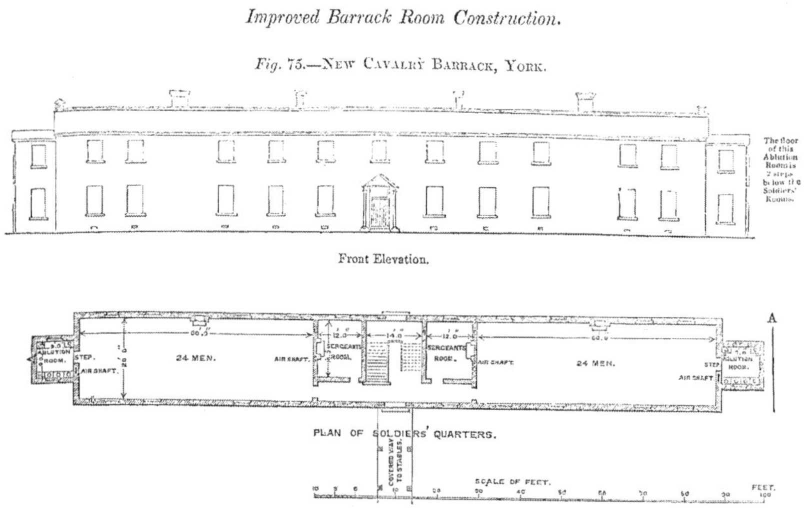

Figure 2.15
New Cavalry Barrack at York – an example of an improved barrack construction. Source: The Commissioners, *General Report of the Commission Appointed for Improving the Sanitary Condition of Barracks and Hospitals*, 1861.

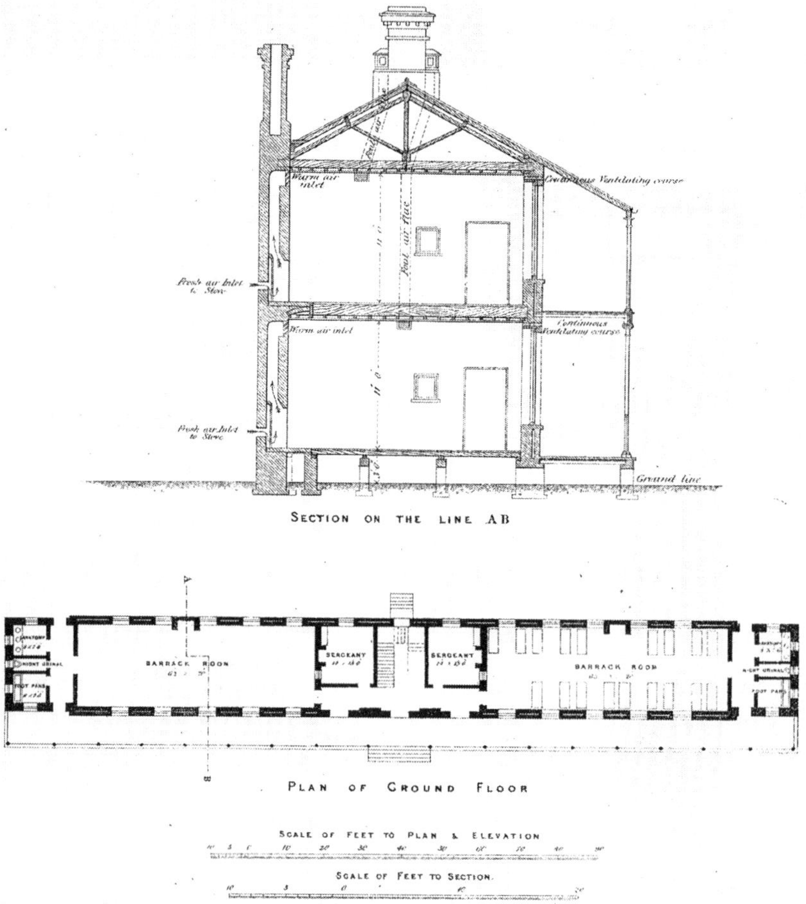

Figure 2.16
Drawings of a two-storey model barrack proposed for the Mediterranean Stations. Source: The Commissioners, *Report of the BHIC on the Sanitary Condition and Improvement of the Mediterranean Stations*, 1863.

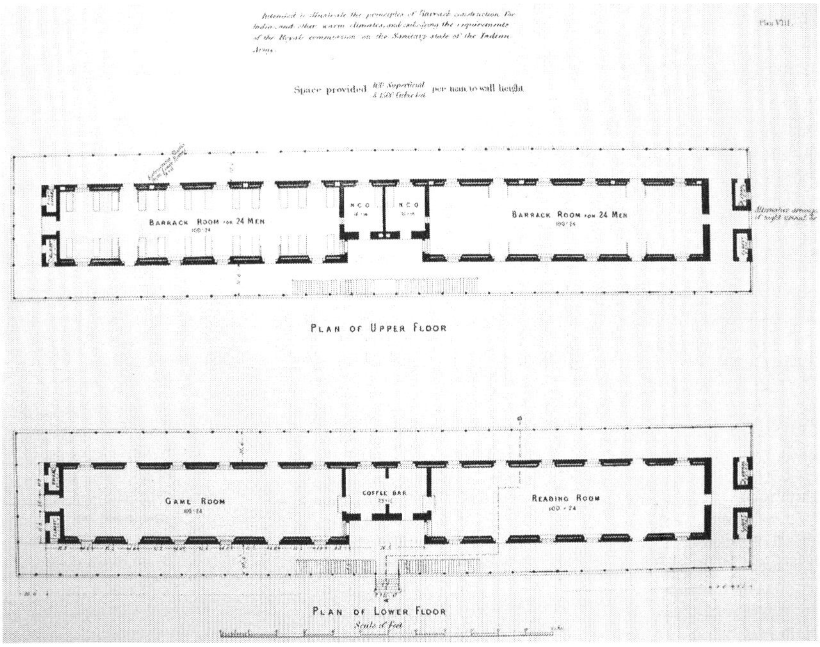

Figure 2.17
Plans of a two-storey model barrack proposed for the Indian Stations. Source: BHIC, *Suggestions in regard to Sanitary Works required for Improving Indian Stations*, 1864.

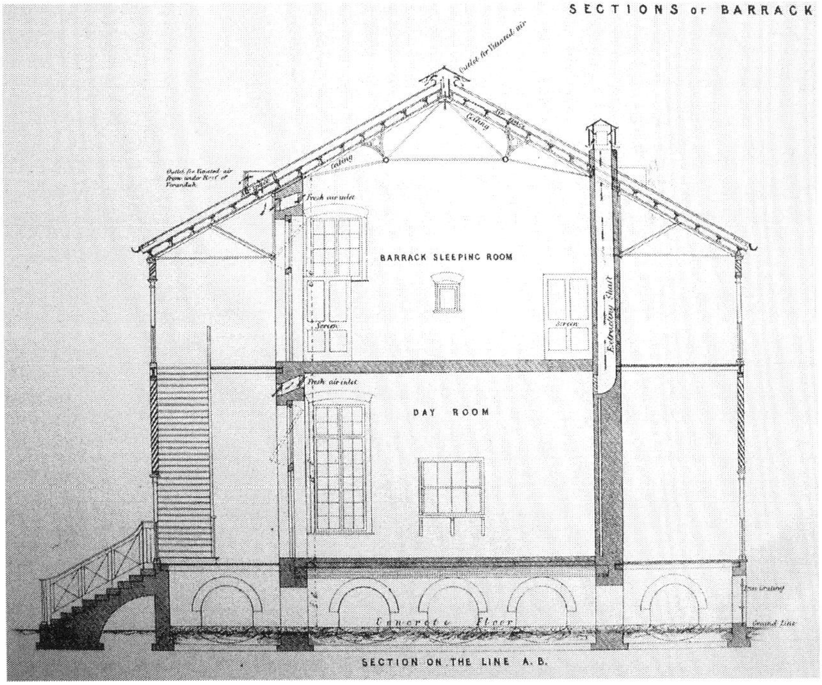

Figure 2.18
Section of a two-storey model barrack proposed for the Indian Stations. Source: BHIC, *Suggestions in regard to Sanitary Works required for Improving Indian Stations*, 1864.

Despite the diverse types of barracks situated in different contexts examined in the three BHICs, all the model barracks proposed were based on the very simple plan of a free standing barrack block open on all sides with a staircase in the center. At the second floor, two sergeant's or non-commissioned officer's rooms flanked the staircase, and the two barrack rooms each accommodating twenty-four men in turn flanked these rooms. At the two ends of the blocks were the ablution rooms or lavatories. This planning arrangement was primarily informed by the miasmatic theories of disease transmission. Ventilation was an important consideration as the circulation of air would dilute the concentration of miasma in the room. Thus, the buildings were to be open on all sides to facilitate the circulation of air around them; the sizes of the room and windows, and the positions of the windows in relation to the beds, were also considered important. Since poisonous miasma would move from one space to another, it was also considered important to separate the different rooms, especially the urinal and ablution facilities, considered to have the highest concentration of noxious vapor because of their stench, from the other spaces. As a result, these facilities were positioned at the extreme ends of the block.

There were other planning and design considerations behind these model barracks that were shaped by the miasmatic theories that will be further explored in the next chapter. For now, it is sufficient to note that the only differences between the plan for the home stations and the plans for the other climates were the verandahs, the dimensions of the rooms, in terms of both floor area and volumetric space, and the types of environmental technologies involved for heating or cooling and ventilating the barracks. Besides the model plans, the variations were also codified into numerical standards. For home stations, the BHIC stipulated a minimum of 60 square feet of floor area and 600 cubic feet of air space per person; for the Mediterranean stations, the same standards as the home stations would be applicable to buildings sited on "airy positions," otherwise a minimum of 70–75 square feet and 750 cubic feet per person would apply for the floor area and the air space respectively.[79] For Indian and other tropical stations, a floor area between 80 and 100 square ft and an air space of between 1000 and 1500 cubic ft would apply.[80]

The BHIC was later turned into a Standing Committee and invested with the "full authority to examine and criticise all barrack and hospital plans, in order to ensure that they were in every respect satisfactory as regards sanitary arrangements."[81] In 1865, this committee became known as the Army Sanitary Committee and it was to exist until 1907 when it was abolished, and its duties of reviewing all aspects of the sanitary arrangements of all barrack designs in the British Empire were transferred to the Army Medical Advisory Board. [82] Not only were the sanitary experts and reformers in the BHIC influential in shaping the design of barracks from the mid-nineteenth century onwards, their reports formed the basis of a definitive standard of military accommodation which was codified into the first edition of *Barrack Synopsis* in 1865. In *Barrack Synopsis*, a standard list of the buildings in the different types of military units in the British Empire was provided, and the floor areas and cubic spaces of the rooms laid down, to form the basis of the designs for any new barrack buildings. The synopsis was also supplemented by a series of "Standard Plans," which, according to Royal Engineer Captain E. N. Stockley, who was once in charge of the Barracks Design Branch of the War Office,

> illustrate how the accommodation may be conveniently arranged; the object of the issue of these plans is to put in convenient form the best points of previous designs, and to avoid the necessity of making an entirely fresh design for each building that is to be erected, by using the standard type modified to suit local conditions.[83]

These "standard plans" were also known as type plans. As we have noted earlier in the planning of Changi Barracks, a type plan was meant to be sufficiently flexible in that it

> should be capable of such alterations as will, without change of general design, admit of its being adapted to changes of site or climate ... [it] should also be capable of extension, so as to suit the larger amount of cubic space required for warm climates.[84]

For example, Major E. H. Hemmings, the head of the barrack design branch in 1900, noted that the type plan of a barrack block for the temperate British Isles with its long axis in the north–south direction and its windows facing east and west to maximize the amount of sunlight in the rooms would have its long axis rotated to be aligned in the east–west direction if it was to be built in the tropics, so that its windows would face north and south to avoid the glaring heat of the morning and afternoon tropical sun. Furthermore, "[p]revailing winds, especially in hot climates, [would] also, of course, temper the above rules, and the exigencies of particular sites and the proximity of existing buildings, if there are any, [would] also require to be taken into account."[85]

Not only were the floor areas and cubic space of the rooms laid down in the synopsis, they were also varied according to the different climates that the barracks were situated in, just as the different BHICs operated and the type plans were designed to be adjusted. However, since *Barrack Synopsis* was continuously revised, modified and purportedly improved, both the climatic classifications of the stations and the space standards prescribed changed. For example, in the 1911 edition of *Barrack Synopsis*, the stations were divided into home, sub-tropical and tropical, loosely following the original BHICs schema of Home, Mediterranean and Indian stations (Figure 2.19). The floor space and cubic space standards also almost corresponded to the minimum stipulated in the BHICs.[86] In the 1923 edition of the synopsis, the climatic classification changed. Instead of the three categories as in the 1911 edition, there were five categories, with the sub-tropical and tropical stations further differentiated into smaller groupings, each with more specific floor space and cubic space requirements (Figure 2.20). Moreover, even the widths of the verandahs and the height of the rooms were specified in the tables.[87] These classifications and specifications were again modified in the 1948 edition of

Table showing Minimum Floor and Cubic Space per Bed to be provided in Barrack Rooms for British Troops.

Note.—The cubic and floor space for Native Troops serving in their own country, or in a similar climate, is the same as that approved for British Troops serving at Home Stations.

Station.	Barracks. Permanent Buildings. Floor Space.	Barracks. Permanent Buildings. Cubic Space.	Barracks. Huts. Floor Space.	Barracks. Huts. Cubic Space.
(1)	(2)	(3)	(4)	(5)
(I.) Home Stations.	Square feet.	Cubic feet.	Square feet.	Cubic feet.
Great Britain and Ireland and Channel Islands	60	600	60	600
(II.) Stations Abroad.				
Scale A, Sub-Tropical. Bermuda .. .. ..; Cape of Good Hope.. ..; Cyprus .. .. ..; Egypt .. .. ..; Gibraltar .. .. ..; Hong Kong (except Victoria); Jamaica (Newcastle and Up Park Camp) .. ..; Malta .. .. ..; Mauritius (Curepipe and Phœnix) .. .. ..; Natal.. .. .. ..; Sierra Leone (Mount Aureol and Tower Hill)	60	720	60	720
Scale B, Tropical. Ceylon .. .. ..; Hong Kong (Victoria) ..; Jamaica (Port Royal) ..; Mauritius (Port Louis) ..; Sierra Leone (King Tom) ..; Singapore	80	1,000	75	850

In barracks where separate dining rooms are provided, not less than 6 feet linear wall space should be allowed for each man

(4004) B

Figure 2.19
Table on minimum space requirements for housing British soldiers in the 1911 edition of *Barrack Synopsis*. Source: WO, *Barrack Synopsis*, 1911.

Barrack Synopsis. The stations were divided into four climatic types – temperate, sub-tropical, tropical A and tropical B – giving the impression that the climatic classification had returned to the earliest tripartite arrangement.

The initial expediency of codifying sanitary principles into type plans and space standards based on climatic classifications by the BHICs of the mid-nineteenth century was to insure that military barracks in the British Empire would adhere to certain ideal spatial configurations and minimum space standards so as to secure the health of the British soldiers in the different military stations. Such practices were also premised on a certain economic calculation that was used to prevent wastage, not just of human life but also of money, as the following statement in all the different editions of *Barrack Synopsis* testifies:

> Any increase in the floor and cubic space of a room beyond what is actually required causes unnecessary outlay in first construction, and entails a continuing excess in charges for maintenance, warming, lighting & c. It is, therefore, most important to ascertain the minimum amounts admissible ...[88]

Table showing Minimum Height and Floor and Cubic Space per Bed to be provided in Barrack Rooms for British Troops.

Stations.	Height to Wall Plate or Ceiling (ft.).	Floor Space (sq. ft.).	Cubic Space (cub. ft.).	Verandahs if provided (width in ft.).
Home Stations.				
Great Britain ... Ireland ... Channel Islands ...	10	60	600	—
Foreign Stations.				
CATEGORY I.				
Gibraltar ... Malta ...	12	60	720	8
CATEGORY II.				
Cyprus ... Ceylon (Hill Stations)... Hong Kong Peak ... Bermuda ...	12	70	840	8
North China (special case) ...	11	70	770	8
CATEGORY III.				
Egypt ... Ceylon (Coast) ... South China (except Hong Kong Peak) ... Mauritius ... West African Hill Stations ... West Indies ...	13	80	1,040	10
CATEGORY IV.				
Soudan ... West Africa (Plains) ... Straits Settlements ...	14	100	1,400	10

Figure 2.20
Table on minimum space requirements for housing British soldiers in the 1923 edition of barrack synopsis. Source: WO, *Barrack Synopsis*, 1923.

These standards and classifications subsequently undergirded the technocracy of the Royal Engineers, which enabled the limited numbers of military engineers and builders to produce large number of buildings required in an efficient manner, without "wasting" time reconsidering barrack design from first principles. As a result, military engineers and builders spread over the vast British Empire produced a fairly uniform military landscape of cantonments and barracks. As Peter Scriver shows in his work on the Colonial PWD in India, such colonial technocracy, with its regularized and standardized practices, served not just to control the physical environment but also to order the cognitive function of the architects and engineers in the bureaucracy.[89] Likewise, it could be argued that the main influence of the space standards and climatic classifications on modern tropical architecture was more a cognitive one, based on the principle that a single architectural type and standard should be varied according to different climates through slight modifications, or more specifically, acclimatized to the tropics.

"GLOBAL FORM" IN COLONIAL SPACES OF EXCEPTION

Having historicized and contextualized the heterogeneously engineered military barracks at Changi in this chapter, we will now situate them in the larger built and socio-political landscapes of colonial Singapore and show how the model cantonment of Changi was an exception rather than the norm in the colonial built environment of Singapore. The isolated location of Changi hinted at the cantonment's exception. The Gillman Commission chose Changi as the location for the cantonment for two main reasons. First, Changi was deliberately isolated and far away from the town, linked to the town of Singapore by "16 miles of tortuous road, the convolutions of which would break the back of a proverbial serpent."[90] Second, Changi was primarily an undeveloped piece of land with very few buildings, "covered partly with rubber plantations and dense jungle" and "partly with swamps or cultivation in the valleys"[91] (Figure 2.21). The Gillman

Figure 2.21
Map of Changi before its development as a cantonment. Reprinted, by permission, from the *REJ*, June 1938.

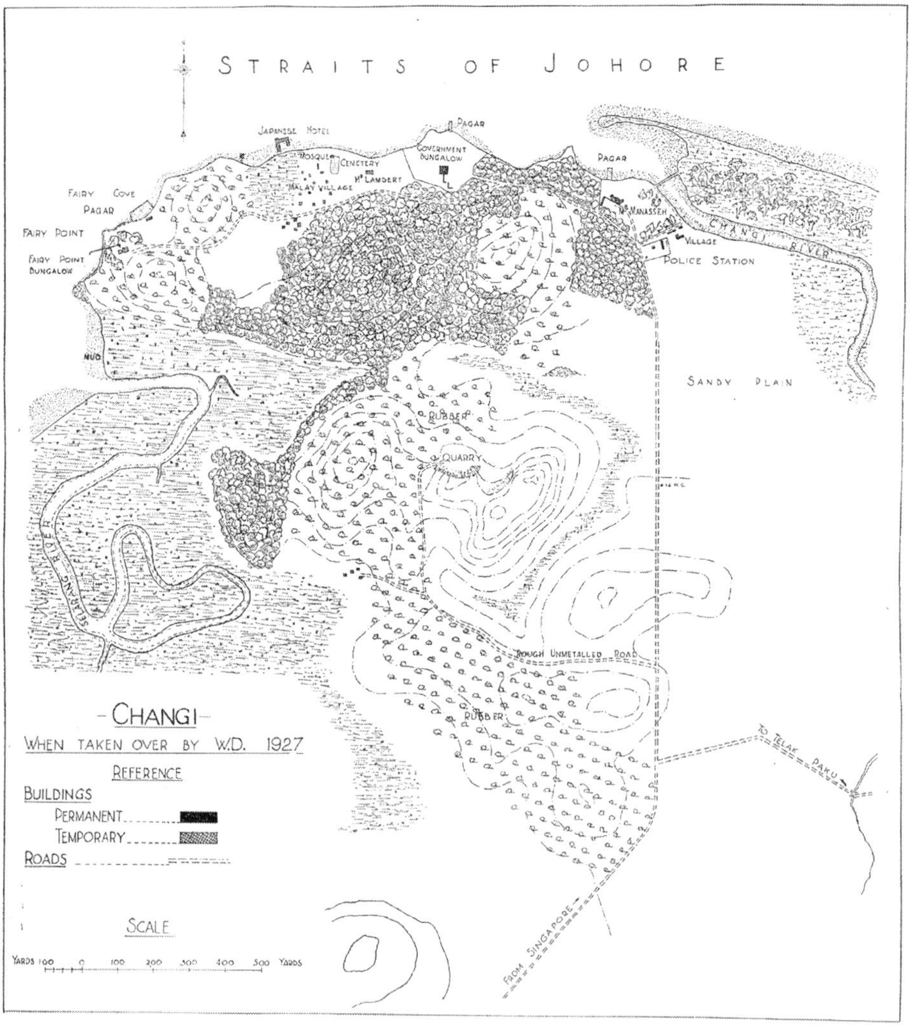

Commission saw these characteristics as advantageous. The remoteness and distance from settlements of the local population meant that the troops were safe from being, as the army saw it, "contaminated" by the local population's insanitary and "immoral" living conditions. The undeveloped state of the site implied that it could be treated as a clean slate for the building of a big model cantonment with all the requisite amenities for exercise and amusements.

Following the Gillman Commission's recommendations, vast tracts of land in the Changi area were acquired and large-scale transformations of the landscape took place. Drawing from the sanitary practices first introduced by the pioneering anti-malarial works carried out by Malcolm Watson in Malaya's plantation estates in the early twentieth century, the swamps were filled, the jungle cleared, and the grounds were drained by the laying of extensive sub-soil drainage pipes.[92] All these were carried out by the hired Chinese contractors and their Chinese and Indian coolies with the aim of eradicating potential mosquito breeding grounds and the possible spread of malaria (Figure 2.22). During the clearing of the jungle, meticulous "care was taken to leave the finest of the forest trees to form an attractive setting to the buildings."[93] Many of the trees that did not interfere with the building sites were left standing and in some cases, the building layouts were adjusted to accommodate the trees. Furthermore, a nursery garden was established under the care of a horticulturalist to provide plants for the cantonment and the soil fertilized to ensure that the trees and plants would grow well.[94]

The Gillman Commission's recommendations that turned Changi Cantonment into a separate and differentiated space were also evident in the earlier establishment of cantonments at Pulau Brani and Pulau Blakang Mati, which in turn could be traced back to the legislations and practices in British India. In fact, as Anthony King shows, the word 'cantonment' derives from the French term 'cantonner,' which means to quarter, divide and separate. Implicit in the planning of any cantonment in British India was what King calls the "separation concept."[95] The cantonment was strategically separated, at a distance of a few miles, from the populous "native" city.[96] It was near enough for the troops stationed at the cantonment to defend the "native" city but far enough not to be "contaminated" by it.

Many of the ideas regarding the siting and planning of the cantonments in India based on the "separation concept" were introduced by the 1863 Report of the RCSSAI, which was in turn informed by the miasmatic theories of disease transmission. As noted earlier, the RCSSAI introduced new forms and norms of barrack design and planning to secure the health of the British soldiers in India. But its sanitary reform did not stop at the boundaries of the cantonments; the commission also noted that:

> [I]t is necessary to include the sanitary state of the native towns and bazaars, because not only is a part of the soldier's time spent in these places, but the mere fact of their proximity to European barracks must necessarily exercise an injurious influence on the healthiness of both barracks and hospitals, if the native dwellings are in an unwholesome condition.[97]

Figure 2.22
Transformation of the landscape at Changi. Courtesy of the REL.

The commission noted that legislative power should be sufficiently effective so that the insanitary "native" bazaars and dwellings could be removed and erected at a "safe distance" to the leeward of the cantonments. "Native" towns and bazaars should also be subjected to sanitary policing with bylaws drawn up to regulate the sanitary conditions and sanitary inspectors employed and empowered to remove sanitary nuisances and punish sanitary infringements.[98]

It has been argued that the clear demarcation between the British and the local population arose also from a widespread fear of miscegenation and the concomitant moral and racial degeneracy that emerged in the nineteenth century.[99] Yet, despite the attempt to separate the cantonments from the "native" towns and bazaars by means of planning, the separation was not, and perhaps could not, be complete given that the cantonments had a parasitic socio-economic relationship with the "native" towns and bazaars.

Various scholars have noted that, in the colonial civilian realm in India, as the British relied on a large retinue of local servants to perform household tasks in their bungalows, the spatial and bodily boundaries between the British and locals were never as clear cut as imagined or planned.[100] A similar situation existed in the military spaces of British Malaya and Singapore, where the British soldiers relied on an array of local servants to support their daily activities (Figure 2.23). For example, in specifying the design of the officers' quarters at Pulau Brani Cantonment in the 1890s, the Commanding Royal Engineer instructed that outbuildings be provided in order to accommodate a range of servants, such as the personal boys of Officers, the cook, *kitchil* (cook's boy), *tukang ayer* (water carrier) and *kebun* (gardener).[101] Reliance on local servants continued up until at least 1966, five years before the British military withdrew from Singapore. Out of 30,000 Singaporeans directly employed at the various military bases, 8,000 were domestic servants.[102] While complicating the "separation concept," the intermingling of British soldiers and locals does not detract from the idea of the cantonment as an exceptional socio-spatial enclave in that it reflected the asymmetrical power relations and also the corresponding disparate commitments of the colonial state's resources between British soldiers and local population. This asymmetry was also manifest in the contrasting spatial qualities and disparities in the provision of amenities and infrastructure between cantonments and "native" towns.

Compared to the congested and insanitary "native" city, the grounds in Changi Cantonment were much more spacious, with buildings located within lush greenery and a good sanitary infrastructure. As we shall see in Chapter 4, since the early twentieth century, the "native" quarters of the Singapore town had been surveyed by sanitary experts and deemed as overcrowded and insanitary. Recommendations for improvement were accordingly put forward. However, the colonial government procrastinated in committing resources and implementing the recommended improvements.[103] In striking contrast, Changi, *terra incognita* when the War Office took over in 1927, was surveyed, comprehensively planned and built as a model cantonment within a fairly short time. Likewise, water supply, drainage and other sanitary works were also undertaken at other military spaces

Figure 2.23
Two British soldiers from Pulau Brani posing with their "native" servants, c. 1910s. Reprinted, by permission, from the REL.

way before similar works were undertaken in the "native" quarters.[104] Such disparities were especially ironic when the Straits Settlements, of which Singapore was a part, made a huge annual financial contribution, drawn from its annual revenue, to build and maintain these military spaces.

From 1867, when the Straits Settlements were transferred from the Government of India's rule to the imperial government's direct rule, it was obligated by the conditions of transfer to bear all the costs of its military and civil requirements. These costs subsequently grew exponentially, becoming a highly controversial subject when Singapore first became an important coaling station in the British Empire in 1880s, and then a strategic base for British imperial defense in the Far East in the 1920s.[105] In 1890, the Straits Settlements, a colony with an annual revenue of £740,000 for 1889, was asked to make a military contribution of £100,000, while the imperial government would only contribute a meager £36,154 for additional fortifications and cantonments perceived locally as serving the imperial purposes of protecting its coaling station and trading interests.[106] This led to ferocious local protests with the issue only temporarily resolved in 1896 when the Straits' military contribution was capped at a fixed percentage of its revenue.[107] Protests over this military contribution were reignited in the 1920s when the imperial government began building the costly imperial naval base along with the associated air and land defenses in Singapore. The imperial government expected the Straits Government to provide an annual military contribution of up to about £600,000 to help finance a base that was again primarily intended not for local defense but for guarding British interests in the Far East. The hefty annual military contribution levied was in addition to the vast tracts of land that the Straits Government had donated earlier for building the bases.[108]

This large military contribution redirected a significant percentage of the Straits Settlements' revenue that was originally intended for meeting urgent colonial development needs in public works, medical services and education. This led the Straits Governor Hugh Clifford to complain that the contribution would "likely prove crippling to the advancement of the Straits Settlements."[109] Moreover, up to approximately one quarter of the colony's revenue was derived from the "tainted source" of opium. In a 1927 letter to Winston Churchill, the Chancellor of the Exchequer, Leopold Amery, the British Secretary of State for the Colonies, wrote that:

> [a]lready between 40 and 50 percent of the military contribution [of the Straits Settlements] is derived from the sale of opium … [and] the Imperial Government [is] thus drawing … from what it is committed to regard as a *tainted source*.[110]

Even though the British imperial government committed itself and its colonies to the abolition of the use of opium after it was subjected to both international and local pressure to do so, and the Straits Settlements government reluctantly took steps in the 1930s to abolish this practice, the "tainted source" of opium revenue continued to account for a large part of the annual revenue of the Straits Settlements well beyond the 1920s.[111] As a percentage of the total revenue, the contribution of opium varied from a low of 15 percent during the early 1930s of the Great Depression to an average of around 22–26 percent in the later 1930s. Britain finally declared it illegal in 1943, and under further international pressure during World War II, opium smoking was totally prohibited throughout the Empire.[112]

Chinese immigrant laborers were the main social group consuming opium. Most only became addicted after they arrived in the Straits Settlements. Their opium addiction was inextricably linked to the conditions of exploitative colonial capitalism in the Straits Settlements. A combination of the strenuous labor many Chinese immigrants had to undertake and the absence of proper and affordable medical services meant that these manual laborers often consumed opium as a sedative drug to alleviate physical fatigue coming from long hours of working and also, used as a remedy for illnesses such as malaria and tuberculosis.[113] The revenue secured by the colonial state's utter disregard of the Chinese immigrant laborers' opium addiction and the consequences on their lives was in turn invested, through its military contribution, in the lives of the British soldiers based in cantonments, such as Changi, providing them with good housing, beautiful landscape, and an array of recreational and sporting facilities.

As we have noted earlier, the cantonment as endowed with these amenities only became the norm after the 1863 RCSSAI report. The RCSSAI noted that "idleness" or the "want of occupation" among the soldiers was the major cause of widespread intemperance, i.e. excessive consumption of alcoholic drinks, ill health and even venereal disease. Hence, both the RCSSAI along with the BHIC proposed new facilities such as workshops, gardens, gymnasia, libraries and reading rooms in the cantonments in order to encourage soldiers to engage in productive craft, agriculture, exercise and other forms of physical and moral improvements, thus occupying their time and diverting them from moral and health vices.[114] The provision of these facilities was a part of the aforementioned medical and sanitary measures proposed by the RCSSAI to intervene into the larger milieu in which the soldiers lived. As noted in the introductory chapter, Foucault understands such practices as part of a new governmental power regime that first emerged in the late eighteenth century, which he calls biopolitics, a regime of governance that sought to invest biopower in order to administer, multiply and optimize the biological life of the population.[115] Foucault contrasts this new biopower with the old sovereign power, famously noting that while sovereign power is the right "to take life or let live," biopower is the opposite power to " 'make' live and 'let' die."[116]

Given that the modern era, especially the twentieth century, was one of the most murderous in the history of humanity, and consisted of continuous wars, genocides and massacres, Foucault was of course acutely aware that there were exceptions to this modern biopolitical power regime of optimizing life.[117] "Given that this power's objective is essentially to make live," Foucault asks, "how can it let die?" Foucault argues that it was the intervention of racism that introduced "a break into the domain of life that is under [biopolitical] power's control: the break between what must live and what must die."[118] In other words, under the modern biopolitical power regime, racism was the precondition for exercising the right "to kill."[119] While Foucault goes on to examine wars and massacres waged against another population for the stake of securing the biological existence of one population, he also makes the qualification that his use of "killing" does not simply mean murder but also every form of indirect murder, for example, of exposing certain people to death or increasing the risk of death for those people. In our case, "to kill" would entail how the colonial government allowed, if not encouraged, a certain segment of the population, specifically the Chinese immigrant laborers, to waste their biological life away and die through opium smoking and addiction.

The opium-smoking exception to the biopolitical power regime of augmenting and optimizing life was not an aberration in the scheme of colonial governmentality. Colonial governmentality was a dislocated form of governmentality, as informed by what Partha Chatterjee calls the "colonial rule of difference," and in violation of its metropolitan liberal conception.[120] With the colonized racialized as the radical Other, the population was divided, first according to race and subsequently, according to relevance to colonial production, into a "discriminatory sanitary order."[121] It was, rather, the colonial military cantonment that was the "space of exception" in the colonial environs; a biopolitical and sanitary haven where the "good life" reigned in the midst of a biopolitical wilderness and insanitary wasteland where "sheer life" ruled.[122]

The use of "space of exception" here is, of course, the inverse of Giorgio Agamben's original conception. For Agamben, the exemplary space of exception is the concentration camp where bare life, politically disqualified life, abandoned by sovereign and reduced to mere biological existence, resides in a state of exception in which law and political normativity are suspended.[123] However, as Aihwa Ong notes, exception need not be associated with Agamben's negative conception of the sovereign marking out excludable subjects who are denied protections. Ong argues that there could be "positive kinds of exception, usually for a minority, who enjoy political accommodation and conditions not granted to the rest of the population."[124] These positive kinds of exception include a greater degree of political autonomy granted to these spaces, unique urban infrastructures developed in them and, most relevant for our purpose, special rights and benefits conferred upon the privileged inhabitants of these spaces.[125] Although Ong's concern lies primarily with the neoliberal present and not with colonial antecedents, I consider the colonial military cantonment a space of exception because I share Ong's attention towards the specific biopolitics and the attendant technologies of governing in these spaces of exception. Likewise, I also share Ong's argument that the spaces of exception could be privileged spaces, inhabited not by "bare life" but by "good life." In other words, the colonial military enclave was a socio-spatial enclave in the sense that it was a privileged space of exception in the milieu of colonial Singapore.

THE INTELLIGIBLE ENCLAVE

In this chapter, we have traced the emergence of standardized barracks in the British tropical colonies in the nineteenth and early twentieth centuries. We have sought to understand how these barracks took on a "global form", an entity that was mobile and stable, and could be replicated at diverse sites in a fairly uniform manner. The word "global," however, could be a misnomer if we assume that global norms oppose local specificities. I have argued that the global form was the commingling of the universal and the local, the abstract and the embodied, episteme and mētis. The global form was, thus, something flexible and sufficiently adaptable to accommodate the different heterogeneous elements and permit the necessary local variations. We have also contextualized the emergence of these tropicalized barracks in relation to a few broader shifts. First, we explored the reforms in the training of the Royal Engineers in building construction and their experimental traditions. Next, we examined how statistical enumeration of high mortality and morbidity rates in the West Indies contributed to the way tropical barracks were designed and fabricated. Finally, we turned to the effects of mid-nineteenth century sanitary reforms, in particular how they led to the formulation of space standards for barracks and type plans based on climatic classifications. These, in turn, shaped the planning and design of tropicalized barracks in the British Empire.

These tropicalized barracks, however, existed only in the privileged socio-spatial enclaves of the cantonments. We have seen that these socio-spatial enclaves were not only characterized by their spatial differences from other colonial spaces, they were also the products of the colonial rule of racialized difference in which a disproportionate amount of resources were invested into these spaces and the biopower of their British inhabitants at the expense of the locals. Following Ong, I have called these enclaves "spaces of exception" and they were the sites where spatial experiments in the building of tropicalized barracks were carried out as part of a new biopolitical regime.

Did these experiments affirm the arguments made by scholars such as Paul Rabinow and Gwendolyn Wright, who, in the context of French colonial urbanism, deduce that the colonies were "experimental terrains,"[126] places where controlled experiments in urban planning and the "new arts of government capable of bringing a modern and healthy society into being" could be carried out?[127] Rabinow and Wright argue that, partly due to the legislative exceptions that could be made in a colonial situation unfettered by metropolitan socio-cultural and politico-economic constraints, these experiments led to innovations that were subsequently brought back to the metropole. As I have noted in the introductory chapter, such arguments about the colonies and the so-called "periphery" as sites of innovation and not merely sites of passive reception of European innovations, have been increasingly foregrounded by historians in recent years.

Was the colonial cantonment an example of such a laboratory where experiments in the design and planning of barracks were carried out? From a Science and Technology Studies perspective, both the laboratory and experiment have more specific conceptions than the metaphorical manner in which they are used in scholarship on colonial urbanism, and they are also ascribed much greater transformative powers. According to Bruno Latour, an experiment in a laboratory works through two key operations. One, it reduces the multifactorial variables from the field into a smaller number of carefully controlled variables so that what was originally invisible in the field could be rendered visible in the laboratory. Two, it involves scalar manipulations such that the field conditions outside could be abstracted into the space of the laboratory and, similarly, the experimental conditions in the laboratory could be extended into the field. In other words, the boundary between the laboratory and the field becomes blurred.[128] Warwick Anderson, however, argues that while the frontier situations of the colonies tended to be represented by the colonizers as a laboratory, their field conditions were frequently too messy and too contested to be reducible to the antiseptic space of the laboratory. Thus, the colonizer's sense of control of the experiment in the laboratory was frequently misleading, if not illusory.[129]

I argue that the case of military barracks in colonial cantonments perhaps falls somewhere between the two above perspectives – the colony as laboratory of experimentation and innovation, and the colony as a messy and disorganized field that was irreducible to any laboratory situation. The military barracks in the colonial cantonment is perhaps best captured in a formulation by David Arnold. In his study of the medical history of colonial India, Arnold argues that, along with prisons and hospitals, military barracks in the cantonments formed specific "enclaves" in which colonial medicine could evaluate India through a series of exploratory or classificatory "grids."[130] A certain grid of intelligibility could be attained in the enclaves because, as regulated spaces, accurate mortality and illness statistics could be obtained and the conduct of the inhabitants, i.e. their diet, attire, exercises and other aspects of their daily routine, could be controlled. Thus, in contrast to the vast and complex colonial world beyond these enclaves, the causes of illnesses and death, and the effectiveness of sanitary measures and curative processes prescribed, were easier to evaluate and know. In other words, these enclaves functioned like laboratories in that multifactorial variables that caused diseases could be reduced into fewer controlled variables. Moreover, manipulation of scales enabled the abstraction of some of the external conditions within the enclaves.

Extending the enclaved conditions into the spaces beyond, however, proved much more difficult, as we shall see in Chapters 3 and 4. Given that the territory within the colonies was uneven, it would not be plausible to imagine that the colonies as a whole presented laboratory conditions for innovative experimentation. Instead it was within clearly delineated exceptional spaces, such as the military cantonments, where extensive resources were committed that experimentations and innovations could take place. In Chapters 3 and 4, we will explore what happened when architectural experimentations with their attendant technologies of government were extended beyond the military enclaves and applied to different sites and building types – medical spaces and the hospital, and urban spaces and the public housing.

Other than contributing to the history of barracks and the military landscapes of the British Empire, this chapter is also significant in that the organized theoretical and practical training of the Royal Engineers was a forerunner to similar organized training in engineering and architecture later in the universities and technical colleges of the British Empire. The building science research undertaken by the Royal Engineers, and the codification of complex building practices into numerical standards and technical norms, were similarly to anticipate the type of mid-twentieth century building science research undertaken by the building research institutions in the British Empire/Commonwealth. The widespread technicalization of architecture and building construction under the hegemonic regime of international development was to follow. Both are discussed in Chapters 5 and 6. As such, the history of barracks and military landscapes discussed here formed the epistemological foundation and constituted one of the early key moments in the genealogy of tropical architecture.

NOTES

1 PRO CO273/538/3, *Committee of Imperial Defence Minutes.*

2 Malcolm H Murfett et al., *Between Two Oceans: A Military History of Singapore from First Settlement to Final British Withdrawal* (Singapore: Marshall Cavendish Academic, 2005). "Gibraltar of the East" was the name given to Singapore by *The Daily Express* at the opening of the Imperial Naval Base at Sembawang in 1938. See Karl Hack and Kevin Blackburn, *Did Singapore Have to Fall? Churchill and the Impregnable Fortress* (London: Routledge, 2004), 23.

3 Henry Probert, *The History of Changi* (Singapore: Changi University Press, 2006 [1965]); J.F.F., "Changi Cantonment 1933–1937," *REJ* 51 (1937).
4 PRO CO273/538/3, *Report of the Gillman Commission*.
5 Probert, *The History of Changi*, 14.
6 Ibid.
7 Cited ibid., 15. Hack and Blackburn, *Did Singapore Have to Fall?*, 105.
8 L. N. Malan, "Singapore: The Founding of the New Defences," *REJ* 52, no. 2 (1938): 216.
9 PRO CO273/538/3, *Report of the Gillman Commission*, 30.
10 Malan, "Singapore," 226.
11 War Office, *Barrack Synopsis, 1923 Edition* (London: HMSO, 1923), 6.
12 PRO CO273/538/3, *Report of the Gillman Commission*, 31.
13 Malan, "Singapore," 216.
14 J.F.F., "Changi Cantonment 1933–1937," 358.
15 War Office, *Barrack Synopsis, 1911 Edition* (London: HMSO, 1911), ii. This statement also appears in the 1923, 1931 and 1939 (India version) editions. A longer version elaborating on the variations for the overseas station appears in the 1948 version of *Barrack Synopsis*.
16 See, for example, Home, "On Engineering Operations on the Gold Coast During the Recent Expedition," *PCRE, New Series* XXIII (1876); E. H. Harvey, "R.E. Works Abroad," *REJ* 11, no. 2 (1927).
17 James C. Scott, *Seeing Like a State: How Certain Schemes to Improve the Human Condition Have Failed* (New Haven: Yale University Press, 1998), 309–41.
18 For a criticism of Scott's formulation of episteme and mētis, see, for example, Tania Murray Li, "Beyond 'the State' and Failed Schemes," *American Anthropologist* 107, no. 3 (2005). See also Michael Polanyi's understanding of the relationship between tacit knowledge and scientific knowledge, Michael Polanyi, *Personal Knowledge: Towards a Post-Critical Philosophy* (Chicago: University of Chicago Press, 1958).
19 McCallum was the only military engineer previously based in Singapore to have a sufficiently illustrious career to be included in the official history of the RE. After his stint as the Straits Settlements Colonial Engineer between 1880 and 1897, he served as Governor of various colonies. See W. Baker Brown, *History of the Corps of Royal Engineers, Volume IV* (Chatham: The Institution of the Royal Engineers, 1952), 435–36.
20 McCallum won the Pollock medal at Woolwich Military Academy and the Fowke Medal at the School of Military Engineering Chatham for proficiency in construction course, a medal named after one of the most prominent builders in the Corps of Royal Engineers, Francis Fowke. B. R. Ward, "The School of Estimating and Construction at the S.M.E.," *REJ* 7, no. 1 (1908); Brown, *History of the Corps of Royal Engineers, Volume IV*. For the distinguished career of Francis Fowke and his various innovations in building construction technologies, see John Weiler, "Army Architects: The Royal Engineers and the Development of Building Technology in the Nineteenth Century" (PhD thesis, University of York, 1987), 279–363.
21 Letter from Acting Governor Anson to Secretary of State for Colonies Michael Beach in PRO CO885/4, *Further Correspondence Respecting Colonial Defences*.
22 Letter from Chard to War Office dated 25 September 1894 in PRO WO33/56, *Correspondence Relating to the Provision of Barrack Accommodation at the Straits Settlements* (1896), 88.
23 Letter from Warren to Governor of the Straits Settlements C. B. H. Mitchell dated 27 March 1894, ibid., 61–63.
24 Official memorandum by McCallum dated 16 April 1894, ibid., 65–66.
25 McCallum's comments dated 7 June 1894, ibid., 73.
26 Letter from the War Office to Chard dated 24 November 1894, ibid., 90–93.

27 Collyer was originally sent to Singapore to propose a defense plan but he was later appointed as the Chief Engineer in 1858.
28 Whye Mun Low, "A History of Tanglin Barracks: The Early Years," *Pointer* 25, no. 4 (1999); Charles Burton Buckley, *Anecdotal History of Old Times in Singapore: From the Foundation of the Settlement under the Honourable the East India Company on February 6th, 1819 to the Transfer to the Colonial Office as Part of the Colonial Possessions of the Crown on April 1st, 1867*, New ed. (Singapore: Malayan Branch of the Royal Asiatic Society, Oxford University Press, 1923).
29 John B. Hattendorf, *The Two Beginnings: A History of St. George's Church Tanglin* (Singapore: St. George's Church, 1984).
30 John Law, "Technology and Heterogeneous Engineering: The Case of Portuguese Expansion," in *The Social Construction of Technological Systems: New Directions in the Sociology and History of Technology*, ed. Wiebe E. Bijker, Thomas P. Hughes and T. J. Pinch (Cambridge, MA: MIT Press, 1987).
31 Andrew Saint, *Architect and Engineer: A Study in Sibling Rivalry* (New Haven: Yale University Press, 2007).
32 Weiler, "Army Architects."
33 B. R. Ward, *The School of Military Engineering, 1812–1909* (Chatham: The Royal Engineers Institute, 1909).
34 Cited in Ward, "The School of Estimating and Construction at the S.M.E.," 33.
35 Weiler, "Army Architects."
36 Ibid.
37 Ward, "The School of Estimating and Construction at the S.M.E."
38 Weiler, "Army Architects," 38.
39 The technical periodicals took on different forms and titles, such *as Papers on Subjects Connected to the Duties of the Corps of Royal Engineers*, *Papers on Subjects Connected to the Duties of the Corps of Royal Engineers – New Series*, *Professional Papers of the Corps of the Royal Engineers – Occasional Papers*, and *Royal Engineers Journal*.
40 Besides the primary materials, my discussions below rely quite heavily on Weiler's Ph.D. thesis.
41 See, for example, William Turnbull, "Practical Essay on the Strength of Cast Iron Beams, Girders, and Columns; in Which the Principles of Calculation Are Exhibited in a Plain and Popular Manner," *PCRE* VI (1843).
42 Home, "On Engineering Operations on the Gold Coast During the Recent Expedition," 85.
43 Cited in Weiler, "Army Architects," 367–68.
44 Harvey, "R.E. Works Abroad."
45 Weiler, "Army Architects," 368–71.
46 Ibid., 377.
47 The formula was taken from Peter Barlow's *An Essay on the Strength and Stress of Timber*, first published in 1817.
48 See, for example, Nelson, "Engineer Details: For the Most Part Collected at Bermuda between April, 1829, and May, 1833," *PCRE* IV (1840).
49 John F. Herschel, "Instructions for Making and Registering Meteorological Observations at Various Stations in Southern Africa, and Other Countries in the South Seas, as also at Sea," *PCRE* II (1844): 215–16.
50 Fife, "The Thickness and Materials of Walls and Roofs of Buildings, Considered in Respect of Coolness in Tropical Climates," *PCRE, New Series* XIII (1864).
51 C.R.E., "Sun-Screens in Sky-Lit Buildings," *REJ* 28, no. 2 (1918).
52 E. C. S. Moore, "Sanitary Engineering Notes," *PPCRE* XVII (1892). J. E. Clauson, "Recent Researches on Malaria," *PPCRE* XII (1887).

53 Captain Smyth, "On the Construction of Barracks for Tropical Climates," *PCRE* II (1844 [1838]): 232.
54 Ibid.
55 Philip D. Curtin, *Death by Migration: Europe's Encounter with the Tropical World in the Nineteenth Century* (Cambridge: Cambridge University Press, 1989).
56 T. Graham Balfour, "The Opening Address of Dr. T. Graham Balfour, F.R.S., &C, Honorary Physician to Her Majesty the Queen, President of the Royal Statistical Society. Session 1889–90. Delivered 19th November, 1889," *Journal of the Royal Statistical Society* 52, no. 4 (1889).
57 A. M. Tulloch, "On the Sickness and Mortality among the Troops in the West Indies I," *Journal of the Statistical Society of London* 1, no. 3 (1838); A. M. Tulloch, "On the Sickness and Mortality among the Troops in the West Indies II," *Journal of the Statistical Society of London* 1, no. 4 (1838); A. M. Tulloch, "On the Sickness and Mortality among the Troops in the West Indies III," *Journal of the Statistical Society of London* 1, no. 7 (1838).
58 Peter Burroughs, "The Human Cost of Imperial Defence in the Early Victorian Age," *Victorian Studies* 24, no. 1 (1980); Tulloch, "On the Sickness and Mortality among the Troops in the West Indies III," 444. See also Chapter 2.
59 Smyth, "On the Construction of Barracks for Tropical Climates," 233–34.
60 Captain H. R. Brandreth, "Memorandum Relative to a System of Barracks for the West Indies Recommended by Colonel Sir C. F. Smith, C.B., R.E., and Approved by the Master-General and Board of Ordnance," *PCRE* II (1844 [1838]): 238.
61 Based on my calculation from the measured drawings.
62 Brandreth noted that: "The properties of miasmata have hitherto escaped detection of analysis; but it is generally assumed that vegetable substances, in the slow decomposition which takes place in them in the process of putrefaction, give out inflammable body of malaria, and renders its operation on the human frame less obnoxious when introduced in particles through the net-work, than in a compact stream through the open window." Brandreth, "Memorandum Relative to a System of Barracks for West Indies," 244–45.
63 However, it was more likely that the gauze screens kept anopheles mosquitoes out of the barrack rooms, thus reducing the rate of malaria infections among the soldiers. Ibid., 242, 44.
64 Weiler, "Army Architects," 415–16.
65 Brandreth, "Memorandum Relative to a System of Barracks for West Indies."
66 Weiler, "Army Architects," 422–25.
67 For an overview of the sanitary reform, see James Douet, *British Barracks 1600–1914: Their Architecture and Role in Society* (London: Stationary Office, 1998), 127–49.
68 "Murdering the Soldier – Portman-Street Barracks – the Commissioners' Report," *The Builder* 16, no. 787 (1858); "Housing the Army – St. George's Barracks – the Tower," *The Builder* 16, no. 788 (1858).
69 David Arnold, *Colonizing the Body: State Medicine and Epidemic Disease in Nineteenth-Century India* (Berkeley: University of California Press, 1993).
70 The Commissioners, *General Report of the Commission Appointed for Improving the Sanitary Condition of Barracks and Hospitals* (London: George Edward Eyre and William Spottiswoode, 1861), B.
71 The Commissioners, *Report of the BHIC on the Sanitary Condition and Improvement of the Mediterranean Stations* (London: George Edward Eyre and William Spottiswoode, 1863).
72 BHIC, *Suggestions in Regard to Sanitary Works Required for Improving Indian Stations* (London: George Edward Eyre and William Spottiswoode, 1864).

73 Florence Nightingale, *Observations on the Evidence Contained in the Stational Reports Submitted to Her by the RCSSAI* (London: Edward Stanford, 1863).
74 The Commissioners, *General Report of the Commission Appointed for Improving the Sanitary Condition of Barracks and Hospitals*, C3.
75 The Commissioners, *Report of the BHIC on the Sanitary Condition and Improvement of the Mediterranean Stations*, A1.
76 The Commissioners, *Report of the RCSSAI. Vol. 1: Précis of Evidence, Minutes of Evidence, Addenda* (London: George Edward Eyre and William Spottiswoode, 1863), xxxi.
77 The Commissioners, *Report of the BHIC on the Sanitary Condition and Improvement of the Mediterranean Stations*, A.
78 BHIC, *Suggestions in Regard to Sanitary Works Required for Improving Indian Stations*, B.
79 BHIC, *Report of the BHIC on the Sanitary Condition and Improvement of the Mediterranean Stations*, A3.
80 BHIC, *Suggestions in Regard to Sanitary Works Required for Improving Indian Stations*, 20.
81 Chas. M. Watson, "Barrack Policy," *REJ* 6, no. 6 (1907): 348.
82 Ibid.; E. H. Hemming, "Progress in Barrack Design," *PPCRE* XXVI (1900).
83 E. N. Stockley, "Barracks," in *The Encyclopedia Britannica: A Dictionary of the Arts, Sciences, Literature and General Information, Vol. 3* (Cambridge: Cambridge University Press, 1910), 427.
84 G. K. Scott-Moncrieff, "The Design of Soldiers' Barracks," *PPCRE* XXI (1895): 126–7.
85 Hemming, "Progress in Barrack Design," 51–52.
86 War Office, *Barrack Synopsis, 1911 Edition.*
87 War Office, *Barrack Synopsis, 1923 Edition.*
88 Defence Department, *Barrack Synopsis (India)* (London: HMSO, 1939), 2; War Office, *Barrack Synopsis, 1923 Edition*, 5; *Barrack Synopsis, 1911 Edition*, B; War Office, *Barrack Synopsis, 1931 Edition* (London: HMSO, 1931), 2; War Office, *Barrack Synopsis, 1948 Edition* (London: HMSO, 1948), 5.
89 Peter Scriver, *Rationalization, Standardization, and Control in Design: A Cognitive Historical Study of Architectural Design and Planning in the Public Works Department of British India, 1855–1901* (Delft: Publikatieburo Bouwkunde, Technische Universiteit Delft, 1994); Peter Scriver, "Empire-Building and Thinking in the Public Works Department of British India," in *Colonial Modernities: Building, Dwelling and Architecture in British India and Ceylon*, ed. Peter Scriver and Vikramaditya Prakash (London and New York: Routledge, 2007).
90 W. M. Blagden, "Temporary Electric Light and Power at Changi," *REJ* 43, no. 3 (1929).
91 PRO CO273/538/3, *Report of the Gillman Commission*, 29.
92 Malcolm Watson, *Rural Sanitation in the Tropics: Being Notes and Observations in the Malay Archipelago, Panama and Other Lands* (London: J. Murray, 1915); Malcolm Watson, "Twenty-Five Years of Malaria Control in the Malay Peninsula," *British Malaya* 1, no. 9 (1927).
93 Malan, "Singapore." PRO CO273/538/3, *Report of the Gillman Commission.*
94 J.F.F., "Changi Cantonment 1933–1937."
95 Anthony D. King, *Colonial Urban Development: Culture, Social Power, and Environment* (London: Routledge & Kegan Paul, 1976), 80.
96 Sten Nilsson, *European Architecture in India 1750–1850*, trans. Agnes George and Eleonore Zettersten (London: Faber and Faber, 1968), 77.
97 The Commissioners, *Report of the RCSSAI. Vol. 1*, ixl.
98 BHIC, *Suggestions in Regard to Sanitary Works Required for Improving Indian Stations*, 32.

99 Ann Laura Stoler, *Race and the Education of Desire: Foucault's History of Sexuality and the Colonial Order of Things* (Durham, NC: Duke University Press, 1995).

100 Anthony D. King, *The Bungalow: The Production of a Global Culture*, 2nd ed. (New York: Oxford University Press, 1995 [1984]); T. Roger Smith, "On Buildings for Europeans Occupation in Tropical Climates, Especially India," in *Papers Read at the Royal Institute of British Architects 1867–68* (1868); Swati Chattopadhyay, "Blurring Boundaries: The Limits of 'White Town' in Colonial Calcutta," *JSAH* 59, no. 2 (2000).

101 WO33/56, *Correspondence Relating to the Provision of Barrack Accommodation at the Straits Settlements*, 87.

102 Ah Poh Lim, "Changes in Landuse in the Former British Military Areas in Singapore" (BA (Hons) Thesis, National University of Singapore, 1974), 39–40.

103 See Chapter 3.

104 PRO WO33/56, *Correspondence Relating to Water Supply at Tanglin Barracks in the Straits Settlements* (1896); PRO WO33/56, *Correspondence Relating to the Provision of Barrack Accommodation at the Straits Settlements*.

105 Murfett et al., *Between Two Oceans*. In fact, the controversies surrounding military contribution started as early as the 1860s when military spending on, what the mercantile community's perceived as, works needed for "the maintenance of a force far beyond all local requirements in its amount and character" used up half of the Colony's revenue in 1863. Walter Makepeace, "The Military Contribution," in *One Hundred Years of Singapore*, ed. Walter Makepeace, Gilbert E. Brooke, and Roland St. J. Braddell (Singapore: Oxford University Press, 1991 [1921]), 380.

106 Frederick Dickson, "Minute by the Colonial Secretary," in *PLCSS 1891* (Singapore: Straits Settlements Government Printing Office, 1892); Cecil C. Smith, "Military Contribution," *PLCSS 1891*.

107 Makepeace, "Medical Work and Institutions"; PRO CO273/541/14, *Military Contribution Committee*.

108 PRO CO273/546/6, *Military Contribution*; Murfett et al., *Between Two Oceans*, 192–97.

109 Letter from the Straits Settlements Governor Hugh Clifford to Secretary of State for the Colonies Lord Amery dated 19 July 1928 in PRO CO273/546/6, *Military Contribution*.

110 Cited in Harumi Goto-Shibata, "Empire on the Cheap: The Control of Opium Smoking in the Straits Settlements, 1925–1939," *Modern Asian Studies* 40, no. 1 (2006): 59 (my emphasis).

111 Speech by the Colonial Treasurer, Proceedings of the Straits Settlements Legislative Council in PRO CO273/529, *Opium Revenue Replacement Reserve Fund*. See also PRO CO273/529, *Replacement of Opium Revenue*. For an overview, see Goto-Shibata, "Empire on the Cheap."

112 Goto-Shibata, "Empire on the Cheap"; E. O. H., "Opium Control in Malaya," *Far Eastern Survey* 7, no. 2 (1937).

113 See, for example, James Francis Warren, *Rickshaw Coolie: A People's History of Singapore, 1880–1940* (Singapore: Oxford University Press, 1986), 240–49; Goto-Shibata, "Empire on the Cheap."

114 The Commissioners, *Report of the RCSSAI. Vol. 1*, lvi–lxvii; BHIC, *Suggestions in Regard to Sanitary Works Required for Improving Indian Stations*, 26–28.

115 This section is taken from Foucault's last lecture of the 1975–76 series, Michel Foucault, *Society Must Be Defended: Lectures at the Collège de France, 1975–76*, trans. David Macey (New York: Picador, 2003), 239–63. The concepts addressed in this lecture were also explored elsewhere in Foucault's other publications, but I choose this lecture because it explores the exception to biopower. For his other related publications, see Michel Foucault, *The History of Sexuality: An Introduction, Volume 1*, trans. Robert Hurley (New York: Vintage, 1990 [1978]); Michel Foucault et al., eds., *The Foucault Effect: Studies in Governmentality* (Chicago: University of Chicago Press, 1991).

116 Foucault, *Society Must Be Defended*, 241.
117 Eric Hobsbawn, *The Age of Extremes: A History of the World, 1914–1991* (New York: Vintage, 1994).
118 Foucault, *Society Must Be Defended*, 254.
119 For an erudite elaboration of Foucault's idea regarding the relation between biopower and racism, see Stoler, *Race and the Education of Desire*, 55–94. See also Achille Mbembe, "Necropolitics," *Public Culture* 15, no. 1 (2004).
120 Partha Chatterjee, *The Nation and Its Fragments: Colonial and Postcolonial Histories* (Princeton: Princeton University Press, 1993); Gyan Prakash, *Another Reason: Science and the Imagination of Modern India* (Princeton: Princeton University Press, 1999), 123–58.
121 Prakash, *Another Reason*, 132.
122 My use of "good life" and "sheer life" here draws from Stephen J. Collier and Andrew Lakoff, "On Regimes of Living," in *Global Assemblages: Technology, Politics, and Ethics as Anthropological Problems*, ed. Aihwa Ong and Stephen J. Collier (Malden: Blackwell, 2005). Collier and Lakoff's conception, in turn, draws from Hannah Arendt. "Sheer life" refers to a life trapped within the biological needs of production and reproduction, never free from labor, whereas good life means a life free from the needs and concerns of mere biological needs and thus a life that could participate in the political sphere.
123 Giorgio Agamben, *Homo Sacer: Sovereign Power and Bare Life*, trans. Daniel Heller-Roazen (Stanford: Stanford University Press, 1998).
124 Aihwa Ong, *Neoliberalism as Exception: Mutations in Citizenship and Sovereignty* (Durham, NC: Duke University Press, 2006), 101.
125 Ibid., 75–118.
126 Gwendolyn Wright, *The Politics of Design in French Colonial Urbanism* (Chicago: University of Chicago Press, 1991), 12.
127 Paul Rabinow, *French Modern: Norms and Forms of the Social Environment* (Chicago: University of Chicago Press, 1989), 289.
128 Bruno Latour, "Give Me a Laboratory and I Will Raise the World," in *Science Observed: Perspectives on the Social Study of Science*, ed. Karin D. Knorr-Cetina and Michael Mulkay (London: Sage, 1983).
129 Warwick Anderson, *Colonial Pathologies: American Tropical Medicine, Race, and Hygiene in the Philippines* (Durham, NC: Duke University Press, 2006), 5–8.
130 Arnold, *Colonizing the Body*, 28.

Chapter 3: Translating Pavilion Plan Hospitals

Biopolitics, Environmentalism and Ornamental Governmentality

In October 1926, at the Annual Dinner of the Straits Settlements Association, Sir Laurence Guillemard, British Governor of the Straits Settlements at that time, boasted that his speedy recovery from ill-health was a "testimony to Malaya as a health resort."[1] Central to Guillemard's boast and his resurrection of the old myth of Malaya as a health resort was the completion of the new Singapore General Hospital (SGH) complex. Guillemard proclaimed:

> With the completion of our new General Hospital and the Mental Disease Hospital at Trafalgar, and the improvement of other curative institutions, Singapore will in this respect be one of the best-equipped centres in the Far East. Her facilities for teaching the practice and art of medicine, including the resources of our new College of Medicine, are unsurpassed.[2]

Guillemard continued to elaborate on the various public health initiatives undertaken by his government – anti-malarial works, infant and child welfare services, hookworm and rural sanitation program, anti-venereal disease program, and, most significantly for this chapter, the unprecedented 10 million dollar program of slum clearance, sanitary improvement and the provision of housing for the poorer classes (see also Chapter 4). Guillemard summed up by noting:

> I hope that what I have said will convince my hearers that Government is alive to its responsibility in the matter of public health though we admit that there is still much to do in the way of improving the conditions of life *out there*.[3]

Guillemard's use of "conditions of life *out there*" in relation to the colonial government's public health initiatives is perhaps revealing. On that occasion, his audiences were members of the elite Straits Settlements Association, who were from the wealthy European mercantile community in the colony. Unlike the indigenous/local population "*out there*," the European population in Singapore received good medical care and was much healthier, and as such, not the target of Guillemard's public health initiatives.[4] The mortality rate of the general population in Singapore, which consisted mostly of the local population, for the year 1926 was 31 per 1,000, which Guillemard described as "not as bad as it looks"[5] although in 1907, the British sanitary expert Professor W J Simpson described similar mortality rates in Singapore as excessive given the youthful migrant population.[6] After years of neglect of the health and sanitary problems of the local population, it seemed that Guillemard's speech marked a new phase in expanding the application of Colonial/Western medical and sanitary sciences, with the attendant commitment of the colonial state's politico-economic resources, "*out there*" into the realm of public health of the local population, beyond the privileged socio-political enclaves of the European residents and soldiers discussed in the previous chapter.

Because of the causalities established between the built environment and health at that time, regulating the built environment was a key component of the British colonial public health initiatives. As a landmark project in the colonial public health initiatives, the new SGH complex and its history encapsulated many of the socio-political aspects, and their contradictions, in regulating the colonial built environment and managing the public health of the local population. In this chapter, I will explore these socio-political aspects by examining the planning and design of the new SGH, and tracing the convoluted history that led to its construction. I also situate the history of the new SGH, a pavilion plan hospital, in the larger history of pavilion plan hospitals in the British imperial context. I outline the "invention," circulation and transformation of the pavilion plan hospital, from its origins in the metropole, to its "tropicalization," standardization and appearance in the colonies.

This overview of the pavilion plan hospital is significant not only because, as noted by scholars in the context of the industrial West, the pavilion plan hospital is one of the earliest modern building types in terms of its spatial organization, methods of construction, and innovations in environmental technologies concerning ventilation, heating/cooling and lighting.[7] As we shall see later, the design of the pavilion plan hospital was very much shaped by the biopolitical concerns for the health of the population and the miasmatic theory of disease transmission. As we have noted, the hot and humid climate of the tropics was perceived as hastening putrefaction and producing even more venomous miasma than the temperate climate. Thus, when the pavilion plan hospital travelled to the tropics and its design modified according to the local conditions, much attention was channeled toward finding ways to cope with the hot and humid climate. The tropical climate continued to be privileged as the key determinant of the architectural form of the pavilion plan hospital even after miasmatic theories of disease transmission had been replaced by germ theories from the late nineteenth century onward. The tropical pavilion plan hospital was hence known for its innovations in environmental technologies, which subsequently became one of the bases for the "tropical architecture" we came to recognize from the mid-twentieth century onwards.

The privileging of the tropical climate as the key determinant of architectural form and the innovations in the environmental technologies in the hospital were not ends in and of themselves. Rather, the emergence of the pavilion plan hospital in nineteenth-century France and Britain was inextricably linked to the larger shift in the social, economic and political order.[8] As noted in the introductory chapter, Michel Foucault describes this larger shift as the emergence of the modern state and its new governmental rationality that saw the "health and well-being of the population in general as one of the essential objectives of political power."[9] That gave rise to, among other things, what Foucault calls the "nosopolitics" in which the urban space and the hospital became new "medicalizable objects," to be controlled and reformed.[10] Spatially, the hospital was configured as both a panopticon and panthermicon, i.e. a disciplinary and thermal space to facilitate the surveillance of the patients and also to safeguard the health of their bodies.[11] In this chapter, through a study of the pavilion plan hospital in the tropics, I extend the scholarship on governmentality and spatiality to understand how the new metropolitan governmental rationality circulated and was translated in the colonial context.

This study of governmental rationality and spatiality entails a number of aspects. One, I attend to the techniques of government, specifically the use of statistics and quantification. I show how military statistics in the early nineteenth century enumerated the high mortality and morbidity rates of British soldiers in the tropics, made visible the socio-economic costs of these rates to the imperial government, and facilitated the political calculation that linked the health of the soldiers to the wealth of the empire. These subsequently led to the sanitary reform in the army and the emergence of the pavilion plan hospital in the military enclaves of the tropics. I argue that statistics and quantification also facilitated government at a distance, prescribing norms and ensuring regularity of practices throughout the British Empire. Even the architecture of the military pavilion plan hospital was prescribed in statistical form, as building specifications couched in numerical terms, to ensure standardization. Statistics and quantification using standardized instruments for taking meteorological measurements also served to "reify climate" in the nineteenth century.[12] Statistically aggregated climate was stable and predictable, unlike the seemingly random and chaotic weather.

Second, I attend to the biopolitical power regime of the new governmental rationality. I argue that the pavilion plan hospital and its environmental technologies prescribed for the military enclaves in the tropical colonies were part of the state's investment of biopolitical power in the soldiers through its proposal of a regime of living that attend to the bodily scale – the soldiers' attire, diet, exercise, labor and means for recreation. Third, I note that the new governmental rationality was premised on the liberal principle of seeing the individual as the locus of freedom, and its implementation depended on an extensive state bureaucracy and a commitment of vast resources. These conditions were absent in the colonial situation and thus I argue that the colonial state's attempt to extend the governmental rationality beyond the European socio-spatial enclaves to the local populace in Singapore through civilian hospitals such as the SGH was partial and incomplete. To compensate for the inadequacies and failings of the partial governmentality, the colonial state resorted to the display of sovereign power through monumental architecture, as part of the performance of spectacle. I call this mix of governmental and sovereign power ornamental governmentality.

LIGHT, AIR AND COOLNESS: THE "NEW" PAVILION PLAN HOSPITAL

The new General Hospital (Figure 3.1), construction of which began in 1923, was completed and officially opened by Guillemard in 1926. Located at the old Sepoy Lines, the new complex replaced the old General Hospital buildings on the same site. The Professor of Medicine at the King Edward VII Medical College, J. S. Webster, on the advisory committee of the building of the new SGH, explained that the elevated site was chosen primarily because of three main considerations – light, air and coolness. The site was "cool and airy," allowed "good natural drainage," and favored "the entrance of sunlight."[13] Moreover, Webster added that the elevated breezy site harbored fewer mosquitoes and was suitable for the execution of anti-malaria measures. The three main environmental factors were to recur in Webster's discussion of the design of the new hospital complex.

The 800-bed hospital consisted of two different schemes and three separate sets of buildings. One set of buildings housed the European scheme while two other sets of buildings house the "Native" scheme.[14] Each of these buildings was organized on the pavilion plan, with pavilion-like wards arranged at right angles to a long central corridor that connected all the pavilions. The pavilions were oriented such that the prevailing direction of wind was at an angle of 45 degrees to the long side of the ward. The emphases of the design of the buildings were on "free ventilation" and "as much light as possible."[15] The wards were designed to facilitate ventilation to the extent of "approximat[ing] an open-air existence." The minimum floor and air spaces of the wards were increased to double or triple those prescribed for hospitals in the temperate zones to obtain "large airy rooms"[16] (Figure 3.2). Ten-feet wide verandahs were designed to line the perimeter of the wards so as to provide breezy spaces while also shading the wards from excessive

Figure 3.1
Panoramic view of the new SGH. Courtesy of the NAS.

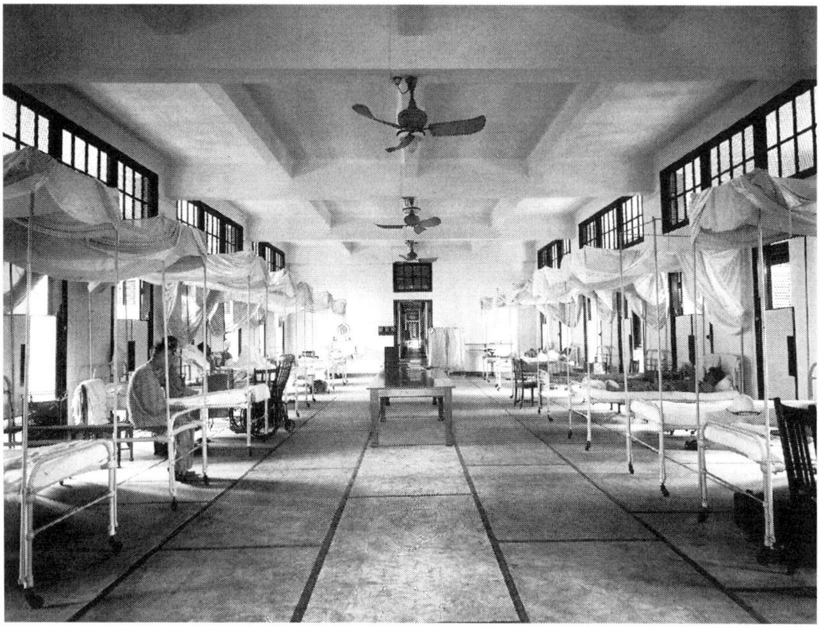

Figure 3.2
View of the interior of one of the native wards of SGH. Reprinted, by permission, from the NAUK.

Figure 3.3
View of a verandah of SGH. Reprinted, by permission, from the NAUK.

heat from the sun (Figure 3.3). Moreover, ventilation holes and large openings were located in the inner walls and outer walls that lined the wards and the verandahs respectively, so as "[t]o avoid the formation of pockets of dead air."[17] The wards were also planned such that the long sides faced north and south to minimize sunlight entering the interior.[18] Besides light, air and coolness, another key environmental consideration was dampness. For example, cement, a material that according to Webster was impermeable to dampness, was used for floor construction so that it was "no longer necessary to raise the building upon arches"[19] to avoid the ground dampness. Furthermore, the wards' walls were plastered and the surfaces were covered with a damp-resisting paint that would give the wall an enameled finish to prevent moisture from seeping in.

Webster claimed that while "the customary requirements of a home [i.e. British] hospital were realized ... the question arose as to what alterations should be made to meet the climatic and other conditions peculiar to the tropics in general and Singapore in particular."[20] He maintained that members in the advisory committee were "forced to rely almost entirely upon their experience" to come up with appropriate recommendations. [21] Webster, however, appears to have overstated the committee's achievement as the new hospital was not even the first pavilion plan hospital to be built in Singapore. The Tan Tock Seng Hospital (TTSH) complex (Figure 3.4), designed and completed by the Straits Public Works Department (PWD) in 1909, was also a pavilion plan hospital. Its design was based on the experimental wards first erected in 1900 at the old TTSH at Serangoon Road, which were, in turn, based on the suggestions provided by Patrick Manson, one of the founders of tropical medicine and the medical advisor to the Colonial Office in the 1890s and early 1900s.[22] The old SGH building, although on a much

igure 3.4
'iew of the pavilion
vards of the Tan Tock
eng Hospital complex.
Courtesy of the NAS.

smaller scale, could also be considered a variation of the pavilion plan hospital. In fact, as early as the 1860s, not long after the first pavilion plan hospitals were established in Europe, a standard design of pavilion plan hospital for the tropics was developed for the British Army. Many of the recommendations made by Webster's committee were not very different from those introduced seventy years earlier in the standard design of the mid-eighteenth century, as we shall see in the next section.

METROPOLITAN ORIGINS AND TECHNOLOGIES OF POPULATION

The pavilion plan gained widespread acceptance as the most suitable configuration for the hospitals in Britain as early as the 1860s through the tireless campaigning of influential sanitary reformers such as the Manchester surgeon Dr. John Roberton, editor of *The Builder* George Godwin, and Florence Nightingale, especially through her *Notes on Hospital* (1863).[23] According to Sir Henry Burdett's magisterial four-volume *Hospitals and Asylums of the World*, the pavilion plan system was distinguished by its wards, each of which is

> a parallelogram, entirely detached on at least three sides, with windows of both its longer sides facing each other, and attached to the main block at one end only ... The essence of the pavilion system is the isolation of wards from the rest of the hospital ...[24]

Advocates of the pavilion system also emphasized that the environmental provisions of the pavilion plan system, for example the big windows in the wards facing each other, let light and air in, and facilitate cross ventilation (Figure 3.5). The planning principle of the pavilion plan hospital was succinctly captured in Nightingale's widely quoted line from her *Notes on Hospital*: "No ward is in any sense a good ward in which the sick are not at all times supplied with pure air, light, and a due temperature."[25]

Underlying the planning principle of the pavilion plan hospital during the mid-nineteenth century was the miasmatic theory of disease transmission, even though this type of hospital continued to be the most commonly adopted planning model during the early twentieth century, years after the germ theory of disease transmission had supplanted the miasmatic theory.[26] As noted in the introductory chapter, miasmatic theory attributed the cause of disease to miasma, a type of noxious vapor from putrescent organic matters that were associated with both the natural and the built environment. It was also purportedly generated by human bodies through breathing and sweating. Miasma was thus perceived to accumulate in large amounts in overcrowded and poorly ventilated interiors. Two types of remedy were usually proposed. The first was through diluting the concentration of miasma in the air. Ventilation was an important means of achieving this and it was therefore emphasized in the planning of a pavilion plan hospital. Similarly, the principle of physically isolating the wards was also emphasized because, as Nightingale noted, "[m]iasma may be said, roughly speaking, to diminish as the

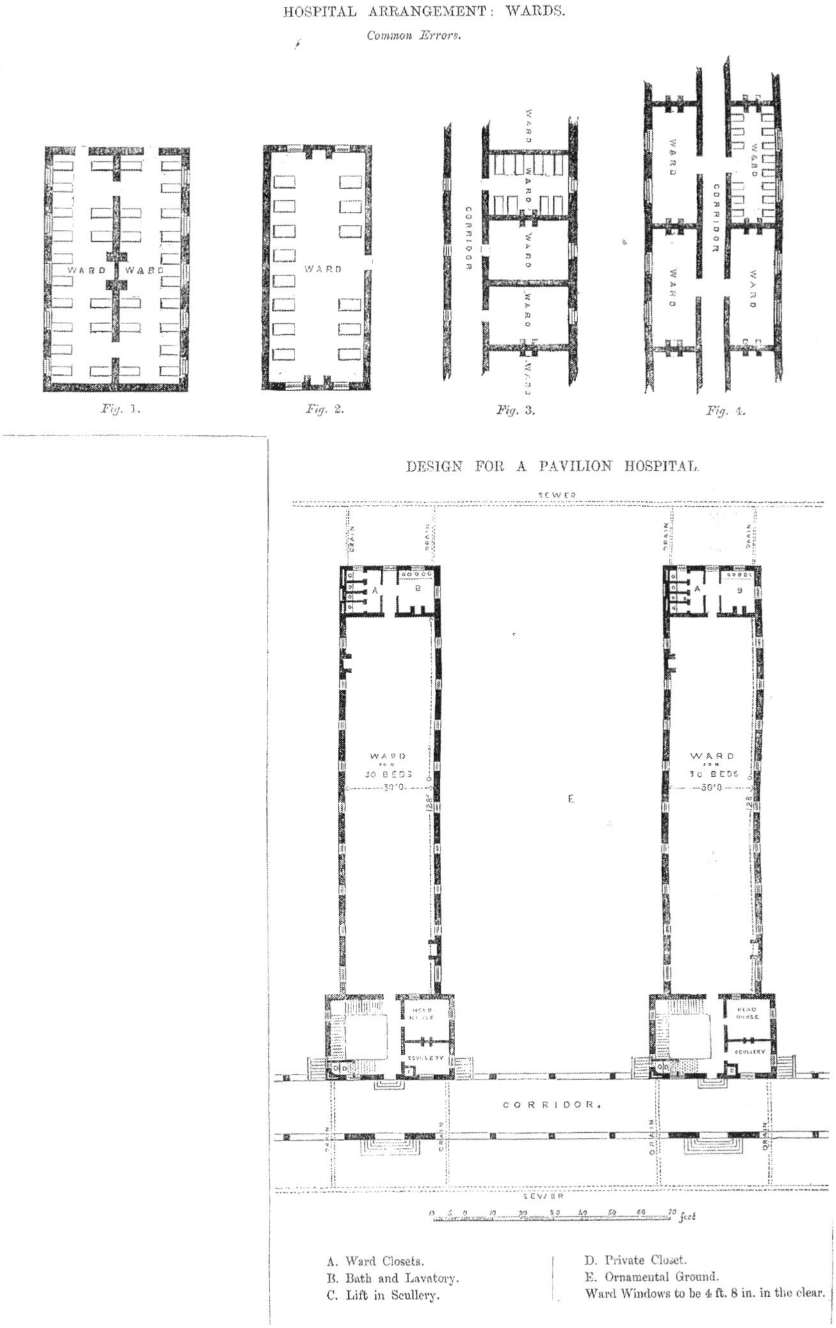

Figure 3.5
"Nightingale wards" (below) as compared to the older plans of hospital wards (above). Source: *The Builder*, 1858.

square of the distance."[27] Besides ventilation and isolation, the prevention of overcrowding and the allocation of sufficient "air space" per person were also stressed. Nightingale prescribed an air space of 1,500 to 1,600 cubic feet per patient in the design of her standard ward.[28] The second remedy was through chemical means, for example, by lime-washing surfaces. Part of this remedy also involved the use of impervious materials such as "Parian cement" in the construction of the pavilion hospital.

The connection between light, the other key consideration in the planning of the pavilion plan hospital, and the miasmatic theory was tenuous. Although light levels could be linked to the rate of putrefaction and, as such, be connected to emanations of the noxious vapor or miasma, it has been argued that its consideration was motivated more by aesthetic and moral, rather than scientific reasons, just as the concentration of miasma was gauged solely through the rather imperfect subjective means of smell.[29] The question of temperature will be considered later.

The pavilion plan hospital adopted in Britain following the efforts of the sanitary reformers was influenced by developments in continental Europe, especially in France. Roberton, Godwin and Nightingale were all familiar with the pavilion plan hospitals built in France during the early nineteenth century. The Lariboisière Hospital, completed in 1854, was an especially significant precedent. It embodied many of the most innovative ideas on hospital planning proposed in the landmark report produced by the committee from the Académie des Sciences appointed by Louis XVI after the major Hôtel-Dieu fire in 1772.[30] Michel Foucault sees the production of the model plan for Hôtel-Dieu and the subsequent building of the Lariboisière Hospital as exemplifying the larger hospital reform in France in which the modern hospital as a "curing machine" for healing sick people emerged out of the old hospital that was a "seat of death," used for housing the sick and other social deviants.[31] As we have noted, Foucault sees these transformations as part of the new governmental rationality of the state that sought to invest in the biopower of the population, improving their health and productivity.[32] The reform of the hospital into a "curing machine" entailed not just the earlier discussed architectural transformations to provide for air, light and thermal comfort, it also meant the spatialization of power.

According to Foucault, a component of the new governmental rationality was the disciplinary regime of biopower that engaged in the micropolitics of separating, knowing, regulating and reforming bodies. Jeremy Bentham's Panopticon, with its apparatus of surveillance and control, was the "strategic exemplar" that Foucault uses to demonstrate this disciplinary regime.[33] Like other modern specialized building types such as the prison, workhouse and lunatic asylum, established in the nineteenth century to manage deviances and normalize the population, the modern hospital shared the panopticon's spatial apparatus of segregation, classification, surveillance and control.[34] Spatially, the different pavilions in the pavilion plan hospital allowed patients to be segregated and classified according to their diseases, thus facilitating regulation and treatment.[35] Furthermore, one of the key planning considerations in Nightingale's pavilion ward was the ease of supervision by the nursing sisters. To facilitate supervision, the ward size was kept manageable and the nurse's room was strategically positioned to have a window overlooking the entire ward so that the nurse "may have all her sick under her eye at once." Furthermore, it was recommended that the beds were to be arranged so that the "patients ... should feel that they [were] continually under the eye of the head nurse." Finally, it was stated: "There should be no dark corners in any part of an [*sic*] hospital ward. Every recess or angle not easily overlooked is ... injurious to hospital discipline."[36] The pavilion plan hospital was planned such that each ward was made the "cul-de-sac of the main circulation system" thus making the whole spatial organization an "effective instrument of surveillance."[37] In many modern building types such as the prison and the hospital, surveillance worked in tandem with environmental regulation of air and light. According to Luis Fernandez-Galiano, Bentham also proposed a heating and ventilating system for his panopticon that guaranteed a homogeneous warmth internally that would "safeguard the health of the bodies in the same way that the vigilant eye tried to reform the ways and safeguard the health of the souls."[38] Fernandez-Galiano thus argues that a panopticon was also a panthermicon, and he gives the example of Pentonville Prison designed by Joshua Jebb.[39]

In the British colonial context, military reorganization and sanitary reform played an important part in the emergence of the pavilion plan hospital. Reformist sentiments in the 1830s led to the start of military statistical work under the likes of Henry Marshall, A. M. Tulloch and Graham Balfour, which compiled and compared the medical returns on the sickness, mortality and invaliding rates of the British soldiers stationed in different parts of the empire.[40] These statistics made visible the correlations between factors such as location of the military station, defects in barrack and hospital design, and high illness rates. They also demonstrated in an unequivocal manner the socio-economic costs to the British government of the high mortality rates caused by defective barrack and hospital designs.[41] As noted in Chapter 2, these contributed to some of the earliest sanitary reforms and the modification of the siting and planning of barracks in the West Indies during the 1830s. The sanitary reform of the British military was given even greater impetus with Nightingale's revelation of the medical mismanagement of the Crimean War, especially the appalling hospital conditions at Scutari. The sanitary fiasco in the Crimea led to a series of Royal Commission inquiries into the sanitary conditions of the army, the management of the military hospitals, and the design of hospitals and barracks.[42]

QUANTIFICATION AND ENVIRONMENTAL TECHNOLOGIES

The pavilion plan principle was proposed for the British Army in the tropical colonies at almost the same time as it was widely adopted in Britain. The 1863 Report of the RCSSAI and the 1864 Report of the BHIC for Indian Stations put forth what were probably the earliest recommendations for military hospitals in British colonies to be built according to the pavilion plan principle.[43] These two reports were produced at a momentous point in British India's history – just after the governance of India was transferred from the East India Company to the Crown after the 1857 Indian revolt and therefore at a time when more British soldiers were to be stationed in India. Following an inquiry that had "unusual extent and duration," two thick volumes – each at around 1,000 pages – of the report of the Royal Commission were published. One of the features that stood out was the "avalanche of printed numbers" compiled in the countless statistical tables in the reports.[44] These statistics were all a part of making sense of the excessive rate of "lives wasted in India." [45] The report opened with two pages of graphic representations that vividly illustrate the high annual mortality rate of the British soldiers stationed in India at 67 in 1,000, a rate that was eight times that of the British Army stationed in Britain and seven times that of the male British civilian population of the same age group. At that rate, the statistics showed that 100,000 British soldiers would be reduced to 9,604 in twenty years of service. It was deduced that in order to maintain an army of 85,856 men, the strength of the British Army in India at that time, 10,000 recruits would be required annually. An even more startling revelation was the economic cost of the high mortality rate. Each soldier was calculated to cost the British government £100 annually to maintain and the commission thus emphasized that "either the loss of his life, of his health, or of his efficiency, is not to be lightly regarded."[46]

Scholars in Science and Technology Studies and governmentality argue that numbers have the power of "turning a qualitative world into information and rendering it amenable to control."[47] Numbers do not merely describe a preexisting reality: they constitute the very reality for political calculations. The statistics of the 1863 report, for example, enumerated the politico-economic costs of the bad sanitary conditions of the British Army in India. Through the processes of quantification and standardization of measurements, different entities distributed across diverse time-spaces could be made commensurable with one another and, as such, also rendered comparable. In the 1863 report, the statistics were compiled and ordered such that mortality rates between not only England and India, but also the different stations in India, could be analyzed and compared. It was through such comparison that the mortality rates of British soldiers in India were deemed abnormally high and costly, thus necessitating political intervention.

It has also been noted that quantification is a "technology of distance."[48] As the results of quantification are outcomes of structured and rule-bound processes, the need for intimate knowledge of a place, or personal trust of the people carrying out the processes, are minimized. Furthermore, the information obtained through quantification is considered more factual and objective because it is the result of disinterested processes. Numbers are in a way like Bruno Latour's concept of immutable mobile that could facilitate action at a distance.[49] This perhaps explains why the Royal Commission only met in London and did not have to visit India. The Commission relied primarily on "an elaborate examination of the available statistical and sanitary documents", i.e. printed answers to the standardized questionnaires they sent out to all the Indian stations, and their interviews with sanitary experts and veterans who had served in India.[50] Statistical information featured prominently in the questionnaires. Besides information on climate, and mortality and morbidity rates that were typically presented in statistical form, information on the built environment, particularly barrack and hospital accommodation, was also quantified in these questionnaires (Figure 3.6). Dimensions of barracks and hospital wards, air space and superficial area (floor area) per person, number and dimensions of windows, and number of occupants were recorded in statistical tables to facilitate cross-checking and comparison with minimum standards.

Such a statistical rendering of architecture as numbers was subsequently adopted as part of the standard annual medical report submitted by the colonies to the Colonial Office.[51] As noted in Chapter 2, such statistical tables were also used to prescribe space standards in the various editions of *Barrack Synopses*. In 1899, Graham Balfour, the president of the Royal Statistical Society and one of the pioneers of sanitary reform in Britain, remarked: "it is upon the [statistical] information so acquired that the labours of the sanitary reformers have been based, and it is by statistics that the success and value of the sanitary work is measured."[52] Statistics were not only used to enumerate and make visible the sanitary problems in the built environment, they also formed the very basis for evaluating the sanitary improvement made.

From the statistics, the commissioners singled out "that subtle, unknown agent, or rather that cause of disease known only by its effect, malaria" as the main culprit of high mortality rates. Introduced in the English-speaking medical world in 1827, etymologically the word 'malaria' was derived from the Italian term, *mal'aria*, which literally means bad air.[53] The etymology suggests that the environmentalist explanations of neo-Hippocratic theories influenced the understanding of malarial fever. Besides the insanitary, overcrowded and poorly ventilated built environment discussed earlier, the medical topographical theories held by many British medical experts in the mid-nineteenth century also attributed the high incidence of malaria to the insalubrious locality and hot and humid tropical climate.[54] Malarial fever was believed to be caused by poisonous miasma, thus it would be accentuated in any locality with topographical features that retard

Figure 3.6
Statistical table on hospital accommodation in Pinang [Penang]. Source: The Commissioners, *The Report of the RCSSAI*, Vol. 2, 1863.

Table of Hospital Accommodation.

The date of the construction of the native artillery and European hospital is not known.
The native infantry hospital was erected in 1860.
Total number of wards, 5.
Total regulation number of beds, 46.

Wards. No.	Regulation Number of Sick in each Ward.	Dimensions of Wards. Length.	Breadth.	Height.	Cubic Contents.	Cubic Feet per Bed.	Superficial Area in Fee per Bed.	Height of Patient's Bed above the Floor.	Windows. Number.	Height.	Width.
		Ft.	Ft.	Ft.				Ft. In.		Ft. In.	Ft. In.
Native Infantry Hospital, 3	14	80	18	19	49,590	1,771	93	2 6	27	2 6	5 0
	7	39	15	19					12	7 0	5 0
	7	39	15	18							ventrs.
European Artillery, 1	10	38	19	10	7,220	722	$72\frac{1}{5}$	2 6	5	5 0	3 6
Golundauze, 1	8	27	18	10	4,860	$607\frac{1}{2}$	27	2 6	4	5 0	3 6

the free circulation of air or retain humidity. Likewise, the frequent rain and intense heat of the tropics were also perceived to increase the decomposition rate of organic matters and the attendant emission of miasma. In the "ubiquitous pathologization of space" in the early to mid-nineteenth century, the tropics were regarded as "the pathological site par excellence."[55]

In addition to the aforementioned collection of mortality and morbidity statistics, and quantified information on the built environment, the Commissioners also asked James Glaisher to prepare a "comprehensive view of the geographical distribution of atmospheric phenomena over this vast and various peninsula."[56] Glaisher was a pioneer meteorologist who helped to standardize the instruments and systematize the collection of meteorological data in the mid-nineteenth century.[57] His synchronic meteorological data contributed to the making of the world's first daily weather maps.[58] For the report, he prepared a weather map of British India (Figure 3.7), which might have been one of the earliest weather maps of the tropics. Although Glaisher's map was rather rudimentary, the quantity of meteorological data and the new mode of representation of these data represent a significant shift in the understanding of climate and space. Until the eighteenth century, climate was largely unquantified and unquantifiable. The availability of precise measuring instruments like the barometer and thermometer in the eighteenth century, and the regularization of observation and measurement methods in the nineteenth century, contributed to the quantification of climate. In the words of Mark Hulme, "order was imposed on seemingly chaotic weather" through statistically aggregating climates from geographically dispersed sites, from which new interpretations and utilities emerged.[59]

Interestingly, evaluating Glaisher's report and the returns from the stations, the commissioners were "struck with the absence of direct allegations against the climate."[60] Indeed, it has been argued that the new understanding of climate assembled from voluminous amounts of quantitative thermometric data challenged some of the assumptions that inhered in the Greco-Roman five-zone system, which was based on the theoretical relation between latitude and climate, and which had prevailed in the Western world from the sixth century B.C.E. to the eighteenth century.[61] It was also one of the bases for the neo-Hippocratic theories on the relation between place, climate and health, particularly the causality between hot and humid tropical climate and ill health. Despite the doubts being cast on the neo-Hippocratic theories, the commissioners insisted that the tropical climate had negative effects on the health of the British soldiers. They also acknowledged, however, that climate was not the sole cause of ill health among the soldiers. Instead, they noted:

> [T]he soldier's health in India, as elsewhere, is the product of all the conditions to which he is exposed. It is not solely the result of climate, nor of locality and dwelling place, nor of diet, habits, nor duties; it is the product of all of these.[62]

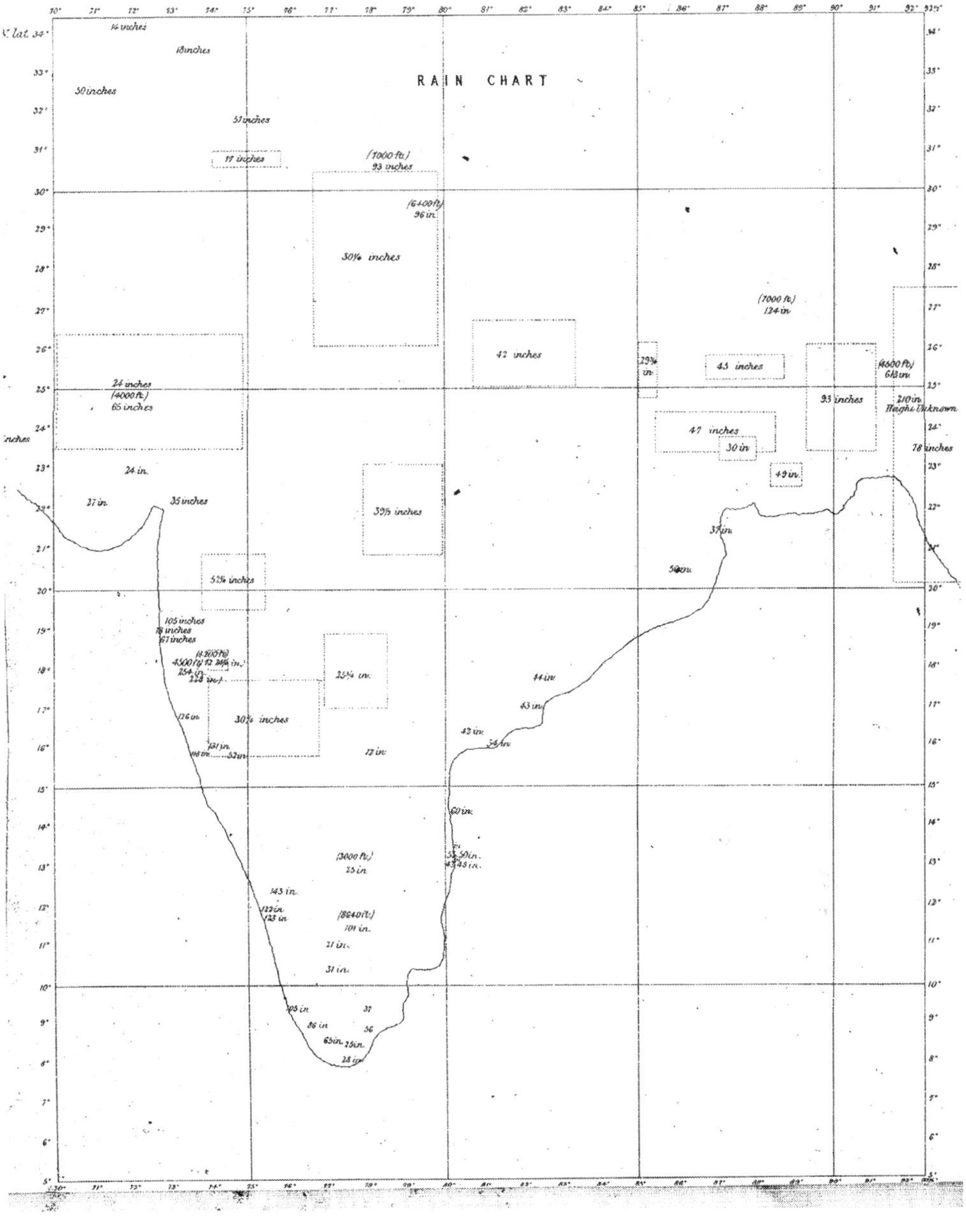

igure 3.7
:artogram of India
vith average rainfall
evels. Source: The
:ommissioners, *The*
eport of the RCSSAI,
'ol. 1, 1863.

This suggests that, despite the quantitative meteorological data pointing to the contrary, the commissioners chose to fall back and rely primarily on the familiar environmental – both built and natural – explanations for ill health.

Given the focus on environmental explanations, the modification of the military built environment in relation to the climate was central to the 1863 Report's recommendations on reducing the mortality rate of the British soldiers in India. These recommendations were followed with even more detailed suggestions, including detailed designs of model barracks and hospitals, in the 1864 report of the BHIC for Indian Stations.[63] From the station reports, the commissioners found that existing hospitals in India, which were built on the same plans as the barracks, tended to be too big, too deep, overcrowded, and not sufficiently ventilated to be healthy to live in (Figure 3.8). Moreover, according to the new sanitary standards in the metropole, most did not have proper water supply, drainage and sewerage systems as manual labor was used to carry water and remove sewerage waste. The ablution and bath facilities and the latrines were similarly defective. As Nightingale noted in her review of the station reports:

> If there be an exception, i.e., if there be a single station in India with a good system of drainage, water supply, and cleansing for itself and its bazaars, with properly planned and constructed barracks and hospitals, provided with what is necessary for occupation and health … I have not found it.[64]

The model hospital design in the report by the BHIC was filled with detailed technical specifications aimed at addressing these deficiencies (Figures 3.9 and 3.10). It was a two-story building raised on a 4-foot-high "ventilated basement" in order for the lower floor to avoid direct contact with the miasma emitted by the ground. This feature addressed the widely held medical belief that "much disease arose from troops being housed on ground level."[65] The building was of two stories so that the sick and convalescent could sleep on the upper floor while the lower floor could be used for auxiliary spaces such as dining rooms and libraries. The wards were designed to accommodate twenty-four beds and were dimensioned such that each patient had 120 square feet of superficial area and 1,800 cubic feet of air space.[66] These numerical standards would ensure that there

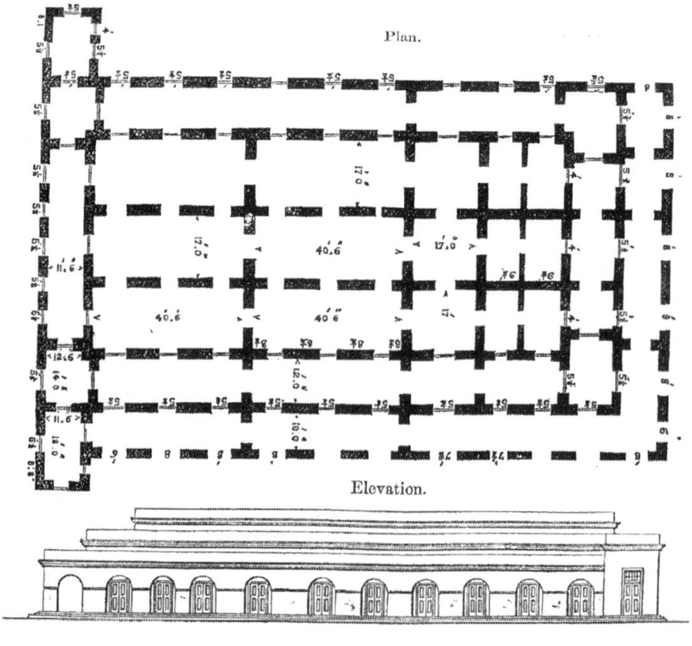

Figure 3.8
Plan of an "improperly ventilated" barrack in Indian stations. Source: Florence Nightingale, *Observations on the evidence contained in the stational reports submitted to her by the RCSSAI*, 1863.

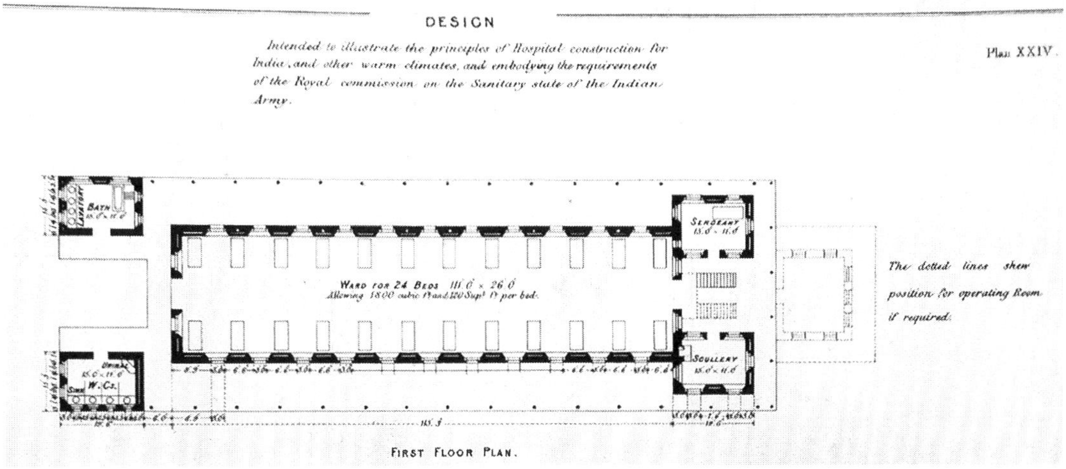

Figure 3.9
Upper floor plan of the model hospital for Indian stations. Source: BHIC, *Suggestions in regard to Sanitary Work required to improve Indian Stations*, 1864.

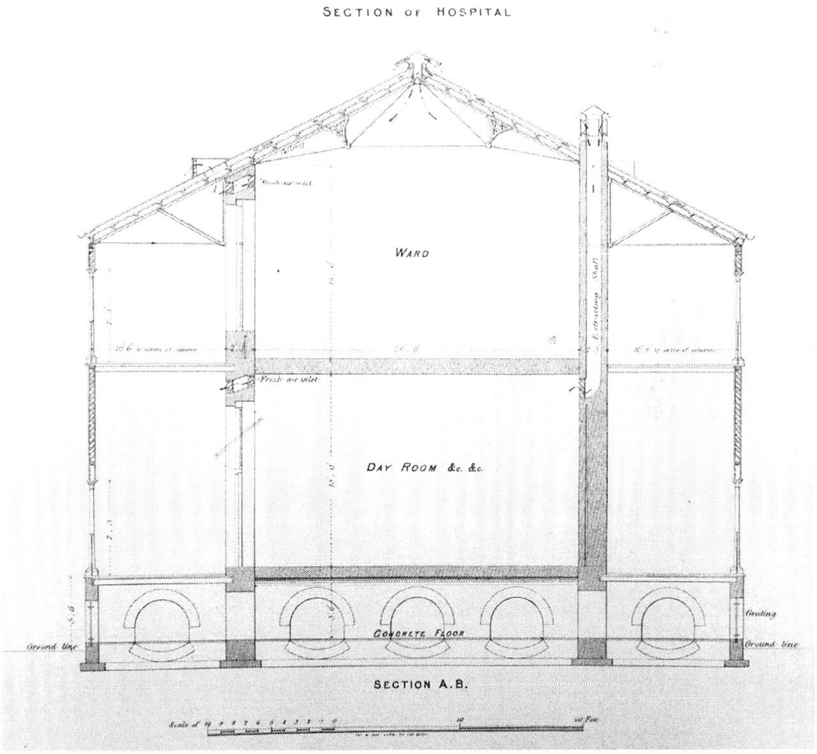

Figure 3.10
Section of the model hospital for Indian stations. Source: BHIC, *Suggestions in regard to Sanitary Work required to improve Indian Stations*, 1864.

would be no overcrowding. As interfaces between the building interior and the external environment, windows and doors controlled the amount of light, air and heat admitted into the wards. Minute considerations were thus given to the specifications of the design and positioning of the windows and doors in the report by the BHIC such that the wards had plenty of daylight and air, and without the heat and draughts. The commissioners also recommended that the windows and doors should not be the only means for ventilation and diluting the miasma. "[V]entilating course(s) of air bricks," ridge ventilation and louvered shafts were recommended to facilitate air movement and the disposal of "foul air."[67]

One particular set of concerns differentiated the recommendations for hospitals in tropical India from those in the temperate climate – cooling. To address cooling, the report dealt with two aspects – the modification of the built form and the use of additional cooling appliances. For the former, the report recommended that the hospital blocks be surrounded with twelve feet wide verandahs and sun-shading louvers be added at the external perimeter of the verandah to shade the wards. In addition, a double roof with a continuous six inches of ventilated air space was to be used to minimize the amount of heat gain through the roof (Figure 3.11). Using the same principles, the report also advocated that "walls should be built hollow, so as to substitute an air space instead of thickness of wall as a means of coolness."[68] On the use of additional cooling equipment, the report first reviewed the existing appliances that were in use in British India – punkah, tatty and thermantidote (Figure 3.12). Both the punkah, a canvas-covered frame suspended from the ceiling that was pulled by a servant, the *punkah wallah*, to circulate the air, and the tatty, a roll-up screen made from fragrant grass that was kept moist by periodic wetting to provide evaporative cooling, were originally adopted from the local inhabitants of India and subsequently modified according to the needs of the British settlers.[69] The thermantidote

Figure 3.11
Details of the double roof construction and roof ridge. Source: BHIC, *Suggestions in regard to Sanitary Work required to improve Indian Stations*, 1864.

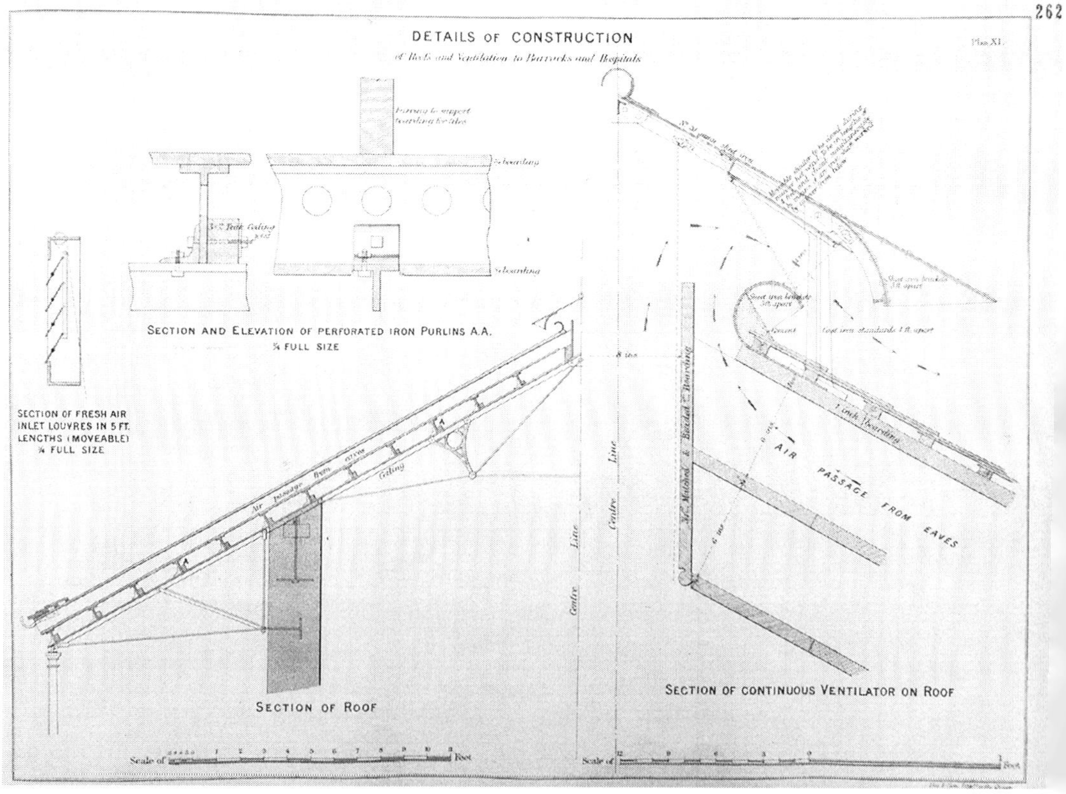

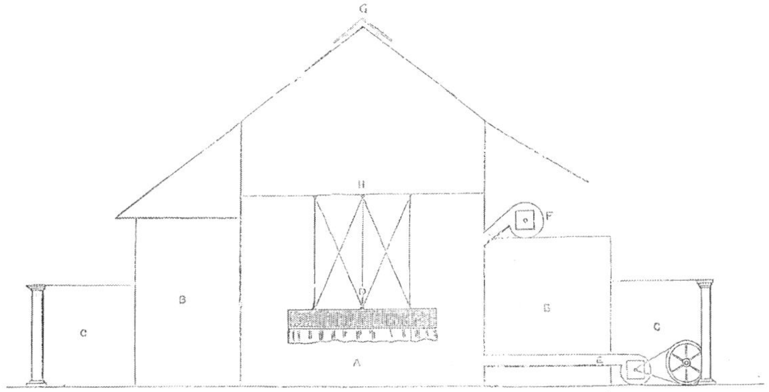

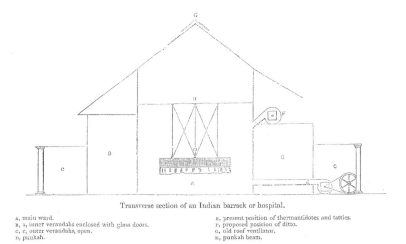

Transverse section of an Indian barrack or hospital.

A, main ward.
B, B, inner verandahs enclosed with glass doors.
C, C, outer verandahs, open.
D, punkah.
E, present position of thermantidotes and tatties.
F, proposed position of ditto.
G, old roof ventilator.
H, punkah beam.

Figure 3.12
Cross section of a typical barrack or hospital showing the thermantidote on the right hand side. Source: The Commissioners, *The Report of the RCSSAI*, Vol. 1, 1863.

introduced by the British was a contraption that combined a fan powered by human or animal muscular power with tatties.[70] The Commissioners found these appliances to be largely unsatisfactory – the punkah was "merely agitat[ing] air already more of less impure", the tatties were "apt to occasion hurtful draughts," and the thermantidote was found to be "most costly, on account of waste of force."[71] After deeming these appliances unsuitable, the commissioners concluded that Dr. Arnott's ventilating air pump, a contraption designed and manufactured in the metropole, should be used in place of these indigenous appliances.

The report also covered the type of latrines and urinals to use and the proper provision of ablution and bath facilities. Again, the commissioners demonstrated a distrust of local practices and a preference for replacing them with appliances manufactured in Britain. The drawings of the model hospital in the report also suggest that the commissioners had in mind the use of prefabricated iron building components, such as columns, beams and purlins, manufactured by one of the many iron foundries in mid-nineteenth century Victorian Britain.[72] The preference for manufactures from the metropole was perhaps not surprising for a commission consisting of metropolitan experts who could be ignorant of local practices in India. Furthermore, as I have noted in Chapter 2, it could also be an attempt to deal with the heterogeneous and heteronomous elements in the production of the built environment in the colonies. For the commissioners, these prescriptions of appliances and prefabricated building components, not unlike statistics and the practices of quantification discussed earlier, served to ensure standardization and control over long distances and on unfamiliar territories.

The detailed prescriptions did not stop at latrines and urinals. The report also elaborated on the types of sewerage pipes, manholes, ventilation shafts, filtration systems, etc. As noted in what Warwick Anderson calls "excretionary colonialism," such colonial obsession with toilet and waste disposal was not simply a concern with environmental sanitation and "matter out of place," it was also an obsession with the disciplining of the body.[73] At the bodily level, the report dealt with the attire and diet of the British soldier. The recommendations for the attire extended the sanitary concerns with the built environment to the intimate scale of the body. Among other things, the report recommended the use of flannel to moderate the heat loss through profuse perspiration and prevent chills.[74] It also proposed the adoption of the "several ingenious improvements" that Julius Jeffreys, a surgeon-inventor and a former resident of India, created.[75] One intriguing invention by Jeffreys was a helmet with a double layered outer shell and ventilated spaces between the wearer's head and the inner surface of the shell so that hot air trapped inside the helmet could escape (Figure 3.13). Jeffreys also proposed to cover the helmet with a reflective metallic surface to minimize absorption of "the sun's ray [*sic*]" and prevent "excessive heat on the brain [which] produces moral depression."[76]

The other aspect of bodily concerns was with the British soldier's diet, more specifically with the "overfeeding" of the soldiers. In the report, "overfeeding" was seen in relation to the little amount of work and exercise that the British soldier in India had to perform. "Idleness" was also perceived as the cause of widespread intemperance, i.e. excessive drinking, among the British soldiers in India. Even venereal disease, another major cause of hospital admission, was seen as "a frequent concomitant of intemperate habit ... fostered by want of occupation."[77] Hence, a good portion of the reports by the BHIC and the RCSSAI dealt with providing means of employment and recreation so as to regulate the soldiers' conduct. Facilities such as workshops, gardens, gymnasia, libraries and reading rooms were provided to encourage the soldiers to engage in productive craft, agriculture, exercise, and other forms of physical and moral improvements.[78]

Like the metropolitan sanitary reform, the military sanitary reform in the tropics was a similar regime of biopower that prescribed better built environments as part of a larger regime of living, except that the target was not the population at large but only the British soldiers. As I have argued in Chapter 2, Western medical and sanitary

Fig. 2.

Fig. 3.

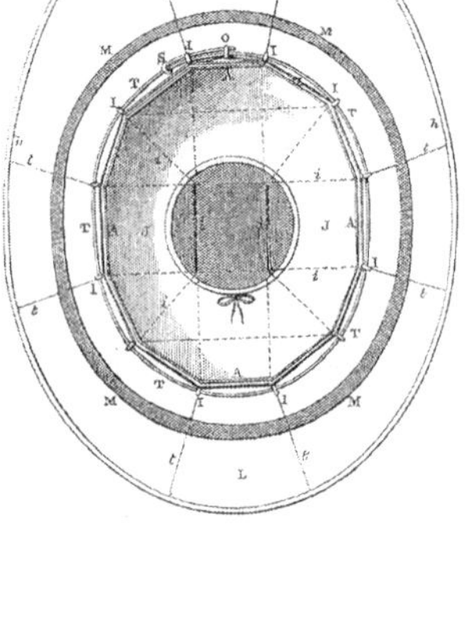

Figure 3.13
Helmet designed by Julius Jeffreys. Source: The Commissioners, *The Report of the RCSSAI*, Vol. 1, 1863.

science was first applied only to the privileged socio-political enclaves in the colonies, in which their effects could be evaluated. The British soldiers in the military space of barracks and cantonments constituted one such socio-political enclave.[79] However, what would happen when these Western medical and sanitary practices escape the limited military enclave into the larger public realm of the civic hospitals and urban sanitation, and engage with the local population at large? How would the medical and sanitary standards, and their attendant technology of population, prescribed for the military enclave be translated? The next section will explore these questions through the case of the various historical buildings of the SGH.

THE "ACCUMULATION OF NEGLECT" BEYOND THE ENCLAVE

Not long after the Straits Settlements became a Crown Colony under the direct control of the Colonial Office in 1867, Governor Sir Henry Ord received a dispatch from the Colonial Office asking him to complete a questionnaire on the state of hospitals and asylums in the Straits Settlements.[80] The questionnaire was first sent out to all the British colonial territories under the charge of the Colonial Office on 1 January 1863. Like many other major inquiries in the history of the British Empire, this inquiry into the conditions of the hospitals and asylums was initiated after "certain evils and defects," and "flagrant abuses and cruelties" had been exposed in the colonies. This time that scandal happened at the public hospital and lunatic asylum at Kingston, Jamaica.[81] The questionnaire used in this inquiry was similar to that used by the RCSSAI discussed earlier in its reliance on the "technology of distance" of statistical returns. From the returns, the inquiry found that:

> generally speaking, the state of the Institutions in the Colonies ... is yet widely and deplorably different from what would be now considered in this country to be consistent with the humane objects they are designed to promote; whilst in some cases ... the state of Colonial Hospitals or Lunatic Asylums would seem to be such as can hardly be deemed to be consistent with humanity itself.[82]

For example, in the West Indies, all the hospitals with the exception of the Port of Spain hospital in Trinidad, were found to run "the same complexion of structural or sanitary defectiveness, of insufficient attendance, internal mismanagement, and want of supervision, resulting, in the case of hospitals, in an unnecessary waste of life and means."[83] Other than a few well-managed and well-planned hospitals and asylums in the larger and richer dominions such as Australia and Canada, the Colonial Office expressed general dissatisfaction and demanded that these deficient hospitals and asylums be improved. The Colonial Office provided a series of recommendations that were not dissimilar to those recommended by the Royal Commissions for the military hospitals discussed earlier. A constant reference in the recommendations laid out was to the "high authority" of hospital design – Florence Nightingale's *Notes on Hospitals*.[84] Behind this reform was a political calculation in which improvement of the hospitals would "in part, if not wholly, be returned indirectly by the economy of management, and of valuable time and lives."[85] An especially significant factor was

> the quicker restoration of the sick to profitable labour [because] in this country, it is calculated that every death of an agricultural labourer at the age of twenty five involves a loss of more than £200 to the wealth of the nation.[86]

In the Straits Government reply to the questionnaire, the General Hospital building then located in the Kandang Kerbau area, which was planned by Captain George Collyer and built by Indian convict laborers, was presented as a well-planned and well-managed building.[87] The reply noted that "[t]he sanitary state [was] satisfactory," the "water supply plentiful and good," and the bathrooms "good, and sufficient." The building was "adapted to the climate" and well ventilated; the temperature of the ward was "equable." From the statistical table, the wards were of the right sizes and each bed enjoyed an air space of 1,800 cubic feet. On seeing the reply, the Colonial Office noted that while there were minor faults, the General Hospital "seem[ed] to be in a state of efficiency."[88] Despite the capacity of quantification and statistics to facilitate government at a distance through gathering objective facts, the Straits Government managed to suppress many of the problems of the SGH in their reply. For example, there was no mention that the hospital was poorly sited on "low and swampy" ground, which led to the sinking of the building's foundation and related structural faults.[89] The reply was also silent on the fact that the hospital was located next to one of the "most objectionable creeks" that was described as producing "the most repulsive odours ... [which were] carried into the wards of the convalescent sick and dying, to retard the progress of the first and to hasten the decay of the last."[90] How should we understand the failure of quantification and statistics in this instance to uncover these problems typical of the colonial hospitals built in nineteenth century Singapore?

One of the prerequisites for the collection of accurate statistics and proper analysis of the statistics collected was a vast state bureaucracy. However, those prerequisites were not always present in a small colony with scant resources such as the Straits Settlements in the nineteenth century. It was noted that when the East India Company became obsessed with the collection of administrative reports and statistics in the early 1850s, the understaffed and underpaid small Straits Settlements administration could not cope. Instead of obtaining statistics and facts, a commentator noted that Calcutta, from where the Straits Settlements was governed, was instead getting "lying figures." He further commented:

> [S]urely there is enough real work in this world to save men from the painful necessity of being set to such a spinning of sand and weaving of moonbeams such as the attempts to manufacture facts by the multiplication of errors must prove.[91]

In 1873, all the patients at the Kandang Kerbau General Hospital were moved to the Sepoy Lines Barracks because of a cholera outbreak. When the outbreak was contained later, the Principal Civil Medical Officer advised against moving back to the Kandang Kerbau site because it was low, swampy and "insalubrious."[92] The patients remained at the Sepoy Lines. This subsequently became a permanent arrangement, and a new hospital building designed by Colonial Engineer John McNair was built in 1882 (Figures 3.14 and 3.15).[93] As McNair noted, the new

Figure 3.14
The SGH building housing European wards. Courtesy of the NAS.

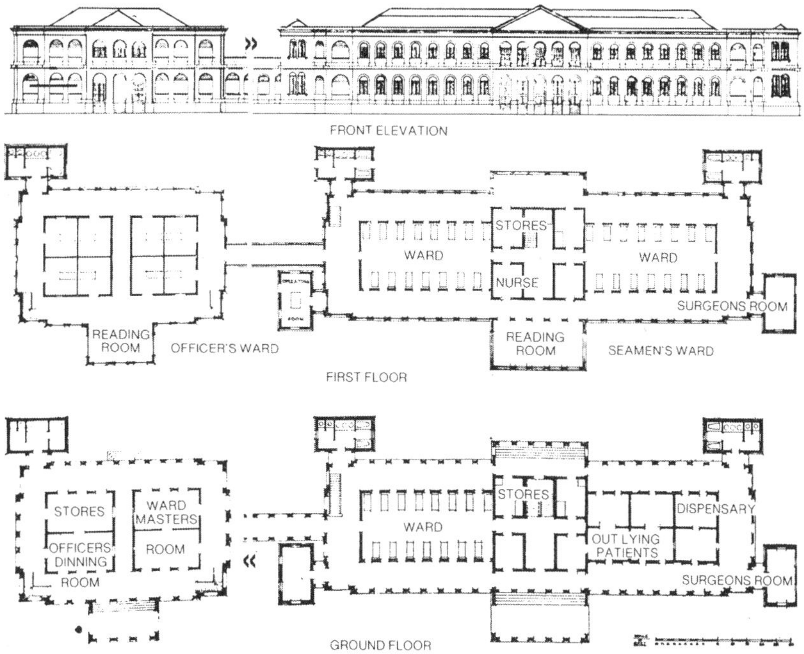

-igure 3.15
-lan of the SGH building -or European wards. -ource: *TMMJ*, 1933.

hospital was "arranged on the pavilion principle," double-storied and elevated on a ventilated arched basement with the ground floor being used for dining and recreation rooms, "built so as to be opened to the prevailing winds, but the beds in the wards are protected from draughts by a suitable arrangement of the doors, windows, and wall space," and it had "baths, lavatories, and latrines built off the wards."[94] Moreover, the wards were spacious and afforded each patient 1,800 cubic square feet; they were also protected from the sun by deep verandahs.

Figure 3.16
John Turnbull Thomson's painting of Tan Tock Seng Hospital (left) and European Seamen Hospital (right) which he designed. Reprinted, by permission, from Hocken Collections, Uare Taoka o Hākena, University of Otago.

This new SGH building represented a significant departure from previous hospital buildings in Singapore. For example, while the first permanent "public" hospital buildings – the European Seamen Hospital and the Tan Tock Seng Pauper Hospital designed by J. T. Thomson and completed in the 1840s on the slope of Pearl's Hill (Figure 3.16) – had rather impressive Palladian exteriors, no water supply and proper ablution facilities were installed.[95] As a result, the senior surgeon observed soon after the building was put in use that:

> the terrace in front of the hospital had been used as a place of easement during the night, and several wretched cripples were crawling up and down the nicely turfed bank already defaced by them for the purpose of washing their sores at the bottom.[96]

Subsequent hospital buildings in Singapore, such as the General Hospital at Kandang Kerbau as noted earlier and the TTSH at Serangoon Road, were similarly fraught with sanitary problems.[97]

The new hospital building at the old Sepoy Line, however, only housed the European wards. The "native" wards continued to be housed in the overcrowded and insanitary old buildings converted from the Sepoy Barracks. This was a reflection of the general segregation of the Europeans from the local population and the disparity in resources allocated to them typical of the colonial governance in general and especially evident in Singapore's colonial medical provision. The colonial medical service in the Straits Settlements was shaped by the colonial political economy of health and its priorities of treatment. From the founding of Singapore as a British settlement in 1819, the hospitals and bare-bones medical service established there by the colonial state served primarily four groups of people essential to the maintenance of Singapore as a free port – the British and Sepoy soldiers, the police and police cases, the convicts, and the sick European seamen passing through the port.[98] The only hospital that the sick person from the local population could seek help from was the pauper hospital, financed and run not by the state but by local philanthropists.

It was only after 1867 when Singapore, as part of the Straits Settlements, became a Crown Colony that the colonial government, as instructed by the Colonial Office, began to take slightly greater interest in the health and welfare of the local population. For instance, in 1872, the Secretary of State for the Colonies, Lord Kimberley, ordered the Straits Government to take over the operation of the pauper hospitals.[99] The colonial government, however, continued to demonstrate an unwillingness to commit financial and administrative resources toward securing the health of the local population. The colonial medical service was still greatly understaffed and the state's medical initiatives were largely restricted to responses to crises, such as outbreaks of plague. It was no wonder that, on the centennial celebration of the founding of Singapore in 1919, a commentator remarked: "The general trend of medical and scientific work in Singapore throughout the century is not especially remarkable for [its] constructive ability or statesmanlike policy."[100]

Some aspects of the "unstatesmanlike policy" were reflected in the many problems with the General Hospital identified in a 1913 report by the Committee on Medical Service and Hospital in the Straits Settlements. The "native" wards, still housed in the converted barracks, were especially condemned by the report. They were overcrowded, dark, and the "chief source of ventilation was through the latrines." The "native" wards were also mismanaged to the extent that "[i]nstances of patients contracting new diseases during their stay in hospital [were] frankly admitted."[101] The report concluded that:

> These wards are a blot on the medical administration of the Colony. In them all the evils conceivable in a hospital have centred … all point to a condition which should never have been permitted to exist, and which demands instant remedy.[102]

The report found the buildings to be so "fundamentally and structurally unsuited for harbouring the sick"[103] that it recommended that the "native" wards be demolished and a new hospital be built immediately. With World War I breaking out the following year and the imposition of wartime fiscal austerity measures on the Straits Settlements and other British colonies, the recommendations of the report were ignored and the "accumulation of neglect"[104] continued until 1920 when Guillemard, as we have seen at the beginning of the chapter, decided to commit the colonial government's resources to deal with mounting public health problems and finally, in his words, to "set our house in order."[105]

COLONIAL MONUMENTS AND ORNAMENTAL GOVERNMENTALITY

To build what Guillemard described as the hospital "on the most modern lines, worthy of this great Colony,"[106] he commissioned two London-based architects, Major P. Hubert Keys and Frank Dowdeswell from H.M. Office of Works, to design the new SGH.[107] They were originally appointed by the Straits Government, through the Crown Agents, as the government architects for The General Post Office Building (also known as the Fullerton Building) in 1920.[108] The engagement of Keys and Dowdeswell was a controversial one. As an unofficial member of the colony's Legislative Council noted, they were "supermen" on "super salaries," generously remunerated by the Straits Government for their services at a time when the colony's economy was in a slump.[109] Despite their generous remuneration, they were controversially involved in private practice while still under contract as government architects.[110] The buildings they designed, especially the General Post Office, were considered luxuries that the colony could ill afford. Their "super salaries" were justified on the grounds of their special metropolitan expertise and the innovations of the buildings they designed. For one, their buildings in the Straits Settlements and British Malaya utilized the latest building technologies. For example, their Perak Turf Club Building was credited with having "the first and only concrete cantilevered stand constructed East of the Suez,"[111] and the General Post Office and the Capital Theatre were the first two buildings in Singapore to install air-conditioning systems.[112] In addition, the reinforced concrete structural system for the General Post Office was purportedly one of the only two in Singapore that had been designed in accordance with the latest London County Council specifications.[113]

Despite the advanced technology employed in these buildings, their exteriors followed what a commentator at that time described as the "modern classic style," one which "evolved from a study of the old Greek and Roman buildings adapted to modern construction and requirements." It was a style that "aims at bigness, simple dignity and the cutting out of superfluous features and decorations" so as to project an image of grandeur and monumentality.[114] The modern classic style was the "style of choice" in three of the most prominent colonial state monuments built in Singapore's city center during the 1920s–1930s – The Supreme Court Building (completed in 1939), The Municipal Building (1929), and The General Post

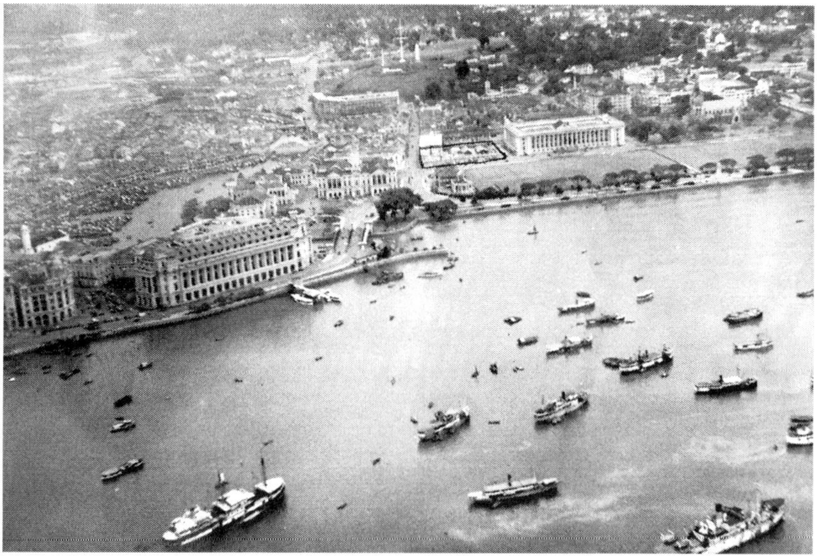

Figure 3.17
The colonial monuments with "modern classic style" in context. Aerial photograph originally used as part of the site study for the new Supreme Court building in the 1930s. The site for the new Supreme Court building is outlined in the center of the photograph. Reprinted, by permission, from the NAUK.

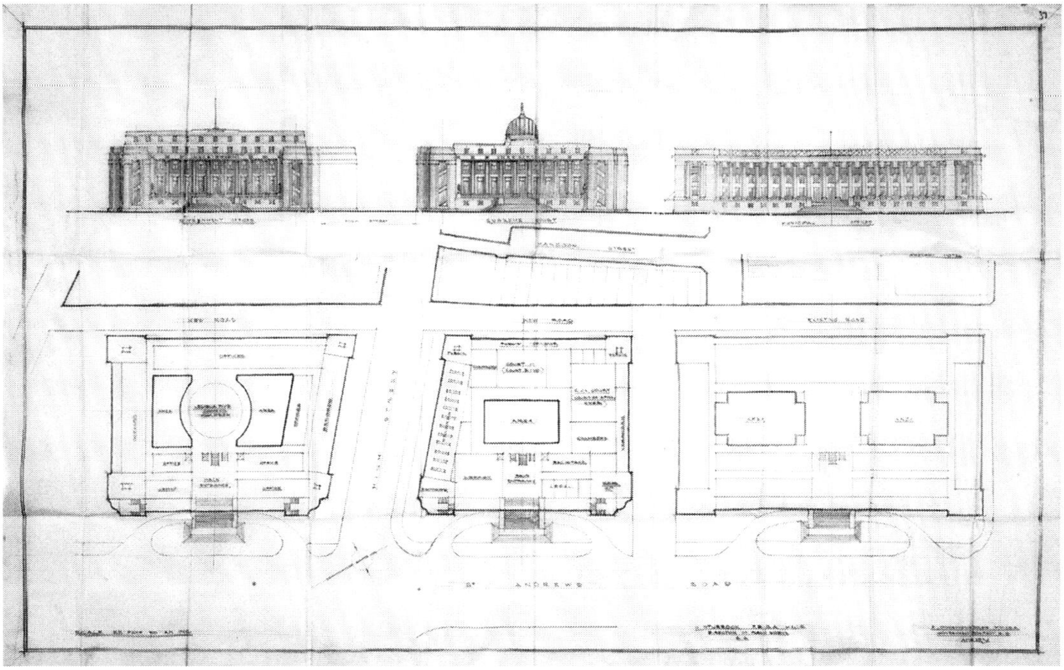

Figure 3.18
The proposed colonnaded buildings in the civic center with the unbuilt Government Offices on the left, the Supreme Court in the middle and the Municipal Office on the right. Reprinted, by permission, from the TNAUK.

Office aforementioned (1928) (Figure 3.17). Even though these buildings were all by different architects, they all share a formal consistency and a sense of monumentality. This monumental idea is especially evident in the masterplan for the civic center proposed by the PWD but not fully realized (Figure 3.18). These buildings were built at a time when the colonial government was embarking on a massive construction program to improve the physical infrastructure of Singapore, injecting symbolic capital into the built environment of colonial Singapore as a reflection of its rising wealth and increasing importance as a trading center.[115]

The new SGH was designed in Keys and Dowdeswell's usual modern classic style – Doric order in a "plain and simple manner" so as to obtain a "good simple architectural effect at the minimum cost" – and it housed two separate schemes within, the European scheme and the "Native" scheme.[116] The estimated 9,151 European population in Singapore was served by a scheme of five pavilions that consisted of 260 beds and was estimated to cost 1.16 million Straits Dollars to build. Elsewhere, the estimated 391,311 "native" population in Singapore was served by a scheme of five pavilions consisting of 538 beds and estimated to cost 1.78 million Straits Dollars.[117] The numbers speak of the disparity of resources committed to each segment of the population. The "Native" scheme, which served a population that was more than forty-two times that of the European population, was allocated only slightly more than double the numbers of beds and 50 percent more money than the European scheme. Not only that, the difference was also subtly encoded in the architectural form. The European scheme was fronted by a three-story building with a clock tower and an entry portico fronted by four pairs of twin Doric columns

Figure 3.19
The clock tower and entry portico of the European scheme. Reprinted, by permission, from the NAUK.

Figure 3.20
The entry portico of the Native scheme. Reprinted, by permission, from the NAUK.

(Figure 3.19) while the "Native" scheme was fronted by a smaller two-storey structure which had an entry portico fronted by four Doric columns (Figure 3.20).

This concern with style and architectural effect contradicted what protagonists of pavilion plan hospitals, such as Florence Nightingale and Douglas Galton, emphasized in their seminal hospital textbooks. In these textbooks, the emphasis was on fitness for purpose, and the authors would typically caution the hospital architect from the pitfall of "striving after architectural effect."[118] Similarly, in the BHIC's general report, the commissioners, of whom Galton was a member, reminded the hospital architect:

> It should never be forgotten that the object sought in the construction of a hospital is the recovery of the largest number of sick men to health in the shortest possible time, and that to this end everything else is only subsidiary. The

Figure 3.21
Exterior view of the Malacca General Hospital. Source: *PWD Annual Report*, 1932.

> intention aimed at is not ... to produce a certain architectural effect, be that good or bad.[119]

Later, they further admonished the hospital architect: "Useless ornament is quite out of place in a hospital. It costs money. It is liable to damage. It harbours dust, and requires extra time in cleaning."[120] As discussed earlier, Nightingale and the commissioners strived to produce a disciplinary space in the hospital through a spatial organization that facilitated surveillance. Their emphasis was on the internal arrangement of spaces, rather than external architectural effects. When the new SGH is compared to the two other General Hospitals being built at around the same time in Penang and Malacca (Figure 3.21), the other two main cities in the Straits Settlements, it also appears unusually historicist, adorned with Doric columns, domed clock tower, and other classical embellishments. How could we understand this stylistic peculiarity of the new SGH? Annmarie Adams argues that the clothing of the modern plans of early twentieth century North American hospitals in historical garb produced the important psychological effects of familiarity and reassurance for the general public.[121] What could then be the possible effects that the modern classic dress of the new SGH sought to produce?

In *Ornamentalism*, David Cannadine argues that spectacles, rituals and honors were central to British imperialism in terms of acting out and symbolizing the hierarchical nature of the imperial society and legitimizing the imperial order of things.[122] He shows the intricate ways in which the British went about devising these elaborate pageantries and how they operated. Although Cannadine does not really discuss it, architecture was central to such pomp and pageantries, not only as a setting but as a display in and of itself.[123] Could the new Singapore General Hospital not be understood along this line, as part of the colonial ornamentalism that sought to symbolize the colonial state's commitment to the health and welfare of the local population? As we have seen earlier, governmentality is situated within the triangle of sovereignty-discipline-government, in which different modalities of power coexist.[124] Drawing on this insight in his study of colonial Delhi, Stephen Legg argues that sovereignty and biopolitics were especially complementary in the colonial context.[125] He also shows how a combination of monumental architecture and hierarchical town planning of imperial Delhi was deployed to showcase imperial sovereignty.

Earlier in the chapter, we saw that Foucault understands the emergence of the modern pavilion plan hospital as part of governmentality, which involved specific techniques of government, such as the statistical enumeration of the problems of the population. This, in turn, required an extensive state bureaucracy and the commitment of vast resources. I have argued that both were lacking in colonial Singapore. Thus, statistics, instead of gathering objective facts, became only capable of producing lying figures that belied political reality. That was further accentuated by illiberal colonial rule and the absence of the need for the colonial state to forge consent from the local population. These factors contributed to the "accumulation of neglect" in terms of the colonial state's failure to secure the health and welfare of its population. This gross neglect on the part of the colonial state was not restricted to the case of the SGH I have described above. It was also evident in the failure of the larger public health reforms, specifically in urban sanitation and housing provision, which were launched together with the hospital building program by Guillemard, as we shall see in the next chapter.

Given the broader failures of colonial governmentality in Singapore, the classical adornments of the SGH complex, which were deemed superfluous and distracting by Nightingale and others for the hospital as a curing machine and an instrument of surveillance, could perhaps be understood as essential in the performance of another role. Could the classical ornaments of the SGH complex not be understood as the compensatory display of sovereign power that, together with the colonial rituals and spectacles, performed the colonial state's commitment to the health and welfare of the local population while also reinforcing colonial norms? Like Tony Bennett's exhibitionary complex, both the apparatus of surveillance of the panopticon and the technology of vision of the spectacle were combined in the colonial pavilion plan hospital of the SGH.[126] However, instead of producing simultaneously both the subjects and objects of knowledge as in the case of the exhibitionary complex, I argue that the combination in SGH sought to produce subordinated subjects. Or, as Lee Kuan Yew, the first Prime Minister of post-colonial Singapore noted, the colonial government built "magnificent monuments to impress the multitude with their superiority and to overawe their subjects into obedience."[127] According to James Francis Warren, that was because "[i]t was easier and more profitable in Singapore ... to embellish its face than sound its depth."[128]

NOTES

1 Laurence Guillemard, "Singapore in 1926: Sir Laurence Guillemard's Speech at the Straits Settlements (Singapore) Association Dinner," *British Malaya* 1, no. 8 (1926): 224.
2 Ibid., 225.
3 Ibid., 226 (my emphasis).
4 In the years of 1924 and 1925, the mortality rates of the European officials were at about a tenth or less than the rate of the general mortality rates of the colony. They were 1.8 and 3.5 per 1,000 as compared to 27.42 and 27.26 per 1,000 respectively. See A. L. Loops, *Annual Straits Settlements Medical Report for 1925* (Singapore: Government Printing Office, 1926); F. R. Sayers, *Annual Straits Settlements Medical Report for 1926* (Singapore: Government Printing Office, 1927).
5 Guillemard, "Singapore in 1926," 224.
6 W. J. Simpson, *The Sanitary Conditions of Singapore* (London: Waterlow, 1907), 6–7.
7 Reyner Banham, *The Architecture of the Well-Tempered Environment*, 2nd ed. (London: Architectural Press, 1984); Robert Bruegmann, "Architecture of the Hospital: 1770–1870" (PhD diss., University of Pennsylvania, 1976); Annmarie Adams, *Medicine by Design: The Architect and the Modern Hospital 1893–1943* (Minneapolis: University of Minnesota Press, 2008).
8 Adrian Forty, "The Modern Hospital in England and France: The Social and Medical Uses of Architecture," in *Buildings and Society: Essays on the Social Development of the Built Environment*, ed. Anthony D. King (London: Routledge & Kegan Paul, 1980); Sven-Olov Wallenstein, *Biopolitics and the Emergence of Modern Architecture* (New York: Princeton Architectural Press and Buell Center/FORuM Project, 2009).
9 Michel Foucault, "The Politics of Health in the Eighteenth Century," in *Power/Knowledge: Selected Interviews and Other Writings*, ed. Colin Gordon (New York: Pantheon, 1980), 169–70.
10 Ibid.
11 Luis Fernández-Galiano, *Fire and Memory: On Architecture and Energy*, trans. Gina Cariño (Cambridge, MA: MIT Press, 2000), 226–33.
12 Mike Hulme, *Why We Disagree About Climate Change: Understanding Controversy, Inaction and Opportunity* (Cambridge: Cambridge University Press, 2009); Theodore S. Feldman, "Late Enlightenment Meteorology," in *The Quantifying Spirit in the Eighteenth Century*, ed. Tore Frängsmyr, J. L. Heilbron and Robin E. Rider (Berkeley: University of California Press, 1990).
13 J. S. Webster, "Hospital Construction," in *Transactions of the Fifth Biennial Congress of the Far Eastern Association of Tropical Medicine Held at Singapore 1923*, ed. A. L. Hoops and J. W. Scharff (London: John Bale and Sons and Danielsson, 1924), 846.
14 Major P. H. Keys, "Memorandum on the New Post Office and New General Hospital, Singapore," in *PLCSS 1922* (Singapore: Government Printing Office, 1923).
15 Webster, "Hospital Construction," 848.
16 Ibid., 849.
17 Ibid., 854.
18 Keys, "Memorandum on the New Post Office and New General Hospital, Singapore."
19 Webster, "Hospital Construction," 855.
20 Ibid., 845.
21 Ibid.
22 See "Correspondence Regarding the Insanitary Site of Tan Tock Seng's Hospital," in *PLCSS 1899* (Singapore: Straits Settlements Government Printing Office, 1900); "New Ward for Tan Tock Seng's Hospital," in *PLCSS 1900* (Singapore: Straits Settlements Government Printing Office, 1901).

23 Anthony D. King, "Hospital Planning: Revised Thoughts on the Origin of the Pavilion Principle in England," *Medical History* 10, no. 6 (1966); Jeremy Taylor, *The Architect and the Pavilion Hospital: Dialogue and Design Creativity in England, 1850–1914* (London: Leicester University Press, 1996).

24 Henry C. Burdett, *Hospitals and Asylums of the World: Their Origin, History, Construction, Administration, Management, and Legislation*, vol. IV (London: J. & A. Churchill, 1893), 99.

25 Cited in Taylor, *The Architect and the Pavilion Hospital*, 1.

26 Forty, "The Modern Hospital in England and France."

27 Florence Nightingale, "Answers to Written Questions Addressed to Miss Nightingale by the Commissioners," in *Report of the Commissioners Appointed to Inquire into the Regulations Affecting the Sanitary Condition of the Army, the Organization of Military Hospitals, and the Treatment of the Sick and Wounded; with Evidence and Appendix*, ed. The Commissioners (London: George Edward Eyre and William Spottiswoode, 1858), 381.

28 Ibid.

29 Bruegmann, "Architecture of the Hospital"; Felix Driver, "Moral Geographies: Social Science and the Urban Environment in Mid-Nineteenth Century England," *Transactions of the Institute of British Geographers* 13, no. 3 (1988).

30 John D. Thompson and Grace Goldin, *The Hospital: A Social and Architectural History* (New Haven: Yale University Press, 1975); Bruegmann, "Architecture of the Hospital."

31 Foucault, "The Politics of Health in the Eighteenth Century." See also Robert Bruegmann, "Review of Michel Foucault, et al., *Les Machines à guerir (aux origines de l'hôpital moderne)*, Paris: Institut de l'environment, 1976," *JSAH* 38, no. 2 (1979). "The Politics of Health" was originally published as a chapter in *Les Machines à guerir*.

32 Michel Foucault, *Society Must Be Defended: Lectures at the College de France, 1975–76*, trans. David Macey (New York: Picador, 2003), 239–54; Michel Foucault, *The History of Sexuality: An Introduction, Volume 1*, trans. Robert Hurley (New York: Vintage, 1990 [1978]), 135–59.

33 Paul Rabinow, *French Modern: Norms and Forms of the Social Environment* (Chicago: University of Chicago Press, 1989).

34 Thomas A. Markus, *Buildings and Power: Freedom and Control in the Origin of Modern Building Types* (London: Routledge, 1993), 95–156; Andrew Scull, "A Convenient Place to Get Rid of Inconvenient People: The Victorian Lunatic Asylum," in *Buildings and Society: Essays on the Social Development of the Built Environment*, ed. Anthony D. King (London: Routledge & Kegan Paul, 1980); Felix Driver, *Power and Pauperism: The Workhouse System 1834–1884* (Cambridge: Cambridge University Press, 1993).

35 I am grateful to Thomas A. Markus for pointing this out to me. See Markus, *Buildings and Power*, 108–14.

36 "Hospital Construction – Wards," *The Builder* 16, no. 816 (1858): 641, 42.

37 Forty, "The Modern Hospital in England and France," 80.

38 Fernández-Galiano, *Fire and Memory*, 229.

39 See also Joshua Jebb, "On the Construction and Ventilation of Prisons," *PCRE* XVII (1845).

40 Peter Burroughs, "The Human Cost of Imperial Defence in the Early Victorian Age," *Victorian Studies* 24, no. 1 (1980).

41 T. Graham Balfour, "The Opening Address of Dr. T. Graham Balfour, F.R.S., &C, Honorary Physician to Her Majesty the Queen, President of the Royal Statistical Society. Session 1889–90. Delivered 19th November, 1889," *Journal of the Royal Statistical Society* 52, no. 4 (1889); A. M. Tulloch, "On the Sickness and Mortality among the Troops in the West Indies I," *Journal of the Statistical Society of London* 1, no. 3 (1838); A. M. Tulloch, "On the Sickness and Mortality among the Troops in the West Indies III,"

Journal of the Statistical Society of London 1, no. 7 (1838); A. M. Tulloch, "On the Mortality among Her Majesty's Troops Serving in the Colonies During the Years 1844 and 1845," *Journal of the Statistical Society of London* 10, no. 3 (1847).

42 The Commissioners, *General Report of the Commission Appointed for Improving the Sanitary Condition of Barracks and Hospitals* (London: George Edward Eyre and William Spottiswoode, 1861); The Commissioners, *Report of the Commissioners Appointed to Inquire into the Regulations Affecting the Sanitary Condition of the Army, the Organization of Military Hospitals, and the Treatment of the Sick and Wounded; with Evidence and Appendix* (London: George Edward Eyre and William Spottiswoode, 1858).

43 The Commissioners, *Report of the RCSSAI. Vol. 1: Precis of Evidence, Minutes of Evidence, Addenda* (London: George Edward Eyre and William Spottiswoode, 1863); BHIC, *Suggestions in Regard to Sanitary Works Required for Improving Indian Stations* (London: George Edward Eyre and William Spottiswoode, 1864).

44 Ian Hacking, "How Should We Do the History of Statistics?," in *The Foucault Effect: Studies in Governmentality*, ed. Michel Foucault et al. (Chicago: University of Chicago Press, 1991).

45 The Commissioners, *Report of the RCSSAI. Vol. 1*, xii.

46 Ibid., xviii.

47 Nikolas S. Rose, *Powers of Freedom: Reframing Political Thought* (Cambridge: Cambridge University Press, 1999), 203. See also David Demeritt, "Scientific Forest Conservation and the Statistical Picturing of Nature's Limits in the Progressive-Era United States," *Environment and Planning D: Society and Space* 19 (2001).

48 Theodore M. Porter, *Trust in Numbers: The Pursuit of Objectivity in Science and Public Life* (Princeton: Princeton University Press, 1995), ix.

49 Bruno Latour, *Science in Action: How to Follow Scientists and Engineers through Society* (Cambridge, MA: Harvard University Press, 1987), 215–57.

50 The Commissioners, *Report of the RCSSAI. Vol. 1*, v.

51 The standard medical report was devised by Patrick Manson in 1900. See Joseph Chamberlain, "Circular from the Secretary of State for the Colonies: Investigation of Malaria and the Training of Medical Officers in the Treatment and Prevention of Tropical Diseases," in *PLCSS 1904* (Singapore: Straits Settlements Government Printing Office, 1905).

52 Balfour, "The Opening Address," 529.

53 Harish Naraindas, "Poisons, Putrescence and the Weather: A Genealogy of the Advent of Tropical Medicine," *Contributions to Indian Sociology* 30, no. 1 (1996).

54 For an overview of medical topographical theories, see David Arnold, *Colonizing the Body: State Medicine and Epidemic Disease in Nineteenth-Century India* (Berkeley: University of California Press, 1993), esp. 28–36.

55 Naraindas, "Poisons, Putrescence and the Weather," 3, 5.

56 The Commissioners, *Report of the RCSSAI. Vol. 1*, xxxi.

57 H. P. Hollis, "Glaisher, James (1809–1903)," rev. J. Tucker, in *Oxford Dictionary of National Biography* (Oxford: Oxford University Press, 2004), online edition, May 2012, accessed 5 January 2016, http://www.oxforddnb.com/view/article/33419.

58 Mark Monmonier, "Telegraphy, Iconography, and the Weather Map: Cartographic Weather Reports by the United States Weather Bureau, 1870–1935," *Imago Mundi* 40 (1988).

59 Hulme, *Why We Disagree About Climate Change*, 6.

60 The Commissioners, *Report of the RCSSAI. Vol. 1*, xxxii.

61 Harry P. Bailey, "Toward a Unified Concept of the Temperate Climate," *Geographical Review* 54 (1964).

62 The Commissioners, *Report of the RCSSAI. Vol. 1*, xxx.

63 BHIC, *Suggestions in Regard to Sanitary Works Required for Improving Indian Stations.*
64 Florence Nightingale, *Observations on the Evidence Contained in the Stational Reports Submitted to Her by the RCSSAI* (London: Edward Stanford, 1863).
65 The Commissioners, *Report of the RCSSAI. Vol. 1*, li.
66 BHIC, *Suggestions in Regard to Sanitary Works Required for Improving Indian Stations*, 28.
67 Ibid., 22.
68 Ibid., 24.
69 Anthony D. King, *The Bungalow: The Production of a Global Culture*, 2nd ed. (New York: Oxford University Press, 1995 [1984]), 34; ibid.
70 The thermantidote blew moisturized air and provided evaporative cooling. An 1850 account of the thermantidote in India described it as an enormous and cumbersome machine with fans turned by two men. It was placed in the verandah and had a projecting funnel that was fixed into the window of a house. Tatties were affixed to the sides of the thermantidotes so that the air drawn was moisturized and these tatties were kept moist by coolies who constantly drenched them. Fanny Parkes, *Begums, Thugs and Englishmen: The Journals of Fanny Parkes* (Delhi: Penguin Books India, 2002 [1850]), 112–13.
71 BHIC, *Suggestions in Regard to Sanitary Works Required for Improving Indian Stations*, 22.
72 Gilbert Herbert, *Pioneers of Prefabrication: The British Contribution in the Nineteenth Century* (Baltimore: Johns Hopkins University Press, 1978).
73 Warwick Anderson, *Colonial Pathologies: American Tropical Medicine, Race, and Hygiene in the Philippines* (Durham, NC: Duke University Press, 2006), 104–29.
74 The Commissioners, *Report of the RCSSAI. Vol. 1*, lviii. For an elaboration of the use of "tropical apparels" such as the flannel and their symbolic, and not just medical, functions, see Dane Kennedy, "The Perils of the Midday Sun: Climatic Anxieties in the Colonial Tropics," in *Imperialism and the Natural World*, ed. John M. Mackenzie (Manchester and New York: Manchester University Press, 1990).
75 The Commissioners, *Report of the RCSSAI. Vol. 1*, lviii; David Zuck, "Jeffreys, Julius (1800–1877)," in *Oxford Dictionary of National Biography*, ed. H. C. G. Matthew and Brian Harrison (Oxford: Oxford University Press, 2004), online edition, May 2007, accessed 5 January 2016, http://www.oxforddnb.com/view/article/14706. See also Julius Jeffreys, *The British Army in India: Its Preservation by an Appropriate Clothing, Housing, Locating, Recreative Employment, and Hopeful Encouragement of the Troops* (London: Longman, 1858).
76 The Commissioners, *Report of the RCSSAI. Vol. 1*, lviii. Fifty years later, American military surgeon Charles Woodruff was to make a similar observation, noting that the excessive "actinic" radiation under the tropical sun produced "tropical neurasthenia." See Charles Edward Woodruff, *The Effects of Tropical Light on White Men* (New York: Rebman Company, 1905); Anderson, *Colonial Pathologies*, 134–42.
77 The Commissioners, *Report of the RCSSAI. Vol. 1*, lxi.
78 Ibid., lvi–lxvii; BHIC, *Suggestions in Regard to Sanitary Works Required for Improving Indian Stations*, 26–28.
79 Anthony D. King, *Colonial Urban Development: Culture, Social Power, and Environment* (London: Routledge & Kegan Paul, 1976).
80 PRO CO273/19, *Colonial Hospitals and Lunatic Asylums.*
81 PRO CO273/19, *Colonial Office Report on Hospitals and Lunatic Asylums*, 1.
82 Ibid.
83 Ibid.
84 Ibid., 19.
85 Ibid., 14.

86 Ibid., 22.
87 Yong Kiat Lee, *The Medical History of Early Singapore* (Tokyo: Southeast Asian Medical Information Center, 1978).
88 PRO CO273/19, *Colonial Hospitals and Lunatic Asylums.*
89 Lee, *The Medical History of Early Singapore*, 52.
90 Cited ibid., 63.
91 Cited in C. M. Turnbull, *The Straits Settlements 1826–67: Indian Presidency to Crown Colony* (London: The Athlone Press, 1972), 82–85.
92 Lee, *The Medical History of Early Singapore*.
93 For the proposed design in 1879, see PRO MR1/1138, *Drawings of the Proposed Singapore General Hospital.*
94 "Correspondence on the Subject of Hospital Accommodation in Singapore," in *PLCSS 1875* (Singapore: Straits Settlements Government Printing Office, 1876), ccclxx–ccclxxi.
95 Forty has argued that the early hospitals in Britain were designed in the Palladian style because they were associated with the patrons whose philanthropy supported these hospitals. Hence, the suggestion of aristocratic taste of these patrons through the Palladian style was important. See Forty, "The Modern Hospital in England and France."
96 Yong Kiat Lee, "Singapore's Pauper and Tan Tock Seng Hospital (1819–1873): Part 2," *JMBRAS* 49, no. 1 (1976): 120.
97 For the sanitary problems concerning TTSH, see "Correspondence Regarding the Insanitary Site of Tan Tock Seng's Hospital" and "New Ward for Tan Tock Seng's Hospital."
98 Gilbert E. Brooke, "Medical Work and Institutions," in *One Hundred Years of Singapore*, ed. Walter Makepeace, Gilbert E. Brooke and Roland St. J. Braddell (Singapore: Oxford University Press, 1991 [1921]); R. B. MacGregor, "A Historical Review of the General Hospital, Singapore," *TMMJ* 8 (1933).
99 "Correspondence Regarding the Insanitary Site of Tan Tock Seng's Hospital"; Yong Kiat Lee, "Singapore's Pauper and Tan Tock Seng Hospital (1819–1873): Part 4, the Government Takes Over," *JMBRAS* 50, no. 2 (1977).
100 Brooke, "Medical Work and Institutions," 489.
101 PRO CO273/396, *Report by Committee on Medical Service and Hospitals*, 21, 22.
102 Ibid., 22.
103 Ibid., 23.
104 These were the words that the committee that reported on the medical service and hospital used in describing the underlying problem with the medical service in the Straits Settlements. Ibid., 2.
105 PRO CO273/502, *Address by His Excellency His Governor to the Members of the Legislative Council at a Meeting Held on the 25th Day of October.*
106 Ibid.
107 Keys and Dowdeswell was frequently described as a Shanghai-based architectural firm, most probably due to the pioneering work of Eu-jin Seow, "Architectural Development in Singapore" (PhD thesis, University of Melbourne, 1973). However, a check of their biographical files and nomination papers at the RIBA Library, London, did not show any Shanghai connections. From P. Hubert Keys' nomination papers for fellowship submitted on 22 October 1920 from Singapore, when he was already appointed as the architect for the General Post Office, it is clear that he had primarily worked only for H. M. Office of Works from 1905 to 1920. He was the architect in charge of the postal section and has designed various post offices in England. From a copy of the contract that he signed with the Crown Agents, who acted on the behalf of the colonial government of the Straits Settlements, it was stated too that he was working at the H.M. Office of Works, Storey Gate, London. See PRO CO273/541/1, *Position of Major P. H. Keys, Government Architect: Petition by Several Architects in Singapore* (1927).

108 Besides these two complexes, they were also asked by the government to design the new King Edward VII Medical College, which was part of the SGH masterplan, and the new Mental Disease Hospital at Trafalgar (later known as Woodbridge Hospital, 1925–28).
109 Mr. Everitt in *PLCSS 1922* (Singapore: Government Printing Office, 1923), B85.
110 See PRO CO273/541/1, *Position of Major P H Keys, Government Architect*. Many of their private commissions were high profile commissions which figured prominently in the local architectural journal. See, for example, "The New Capitol Theatre Building," *JSSAI* 2, no. 4 (1930); "The New China Building," *JSSAI* 1, no. 2 (1930); "Perak Turf Club Extensions Competition," *JSSAI* 1, no. 6 (1930); "The New K. P. M. Building," *JSSAI* 4, no. 4 (1931).
111 "Extension to Ipoh Grand Stand for the Perak Turf Club," *JIAM* 1, no. 4 (1931): 14.
112 Both systems were designed and installed by E. H. Hindmarsh for United Engineers. See E. H. Hindmarsh, "Air in the Tropics – Particularly Malaya," *JIAM* 4, no. 4 (1933).
113 The Colonial Engineer J. H. W. Park's assertion. The regulations of Singapore Municipality then was lagging quite a few years behind LCC's regulations. See *PLCSS 1922*, B85.
114 A. Gordon, "The Old Order Changeth," *JSSAI* 3, no. 6 (1930): 2.
115 The comprehensive building program included other equally visible buildings such as Tanjong Pagar Railway Station (1932), Clifford Pier (1933), and the Singapore Civil Aerodrome (1937), the main terminals for rail, sea, and air transport respectively, security and defense installations such as Hill Street Police Station (1931), Pearl's Hill Sikh Police Barrack (1932), and Changi Goal (1936). See Yunn Chii Wong, "Public Works Department Singapore in the Inter-War Years (1919 – 1941): From Monumental to Instrumental Modernism" (Unpublished Research Report, National University of Singapore, 2003).
116 Keys, "Memorandum," C219.
117 Costs estimates from ibid., population estimates for the year 1920 from A. L. Hoops, *Annual Straits Settlements Medical Report for 1921* (Singapore: Government Printing Office, 1922).
118 Taylor, *The Architect and the Pavilion Hospital*.
119 The Commissioners, *General Report of the Commission Appointed for Improving the Sanitary Condition of Barracks and Hospitals*, 175.
120 Ibid., 197.
121 Annmarie Adams, "Modernism and Medicine: The Hospitals of Stevens and Lee, 1916–1932," *JSAH* 58, no. 1 (1999).
122 David Cannadine, *Ornamentalism: How the British Saw Their Empire* (Oxford: Oxford University Press, 2007).
123 See Thomas R. Metcalf, *An Imperial Vision: Indian Architecture and Britain's Raj* (New Delhi: Oxford University Press, 2002 [1989]).
124 Michel Foucault, "Governmentality," in *The Foucault Effect: Studies in Governmentality*, ed. Michel Foucault et al. (Chicago: University of Chicago Press, 1991).
125 Stephen Legg, *Spaces of Colonialism: Delhi's Urban Governmentalities* (Malden: Blackwell, 2007), 1–36.
126 Tony Bennett, "The Exhibitionary Complex," in *Representing the Nation: A Reader*, ed. Jessica Evans and David Boswell (London; New York: Routledge, 1999).
127 Kuan Yew Lee, "Message" in Housing Development Board, *Homes for the People* (Singapore: HDB, 1965), 1.
128 James Francis Warren, *Rickshaw Coolie: A People's History of Singapore, 1880–1940* (Singapore: Oxford University Press, 1986), 213.

Chapter 4: Improving "Native" Housing

Sanitary Order, Improvement Trust and Splintered Colonial Urbanism

> But the plain unvarnished truth is that Singapore is a disgrace to British administration. There is no fouler, less-cared for place in the Empire. If it were not for the constant heavy rains which automatically wash out the side channels, there is not a street in the more closely populated portion of the city where life would be supportable. Even with all the natural advantages we have a death-rate that is positively scandalous.[1]

The above, an excerpt from a 1910 newspaper report on "Insanitary Singapore," reflects a prevalent sentiment towards the British colony in the early twentieth century. It was a view that persisted, prompting major housing and sanitary reform in the post-World War II period. Indeed, perceptions of Singapore as a singularly "insanitary" city and a "disgrace" to the colonial administration underlay what might aptly be called a "sanitizing fervor" which brought about housing and planning improvements.

A sanitary movement emerged in England in the mid-nineteenth century, motivated in part by outbreaks of cholera from the 1830s.[2] During the course of the century, public health initiatives in Europe led to improved standards of urban housing for the poor. However, these metropolitan sanitary and public health reforms had a very different impact and outcome in the colonies. As we have seen in Chapters 2 and 3, they had led to the emergence of highly sanitized and regulated military and medical enclaves. But these reforms had little impact upon and made minimal headway in the colonies during the same period, at least in relation to the housing of the colonized population. This inaction began to change at the turn of the twentieth century, particularly with outbreaks of bubonic plague and malaria in various parts of the British Empire. Another impetus for the shift in policy was the series of colonial development initiatives associated with the colonial secretary Joseph Chamberlain. Under his "constructive imperialism," the Colonial Office funded research in tropical medicine and sanitation as a means of eradicating some of the problems that were deemed to be inhibiting the socio-economic development of Britain's tropical colonies. Experts in tropical medicine and sanitation, for example, were dispatched from the metropole to various colonies to investigate the causes of disease and to recommend remedies and preventive policies.[3] These measures contributed to the aforementioned sanitizing fervor in the early twentieth century and gave rise to a veritable proliferation of discourses on urban sanitation in the tropics.[4]

It was against this background that an imperial sanitary expert, William Simpson, was appointed by the government of the Straits Settlements in 1906 to investigate the sanitary conditions in Singapore. Prior to Simpson's appointment, the high mortality and morbidity rates of the "native" population in Singapore, especially the increasing numbers of death from tuberculosis, had been brought to the attention of the Straits Government. Following reports from his medical officers and after his own inspection, Straits Governor John Anderson cited overcrowded and insanitary housing as the principal cause of the high mortality and morbidity rates. He appointed a committee, consisting of the Principal Civil Medical Officer, the Health Officer and the Municipal Engineer, to look into the problem and to advise him on the appropriate course of action. In its report, the committee recommended that the sanitary conditions of these areas be rectified by rebuilding the houses according to a new town and housing plan. As the power conferred by the municipal ordinance was insufficient for executing the clearance and improvement of these insanitary houses, a new bill dealing with the insanitary areas was considered by the Legislative Council. The council decided that an independent expert from the metropole should be appointed to investigate the sanitary problem in further detail and to furnish the Straits Government with supporting evidence and recommendations for introducing the new bill.[5] On the advice of the Colonial Office, Simpson was therefore appointed and he issued a report that was to shape housing and town planning in pre-World War II Singapore in significant ways. Among other things, the report established the technical framework for sanitary improvement and town planning, which in turn influenced the subsequent practices of town improvement and housing provision in colonial Singapore during the pre-World War II years. The report's recommendations also led to the formation of the Singapore Improvement Trust (SIT), the key colonial agency that undertook the work in town improvement and housing provision, in 1927.

Most accounts of the work of SIT focus primarily on what it achieved in the post-World War II years as SIT built much more housing in those years than in the prewar years. The prewar years of SIT was very much regarded as a history of belatedness, indecisiveness and piecemeal execution in dealing with the town planning and housing problems of colonial Singapore. This chapter will nevertheless examine the prewar history of SIT, specifically what happened between 1907, when the landmark Simpson's report was published, and 1942, when British colonial rule temporarily ceased with the Japanese occupation of Singapore. Though neglected, this history is significant because the various inadequacies captured what happened when the application of technologies of sanitary improvement and governance expanded beyond the military and medical enclaves (discussed in the last two chapters) to engage directly with the health and well-being of the majority of the colonized population in urban Singapore. The expansion of these technologies of improvement and governance, in terms of dealing with a much larger number of the governed and a much bigger area, brought about a different set of challenges.

In attempting to overcome the difficulties of dealing with the much larger colonized urban population, a broader set of technologies of identifying and "knowing the governed" was deployed.[6] Besides statistics and enumeration that were discussed earlier, this chapter explores the use of mapping, photography, inspection and drawing to visualize and understand the spatial distribution and environmental causation of the health and illnesses of the population. Despite the deployment of a broader set of technologies, this chapter argues that the colonial state's unwillingness to commit resources and the resultant lack of a sociotechnical infrastructure of people, knowledge and practices meant that the colonial state did not really know the governed.

To improve the health of the larger population distributed over the built environment in a larger territory, the colonial state sought different strategies of intervention. Unlike what we saw in Chapters 2 and 3, where the colonial state was directly involved in the comprehensive planning and design of the buildings in the military and medical enclaves, this chapter shows how the colonial state attempted to indirectly control the built environment through the acquisition of legislative power that enabled it to engage in town planning, sanitary improvements and building regulation using bylaws. When SIT was finally empowered to build housing for the colonized population, it experimented and built multiple housing typologies for the different socio-economic classes of the colonized population instead of the singular hierarchical system produced for both military barracks and hospitals.

In previous chapters, we explored various aspects of colonial connections and the circulation of people, ideas and practices through actors like military engineers, medical experts and architects, and the building types of barracks and pavilion plan hospitals. In this chapter, we will extend the discussion to another group of specialists of space and building types associated with public housing. Sanitary and town planning experts, engineers and architects involved in the planning of other British colonial cities came to Singapore in the early twentieth century and influenced subsequent housing and town planning practices there. Their influences were most evident in three interrelated forms of outcome. The first is the formation of the SIT as an organization to carry out housing improvement and town planning. The institutional form of the Improvement Trust, with its improvement legislations and practices, had precedents in other cities of the British Empire, such as Glasgow, Calcutta, Bombay and Rangoon. The second is the undergirding of housing improvement and town planning practices with a sanitary calculus on the environmental variables that affect health, focusing particularly on the air and light. Although the sanitary calculus was based on scientific knowledge and was thus purportedly objective and universal, its application in colonial Singapore was challenged. Rob Imrie and Emily Street argue that the proliferation of new mechanisms and techniques of regulating different aspects of the built environment in Europe and North America from the nineteenth century onward to secure the physical and social health of the population had led to the normalization of the larger urban built environment.[7] In colonial Singapore, that did not take place. Instead, I argue that differences and deviations persisted. The third and final outcome is evident in the housing types that the SIT built after its failure to bring about housing improvements through design regulation and planning control. The various housing types that the SIT experimented with in the prewar years included urban tenements, cottage houses, artisan quarters and flats. Many of these were adapted from metropolitan or colonial models from other parts of the British Empire. In colonial Singapore, none of these types became the primary type because none of them was considered to be sufficiently successful to be replicated at a larger scale.

KNOWING THE GOVERNED, REGULATING THE ENVIRONMENT

The Sanitary Conditions of Singapore was a landmark report in Singapore's housing and planning history.[8] Its author, William John Ritchie Simpson (1855–1931), Professor and Chair of Hygiene at King's College, London, and one of the co-founders of the London School of Tropical Medicine and the Ross Institute, was regarded as one of the foremost sanitarians in the British Empire at that time.[9] Simpson's report is the first comprehensive study of the housing and town planning problems of Singapore's colonized population, particularly the immigrant Chinese laborers. It made visible the seriousness of the problem and recommended a set of improvements that shaped subsequent colonial housing policies in important ways. Simpson did so by deploying what scholars of governmentality have called technologies of identifying and "knowing the governed" and the built environment they reside in, so as to facilitate state interventions.[10]

These technologies involved techniques of quantifying, surveying, mapping, photographing and drawing. Simpson examined the statistical information on the population, especially that pertaining to mortality rates, and concluded that the mortality rates of Singapore's "native" population were excessive and extraordinary, particularly since the immigrant population of Singapore was "essentially a population at the most vigorous period of life, viz. between fifteen and fifty-five years of age."[11] He attributed the high mortality rates to overcrowded and insanitary housing. One of the main causes of death was tuberculosis; Simpson mapped the number of deaths from tuberculosis recorded over a period of five years at two blocks of shophouses in Upper Nankin Street and Upper Chin Chew Street. The map Simpson produced shows the spatial distribution of death and illnesses, and illustrates his argument that the insanitary housing conditions, particularly the deficiencies in light and air, of some of the shophouses led to the greater recurrence of tuberculosis. Simpson also inspected and described in detail how the narrow and deep shophouses were subdivided into tiny windowless cubicles "pitch dark in their interior."[12] His descriptions were augmented with photographs of the interiors (Figure 4.1) and measured drawings (Figure 4.2) of the plans and sections of the shophouses.

Figure 4.1 Photograph of the interior of an insanitary shophouse in Simpson's report. Source: Simpson, *The Sanitary Conditions of Singapore*, 1907.

In Chapters 2 and 3, we discussed some of these technologies of knowing the governed, specifically statistics and enumeration, and in this chapter, we extend the discussion to technologies such as photographs, mapping and drawing. Like enumeration that constructs and constitutes the reality that it purportedly describes, photographs do not just visually record the reality. Photographs have been described as operating in the manner of the Foucauldian gaze that "penetrated the hidden recesses" of the insanitary housing, exposing the visual disorder of the overcrowded and insanitary interior, implicitly calling for intervention to order and clean up the interior.[13] In a similar manner, the drawings and maps also (re)construct and (re) present the reality. Simpson noted that one of his maps

> very graphically illustrates the great incidence of the disease in houses of a class which are numerous in town … The disease once in a house tends to recur, some years being worse than others, until it almost assumes an epidemic form. The

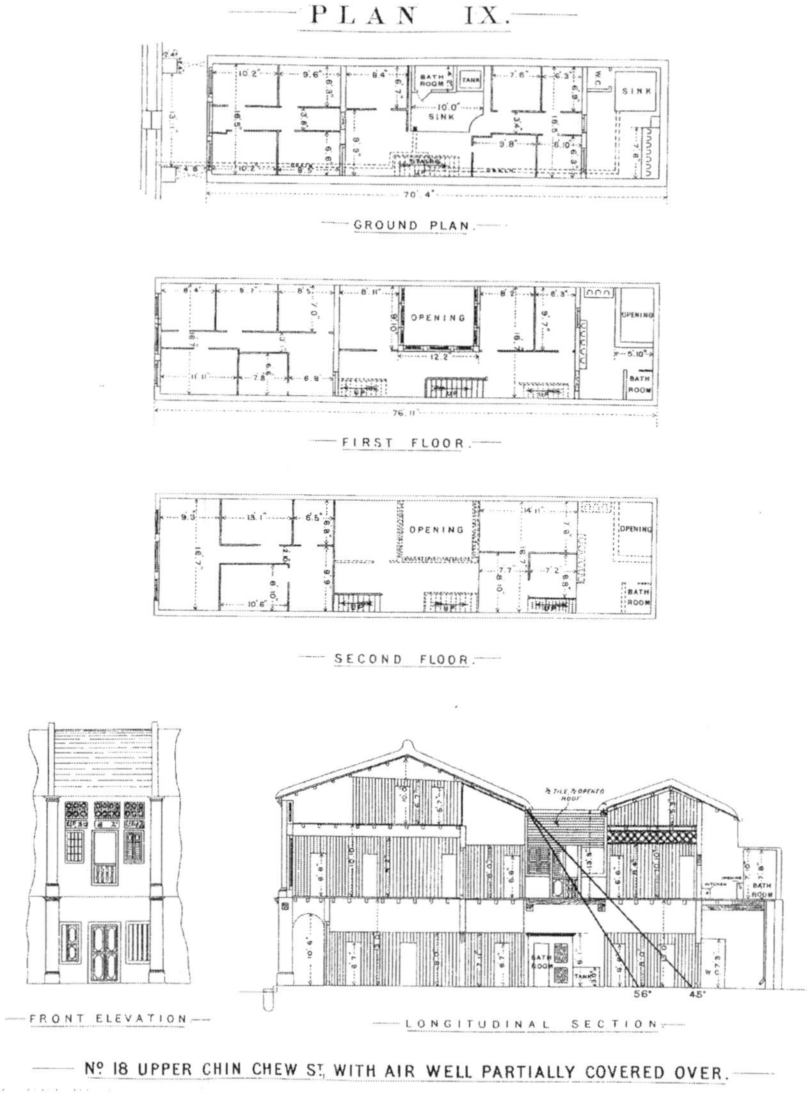

Figure 4.2
Drawings of a shophouse converted into tenements with small cubicles in Simpson's report. Source: Simpson, *The Sanitary Conditions of Singapore*, 1907.

> conditions as regards light and air in a house that are favourable to phthisis are also those which are favourable to plague whenever this disease acquires a firm hold in a town.[14]

In other words, Simpson's maps showed the spatial distribution of the deaths and illnesses, making visible the causality between health and environment.[15] If the photographs exposed the visual disorder, the drawings rendered the "disorders" legible by simplifying them and representing them in scaled plan and sectional drawings as geometrical and measurable spaces that could be evaluated in quantitative terms through the proportion of open spaces and the depth of the buildings. Thus, the photographs, drawings, and maps were visual tools that operated in a similar manner to statistical enumeration – they represented reality in ways that facilitated the disciplining of that reality.[16]

The recurring themes in Simpson's enumeration, visual representation, and description of the insanitary shophouses were overcrowding and the "obstructions to the admission of light and a free circulation of air."[17] For example, Simpson noted that the shophouse interiors were subdivided into cubicles that had no windows to admit sunlight and fresh air; additions were made that further contracted the small courtyards and obstructed the entry of light and air; and the shophouses were so tightly packed that there was insufficient open space within and between them. He calculated that the percentage of open spaces in a shophouse plot was only about 6–7 percent, when a much higher percentage was required in the sanitary discourse.

As a consequence of his diagnosis of the problems, Simpson put forth a list of recommendations that aimed at "opening up the dark and airless portions of the houses."[18] These included inserting either back lanes of between 15 to 20 feet wide or larger open spaces to separate the existing back-to-back shophouses and to open up the center of the shophouse block (Figures 4.3 and 4.4).[19] Simpson proposed that new bylaws be drawn up to limit the depth of buildings to not more than 45 feet unless "lateral windows" were provided. He stipulated that, following the bylaws adopted in Hong Kong and Calcutta, at least one-third of the building plot should remain as open space. In addition, Simpson recommended that the proportions of open spaces and courtyards in relation to buildings be regulated by the new bylaws. He noted that the height of a building next to an open space or

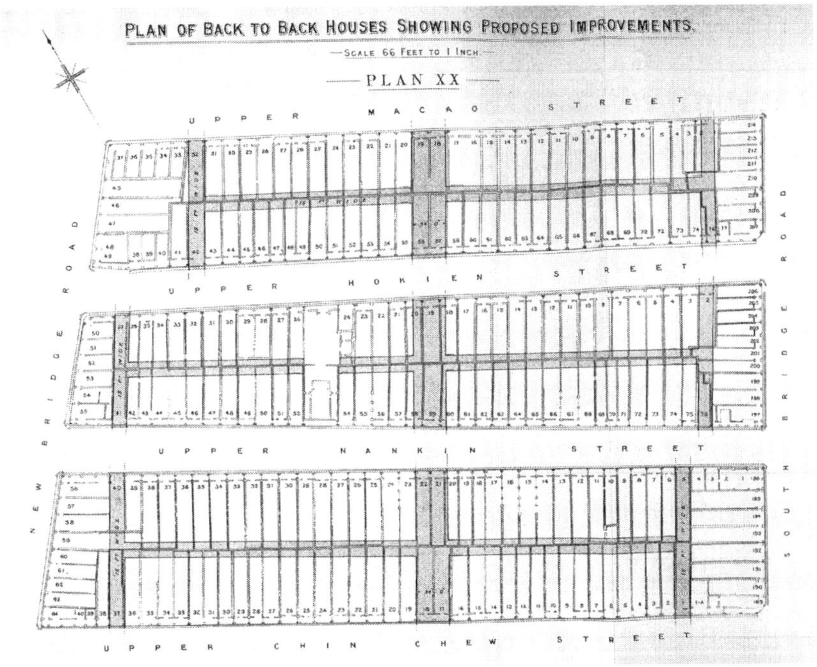

igure 4.3
\ back lane scheme
proposed in Simpson's
eport to open up the
ack-to-back shophouses.
ource: Simpson, *The*
anitary Conditions of
ingapore, 1907.

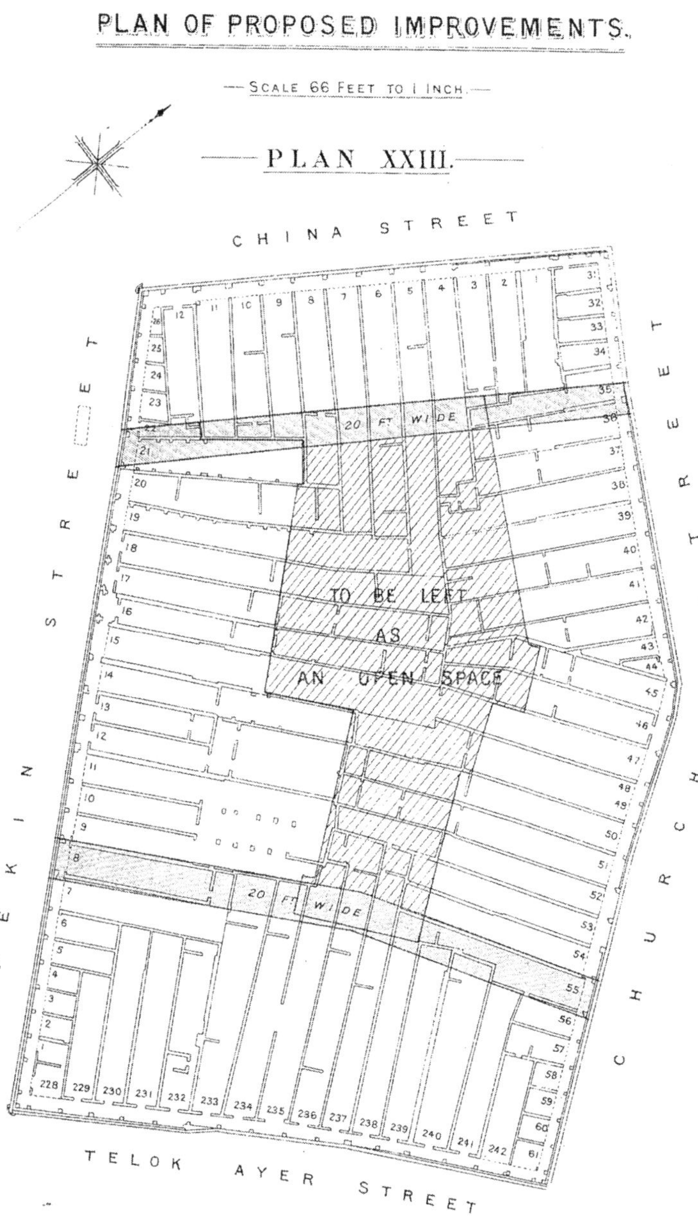

Figure 4.4
A larger open space scheme proposed in Simpson's report. Source: Simpson, *The Sanitary Conditions of Singapore*, 1907.

courtyard should not be more than one and a half times the width of that open space or courtyard, and that the minimum width of the courtyard should be kept at 10 feet. The new guideline on the proportion of a building height next to an open space is represented by the 56-degree line, or light plane, that was drawn over the sectional drawings of a shophouse (see Figure 4.2) in Simpson's report. Finally, Simpson proposed that a new ordinance based on the English precedents "to provide for the abolition of unhealthy dwellings, and for the sanitary condition of the town" should be put up to effect the improvements he recommended.[20] Although many of these recommendations were based on established bylaws and precedents in England or other parts of the Empire, and they were apparently based on scientific principles and articulated in the unambiguous certainty of numbers, their implementation in colonial Singapore proved to be difficult.

This preoccupation with light and air was a feature not just of early twentieth-century sanitary discourse as practiced by Simpson and his contemporaries but of architectural and town planning discourses of that time in general. As Chapters 2 and 3 show, the understanding of air, specifically "pure air," as a precondition for health could be traced to at least the nineteenth-century medical and sanitary discourses, if not the much earlier Hippocratic theories. In these discourses, ventilation was seen as the key to removing the impurities in the air. In the built environment, pure air and ventilation was secured through the stipulation of minimum space standards, in terms of volumetric space and floor area per person, and the proposal of buildings with shallow sections to facilitate cross ventilation. In the tropics, these measures manifested most evidently in building types such as military barracks and hospitals. Although germ theories of disease transmission had replaced miasmatic theories as the main medical doctrines for understanding disease transmission from the late nineteenth century, the concerns with air and ventilation continued through a hybrid theory that Prashant Kidambi calls "contingent contagionism," which blended contagionist doctrines of germ theories with environmentalist doctrines of miasmatic theories.[21] Spacious and well-ventilated bungalows and quarters continued to be built as they continued to be endorsed by British imperial scientists and medical experts, such as Ronald Ross and Malcolm Watson.[22]

The concerns with air and ventilation were in fact extended from the design of buildings to the planning of towns. In his manual on tropical sanitation, Simpson noted that streets should be wide, straight, and intersecting at right angles, with the main avenues oriented in the direction of the "most prevalent and healthy winds" so that they would "act as ventilating conduits to town or village."[23] Simpson's prescription of regular and well-ventilated streets served as a counterpoint to what he considered the typically chaotic town in the tropics, "the narrow streets, the winding alleys, the crowding together of houses, [that formed] an insanitary labyrinth, which [could not] be efficiently cleansed nor be purified by a free circulation of air"[24] (Figure 4.5). Besides streets, the open spaces between and within buildings were articulated in the sanitary discourse as "lungs" that should also be regulated according to ventilation needs. Much of these concerns with air and ventilation were subsequently incorporated into the building science research when tropical architecture was institutionalized in the mid-twentieth century, as we shall see in Chapters 5 and 6.

One oft-repeated quote in early twentieth-century sanitary writings captures the significance of light and sunshine for sanitarians: "Second only to air, is light and sunshine essential for growth and health."[25] Although the rationale for the medical benefits of light under miasmatic theories was unclear, light was

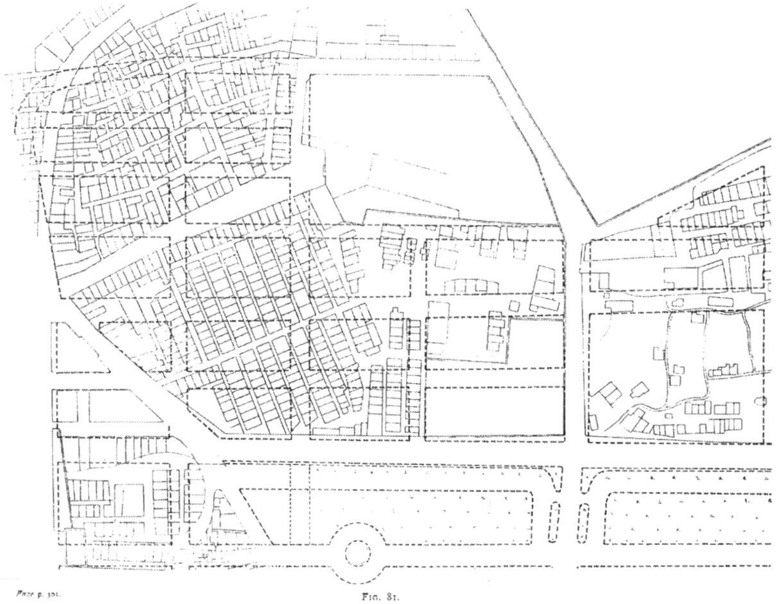

Figure 4.5
Wide, straight streets intersecting at right angles as "ventilating conduits" in dotted lines superimposed on what appears to be an insanitary city with narrow, irregular streets. Source: Simpson, *The Principles of Hygiene as Applied to Tropical and Sub-Tropical Climates*, 1908.

nonetheless valued by Victorian sanitary reformers for aesthetic and moral reasons.[26] With the advent of germ theories, light – specifically direct sunlight – was discovered to have antiseptic properties and to be particularly useful for treating diseases such as tuberculosis.[27] Thus, the presence of direct sunlight in both interior and exterior spaces became desirable for health reasons.

Many attempts were made to quantify the amount of light so as to facilitate its measurement, regulation and optimization. However, from the nineteenth century to the early twentieth century, there was no agreed way to quantify the amount of light with any precision. This was most evident in the outcome of the numerous court cases heard over the violation of the English common law on "ancient light," which dated from 1189 but was incorporated into the 1832 Prescription Act that stipulated that the erection of a new building should not obstruct the access to light of the adjoining buildings. In the second half of the nineteenth century, numerous court cases were heard over the violation of this law. Despite the importance attached to light access, the outcome of the cases appeared to be arbitrary. An 1875 article in the *Architect* journal noted that the cases demonstrated "a succession of new principles of adjudication" and there was no standard "but the personal opinion of a jury or a judge" that the architect could follow.[28] In face of such arbitrariness, the use of the 45-degree angle as a guide was proposed by a few experts. This 45-degree angle was based on a bylaw passed by London's Metropolitan Board of Works in 1856 that stipulated, among other things, that the width of a street within the metropolis of London should at least be equal to the width of the tallest building lining it. If a line is drawn from the opposite side of the street to the height of the tallest building, it should not exceed an angle of 45 degrees. Although the angle provided numerical certainty to the dispute, it was not relied upon as there were questions about where the 45-degree angle should be measured from.[29] Despite the uncertainties, Simpson applied the 45-degree light plane as an unambiguous rule that represents a "better" guide for the proportion of open spaces. He also supplemented that with the 56-degree light plane as the "recommended" guide (see Figure 4.2).

This perceived desirability of direct sunlight in the built environment from the late nineteenth and early twentieth centuries onward led not just to attempts at regulation through stipulating the minimum standard but also to attempts at optimization, such as studies on how buildings could be designed and towns planned to benefit from solar radiation. Such studies also explored how these benefits could be systematically codified into a set of abstract design guidelines or bylaws. For example, Boston architect William Atkinson produced a series of visual studies of the distribution of sunlight on both the exterior and interior of buildings at different times of the year to obtain, among other things, the ideal orientation and proportion of building to street (Figure 4.6).[30] The renowned British town planner Raymond Unwin likewise used sun path diagrams to study the relative advantages and disadvantages of different building orientations in order to rationalize the housing layout in his town planning projects.[31] Later, Unwin was to play an instrumental part in the establishment of the Building Research Station in the post-World War I years to carry out systematic building research to deal with Britain's mass housing problem.[32] During Unwin's tenure as the President of the Royal Institute of British Architects (RIBA), the 1933 RIBA report *The Orientation of Buildings*, probably the most comprehensive technoscientific report on sunlight in relation to the built environment from the pre-World War II period, was published. One of the report's primary objectives was to provide information on insolation in a manner that could be adopted by practicing architects. It reviewed the various methods of graphically measuring insolation in the built environment and recommended two straightforward and practical methods. To further simplify things, the report also introduced the use of two new instruments, i.e. the heliodon and the pinhole camera, for time-saving ways of visualizing and measuring insolation. Based on investigations of insolation using these new methods and instruments, the report provided recommendations for the design of hospital, school, housing, and town planning (Figure 4.7).[33] What came to be known as the subfield of building science has its beginning in early twentieth-century concerns with health and housing. Indeed, studies on sunlight were frequently carried out in relation with the town planning and housing research on the "optimum" building density, building height, spacing between buildings, setbacks and other aspects of the built environment, so that bylaws could be modified or refined accordingly.[34]

By using the "natural" variables of light and air as the common denominators for evaluating sanitary conditions, buildings from different parts of the world could be compared based on the purportedly objective variables while their specific socio-political differences were ignored. This was especially valuable for an imperial

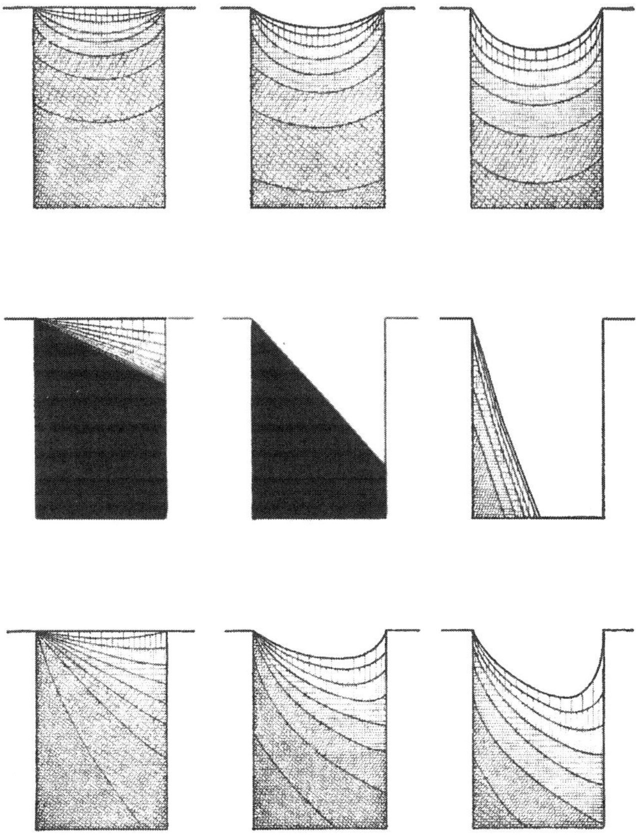

Fig. 70. — Sunlight curves in streets. The three upper diagrams are for a street running north and south, the three middle diagrams for a street running east and west, and the three lower diagrams for a street running at an angle of 45 degrees with the meridian. The diagrams of the left-hand column are drawn for the winter solstice; of the center column for the vernal and autumnal equinox; and of the right-hand column for the summer solstice. The zones between the curves are shaded in a series of tints, the lightest zone being in sunlight between eight and nine hours, and the solid black being without sunlight.

Figure 4.6
Chart showing hours of sunlight in streets of different widths and orientations. Source: Atkinson, *The Orientation of Buildings or Planning for Sunlight*, 1912.

sanitary expert like Simpson, as he moved between different parts of the British Empire, advising the various colonial governments on how to improve the sanitation of their towns and villages. In one of his manuals on tropical sanitation, drawings of both the Chinese shophouse from Singapore – culled from his sanitary report on Singapore but unidentified in his manual – and another unidentified house were presented as instances of the typical insanitary dwelling in the tropics: both failed to provide sufficient open space between buildings that could fit the 45-degree line known as the light plane (Figure 4.8). Besides the use of light planes, Simpson also recommended other solutions, as discussed earlier, based on the codification of light and air requirements into simple numerical rules. These rules could be used as technical design guides or legislated as building bylaws to regulate built form for securing the health of the inhabitants.

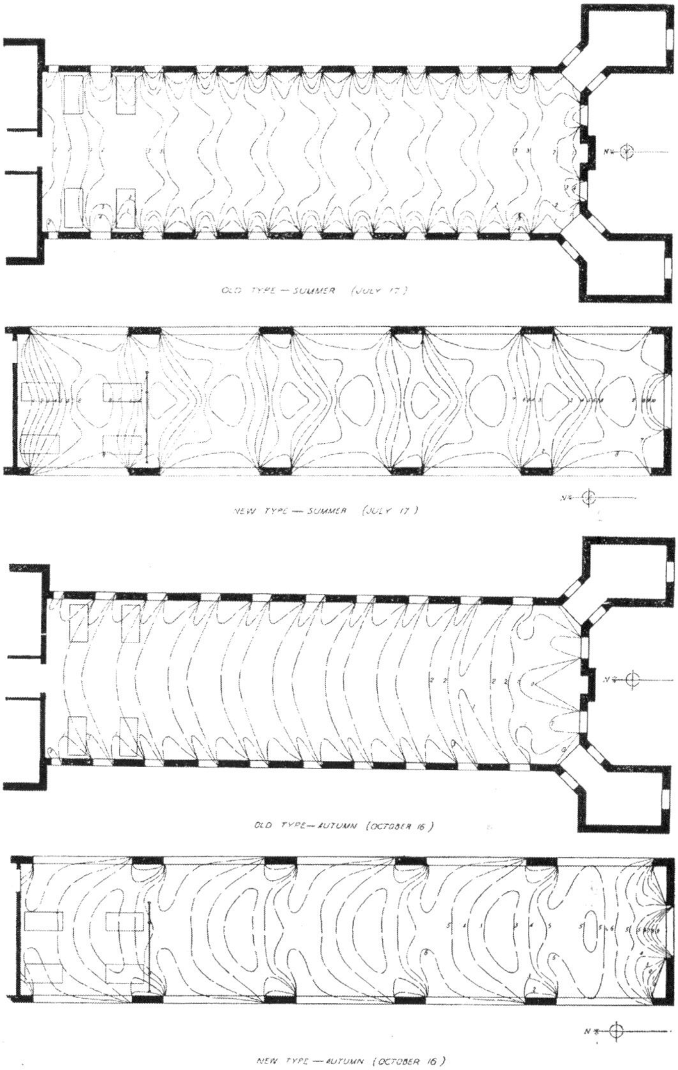

Figure 4.7
Plan drawings comparing the sunlight distribution in the old pavilion plan ward with the new "verandah" ward. Source: The RIBA Joint Committee on the Orientation of Buildings, *The Orientation of Buildings*, 1933.

The use of building bylaws to regulate, order and improve the light and air of the built environment in colonial Singapore could be understood in relation to what Rob Imrie and Emily Street characterize as the rise of "regulatory society" in Europe and North America during the nineteenth century.[35] While various methods of controlling the built environment had existed much earlier, building regulation in the nineteenth century was distinguished by two key differences. First, building regulation in the nineteenth century was based on a technical and purportedly objective system that explicitly "spelled things out in great mathematical precision".[36] Second, new mechanisms and techniques of regulation proliferated and were applied to different aspects of the built environment because the state was concerned with the various risks and hazards in the urban environment and

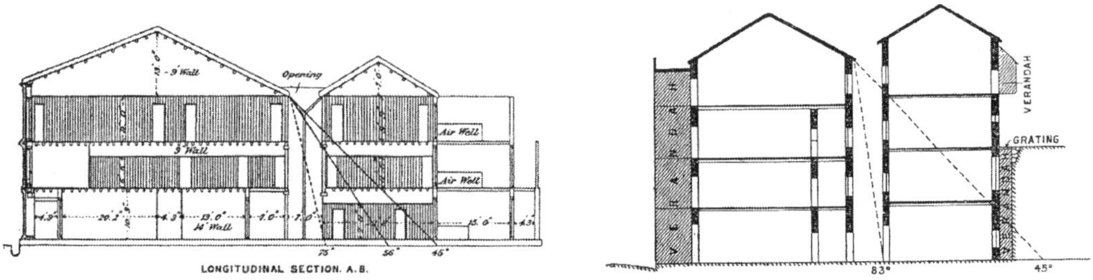

Figure 4.8
Sections of two houses that have open spaces that could not fit the 45-degree light plane. Source: Simpson, *The Principles of Hygiene as Applied to Tropical and Sub-Tropical Climates*, 1908.

sought to secure the physical and social health of the population through the normalization and correction of deviations in the built environment. Both distinctions were clearly evident in Simpson's report and the context that gave rise to the report. Imrie and Street's understanding of building regulation overlaps with my argument in previous chapters that connected the rise of sanitary concerns with Foucauldian biopolitics and governmentality. As with previous chapters, I am interested to explore how these metropolitan ideas and theories translated into practices and were implemented in the colonial urban context outside of the socio-spatial enclaves of the cantonments and hospitals.

On top of improving insanitary buildings through improvement schemes – like the back lane and open space schemes we saw earlier – and the introduction of bylaws to regulate the built environment, Simpson also recommended a town plan specifying housing densities, zoning of uses, open spaces, layout of streets, and other aspects that were required to regulate the future growth of the town in an orderly manner. In order to effect the improvements he recommended, Simpson proposed that a new ordinance based on the English precedents "to provide for the abolition of unhealthy dwellings, and for the sanitary condition of the town" was necessary. Since the improvement schemes would be far too large for the Municipality to deal with and a new executive power was required, Simpson suggested that an organization along the lines of the Improvement Trusts in Bombay and Calcutta should be established.

DEFICIENT "INFORMATION ORDER" AND BELATEDNESS

The recommendations in Simpson's report were enthusiastically received by Singapore's Legislative Council. However, no improvement work was undertaken and no news about the establishment of the Improvement Trust was heard for more than ten years. To understand the inaction and delay, we might have to examine the nature of the Improvement Trust. The metropolitan origin of the model was the Glasgow City Improvement Trust. It was established through the 1866 Improvement Acts, which gave the Trust the power to carry out improvement schemes through the acquisition, demolition and redevelopment of the slums in

Glasgow city center. The key feature of the Improvement Acts was the sanctioning of a public authority, in this case the Trust, with the power to seize insanitary and overcrowded private property in the name of public interest.[37] It represented the first extensive municipal intervention in Britain to deal with housing problems. The establishment of the Glasgow Improvement Trust came from the awareness that the free market and private philanthropies could not deal adequately with the housing problems of the poorest classes.[38]

The immediate referent for Simpson and others in colonial Singapore was not Glasgow but the Indian model, specifically Bombay and Calcutta Improvement Trusts, the two earliest Trusts in the British Empire outside Britain established in 1898 and 1911 respectively.[39] Both were established after the crisis of the 1896 plague in India, upon the colonial state's realization that insanitary housing "played such a terrible part in spreading plague and other infections and contagious diseases."[40] Underpinning their establishment was the belief among colonial officials that "strong executive action unencumbered by accountability to representatives of local self-governing institutions was the only way to achieve decisive results in [colonial] civic affairs."[41] The Improvement Trust subsequently became a widely adopted model in the British Empire and was established in colonial cities such as Rangoon in 1920, Lagos in 1928, and Delhi in 1937.[42] The strong executive power required by the Improvement Trust, however, led to opposition from the property-owning class, as represented by what a former Municipal Commissioner Roland Braddell called "vested interests" among the Unofficial Members of the Legislative Council in colonial Singapore.[43] The property-owning class feared that the value of their properties might be affected, particularly if they were deemed insanitary.

Inaction by the colonial state and the concurrent increase in population led to the worsening of the housing problem and in 1917, Straits Governor Arthur Young had to appoint a new housing commission to reexamine the acute problem. The new housing commission, which published its report in 1918, relied on methods of investigation similar to the ones employed by Simpson, to the extent of reproducing photographs from Simpson's report. Unsurprisingly, the commission reached similar conclusions.[44] Like Simpson, they found that there was severe overcrowding and inadequate housing. In fact, the conditions had been further exacerbated since 1907. Their recommendations were largely similar to Simpson's and they reiterated the importance of having an improvement ordinance and the need to form an Improvement Trust along the lines of those in other British colonial cities such as Bombay and Calcutta.

The Housing Commission's recommendations were accepted by the colonial government, which, in the following year, decided to appoint a technical expert to be the Deputy Chairman of the future Trust; this person would "investigate the city's problems and get to work prior to the creation of the Trust, and passing of new legislation to endow the Trust with efficient powers to carry out improvement, housing, town-planning and development."[45] This led to the appointment of Captain Edwin Percy Richards, a founding member of the Town Planning Institute and chief engineer of the Calcutta Improvement Trust between 1912 and 1913.[46] Richards was best known for the voluminous 400-page report *On the Condition, Improvement and Town Planning of the City of Calcutta and Contagious Areas*, published in 1914. This influential report was summarized and commented upon by Henry Vaughan Lanchester in the *Town Planning Review*;[47] renowned town planner Patrick Abercrombie hailed the report as "a fine achievement and shows a good grasp of a problem of amazing intricacy."[48]

As with the appointment of the previous technical expert, William Simpson, the arrival of Richards in Singapore did not lead to any immediate and significant changes to the status quo. His attempts at drafting an "equitable, up-to-date legislation" to empower the SIT with "the *sine qua non* for reformation of present evils and for the future healthy, orderly, prosperous growth of Singapore" were repeatedly thwarted.[49] Richards resigned in 1924, three years before the Singapore Improvement Ordinance was eventually passed and SIT was formally established.[50] Likewise, Richards faced many challenges when he attempted to plan for town and housing improvements. As other science and technology scholars have noted, the implementation of any technical practice requires a specific sociotechnical network of people, things, knowledge, and practices to be in place, just as governmentality scholars have noted that intervening in the governed necessitates "knowing the governed."[51]

Scholars of planning history in colonial Indian cities note that colonial urban governance was underpinned by an "information order" that consisted of "vast amounts of cartographic knowledge and statistical data" gathered through extensive formal and informal mechanisms of information collection about the settlements and their inhabitants.[52] Richard Harris and Robert Lewis even argue that the creation of the Improvement Trust in Bombay resulted in the innovative Indian Census of 1901, "a census of unprecedented accuracy, scope and detail" even when compared to European and American censuses.[53] Colonial Singapore, however, seemed to be the exact opposite case. One of the key challenges Richards discovered was the lack of an up-to-date contoured survey map of Singapore, as the survey department had been understaffed for many years and lacked the resources to carry out a new survey. Without contoured surveys, Richards was unable to plan accurately, as Singapore was "four-fifths hilly."[54] He had to establish his own team to carry out the surveys.[55] Although his team managed to complete a four-chain contoured topographical survey of the city in 1924, after four years of work and much financial outlay, it was still insufficiently accurate for preparing a detailed layout of roads.[56] Moreover, the problems faced by Richards were compounded by the lack of accurate census information, which had already been highlighted in both Simpson's Report and the 1918 Housing Commission's Report.[57] Like the lack of reliable statistical information on the governed in the case of the census, the absence of accurate spatial information on the environment in the case of the map could be attributed to the want of an operational sociotechnical network, or what Collier and Ong describe in another context as the "technical infrastructure" and "administrative apparatuses."

In the absence of new legislation and the necessary survey map for comprehensive town planning and housing improvement, W. H. Collyer, who replaced Richards as the Deputy Chairman of the Improvement Trust, could only propose "a very modest programme of works" in the mid-1920s on an experimental basis and as a stopgap measure to address the worsening overcrowding and insanitary conditions in the colony. Back lane schemes were implemented in 1924. Open space schemes for creating "lungs to let a little fresh air into the city" were also proposed for houses in the Chulia Street–Church Street block and Beach Road, where houses were described as "a rabbit warren of dangerously insanitary structures."[58] These schemes were proposed for areas deemed improvable by the health officers, where partial demolitions to create back lanes or open spaces were considered sufficient. For areas where the insanitary conditions were deemed beyond redemption, more drastic measures of total demolition and rebuilding were necessary. These more drastic schemes, which also entailed clearing the slums and rehousing the affected population, were called "improvement schemes," as differentiated from the back lanes and open spaces schemes.[59] Although they adhered to the improvement schemata in Simpson's report, they were not part of any comprehensive plan of wholesale change as originally envisioned by Richards because of the uncertainty surrounding the proposed improvement bill at that time. This piecemeal approach to housing and sanitary improvement was primarily undertaken to gauge the funds required for more comprehensive improvement works.

After much delay, the SIT was finally founded in 1927 with the passing of the Singapore Improvement Ordinance. The ordinance provided the Trust with some of the executive power it needed to carry out improvement schemes and to prepare the general town plan.[60] However, glaringly missing in the ordinance was anything on the provision of housing for the general population besides those displaced by the improvement schemes. In a public lecture, Collyer noted that most of the Trust's activities were directed at "developing land," i.e. the building of roads to access plots of land outside the town and making these plots of land suitable for the erection of new housing.[61] The actual erection of the houses was left to the private enterprises. Besides "developing land," the other primary role of the Trust was slum clearance and improvement, as noted earlier. This approach was endorsed by a certain Professor W. W. Johnson, a "leading health expert" from the London School of Hygiene and Tropical Medicine who visited Singapore in the 1930s. Johnson noted,

> The problem of housing as it affects public health is largely from the point of view of slum clearance, and that is the line from which it is being approached at home today. Provision of houses is not regarded now as so important as elimination of overcrowding and of insanitary dwellings.[62]

Johnson's statement suggests that the neglect of housing was linked to the prioritization of public health concerns over the broader consideration of the housing needs of the local population. Thus, the Trust's activities favored the eradication of insanitary nuisances and the elimination of health threats, which were presumably more economical than the provision of mass housing. The prioritization of slum clearance and the development of suburban land would, however, soon run into difficulties, as we shall see below.

The other problem of the 1927 ordinance was a lack of clarity in terms of funding. Although in 1926 the colonial government committed a sum of 10 million Straits dollars for the purpose of dealing with Singapore's slum problem, a commentator noted that "the fund was never clearly defined in nature and purpose, and has not been operated as a 'trustee fund.'"[63] Up until the mid-1930s, SIT only built to accommodate those displaced by its improvement schemes. According to one estimate, the housing built up until the mid-1930s housed only about 4,500 people.[64] As such, these housing measures did little to alleviate the problems of housing shortage and overcrowding. The original plan of addressing the housing shortage through private enterprise with the assistance of the Trust – by having the Trust improve lands outside the town and then selling them to private enterprises – did not come to fruition. By the mid-1930s, the housing problem was further aggravated by the further increase in population.

THE DEFINING PROBLEM

As we have seen earlier, the Trust encountered many problems in the early years of its existence. What came to be known as the "Bugis Street case"[65] was a defining problem that shifted the course of the Trust's history. One of the powers conferred upon the Trust by the 1927 ordinance was the right to declare a building "unfit for human habitation," which would require the building to be demolished by either the owner or the Trust. In such a case, the Trust would need only to compensate the owner for the price of the site but not for the building itself. The evaluation of the fitness of a building for human habitation was to be based on the sanitary assessment by the municipal health officer using the same technical – and thus purportedly objective – criteria that Simpson first used decades ago for determining whether the light and air (or ventilation) in the interior was adequate, and if the water supply, sewage, drainage, and refuse and night soil disposal arrangements were satisfactory.[66] However, even such technical and purportedly objective evaluations did not go unchallenged.

In 1933, when the Trust declared numerous shophouses in the city unfit for habitation and wanted to demolish them, the owners of eight of these buildings challenged the Trust's right to do so in the Court. Two of these shophouses, owned by the wealthy Chinese businessmen Eu Tong Sen, were located on Bugis Street.[67] This challenge subsequently developed into a prolonged saga known as the "Bugis Street case," which was only resolved in 1937. The owners' appeal against the Trust's decision went all the way to the Privy Council in London, which ruled against the Trust. A main point of contention in this case was whether the houses were fit for habitation. The Trust and the Acting Municipal Health Officer Dr. W. Dawson deemed them as unfit for habitation based on their bad ventilation, poor water supply and drainage, and the lack of a proper sewerage system. But another medical expert, the former Principal Civil Medical Officer Dr. A. L. Hoops, argued that while the houses were "insanitary and in need of improvement," they were not "unfit for human habitation," which "could only be justified by very much worse conditions than were founded [*sic*] in those houses."[68] As there was no "insanitary calculus" in the 1927 improvement ordinance, the health officer's assessment of unfitness for human habitation was based on the standard established by the Ministry of Health in England. The Privy Council ruled that England's standard was not applicable to Singapore, and thus the Trust had no legal right to declare the buildings insanitary.[69]

The Bugis Street case meant that the sanitary calculus that the Trust inherited from Simpson's report could not be applied for slum clearance purposes in Singapore. The Trust's other strategy of addressing the housing problem – through the sale of land acquired and improved by the Trust in the suburb to private developers to build housing – also did not work as no private developer was interested. These two setbacks brought into focus important questions about the role of the Trust and what it could do to address the housing problem in colonial Singapore. It led to a review of the power of the Trust and helped to transform it from a town improvement agency into a proper housing agency. Arnold Robinson, a former senior unofficial member of the Straits Settlements Legislative and Executive Council and a prominent figure in the Colonial public sphere, was instrumental in bringing about the change. He considered slum improvement as a "big issue" and said that it should be seen as an essential "social service." He argued that back-lane and other improvement schemes carried out by the Trust were inadequate as the houses continued to be insanitary. He thus suggested that the Trust should "erect model houses on a moderate scale" and he urged the Trust to "study English methods."[70]

In response to Robinson's suggestions, the Straits Governor Shenton Thomas issued a memorandum – regarded by the newspapers as "a document of outstanding interest"[71] – that agreed in principle that the power of the Trust should be extended to allow it to build houses and that the Trust should investigate and report on the latest methods of slum clearance and housing.[72] Langdon Williams, the SIT manager, was sent to Britain to carry out the latter task and also to attend the International Town Planning Congress in London in 1935. Upon his return, Williams submitted a report that addressed the issues of slum clearance and public housing. From his survey of the housing policy in Britain, he argued that affordable housing for the working class could be built only by the authorities with state subsidies, not by private enterprises.[73] Public opinion expressed in the local newspaper also advocated the use of public funds to subsidize housing for the poorer classes of the local population.[74] All these led the Straits Governor Shenton Thomas to declare in 1936 that SIT should put up a ten-year housing program that would take "concrete shape in much larger schemes than have been attempted hitherto."[75] The use of public funds to subsidize housing was endorsed by the Weisberg Committee's Report and became the official policy in 1938. The Weisberg Committee argued that slum eradication was not just about "destroying bad houses," but about building housing that the poorer classes could afford.[76] Since private enterprises expected a return on their financial outlay that the working-class housing could not possibly yield, the Weisberg Committee saw "no alternative to the provision by Government of subsidized accommodation for the poorer working class."[77] With the recommendations of the Weisberg Committee, SIT became the official housing agency of the colonial state, empowered to build subsidized housing.

HOUSING EXPERIMENTS FOR A VARIEGATED "PUBLIC"

Before SIT was given the mandate to plan, design and build mass housing, the colonial state's involvement in housing was rather limited. Besides building palatial bungalows for its European staff, various colonial state agencies – such as the Public Works Department and the Municipality – were involved in the building of small number of houses for their employees. For example, during the housing crisis in the 1920s, the municipality was instructed to provide housing for its own employees, particularly its junior staff and coolies. As a result, subordinate quarters and coolie lines were built at Bukit Timah and Kampong Kapor respectively. A newspaper article that reviewed the coolie lines hailed their quality:

> These lines would indeed appear to come as near perfection as is possible where coolies are concerned, and they are probably unique in Singapore. They are solidly constructed of concrete, with wide spaces of grass between them for the children to play on; they have good verandahs ...[78]

In describing these coolie lines designed by municipal architect S. Douglas Meadows in such glowing terms, the journalist was also implicitly participating in the contentious debate on how to house the poorer classes in colonial Singapore.

A few minor, piecemeal and controversial attempts were made by the colonial state to ameliorate the housing conditions of especially the poorer classes after the 1918 Housing Commission. Two main types of housing were provided. The first type was the multi-storied tenement housing built in the city center. An example of this was the model tenements erected on Cross Street that consisted of three blocks of four-storey buildings built in reinforced concrete that provided 396 apartments.[79] The second type was the single-story or double-story housing built in the suburb, typically provided with open spaces. Two examples were the model coolie lines built by the colonial state at Keppel Road and Kampong Bahru, on land leased from Singapore Harbour Board.[80]

Both types of housing had their critics. One anonymous critic of the tenement argued that "close-build, tall barrack-tenements, devoid of adjoining play-grounds or recreation places, and erected on costly land, in congested streets" should not be erected to house the coolies and their families after slum clearance because "[a]ll amenity, the pleasantness of home, the essentials of fresh air and quiet, are absent" in these tenements.[81] Furthermore, the critic claimed that tenements had failed in English cities and were even more likely to fail in colonial cities like

Calcutta and Singapore because the population densities were even greater, so there was no way they could be rehoused on the same urban sites from where the insanitary slums were demolished. Instead of building tenements, the critic's proposal was to adopt town planning and plan for new roads to open up new land outside the city for housing development. According to the critic, this would encourage private developers to build housing on this cheap land, which would in turn relieve the overcrowding in the city.[82] In other words, what the critic proposed was the Empire-wide planning orthodoxy that was adopted by the Trust in its early years, as we have seen.[83]

Another expert, Oscar Wilson – the secretary of the Singapore Society of Architects – held the opposite view. He claimed that overcrowding in tenements could be overcome by having tall and "lofty" tenements because, in the tropics, "you get so much vertical sunlight that you can afford to have higher buildings than you can in Northern and Southern latitudes where you do not get the same amount of vertical sunlight." He further argued,

> The day has gone by now when you can house the poorer classes in individual houses. They cannot pay the necessary financial return that land owners and property owners require. In America, France and Germany the poorer classes are housed in apartments and blocks of flats. It is looked to as the only solution of the housing problem.[84]

Referring to cases in colonial Singapore, he noted that efforts to move the poorer classes to the outskirts had not been sound because the amount they saved from cheap rent had to be spent on transport to their places of work. Indeed, the colonial state had great difficulty renting out the coolie lines it built at Kampong Bahru and Keppel Road. A report noted that "[t]he lines remained vacant for quite a long time, till 'the poor, the real poor could be found'"[85] because the sites were considered by the coolies as too far from the town and the monthly rent of six dollars was not regarded as sufficiently low.

A newspaper journalist remarked that "[t]he coolie was the most difficult person to house because he could not afford a rental." It was made in response to Collyer's pronouncement at a lecture that "it may turn out that coolies cannot be housed in a sanitary manner at an economical rental."[86] The key phrase here was "economical rental." The root of the problem seemed to be that the typical coolie was earning far too little. The coolie could not afford to pay a rental for any form of housing that met the minimum sanitary standards while also allowing the property owner to profit from his or her investment. In other words, if the socio-economic structure remained unaltered, the only way for the rental to be sufficiently affordable to the coolie was for the colonial state to subsidize the housing. Further compounding the unsettled question of the suitable type of housing and issues surrounding housing affordability was the problem of the colonial state "not knowing the governed" in Singapore. Thus, when the Trust became a housing agency, it "experiment[ed] with various types of houses to suit different classes"[87] of the local population.

One of the earliest types that the Trust built was "tenement housing," as part of the 1920s improvement schemes discussed earlier, such as those at Dickinson Hill, Albert Street, and Lorong Krian. As the tenement housing was rented out at low rates to the poorest classes, they were designed according to bare minimum standards. In fact, one could even argue that they were substandard, as each family was typically allocated only a single room, with the kitchens and toilets as common facilities to be shared among the various families. Putting a whole family into a single room or cubicle was one of the main criticisms directed at the cubicles in the shophouses as they did not allow privacy for the adults in the family.[88] Reproducing the same problem in tenement housing was clearly an indication that the other types of SIT housing discussed below were not sufficiently affordable for the poorer classes of the local population.[89] However, with the emergence of the Bugis Street case in the 1930s, the Trust could no longer undertake slum clearance and large-scale improvement schemes within the city. The Trust thus shifted its attention to building in the suburbs.

One of the earliest suburban housing schemes that the Trust planned was one originally intended for the coolies. The scheme was located at Balestier, an area to the north right outside the limits of the city, and they were built over different phases during the 1930s (Figures 4.9 and 4.10).[90] Balestier was originally a low-lying area that consisted of 75 acres of agricultural land occupied by a village. The colonial health authorities saw it as a "fruitful source of disease" as it was "covered with filthy wood and *attap* houses and densely overcrowded," and the many stagnant pools there were regarded as "ideal breeding grounds for mosquitoes." [91] It was initially intended as a scheme of village clearance and resettlement of the pig breeders and vegetable growers. At the beginning, the plan was to build "small coolie dwellings of 3 rooms" at a monthly rental of about three to four dollars. But later, the houses built were called "artisan quarters" instead. "Artisan" was used to describe the class of skilled workmen who earned more than the unskilled coolies and were more likely to be able to afford the rent that the Trust was charging for the quarters at Balestier. These quarters were one- or two-bedroom terrace houses, each with its own kitchen, toilet and backyard. The units were arranged in blocks of six and eight, organized around internal courtyards and clustered around open spaces that provided plenty of light and air. Built in white-washed concrete, topped with flat roofs and enclosed with unadorned surfaces common to modern architecture, these quarters were described as providing an "atmosphere of brightness and spotless cleanliness" in contrast to the dim and dirty *attap* huts built of timber and thatch that they replaced.[92]

The artisan quarters at Balestier were sometimes described as "cottage houses." According to Robert Home, the cottage housing type in the British colonies was probably derived from the British garden suburban single-family dwelling, which was popular in the early twentieth century because it helped to secure more "light and air" for the inhabitants. Home also notes that town planners such as Richards considered the built environment of cottage housing to be more conducive to the production of "good citizens" than the "block dwellings" of the tenements.[93] In colonial Singapore, only a small number of units

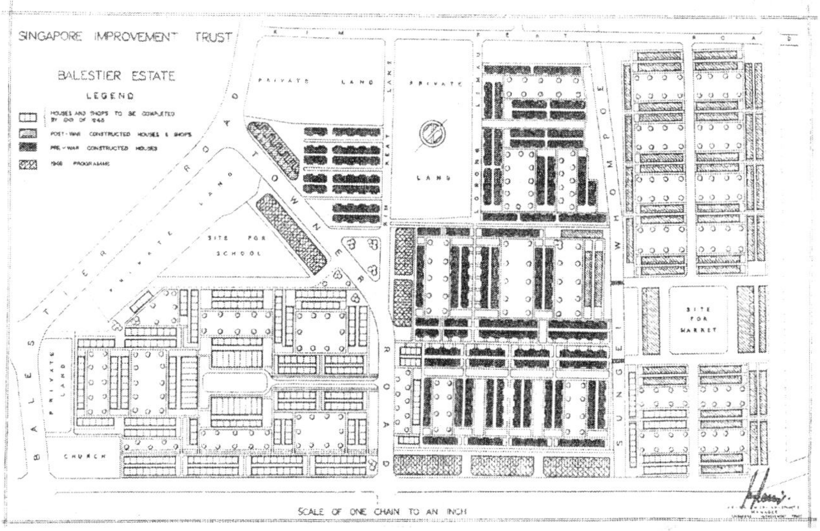

Figure 4.9
Plan of Balestier Housing by SIT. Source: Fraser, *The Work of the Singapore Improvement Trust 1927–1947*, 1948.

gure 4.10
hoto of Balestier's artisan uarters. Source: Fraser, *he Work of the Singapore nprovement Trust 927–1947*, 1948.

of actual cottage housing were built. Most of these were erected before the Trust became a housing agency in two schemes. The first scheme was a "model village" with 65 double tenancy houses erected in 1925 on 10 acres of land owned by the municipality at the junction of Alexandra Road and Henderson Road for the residents displaced by the Trust's improvement schemes.[94] The second was the Lavender Road Housing Scheme of 1928 designed by Williams, in which 118 units of cottage housing were built for those displaced by the Lorong Krian Improvement Scheme.[95] Williams contrasted the "cottage type of house, one room deep with ample kitchen, living room accommodation and all rooms well lighted and ventilated" that he designed for the Lavender Road scheme with the "long narrow barrack" built form of the shophouse.[96] As the cottage houses tended to be bigger than artisan quarters, they cost more to build and the rent was naturally higher. They were thus conceived as primarily catering to the "clerical class." Besides the aforementioned two schemes, the other SIT "cottage" housing scheme was a very small scheme in the Old Race Course area, where seventeen two-storey houses were completed in 1941 (Figures 4.11 and 4.12).[97]

The largest prewar housing scheme by the Trust and one that survives till today is the Tiong Bahru estate. Located just outside the city, a short distance from the congested Chinatown and opposite the Singapore General Hospital, the land was originally "partly swampy, partly disused graveyard and hills … crowded with squatters' huts."[98] The land was acquired between 1925 and 1926 based on the Municipal Health Officer P. S. Hunter's recommendation that "a well-planned suburb near the Singapore China Town was necessary to provide for future expansion to relieve congestion."[99] Improvement works were subsequently carried out with the aim of selling the land to private developers to build housing. The Trust was, however, unsuccessful in attracting any interests and it decided to build in the mid-1930s when the Trust became a housing agency.

Figure 4.11
Overall site plan of the SIT cottage housing at Old Race Course Road. Only those shaded in dark grey were built. Courtesy of the NAS.

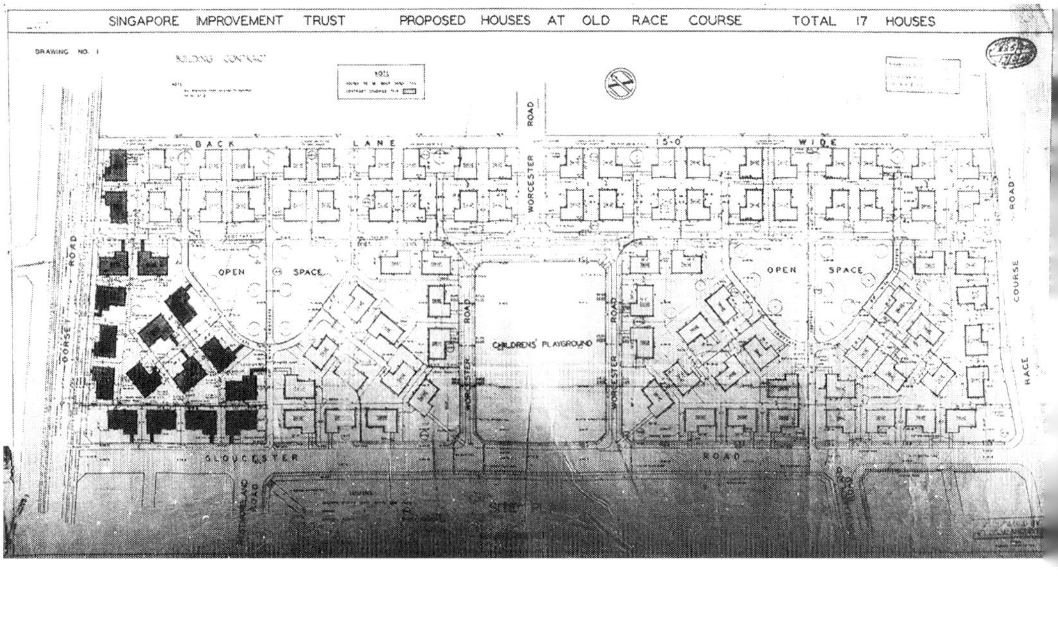

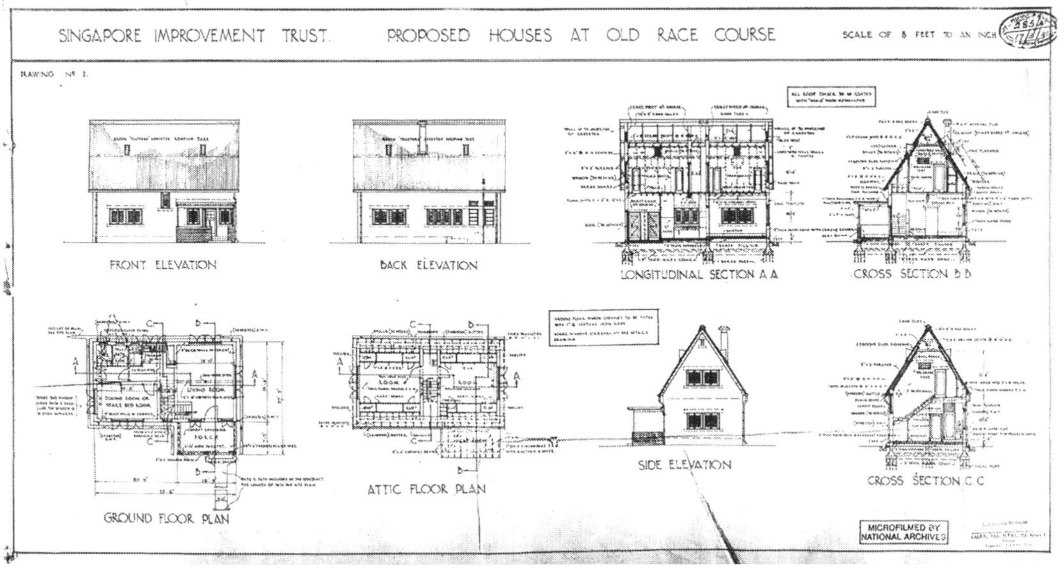

Figure 4.12
Section of Old Race Course Road Scheme. Courtesy of the NAS.

igure 4.13
lean lines and treamlined curvilinear orms of the SIT flats at iong Bahru. Author's hotograph.

Between 1937 and 1941, when building activity stopped due to the imminent Japanese Occupation of Singapore, the Trust built 784 flats, 54 tenements, and 33 shops in the estate.[100] As the main building type in Tiong Bahru, the flats were regarded as some of the most modern buildings of their time (Figures 4.13 and 4.14). Not only were they built using modern materials such as hollow concrete blocks and steel windows, they were also designed in a simple and abstract architectural language that accentuated clean lines and streamlined curvilinear forms.[101] They were planned in such a way as to let the residents enjoy plenty of light and air, featuring individual flats with balconies for "sitting out," light wells in the middle of the blocks, and a "children's grassed playground" for the children to enjoy fresh air. Williams, who was also the architect of the flats, proudly claimed that they provided "modern comfort" and were comparable to similar schemes in Britain. These flats were, however, not intended for the poorest classes. They were meant for the "clerical class" that could afford the fairly high monthly rental.[102] Despite their modern appearance, the Tiong Bahru flats were obviously influenced by the shophouse, especially in terms of the types of improvement that Simpson proposed. Individual units were narrow and deep and the layout of the units made use of light

Figure 4.14
Plan of two connected blocks of SIT flats at Tiong Bahru enclosing a "Children's Playing Field" in the middle. Courtesy of the NAS.

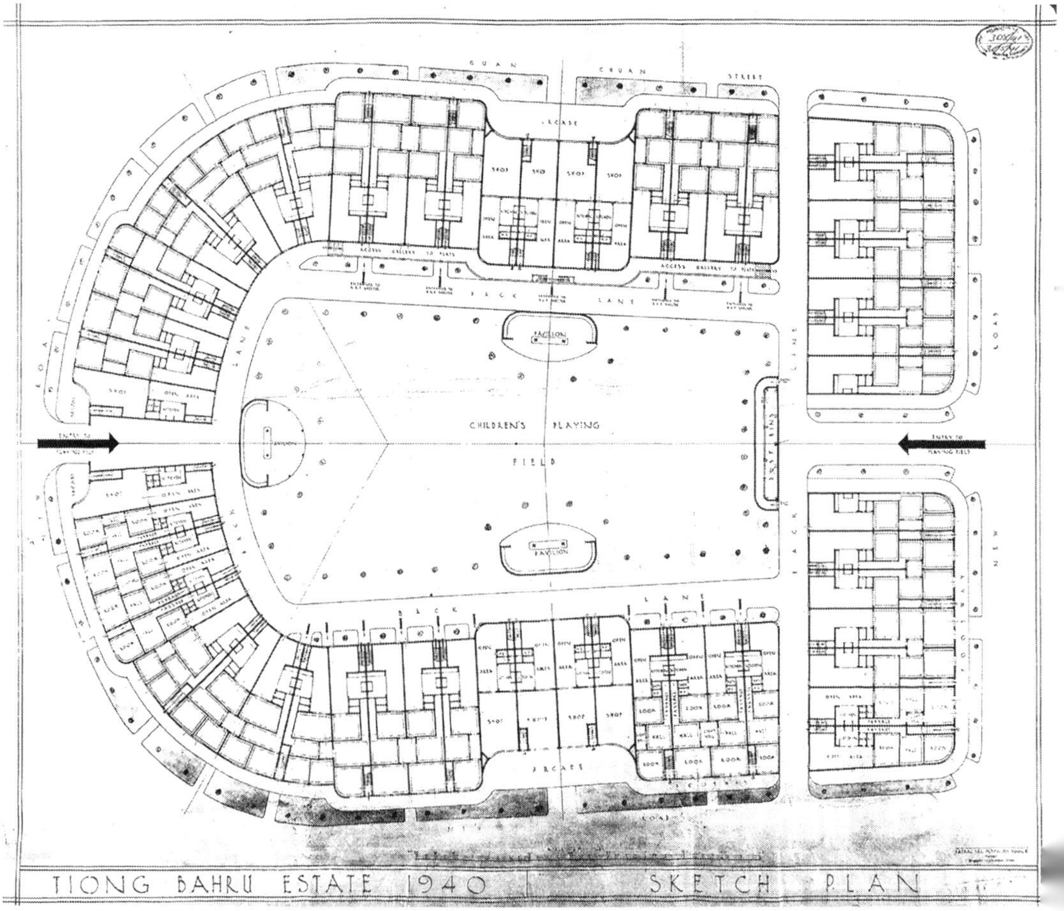

wells, around which rooms were grouped.[103] Furthermore, the rear of the units lined back lanes in almost the same manner as the reconstructed rear of the shophouses after back-lane improvements.

THE ANATOMY OF A FAILED CASE

The ways in which technologies of sanitary and environmental improvement expanded beyond the military and medical enclaves in colonial Singapore could be understood in a few ways. Many of the ideas and practices of town planning and housing in colonial Singapore were of course shaped by "global" norms elsewhere, particularly those within the British Empire. But they were also translated in manners that were particular to the socio-political conditions of colonial Singapore. It is by understanding how the global and the local, the general and the specific interacted that we can understand the specific outcomes of town and housing improvements in colonial Singapore during the prewar years.

One of the main reasons behind the delays and piecemeal implementations in town and housing improvement in colonial Singapore was that the colonial state did not know the governed. Despite the array of technologies of knowing the governed applied, the colonial state had inaccurate information and knowledge about the colonized population. The minute information order that characterized many metropolitan and even colonial societies, and was necessary for devising proper strategies for intervening in the lives of the population, was absent in colonial Singapore. The Singapore colonial state's lack of knowledge of the governed was not due to the inherent deficiency of the technologies it deployed. Rather, it could be attributed to the colonial state's unwillingness to commit the requisite resources needed to fund and undertake the gathering of vast amounts of information. Not knowing the governed had important implications for the subsequent implementation of town and housing improvement. It led to delays in the proposal of town improvement schemes and it also contributed to the colonial state and SIT's uncertainties about the right housing type – in terms of standards, location and affordability – for the poorer classes of the colonized population.

Other than the deficient information order, the delays in implementing town and housing improvements in colonial Singapore could also be attributed to a few other reasons. One of the main reasons was the confluence of the colonial state's unwillingness to commit resources to undertake the improvements and the opposition from the powerful property-owning class in colonial Singapore. Despite the colonial development initiatives put forward by the Colonial Office in the early twentieth century, British colonies were in general expected to be fiscally self-sufficient – and in the case of Singapore, it even had to contribute to the building and maintenance of imperial military defense, as we saw in Chapter 2. Thus, as many scholars of colonial cities show, most British colonial sanitary and housing improvement programs for the colonized population were typically underfunded.[104] The lack of funding and the chronic insanitary conditions of the local housing were sometimes justified through colonial discourses of racial and cultural difference. It was, for example, reasoned that, due to their fundamental "Otherness," the "ignorant and habitually uncleanly natives,"[105] who were "filthy in their habits beyond all European conception of filthiness,"[106] were incapable of observing hygienic practices and maintaining the environment in a sanitary condition.

However, as we saw, the colonial state began to realize from the mid-1930s, following the Bugis Street case and advocacy from respected members of colonial society like Robinson, that the only way to deal with the intractable sanitary and housing problems was for the colonial state to be directly involved in the building of subsidized housing for the colonized population. That shift in policy was accompanied by a different discourse on the colonized population. This new discourse refuted the earlier stereotypes and argued that "there [were] very few inveterate, incurable ["native"] slum-dwellers"[107] and that the colonized population "[would] observe clean habits if only they [were] properly housed."[108] The policy shift to the colonial state building subsidized housing was only implemented in the later part of the 1930s and it was halted in a few short years with the advent of World War II. It therefore did not bring about the completion of a sufficiently large quantity of housing to make a significant dent on the housing problem. Despite that, the policy shift was significant in that it anticipated the postwar colonial welfare policies in general (to be discussed in Chapter 5) and the postwar housing policy in particular, which brought about the completion of a substantial quantity of subsidized housing by SIT.

The "vested interest" within the colonial Legislative Council of Singapore, specifically that of the property owning class within the council, also contributed to the delays in implementing town and housing improvements by opposing the passing of the legislation needed for the formation of the SIT. When the SIT was finally established, its power to declare a building unfit for human habitation was challenged in the landmark Bugis Street case. Although the criterion of declaring a building unfit for human habitation was based on a purportedly scientific and thus objective sanitary calculus, the calculus was deemed to be based on metropolitan norms and thus inapplicable to the colonial context of Singapore. As a result, SIT could not bring about sanitary improvement indirectly through only bylaws and building regulation. The regulatory society and the attendant normalization of the built environment that happened in metropolitan societies in tandem with the rise of building regulation did not actualize in colonial Singapore. While the sanitary calculus could not withstand the legal challenge, its underpinning technoscientific methods of privileging and quantifying air and light as desirable environmental variables continued to be influential. Not only did it shape the ways buildings were designed and planned in colonial Singapore and the tropics, these technoscientific methods also became the basis for the architectural subfield of building science and institutionalized tropical architecture, as we shall see in Chapters 5 and 6.

The colonial state's inadequate knowledge about the colonized population also shaped the types of housing SIT built. Unlike the clearly defined building types produced by previous reforms in sanitation and governance at the socio-spatial enclaves we saw in Chapters 2 and 3, this attempted sanitary reform outside the enclaves led to SIT experimenting with different housing typologies in an attempt to house the different socio-economic classes of the colonized population. The absence of a consistent planning principle behind the different types of housing, and the colonial state's struggle to provide affordable and adequate housing for the "poorer classes," especially the coolies, suggest that the diversity of solutions was not an intended outcome. The delays and postponements in implementing housing improvement and the absence of a clear housing policy further reinforced the impression that the colonial state lacked a clear vision and did not know what to do.

Although recent scholars of colonial cities have argued that spatial boundaries between the European and "native" towns were not clear and distinct but blurred, the discrepant sanitary provisions and housing conditions in colonial Singapore between the European residential and military enclaves on the one hand, and most of the "native" city on the other suggests that there were undeniably generalizable differences between the two.[109] Indeed the case of colonial Singapore reinforces the enclave nature of colonial cities that Anthony King first theorized in the 1970s and this book has tried to show in Chapters 2, 3 and 4.[110] While the colonial state's technologies of sanitary improvement and governance were applied outside the enclaves, their application was piecemeal, fragmentary and on a negligible scale. It was not until the postwar years that further aggravated housing problems were sufficiently dealt with on a much larger scale by both the colonial state and, more significantly, the post-independence state.

NOTES

1 "Insanitary Singapore," *ST*, 13 September 1910.

2 Martin V. Melosi, *The Sanitary City: Urban Infrastructure in America from Colonial Times to the Present* (Baltimore, MD: Johns Hopkins University Press, 2000), 28–39.

3 Ronald Ross, *Report of the Malaria Expedition to the West Coast of Africa 1899* (Liverpool: Liverpool School of Tropical Medicine, 1900); W. J. Simpson, *Report on Sanitary Matters in Various West African Colonies and the Outbreak of Plague in the Gold Coast, Presented to Parliament by Command of His Majesty* (London: HMSO, 1909); Mary Sutphen, "Not What, but Where: Bubonic Plague and the Reception of Germ Theories in Hong Kong and Calcutta, 1894–1897," *Journal of the History of Medicine* 52 (1997).

4 See, for example, Birendra Nath Ghosh and Jahar Lal Das, *A Treatise on Hygiene and Public Health, with Special Reference to the Tropics*, 2nd ed. (Calcutta: Hilton and Co, 1914); W. J. Simpson, *The Principles of Hygiene as Applied to Tropical and Sub-Tropical Climates* (London: John Bale, Sons & Danielsson, 1908).

5 Anderson to Lyttelton, 12 September 1905, in PRO CO273/310, *Sanitary Condition of Singapore*.

6 Patrick Joyce, *The Rule of Freedom: Liberalism and the Modern City* (London: Verso, 2003).

7 Rob Imrie and Emma Street, *Architectural Design and Regulation* (Oxford: Wiley-Blackwell, 2011).

8 The seminal study on Simpson's report in relation to sanitary improvement and town planning in colonial Singapore is Brenda S. A. Yeoh, *Contesting Space: Power Relations and the Urban Built Environment in Colonial Singapore* (Kuala Lumpur: Oxford

University Press, 1996). My chapter is of course indebted to Professor Yeoh's study although my focus is different and I deploy different theoretical frameworks.

9 Sutphen, "Not What, but Where"; Malcolm Watson, "Simpson, Sir William John Ritchie," rev. Mary P. Sutphen, in *Oxford Dictionary of National Biography* (Oxford: Oxford University Press, 2004), online edition, Jan 2008, accessed 5 January 2016, http://www.oxforddnb.com/view/article/36106.

10 Joyce, *The Rule of Freedom*.

11 W. J. Simpson, *The Sanitary Condition of Singapore* (London: Waterlow, 1907), 7.

12 Ibid., 15.

13 Yeoh, *Contesting Space*, 104.

14 Simpson, *The Sanitary Condition of Singapore*, 10.

15 The modes of representation in Simpson's maps and drawings could be traced to the practices of medical mapping in Victorian Britain premised on medical topography and the miasmatic theories of disease transmission. See Pamela K. Gilbert, *Mapping the Victorian Social Body* (Albany: State University of New York, 2004).

16 For maps, see Joyce, *The Rule of Freedom*, 35–56; Nikolas S. Rose, *Powers of Freedom: Reframing Political Thought* (Cambridge: Cambridge University Press, 1999), 36–40.

17 Simpson, *The Sanitary Condition of Singapore*, 25–26.

18 Ibid., 29.

19 The building of back lanes was proposed by the local officials in their 1905 initial report on sanitary improvement. See Yeoh, *Contesting Space*, 148–57.

20 Simpson, *The Sanitary Condition of Singapore*, 37.

21 Prashant Kidambi, "Planning, the Information Order, and the Bombay Census of 1901," *PP* 28, no. 1 (2013): 121. For a French colonial example, see Laura Victoir, "Hygienic Colonial Residences in Hanoi," in *Harbin to Hanoi: Colonial Built Environment in Asia, 1840 to 1940*, ed. Laura Victoir and Victor Zatsepine (Hong Kong: Hong Kong University Press, 2013).

22 See, for example, Ronald Ross, *Report on the Prevention of Malaria in Mauritius* (London: J. & A. Churchill, 1908); Malcolm Watson, "Memorandum on Insanitary Houses in Selangor," 1908 in ALSHTM, *Ross/140/01/08*.

23 Simpson, *The Principles of Hygiene*, 305.

24 Ibid., 294.

25 Cited in William Atkinson, *The Orientation of Buildings or Planning for Sunlight* (New York: John Wiley & Sons, 1912), 1.

26 Felix Driver, "Moral Geographies: Social Science and the Urban Environment in Mid-Nineteenth Century England," *Transactions of the Institute of British Geographers* 13, no. 3 (1988). See also Chris Otter, *The Victorian Eye: A Political History of Light and Vision in Britain, 1800–1910* (Chicago: University of Chicago Press, 2008), 62–98.

27 The RIBA Joint Committee on the Orientation of Buildings, *The Orientation of Buildings, Being the Report with Appendices of the RIBA Joint Committee on the Orientation of Buildings* (London: RIBA, 1933).

28 Cited in Bannister Fletcher, *Light and Air: A Text-Book for Architects and Surveyors* (London: B. T. Batsford, 1895), 91.

29 Ibid., 92–93.

30 Atkinson, *The Orientation of Buildings*.

31 Raymond Unwin, *Town Planning in Practice: An Introduction to the Art of Designing City* (New York: Benjamin Blom, 1971 [1909]).

32 George Anthony Atkinson, "Raymond Unwin: Founding Father of BRS," *RIBAJ* 78 (1971): 448.

33 The RIBA Joint Committee on the Orientation of Buildings, *The Orientation of Buildings*.

34 F. Longstreth Thompson, "Suggested Regulations Regarding Density, Proportion of Curtilage to Be Built Upon, and Height of Buildings," *JTPI* 9, no. 8 (1923). See also A.

Trystan Edwards, "Sunlight in Streets," *TPR* 8, no. 2 (1920); A. Trystan Edwards, "Sunlight in Streets II," *TPR* 9, no. 1 (1921).

35 Imrie and Street, *Architectural Design and Regulation*.

36 Howard Davis, *The Culture of Building* (Oxford: Oxford University Press, 1999), 210. See also Rob Imrie, "The Interrelationships between Building Regulations and Architects' Practices," *Environment and Planning B: Planning and Design* 34 (2007). For an overview of the history of building regulation, see Eran Ben-Joseph, *The Code of the City: Standards and the Hidden Language of Place Making* (Cambridge, MA: MIT Press, 2005).

37 Prashant Kidambi, "Housing the Poor in a Colonial City: The Bombay Improvement Trust, 1898–1918," *Studies in History* 17, no. 1 (2001): 58.

38 Geoffrey Best, "The Scottish Victorian City," *Victorian Studies* 11, no. 3 (1968): 338–44; George Allan, "The Genesis of British Urban Redevelopment with Special Reference to Glasgow," *The Economic History Review* 18, no. 3 (1965).

39 "The Calcutta Improvement Trust," *Garden Cities & Town Planning, incorporating the Housing Reformer* 6, no. 5 (1921).

40 J. M. Linton Bogle, "Town Planning in India," *JTPI* 15, no. 5 (1929): 159.

41 Kidambi, "Housing the Poor in a Colonial City," 58.

42 Raj Bahadur Gupta, *Labour and Housing in India* (Calcutta: Longmans Green & Co., 1930), 158–69.

43 Roland Braddell, "Public Health and Town Improvement," *ST*, 5 September 1923.

44 Singapore Housing Commission, *Proceedings and Report of the Commission Appointed to Inquire into the Cause of the Present Housing Difficulties in Singapore and the Steps Which Should Be Taken to Remedy Such Difficulties*, vol. 1 (Singapore: Government Printing Office, 1918).

45 E. P. Richards, "Appendix H, Improvement Trust for Singapore: Report by Deputy Chairman, May to December 1920," in *ARSM 1920* (Singapore: The Straits Times Press, 1921), 125–27.

46 Robert K. Home, *Of Planting and Planning: The Making of British Colonial Cities* (London: Spon, 1997), 81.

47 H. V. Lanchester, "Calcutta Improvement Trust: Précis of Mr. E. P. Richards' Report on the City of Calcutta, Part I," *TPR* 5, no. 2 (1914); H. V. Lanchester, "Calcutta Improvement Trust: Précis of Mr. E. P. Richards' Report on the City of Calcutta, Part II," *TPR* 5, no. 3 (1914); H. V. Lanchester, "Notes on the Calcutta Report of Mr E. P. Richards, Summarised in Nos. 2 and 3 of Vol. V," *TPR* 6, no. 1 (1915).

48 Patrick Abercrombie, "Town Planning Literature: A Brief Summary of Its Present Extent," *TPR*, no. 2 (1915): 93.

49 E. P. Richards, "Appendix E, Improvement Trust for Singapore: Report for 1921 by Deputy Chairman," in *ARSM 1921* (Singapore: The Straits Times Press, 1922), 101.

50 There were different accounts of why Richards resigned. One noted that he was in the bad books of the president of the municipal commissioners. See Han Hoe Tan, "A Study of the Singapore Slum Problem, 1907–41: With Special Reference to the Singapore Improvement Trust" (Unpublished Academic Exercise, University of Malaya, 1959). Another noted that Richards was "[l]ike all planning pioneers... regarded as an unrealistic dreamer and ... gave up the unequal struggle." J. M. Fraser cited in Home, *Of Planting and Planning*, 84.

51 See, for example, Joyce, *The Rule of Freedom*; Bruno Latour, *Science in Action: How to Follow Scientists and Engineers through Society* (Cambridge, MA: Harvard University Press, 1987).

52 Kidambi, "Planning, the Information Order, and the Bombay Census of 1901," 117.

53 Richard Harris and Robert Lewis, "Introduction," *PP* 28, no. 1: 113–14. See also Richard Harris and Robert Lewis, "A Happy Confluence of Planning and Statistics: Bombay and Calcutta in the 1901 Census," *PP* 28, no. 1 (2013).
54 Richards, "Appendix H," 126.
55 Ibid.
56 W. H. Collyer, "Appendix B, Improvement Trust for Singapore: Report for 1924 by Deputy Chairman," in *ARSM 1924* (Singapore: The Straits Times Press, 1925), 1–12; W. H. Collyer, "Appendix B, Singapore Improvement Trust," in *ARSM 1925* (Singapore: The Straits Times Press, 1926), 1–35.
57 The 1918 Report describes the data from the colonial decennial censuses as "estimating in a very high form." Singapore Housing Commission, *Report of the Commission on Housing Difficulties*, 1, A3.
58 Collyer, "Appendix B," 28.
59 Ibid., 3.
60 See the ordinance "Town Planning in Malaya" in PRO CO273/539/1, *Town Planning in Malaya*.
61 "Singapore's Housing Problem: Mr. W. H. Collyer's Lecture," *ST*, 12 July 1930.
62 "Singapore Impresses Health Expert," *ST*, 6 March 1934.
63 J. M. Fraser, *The Work of the Singapore Improvement Trust 1927–1947* (Singapore: Singapore Improvement Trust, 1948), 4.
64 *Report of the Housing Committee Singapore, 1947* (Singapore: Government Printing Office, 1947), 48.
65 Fraser, *The Work of the Singapore Improvement Trust 1927–1947*, 6.
66 See, for example, the Health Officer's reports in NAS HDB1079 SIT29/8/27, *Victoria Street Nos. 256, 258, 260, 262 & 264*.
67 "Test Case against Singapore Improvement Trust Continues," *ST*, 24 January 1935.
68 "Vested Interests," *ST*, 7 August 1935; "Worthless Houses," *ST*, 6 August 1935.
69 Tan, "A Study of the Singapore Slum Problem, 1907–41," 35–36.
70 "Slum Clearance Is 'a Big Issue'," *ST*, 31 August 1935.
71 "Multum in Parvo," *SFPMA*, 18 April 1935.
72 "Governor's Searching Survey of Slum Clearance," *SFPMA*, 18 June 1935.
73 "Clearing Singapore Slums: Report on Home Policy," *ST*, 29 April 1936.
74 "Rehousing Slum Tenants," *ST*, 18 May 1936.
75 "Eastern Slums and Western Cities," *ST*, 4 May 1936.
76 NAS HDB1061 SIT70/41, *Weisburg Building Policy Report*, 3.
77 Ibid., 6.
78 "A Review of Municipal Activities," *ST*, 13 January 1925.
79 "Housing Problems: What the Government Is Doing," *SFPMA*, 2 December 1920.
80 "Houses for the Poor," *SFPMA*, 25 January 1922.
81 "Town Planning: For Singapore and Penang, Barrack Tenements, Part III," *SFPMA*, 10 May 1923.
82 This view was also shared by Dr. P. S. Hunter, the municipal health officer. "Singapore's Chinatown: Overcrowding Evil Still Unsolved," *ST*, 23 August 1928.
83 See for another example of planning orthodoxy, Partho Datta, "How Modern Planning Came to Calcutta," *PP* 28, no. 1 (2013): 141.
84 "Housing in Malaya: Singapore Architect Interviewed," *SFPMA*, 21 August 1929.
85 "Houses for the Poor."
86 "Tackling Singapore Congestion," *SFPMA*, 16 July 1930.
87 "Singapore's Housing Problem."
88 For the Victorian origin of such an argument, see Robin Evans, "Rookeries and Moral Dwellings: English Housing Reform and the Moralities of Private Space," in *Translations from Drawing to Building and Other Essays* (London: Architectural Association, 1997).

89 This was a point repeatedly raised in many reviews of prewar SIT housing; it was not adequately addressed until the postwar housing reform. See, for example, "Housing Position Has Reached a Dangerous Point," *ST*, 6 November 1937; "Just Another Report?," *ST*, 18 August 1948.
90 Fraser, *The Work of the Singapore Improvement Trust 1927–1947*, 10.
91 "A Healthier Singapore," *The Malayan Architect* 5, no. 5 (1933): 105; "Slum Clearance in Singapore," *ST*, 29 March 1930.
92 "Another Big Step Forward in Slum Clearance Scheme," *ST*, 2 July 1937.
93 Home, *Of Planting and Planning*, 113.
94 Collyer, "Appendix B."; NAS HDB1003 SIT148/25, *Housing Scheme at Henderson Road*.
95 "Bad Housing and Disease," *ST*, 4 October 1932; NAS HDB1079 SIT582/25, *Improvement Trust Housing Off Lavender Street*.
96 NAS HDB1080 SIT28/26, *Amended Layout of Lavender Street Housing Scheme*.
97 "Trust to Build Detached Two-Storey Houses," *ST*, 13 November 1940.
98 Collyer, "Appendix B," 23.
99 "Tiong Bahru Housing Plan," *ST*, 20 April 1935.
100 NAS HDB1080 SIT744/50, *History and Development of Tiong Bahru Estate*.
101 NAS HDB1079 SIT242/35, *Steel Windows for Tiong Bahru*.
102 "Bomb-Proof Shelters for New Blocks of Flats," *ST*, 28 June 1939; "Tiong Bahru Flats Will House 1000 by End of 1938," *ST*, 13 October 1937.
103 James M. Fraser and Lincoln Page, "Singapore Improvement Trust, 1950 Programme: Two Blocks of Flats and Shops in Tiong Bahru Road, Singapore," *QJIAM* 1, no. 2 (1951).
104 Matthew Gandy, "Planning, Anti-Planning and the Infrastructure Crisis Facing Metropolitan Lagos," *Urban Studies* 43 (2006); Colin McFarlane, "Governing the Contaminated City: Infrastructure and Sanitation in Colonial and Post-Colonial Bombay," *International Journal of Urban and Regional Research* 32, no. 2 (2008); Vijay Prashad, "The Technology of Sanitation in Colonial Delhi," *Modern Asian Studies* 35, no. 1 (2001).
105 "A Beneficial Epidemic," *Eastern Daily Mail and Straits Morning Advertiser*, 3 May 1906.
106 "Editorial," *ST*, 4 July 1907.
107 "Colony Cavalcade: Another Chinatown Tour – the Brighter Side from the Back-Yard – Lanes in Human Antheaps," *ST*, 24 May 1936.
108 "Another Big Step Forward in Slum Clearance Scheme."; "From Hovels to Modern Housing in Singapore," *ST*, 3 July 1937.
109 Swati Chattopadhyay, "Blurring Boundaries: The Limits of 'White Town' in Colonial Calcutta," *JSAH* 59, no. 2 (2000); William Glover, *Making Lahore Modern: Constructing and Imagining a Colonial City* (Minneapolis: University of Minnesota Press, 2008).
110 Anthony D. King, *Colonial Urban Development: Culture, Social Power, and Environment* (London: Routledge & Kegan Paul, 1976).

Part II
Research and Education

Chapter 5: Constructing a Technoscientific Network

Building Science Research, "Rendering Technical" and the Power-knowledge of Decolonization

In Part I of the book, we have explored the histories of four building types in the genealogy of tropical architecture from the eighteenth to the mid-twentieth centuries. These histories took place before the institutionalization of tropical architecture in the mid-twentieth century. In the second part of the book, we continue chronologically from where we left off in the 1940s and explore the histories of tropical architecture in the mid-twentieth century. As we are dealing with tropical architecture during and after its institutionalization in this part, we are no longer attending to relatively esoteric colonial knowledges and practices of building in the tropics. Instead we are encountering tropical architecture from a period that has been fairly extensively covered by a body of new scholarship. Emerging in the past decade or so, this body of scholarship goes beyond the established scholarship on Brazilian tropical architecture and Le Corbusier's work in India (Figure 5.1) to shed new light on previously unknown or little-known buildings and architects associated with modern tropical architecture.[1]

gure 5.1
ɔwer of Shadow with the igh Court Building in the ɜckground, Chandigarh. ɔth were designed by ɜ Corbusier. Author's ɿotograph.

One of the most fascinating aspects of this new scholarship is its departure – to various extents and different degrees of success – from what Greig Crysler calls "life-and-work" narrative genre of traditional architectural historiography.[2] This new scholarship situates tropical architecture in the complex social, cultural and political contexts of decolonization, international development regimes and narratives of nationalist modernization in the mid-twentieth century. Drawing on postcolonial and other interdisciplinary theories, the best of this scholarship provides grounded perspectives that interrogate the binary structure of colonist and colonized, center and periphery, and tradition and modernity to show the transcultural subjectivities, hybrid knowledge and contradictory social relations involved in the production of tropical architecture. Some of this scholarship also goes beyond the center–periphery diffusionist narrative to examine the complex networks in which the agents, knowledge and objects of tropical architecture circulated between the different geographic localities. Not only do the networks that this scholarship uncovers interrogate the old metropole–colony dichotomy, they also question the validity of the east–west bipolarity assumed in the cold war politics of the mid-twentieth century.[3]

I see this and the next chapter as part of the broader scholarship in expanding our historical knowledge of modern tropical architecture and also the revision of the underlying historiographical and theoretical frameworks. I share some of this new scholarship's interest in examining the work of what Łukasz Stanek calls "aggregate actors" – lesser known architects or even non-architects responsible for the production of the built environment working in large institutions like governmental departments and development agencies – and in mapping and understanding the complex networks in which actors, knowledge and objects of modern tropical architecture circulated.[4] But given that the genealogy of this book is primarily concerned with subjugated knowledges and their power configurations, the two chapters in this part will explore specific dimensions of modern tropical architecture that even this new scholarship has thus far overlooked – the technoscientific aspects. To do that, the approach I take in Part II will differ significantly from that taken in Part I. Instead of focusing on building types, this and the next chapter explore two key institutions and their production of technoscientific knowledge that undergirded modern tropical architecture.

THE MISSING TECHNOSCIENTIFIC DIMENSIONS

The mid-twentieth century witnessed the establishment of numerous building research stations that focused on tropical building problems. Within the British Commonwealth, building research stations were first established in the British Dominions – the National Building Research Institute in Pretoria, South Africa in 1942, and the Commonwealth Experimental Building Station in Chatswood, Australia in 1944.[5] That was followed by the founding of the Central Building Research Station in Roorkee, India in 1947 after India's independence.[6] The West African Building Research Institute was set up in Accra, Gold Coast in 1952, four years after a report on its proposed structure and scope was finalized and approved (Figure 5.2).[7] Similar proposals to establish regional building research stations in British West Indies and Malaya in 1948 were, however, not realized due to the lack of funds.[8] The setting up of building research establishments was not a phenomenon confined to the British Commonwealth. The French have their own Centre Scientifique et Technique du Bâtiment, which was set up in early 1948 at the request of the Ministry of Reconstruction and Town Planning to carry out building research and advise the French colonial governments.[9] In the first edition of their seminal book *Tropical Architecture in the Humid Zone* (1956), Maxwell Fry and Jane Drew provide a list of "principal building research stations that deal with the problems of building in the tropics."[10] Besides the aforementioned building research stations in the British Commonwealth, they also list the Building Research Station, Israel Institute of Technology, Haifa, the Building Research Advisory Board, Washington D.C., and the Inter-American Housing Centre (Centro Interamericano de Vivenda) at Bogota, Colombia. The formation of building research stations appears to be a fairly widespread, if not global, tendency in the mid-twentieth century.

Indeed, in a 1950 report on housing in the tropics, the United Nation's Department of Social Affairs affirms this trend, noting the "[g]rowing emphasis on scientific research and experimentation aimed at improving building methods and design." In the same report, it observes that, as far as tropical buildings were concerned, this international emphasis was a new one as "[u]ntil recently, there has been little co-ordinated scientific research into the design of suitable buildings for tropical climates."[11] (Figure 5.3) When the UN Tropical Housing Mission was dispatched to South and Southeast Asia between November 1950 and January

gure 5.2
uilding research carried
ut at a station in Kumasi,
old Coast in 1944,
efore the West African
uilding Research Station
as formally established.
eprinted, by permission,
om the NAUK.

1951, the experts in the mission – Jacob Crane, Jacobus Thijsse, Robert Gardner-Medwin and Antonio Kayanan – found

> a great amount of research, experimentation and small-scale demonstration going on in South and South-East Asia. In India alone there are a dozen of research establishments and literally hundreds of experiments and demonstrations devoted wholly or in some part to the problems of housing and community development … In Indonesia, several laboratories and field trials are developing new and very promising materials and methods.[12]

Their report suggests that, besides the principal building research stations identified earlier, there were many other establishments in the tropics conducting research on problems of building in the tropics (Figure 5.4). The centrality of the technoscientific research in modern tropical architecture is also evident in the numerous technical conferences and specialist meetings that were held to explore the challenges of building in the tropics during the 1950s. Besides the well-known "Conference on Tropical Architecture" held at University College London in 1953,

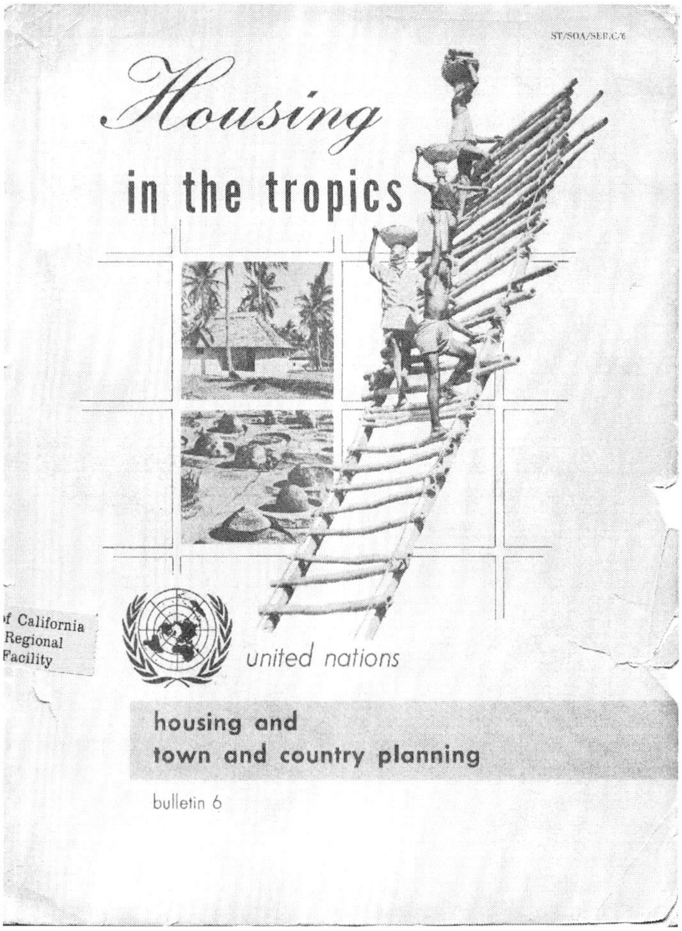

Figure 5.3
Cover of a special issue of United Nations' *Housing and Town and Country Planning* published on "Housing in the tropics." Reprinted, by permission, from the UN.

Figure 5.4
Tropical housing mission – Jacob Crane (fifth person from left), Jacobus Thijsse (sixth person from left), Robert Gardner-Medwin (third person from right) and Antonio Kayanan (third person from left) – visiting a housing project in India. Reprinted with the kind permission of the University of Liverpool Library.

there were the 1951 informal meeting preceding the Building Research Congress on building problems in the hot climates, the 1952 UNESCO conference on "Scientific Principles and their Application in Tropical Building Design and Construction" held at New Delhi, and the 1957 Symposium on "Design for Tropical Living" held at Durban.[13] On top of conferences, the many technical textbooks and manuals on tropical architecture published in the 1950s and 1960s further reinforced the technoscientific nature of modern tropical architecture.[14]

An important precedent for these research stations was the Building Research Station (BRS), which was first established in 1921. BRS was regarded as the model for state-funded building research that became replicated not only in the Commonwealth but throughout the world from the mid-twentieth century onward.[15] The South Africans, Australians and Indians all consulted the general organization and scope of research at BRS before establishing their respective research stations.[16] The West African Building Research Institute was likewise based on a proposal written by two staff members of the BRS in 1947.[17] Mark Swenarton went as far as to argue that the BRS pioneered a systematic approach to technoscientific research on building problems "even if it did not actually invent building science as a discipline."[18] BRS was also singled out by the UN Department of Social Affairs in 1950 for having "done particularly outstanding work, with regard to the British Commonwealth, in the development of experimental techniques and the dissemination of its findings" for building in the tropics.[19] BRS was, however, originally established to deal with housing and other building problems in Britain. It was only in 1948, when a Colonial Liaison Unit (CLU) was established with the appointment of George A. Atkinson as the Building Liaison

Officer that it started to address building problems in the tropics and became intimately connected to technoscientific research of modern tropical architecture. The CLU was later expanded and renamed Tropical Building Division (TBD), clearly signaling its research focus.

The history of technoscience in architecture has been a much-neglected area. Although the history of the BRS has received some attention, including a few official accounts, none of these historical accounts of BRS dedicate much, if any, space to the CLU or TBD.[20] This chapter seeks to rectify this omission by examining the short history of the CLU and TBD from the 1940s to the 1960s. This chapter shows that the CLU and TBD, through their organization, coordination and dissemination of technoscientific research, were central to the production of modern tropical architecture in the mid-twentieth century. This chapter hopes to add to the scholarship on modern tropical architecture in the mid-twentieth century by examining how architectural technoscience was shaped by, as well as shaped, the complex socio-political configurations at the end of the British Empire.

By connecting technoscience with socio-political configurations, I am subscribing to the well-rehearsed argument in Science and Technology Studies that science and technology are social constructions.[21] I do not mean that in the epistemologically relativist sense, but in the sense that science and technology are what Donna Haraway calls "situated knowledge," i.e. what is assumed to be universally true and objective scientific knowledge is necessarily local, mediated, situated and partial to begin with.[22] In other words, the production of technoscientific knowledge could never be understood in isolation from the socio-politico-cultural context. Recent scholarship on (post)colonial technoscience has argued that the significance of socio-politico-cultural context is even more accentuated in the production of colonial technoscience. In that context, the asymmetrical development in scientific knowledge and technological power between the colonist and the colonized was overlaid with similarly lopsided socio-politico-cultural power relations in colonial societies.[23] In this chapter, I deploy Actor Network Theory (ANT), as put forth by Bruno Latour and others, as a theoretical framework to understand such a moderate form of social constructivism. ANT does not privilege the social in understanding how science and technology are constructed. Its emphasis is on the heterogeneous ensemble that includes both the social and the non-social forces, the human and the non-human actants. Furthermore, it also provides a way to account for how specific technological infrastructure of instruments, tools and manuals are deployed alongside institutions and personnel to facilitate the production of technoscientific facts.

THE COLONIAL RESEARCH MODEL

The Tropical Division of BRS had its origin in the recommendations put forward in a report by the Colonial Housing Research Group in 1945.[24] The Group was formed around 1944 to advise the Colonial Office on the organization of housing research in the colonies.[25] It was chaired by I. G. Evans, the acting director of BRS, and it involved key colonial housing experts such as Professor D. B. Blacklock of the Liverpool School of Tropical Medicine who authored a book on the "empire problem" of housing in the early 1930s[26] and Major Granville St. John Orde Browne, the labor advisor to the Colonial Office and an expert on colonial labor issues.[27] The Group convened several meetings and interviewed British officials who were, in various capacities, involved in colonial housing. They included Frank Stockdale, then Comptroller for Development and Welfare in the West Indies, Jane Drew, then Assistant Town Planning Advisor in Nigeria, and various officials from the Colonial services such as Public Works Department and Forestry Services.

In their report, the Group recommended making a coordinated effort in housing research to deal with the immense housing problems in the colonies. Valuable work on housing research was being carried out in many of the colonies, they noted, but those efforts were dispersed and uncoordinated. The knowledge gained from these efforts in a colony was thus not available to those in other colonies, leading to the inefficient and uneconomical duplication of work. To deal with this problem, the Group made two recommendations – the establishment of a center, which the Group called the Colonial Housing Bureau, for the collection and dissemination of information concerning colonial housing research in the metropole, and the setting up of regional research establishments in the colonies. The center in the metropole was to be a depository in which information such as "type plans, reports on various materials and on the performance, cost and suitability from various points of view of various designs might be accumulated and be available for consultation." The center would also be disseminating the knowledge accumulated to the various colonial departments through the publication of periodical digests. A Colonial Liaison Officer was subsequently appointed by the Colonial Secretary to take charge of this metropolitan center, i.e. the CLU. Besides establishing the metropolitan center, the Group also recommended the setting up of four regional research centers in the periphery, with the West Indies, East Africa, West Africa and Malaya being mentioned as the probable locations.[28]

It is striking that similar ideas of organizing building research were arrived at by others, quite separately, at around the same time. For example, in his review of *Report on Housing in the West Indies* (1945), Anthony M. Chitty suggests that a great deal of building research has been carried out in Britain and the knowledge acquired has been successfully applied in field conditions.[29] He then argues that the expertise and experience acquired could be applied to address housing problems in the West Indies and other colonies. Chitty ends the review by recommending that

> a Planning and Housing Bureau be set up at once at the Colonial Office to collect, correlate and disseminate technical information on the problems and their solution; to implement the recommendations of the mission on exchange of personnel and ideas and to achieve a really close liaison between technicians and administrators at home and in the Colonies.[30]

Just as Chitty's review was published, John MacPherson, the comptroller of Development and Welfare in the West Indies, proposed having a building research officer appointed to coordinate and advise building research activities in the West Indies. The duties of the proposed building research officer included those of executing a research program "aimed at immediate economy in building projects," serving as a liaison officer between the different colonies in the West Indies "collating existing information, co-ordinating research activities and circulating useful information;" and also maintaining contact with other research organizations, particularly the BRS.[31] The simultaneity of these proposals suggests that the Group's recommendations should not be seen as an isolated case. They reflected broader ideologies of that historical moment which I contextualize below.

First of all, these recommendations spelt the first time that a major coordinated effort matched by a large sum of funding had been made by the Colonial Office to deal with the much-neglected problem of colonial housing. Of course there had been earlier efforts that addressed the colonial housing problems. For example, in the early twentieth century, various initiatives were undertaken by the municipal and colonial governments in different parts of the British Empire to improve housing conditions for certain segments of the "native" population through Improvement Trusts, as we saw in Chapter 4. However, these earlier efforts were smaller scale local initiatives at the municipality level which tended to be underfunded and/or were not backed by strong political will. The new concerted effort taken to address the colonial housing problem prompted a senior staff member of the Colonial Office to remark in 1947 that: "Colonial Housing and Building, hitherto a Colonial Office Cinderella, has suddenly come very much on the tapis here."[32] This unprecedented attention given to the colonial housing problem was, however, not limited to the British. It was part of what a 1950 UN report describes as, "a period of greater housing consciousness" that sprung up only in the 1940s, when there was broad international recognition of the tropical housing problem and concerted efforts taken to address it.[33]

Alongside the efforts of the Colonial Housing Group, other housing initiatives, such as the appointment of Professor William Graham Holford as the Honorary Town Planning Advisor to the Secretary of State for the Colonies and the setting up of a Housing Advisory Panel, were also made in the 1940s. The position on housing taken by the Colonial Housing Research Group that "general economic development must be pursued concurrently with improved housing" reflects the official view, following the passing of the Colonial Development and Welfare Act (CDWA) in 1940.[34] The equal emphases on both economic development and the welfare of the "natives," through making provision in areas such as health, education, and housing, were seen by the British officials as a disavowal of any intention to merely exploit the colonies more effectively.[35] This emphasis on welfare and its implementation through comprehensive provision set the CDWA apart from earlier development schemes. Previously, development priorities had been unambiguously economic in focus although the British administrators did pay lip service towards their mandate of taking care of the welfare of the "natives" and "civilizing" them as a way of legitimizing colonial rule.[36] But the new post-1940 concern for the welfare of "natives" did not merely arise from the "benevolence" of the British imperial government. Rather, welfare was seen as an antidote to the "disorder" in many colonial territories. After all, the CDWA was formulated primarily to deal with what the British called "disturbances" – both labor unrests and anti-colonial nationalist movements – in colonies such as Northern Rhodesia, Mauritius, West Africa and, especially, the West Indies.[37]

Central to this shift in colonial development policy was the report of the West Indian Royal Commission. It was submitted in 1939 but its findings were so critical of colonial policies that its publication was delayed until 1945. Among other criticisms of the inadequacies of social services and welfare provisions in the report were criticisms of the housing conditions. The Commission noted that in the West Indies, "[h]ousing is generally deplorable, and sanitation primitive in the extreme."[38] Frank Stockdale, the Comptroller for Development and Welfare in the West Indies, later stressed that "[h]ousing ranks as one of the largest and most pressing problems of the West Indies." [39] Thus, some of the earliest large scale colonial housing initiatives, including research, were undertaken in the West Indies in the early 1940s under Stockdale and his architecture and town planning team that included Robert Gardner-Medwin, Leo de Syllas, Gordon Cullen and Joan Burnett.[40]

Second, the recommendations made by the Colonial Housing Group were shaped by prior models of colonial scientific research. This is perhaps not unexpected as the Group consisted of members from the Colonial Office, the Crown Agents, and also experts from organizations that had previously been engaged in colonial research, such as the Liverpool School of Tropical Medicine, Imperial Institute, and Department of Science and Industrial Research (DSIR).[41] Following the practice adopted for the Imperial Agricultural Bureau, the proposed Colonial Housing Bureau was to be attached to an existing metropolitan institution working on similar problems. In this case, the Bureau was to be attached to BRS, which, as mentioned earlier, was first established in 1921 as part of the DSIR to carry out scientific research on building materials and construction methods in order to address post-World War I housing shortages.[42] The regional research establishments in the colonies were also to be organized on the metropolitan model.

Methodologically, the Group proposed that colonial housing research follows that of colonial nutrition. Michael Worboys has noted that British colonial nutrition research in Africa followed the technical problem-solving approach in which the problem of undernourishment was isolated from the larger socio-economic conditions of poverty and turned into a specialized medical problem that required professionalized expertise to solve.[43] As a result, the prescribed solution for the colonial nutrition problem overlooked the larger structural conditions that caused poverty and undernourishment in the first place.[44] In a not dissimilar manner, the Group proposed that housing research be compartmentalized into different spheres of specializations and the colonial housing bureau should concentrate on the "study of the more physical and material aspects." This was despite the Group's recognition that "[h]ousing research … is not a mere matter of materials and construction" and "without a broad medico-sociologico-economic background of knowledge, house design and the planning of housing schemes are bound to suffer." [45]

Even though the colonial model of research was derived from the metropolitan model, there was a major difference between them. It has been noted in the case of tropical medicine that there was a division of labor between the specialist research work in the metropolitan institutions to discover the causes of tropical diseases and the general practitioners in the colonies treating the diseases.[46] A similar hierarchical division of labor was also assumed between the center and the periphery in the proposed organization of building research institutions.[47] It was stated in the Group's report that the primary roles of the regional centers would be to "act as local centres of information, and to carry out those investigations which must necessarily be done on the spot." In contrast, "[c]ertain other investigations of a specialist character or of a more long-term or general nature might well be undertaken in [Britain]" at the metropolitan institutions such as the BRS and the Imperial Institute.[48] This center–periphery division of labor in scientific research corresponded to the prevailing view of the center–periphery economic relations, in which tropical colonies in the periphery produced raw materials for the industrial production in the temperate metropole.[49] Such a welding of the peripheral tropical production to the metropolitan temperate industrialization means that the tropical economy was caught up in a relationship of dependency with the temperate economy – not only subjected to their economic exploitation and vulnerable to the fluctuations of their economic cycles, but also perpetually relying on their capital and expertise.

Finally, underlying the Group's recommendation is a fundamental faith in the transformative power of science and technology, especially in terms of how the application of technoscientific knowledge would enable socio-economic development and provide for welfare. Recent scholarship in social studies of science, especially in relation to colonial technoscience, has argued that scientific research has never been a disinterested pursuit for its own sake.[50] Instead, colonial technoscience has been understood as an instrument of economic development; to further the exploitation of natural resources by increasing the productive capacity of soil and identifying the properties and the potential commercial uses of natural resources. State-sponsored colonial scientific research was first initiated in a systematic manner in the late nineteenth century after Joseph Chamberlain became the Colonial Secretary in 1895. As we saw earlier in Chapter 4, Chamberlain's years as Colonial Secretary marked the beginning of the shift from the *laissez-faire* approach towards colonial economies in the Victorian era to a more systematic approach of economic planning and development that eventually contributed to the passing of the CDWA. Other than providing loans and grants to the colonies for infrastructural projects of railway, port and road construction, the Colonial Office under Chamberlain also organized and funded scientific research in tropical medicine and agriculture to alleviate colonial health and agricultural problems. Initiatives related to Chamberlain included the founding of the Liverpool and London Schools of Tropical Medicine, the Imperial Department of Agriculture, and the appointment of Patrick Manson as the medical advisor to the Colonial Office.[51]

Later in the post-World War II years, with more funding from the CDWA and following the recommendations of Lord Hailey's *African Survey* and E. B. Worthington's *Science in Africa*, technoscientific research on British colonial problems was greatly broadened and intensified. Its scope expanded beyond the traditional fields of medicine, agriculture and geology to include, among other areas, social sciences, economics, veterinary, fisheries, road building and, of course, building.[52] There was also a huge increase in the number of scientists and technical experts deployed in the colonies, leading to what some described as a "second colonial occupation." [53] The enormous expansion of technoscientific research in the British colonies was, however, more than the increase in topics of research and the number of researchers. It also led to a technocratic turn in colonial governance, particularly the reliance on scientific approaches to rationalize and plan the development process. Colonial housing research was thus an inextricable part of the broader expansion in British colonial research and the technocratic turn in British colonial governance in the mid-twentieth century. Furthermore, with the beginning of the end of the British Empire, and the shift into a new "world order" as shaped by cold war politics and the division into "developed" and "underdeveloped" countries, development was of course not restricted to the geopolitical confines of the British Empire. Development was internationalized under the aegis of the United States and new development agencies, such as the World Bank, the International Monetary Fund, and the various United Nations development organizations.[54] The faith in science and technology of this new development regime was even greater than before. This was exemplified in United States president Henry Truman's Point Four Program in which he promised that the developed countries, as led by the United States, would use their technical knowledge to help the underdeveloped countries eradicate poverty and its attendant social problems. That became manifested in the many technical assistance and technology transfer schemes rendered by the developed world to the developing one. The faith in technoscience brought about the further expansion of technoscience into every possible social field, creating new forms of knowledge where there were none, elaborating new objects, concepts and theories, so much so that some critics claimed that these technoscientific development discourses "colonized reality."[55]

NETWORK BUILDING AND THE TROPICAL BUILDING DIVISION

After an almost-three-year search, George Anthony Atkinson was appointed as the Colonial Liaison Officer in June 1948. After Atkinson's appointment, each British colony was to assign a technical officer as his correspondent in order to facilitate his work of collecting, organizing and disseminating information on colonial housing and building. Atkinson was deemed suitable because of his overseas work experience, specifically his wartime experience of working with the Royal Air Force

Airfield Construction Service in West Africa, North Africa and the Middle East.[56] (Figures 5.5 and 5.6) The scope of Atkinson's work extended beyond the original proposed focus on colonial housing to include colonial building in general. That was because, besides social housing, CDWA was also funding other schemes that involved the building of schools, hospitals, and offices. Moreover, there was the "recognition of the difficulty of separating the physical problems of building from those of general housing and planning policies in the overseas territories."[57]

Other than the aforementioned "discovery" of colonial housing problems in the 1940s, another impetus behind the appointment of a Colonial Liaison Officer

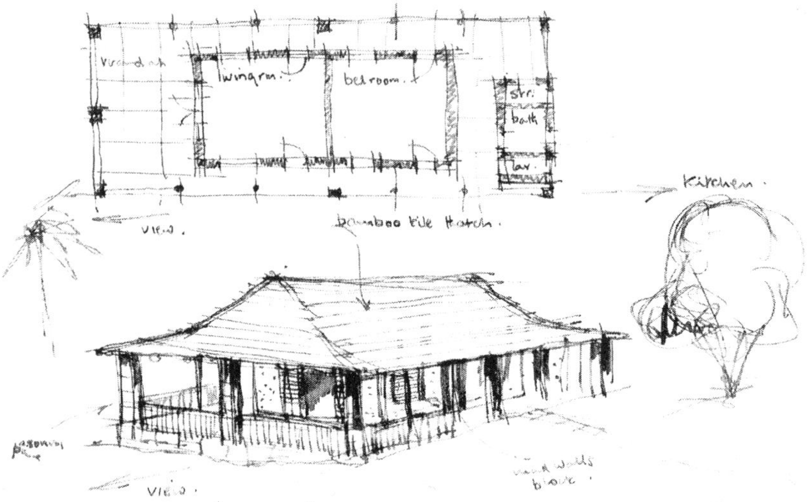

Figure 5.5
The bungalow George Atkinson designed and built for himself at the Waterloo Airfield in Sierra Leone, 1941. Courtesy of George Atkinson.

Figure 5.6
A caricature of George Atkinson drawn in 1991 on the occasion of his testimonial dinner. Courtesy of George Atkinson.

was the need to control the escalating costs of building construction in the colonies, especially those sponsored by CDWA funds. Although the escalating costs of building construction could be partially accounted for by the shortage of building materials in the immediate postwar years, the Colonial Office also attributed the cause to the lack of well-defined minimum building standards, which led "imperceptibly to somewhat extravagant schemes." To reduce costs, the Secretary of State went as far as expressing his anxiety that "colonies should avoid the error of constructing buildings of a more permanent character than circumstances warrant."[58] As a result, one of the earliest tasks for Atkinson was to formulate minimum standards for building in the tropics.[59] Here, standards referred not only to standard plans for building types such as bungalow and barracks, which have been in existence in the British Empire since the nineteenth century, as we saw in Chapters 1 and 2. Standards here should also be understood in relation to building science research. According to Frederick Lea, the director of BRS from 1946 to 1965, scientific methods were first systematically applied to building research from the 1920s with the establishment of the BRS in order to overcome the limitations of a building industry that was largely craft-based. Traditional craft which depended on rules of thumb established through generations of trial and error was deemed inadequate in keeping up with the array of new construction materials that industrialization brought about. Lea argued that "[w]ith new materials tradition could be no guide and its blindfold application to them was a gamble" that supposedly caused many building failures.[60] In contrast to craft, the application of scientific methods to building research sought to achieve *predictability* in performance and *replicability* in different sites and contexts. To accomplish that, not only were new building standards required, it also "infer[red] the dissemination of the knowledge gained, a new outlook and new methods in architectural and technical training and a new conception of the fundamentals of architecture on the part of its practitioners."[61]

Building standards would be useless if they were not adhered to outside the building research stations where they were formulated or if they were not adopted by people besides the building scientists who formulated them. For standards to work, the knowledge gained from building research has to be disseminated, the building industry has to be trained to follow established norms of practices, and new tools and instruments might be required. In other words, building standards have to remain constant when circulating between different sites and situations – such as building research stations, construction sites, architectural studios, and building material factories – and different people – such as building scientists, architects, building contractors, and building material suppliers. In many ways, building standard approximates what Bruno Latour calls immutable mobile, an entity that is mobile, stable, and combinable in that it is an entity that could circulate without distortion, corruption or decay. According to Latour, immutable mobile only remains immutable and combinable *inside* the network.[62] Producing building standards thus entails network building, i.e. bringing the heterogeneous elements of people and things, institutions and practices from different sites, that were needed to sustain the standard, into alignment.[63]

The work undertaken by Atkinson after his appointment as the Colonial Liaison Officer could be understood along the line of network building. One of the first things that Atkinson did after his appointment was to set up a network of correspondents. Colonial governments were asked to nominate representatives to be Atkinson's correspondents to "facilitate the interchange of [building] information" between Atkinson and the colonial territories.[64] Atkinson also traveled extensively to visit the different colonial territories. At these places, he would carry out diverse activities, such as survey and advise on the colonial building developments, lecture and publicize the work undertaken in colonial building research, and encourage the setting up of building research stations.[65] Besides that, Atkinson also publicized the work of colonial building research by publishing extensively in different periodicals linked to the building industry – from metropolitan architectural journals such as *RIBA Journal*, *Architectural Association Journal*, and *Architectural Review*, to trade journals such as *Prefabrication*, to journals on society and politics such as *African Affairs*.

One of Atkinson's main tasks as a Colonial Liaison Officer as spelt out in the Secretary of State's circular was the publication of a periodical digest disseminating the information and knowledge of colonial building gathered at the Unit. The periodical digest was initially called "Colonial Building Circular Letters." It was later formalized and took the form of *Colonial Building Notes* (1950–58), which was renamed *Overseas Building Notes* (1958–84) (Figure 5.7) in 1958 in view of the changing geopolitical landscape of the decolonizing British Empire. These periodicals, which were published at irregular intervals, varying from a month to a few months, consist of various types of articles that covered a wide range of topics. The topics covered could be classified into three main overlapping areas – information on exemplary building and planning schemes in the tropics; building construction materials and building methods for the tropics; and climatic design, especially in terms of sun-shading, natural ventilation and thermal comfort. By 1984, when *Overseas Building Notes* ceased publication, 191 issues had been published and widely circulated. For example, in 1961, the circulation for each issue was about 1,400 copies.[66] The Unit also published five issues of *Tropical Building Studies* from 1960 to 1963, each of which was an in-depth research report on a particular technical aspect of building in the tropics.

Atkinson took on educational initiatives too. From around 1950 to 1961, he helped to organize short courses for overseas officers – architects, civil engineers, and quantity surveyors – in government services[67] (Figure 5.8). Atkinson also taught at the Department of Tropical Architecture at the Architectural Association.[68] In addition, the Unit provided advisory services to the different colonial governments and to special committees working on building projects funded by the CDWA. They included the Inter-University Council for Higher Education in the Colonies and the Colonial University Grants Advisory Committee, which were building universities in colonies like Gold Coast, Uganda, the West Indies and Nigeria, as we shall see in Chapter 6. The Unit also provided consultancy services to British architects and builders who wished to or were already working in

DEPARTMENT OF SCIENTIFIC AND INDUSTRIAL RESEARCH

COLONIAL BUILDING NOTES

No. 31

July, 1955

A. COMMONWEALTH COUNTRIES WITH WARM CLIMATES: RESEARCH INTO WARM CLIMATE BUILDING PROBLEMS

[The following paper was prepared by the Colonial Liaison Office, Building Research Station. It was originally published in the United Nation's Housing and Town and Country Planning Bulletin No. 8. It reviews building and housing research in the Commonwealth outside the United Kingdom, Canada, Australia and New Zealand. Most of the countries included have warm or tropical climates; the review therefore deals largely with research into warm climate building problems. Organisations which have been established, or are planned to study such problems in India, South Africa and in some of the British Colonial territories, are described. No information, unfortunately, is available on recent development in Ceylon and Pakistan.

The United Nation's Housing Town and Country Plannung Bulletins are prepared by the Housing and Town and Country Planning Section, Department of Social Affairs, United Nations, and are published periodically in English and French editions. Copies can be obtained in the United Kingdom from H.M. Stationery Office, P.O. Box 569, London, S.E.1. They can also be obtained through a number of overseas book-sellers.]

Fig. 1: United Nations Regional Seminar on Housing & Community Improvement, New Delhi, India, 1954. United Nations expert discusses a type of semi-precast roof with representatives from the United Nations, India, Iran, Pakistan, Singapore, Greece and Indonesia.

CONTENTS OF NOTE No. 31

(90857) 1

PREPARED BY THE COLONIAL LIAISON OFFICER, BUILDING RESEARCH STATION, WATFORD, HERTS.

gure 5.7
over of an issue of
olonial Building Notes.

Figure 5.8
Colonial architects and civil engineers taking a course at the Building Research Station. Source: *Colonial Building Notes*, No. 31, July 1955.

the colonial territories. For example, Architects Co-Partnership in Nigeria collaborated with the Unit to make a "strenuous enquiry into the performance of each successive building" it designed.[69]

One of the most important aspects of the Unit's and Atkinson's network building entailed assisting the establishment of regional building research stations in the colonies, as envisioned in the Colonial Housing Group's recommendations, and also maintaining contacts and sharing research findings with these research stations. As discussed earlier, BRS served as the model for the different building research stations in the British Commonwealth and beyond. Besides his connections with the research stations in the British Commonwealth, Atkinson also linked up with other research establishments working on building problems in the tropics, such as the French, Belgian and UN organizations.[70]

Network building was more than gathering and disseminating information through publication, training expertise through educational work, or establishing a technical infrastructure through the building of research stations. According to Latour, network building also entails a series of translations of interest and the enrollment of allies so that more entities (both human actors and non-human actants) participate in the construction of fact, slowly transforming "a claim into a matter of fact." [71] By translation, Latour meant "the interpretation given by fact-builders of their interests and that of the people they enroll" so that associations and alliances can be formed to control the actions of others and make them predictable.[72] Active translation of interest and enrollment of allies is quite apparent in various of Atkinson's writings and published speeches. Atkinson articulated the benefits of building research in different ways, catering specifically to the interests of his targeted audience. In his famous speech to an audience consisting mainly of

British architects at the Architectural Association in April 1953, Atkinson impressed on his audience the abundant building opportunities available in the tropics and the importance of acquiring the appropriate technical expertise of building in the tropics if they wished to seize these opportunities.[73] However, when Atkinson was lecturing in Singapore, he shifted his earlier emphasis on how technical knowledge would privilege the metropolitan architects to show that it would instead benefit the local building scene. He noted that the establishment of a regional building research center in Malaya would mean that "results of research and technical development throughout the World can be applied to Malayan conditions" and "where problems, particular to Malaya can be studied."[74] In another instance, when Atkinson was writing in a trade journal for the building prefabrication industry, he reviewed the existing building techniques and the state of the building industry in the colonies and advised on the opportunities available to the British manufacturers to export their equipment for producing building materials, such as concrete block-making presses, to these places, as we shall see later.[75]

Other than enrolling human actors, Latour also argued that non-human actants are crucial to the construction of facts. By non-human actants, Latour referred to entities such as tools, instruments, or even something as simple as a graph. These tools or instruments might be critical in the conduct of an experiment so that a hypothesis could be proven and the graph might help one visualize particular data and facts. In the case of building science and the work of the CLU of the BRS, instruments such as the heliodon and graphical representations such as the sun path diagram and thermal comfort charts were especially important in the attempt to enroll more architects in the construction of tropical building science. As Henry Cowan, the self-professed first professor in building science, noted, "the average architect is receptive to visual demonstrations, but that he does not respond well to mathematical treatment."[76] The heliodon (Figure 5.9), which was invented by A. F. Dufton and H. E. Beckett of the BRS in 1928, is one such instrument that provides effective visual demonstration.[77] It is a powerful "device for determining the natural lightings of rooms, and the shadows cast on, and by, buildings."[78] It shows the sunlight and shadow cast three-dimensionally by simulating the sun with a light bulb, the earth's surface with an adjustable flat board, and the building with a model. The heliodon was designed to allow it to simulate the sun's position for all latitudes for all days of a year and all the sunlight hours of a day. It is thus a useful design aid that could be used to predict various aspects of the building performance related to sun-shading and sunlight penetration.

Most of the works described above were of course not undertaken by Atkinson alone as the CLU expanded fairly rapidly after his appointment as Colonial Liaison Officer in 1948. In 1951, an assistant architect and an experiment officer were appointed. Later on in 1954, a senior architect and a town planner were added to the Unit. Three years later, a tropical paint research fellow was appointed to specifically investigate the performance of paints suitable for tropical buildings. The Unit applied unsuccessfully for funds in 1956 to expand and carry out research in areas such as building climatology, thermal conditions, natural

Figure 5.9
A researcher placed the model of the Dining Hall at University College, Ibadan, Nigeria (architects: Maxwell Fry and Jane Drew) on the heliodon to study the effectiveness of the sun-shading. Source: Foyle ed. *Conference on Tropical Architecture 1953: A Report of the Proceedings of the Conference Held at University College*, 1953.

ventilation, daylighting, and the use of solar energy in the tropics. In 1959, it made another failed application for funds to study the field conditions of thermal discomfort. In the same year, the Unit was also renamed as TBD, becoming one of the three tropical units in DSIR. The other tropical units were the Tropical Products Institute and the Tropical Unit in Road Research Laboratory.[79] The change in name reflected the change in emphasis from a "colonial" focus on dependent countries and countries in the British Commonwealth to a broader "tropical" coverage that included countries newly independent and even those outside the Commonwealth. In 1960, the unit came under the administration of the Department of Technical Cooperation as it took over the former functions of the CO. In the same year, the division expanded from wholly advisory work to conducting some research work of its own.[80] In 1961, Atkinson was promoted to become the Chief Architect of the BRS succeeding William Allen, who was appointed the Principal of the AA. Wilfred Woodhouse, a senior architect in the Division who had previously served as the Building Research Officer in the West Indies, took over Atkinson's position.[81]

Due to changes in British foreign policy and its administration of development aid as the empire gradually dissolved in the 1960s, the TBD similarly underwent many changes in the 1960s. In 1964, it came under the administration of the Ministry of Overseas Development and the division was renamed as the Overseas Division in 1966.[82] The change in name perhaps signaled the expansion of the division's sole focus on the tropics to include research work in developing countries located outside what is conventionally regarded as the tropics, such as Malta, Nepal and Iran. Although the Overseas Division still engaged in "tropical research" – primarily in African and Caribbean territories – its influence on the production of tropical architecture seemed to have diminished.[83] As I have argued earlier, a great amount of work is involved in building and sustaining a network. "Vigilance and surveillance have to be maintained," or the contingent alignment of heterogeneous "elements will fall out of line and the network will crumble."[84] Despite its subsequent decline, the Overseas Division of BRS and its predecessors nevertheless played an important part in providing the technoscientific foundation for tropical architecture in the British Empire/Commonwealth for about two decades.

At this point, it is perhaps pertinent to ask – what did the network achieve besides enabling the circulation of immutable mobiles? What were the other effects of the network? Spatially, as Latour noted, a network "indicates [that] resources are concentrated in a few places – the knots and the nodes – which are connected with one another – the links and the meshes: these connections transform scattered resources into a net that may seem to extend everywhere."[85] Within the network, events, places and people could be turned into abstract, transportable and combinable information – that is immutable mobiles. This information could then be circulated from one point of the network to another, often from the edges or peripheries of the network to the nodes or centers, facilitating the accumulation of knowledge at these centers. According to Latour, the accumulation of knowledge is also the accumulation of power because it allows a point, or a few points, in the network to become center(s) of calculations which can act on distant places because of its familiarity with things, people and events there. Cycles of accumulating knowledge create and reinforce an asymmetry of power between the centers and the peripheries of the network, thus allowing the centers of calculation to dominate others. Even as such an understanding of the working of the technoscientific network might reinforce the insight of the world system theory on center–periphery relations, this understanding is not based on a dominant capitalist logic. Instead, it is contingent on multifarious sociotechnical processes. Moreover, ANT does not conceive the center as a fixed or static entity. Rather, the center of calculation is seen in a fluid and dynamic manner, dependent on the processes of network building. Just as a center could emerge and become dominant, it could also decline, lose control or be surpassed and replaced by other newly emerging center(s) as long as they could build better and stronger networks.

Historians who have recently used the networked spatial conception to study and analyze the British Empire further contributed to the insights gleaned from ANT. These historians have distinguished themselves and their works from the old writings on the Empire that relied on the binary spatial concept of core and periphery. Surveying these new writings, Alan Lester notes that they sought

> to examine the multiple meanings, projects, material practices, performances and experiences of colonial relations rather than locate their putative root causes … These relations were always stretched in contingent and non-deterministic ways, across space, and they did not necessarily privilege either metropolitan or colonial spaces. They remade both metropolitan and colonial spaces in the act of connecting them.[86]

The emphases were on multiplicity, relationality and contingency of the colonial network conception. Lester argues that the complexity of colonialism was irreducible to a single European colonial project or discourse. There were bound to be tensions and even contradictions between the different projects or discourses of colonialism. Lester stresses that colonial networks were provisional or even ephemeral and he cautions us against seeing the network as a reified or ossified structure. The technoscientific network centered on TBD was indeed a provisional one. TBD's role as a center of calculation in the field of tropical architecture declined in the 1960s, when the British Empire was disintegrating with many of its former colonies gaining independence. The original technoscientific network became much weaker, if not disintegrated, with decolonization. Without further cycles of accumulation of knowledge through the network, TBD could not function as a center. In the next section, I will combine the insights of ANT with those of the networked spatial conception of the British Empire to examine in greater detail TBD's work in climatic design and thermal comfort to illustrate some aspects of the multiplicity, relationality and contingency of the technoscientific network.

(IM)MUTABLE MOBILES AND CLIMATIC DESIGN

One year into his appointment, Atkinson submitted a report to the Colonial Research Council. Besides reporting on the work his unit had done, Atkinson also discusses the type of future building research his unit would be carrying out in the report. Atkinson frames the problems of colonial building as essentially those of building in the tropical climate, which were in turn entwined with that of low level of socio-economic development. In the report, he writes:

> The special features of Colonial life which generally affect buildings in the Colonies are climate and relatively low standards of social and economic development ... They are, most obviously, interdependent. Many aspects of development are due to climate and, because of low standards of development, man is often more dependent on climate.[87]

Atkinson then goes on to identify four main areas of research, including thermal comfort and the design of buildings, on which we will focus.

In the early 1950s, Atkinson published two widely referenced articles in the area of thermal comfort and the design of buildings in the tropics.[88] These were two of the earliest articles on climatic design, an emerging field in the mid-twentieth century.[89] The earlier chapters in this book have shown that climate, especially the hot and humid tropical variant, and its influence on the built environment have featured prominently in British colonial architectural discourses for more than a century prior to the mid-twentieth century. As we have noted, for much of the nineteenth and early twentieth centuries, the prevalence of miasmatic theories of disease transmission and other related environmental discourse meant that much attention was channeled toward developing systematic knowledge on the built environment in order to mitigate the supposedly pernicious effects of tropical climate on white men. The colonial environmental discourse on climate was not simply a neutral scientific knowledge describing natural phenomena; it was entwined with the politics of colonial governance and the related constructions of race and culture.[90]

With the miasmatic theories of disease transmission discredited and replaced by germ theories of disease transmission in the early twentieth century, the hot and humid tropical climate was subsequently no longer deemed as the cause of ill health, although old ideologies and habits persisted. Furthermore, the success of tropical medicine in finding the causes of major tropical illnesses and the expansion of public health programs in many parts of the colonial tropics during the early twentieth century led to a significant reduction in the mortality and morbidity rates of both European and "native" populations in the tropics. Although the socio-medical perception of the tropical environment has changed, the lingering influence of colonial tropicality meant that the hot and humid climate of the tropics continued to be seen in largely negative terms, as the cause of bodily discomfort, which purportedly led to a low level of labor efficiency and contributed to the economic backwardness in the tropics. Thus, in the mid-twentieth century, living in the tropics was no longer a matter of life and death. It was more a matter of thermal comfort.

The emerging field of climatic design in the mid-twentieth century drew on two bodies of technoscientific knowledge – physiology and climatology. At that time, researchers in physiology were already aware that their findings about thermal comfort would necessarily vary, depending on the experimental subjects they surveyed and the contexts in which they carried out the experiments. For example, "natives" and acclimatized subjects in the tropics were found to have higher tolerance for heat and humidity than Europeans in the temperate zone and non-acclimatized subjects in the tropics.[91] Since the researchers working in North America and Britain studied primarily white men in a temperate climate, their findings had to be supplemented by researchers who studied the comfort zones of both Europeans and natives in tropical climates before Atkinson could use them to construct an accurate thermal comfort zone for climatic design in the tropics. Atkinson, however, noted that most of the physiological research on the tropics done prior to 1950 were those of "hot climate physiology" dealing with "extreme conditions when heat exhaustion and collapse are imminent," whereas he was interested in "the less clearly defined problems of comfort over long periods in ordinary tropical, or summer, conditions."[92]

The importance of climatology to climatic design is evident in Atkinson's note "The Role of Meteorology and Climatology in Tropical Building and Housing" written in June 1954 and issued in January of the following year, together with the Colonial Secretary's circular of the same title. They were sent out to the colonies requesting meteorological data that was deemed critical to tropical building and housing. In the note, Atkinson criticizes the existing summaries of meteorological data from the colonies. He regards them as patently inadequate because "the summarised records of the different [climatic] variables do not refer to the same observation hour."[93] As a result, an important indicator of thermal comfort such as effective temperature – which is a combination of air temperature, relative humidity and air movement – could not be determined from these records. Furthermore, Atkinson argues,

> Building design should not be related to average conditions. It should take into account the range of weather likely to be encountered. It is more useful for a designer to have before him summaries of the conditions prevailing with a particular type of weather, and some indication of its frequency, than to have monthly means which, being based on observations of all types of weather, often obscure the essential requirements.[94]

In the note, Atkinson provides a few examples from the colonial territories to illustrate how the averaging of climatic data over a long duration is deceptive as it conceals the fluctuations in climatic data and masks meteorological phenomena such as daily land and sea breezes. In criticizing the existing meteorological data, Atkinson perhaps had in mind the type of meteorological data to which his North American counterparts have access. In the American Institute of Architects' *House Beautiful Climate Control Project*, cited as one of the models of building climatology in his report, comprehensive climatic data were collected, aggregated, analyzed and visualized in a detailed manner. For the project, raw climatic data consisting of hourly readings of wet and dry bulb temperatures and wind velocities at 110 weather bureau stations were recorded on IBM punch cards and analyzed (Figure 5.10).[95]

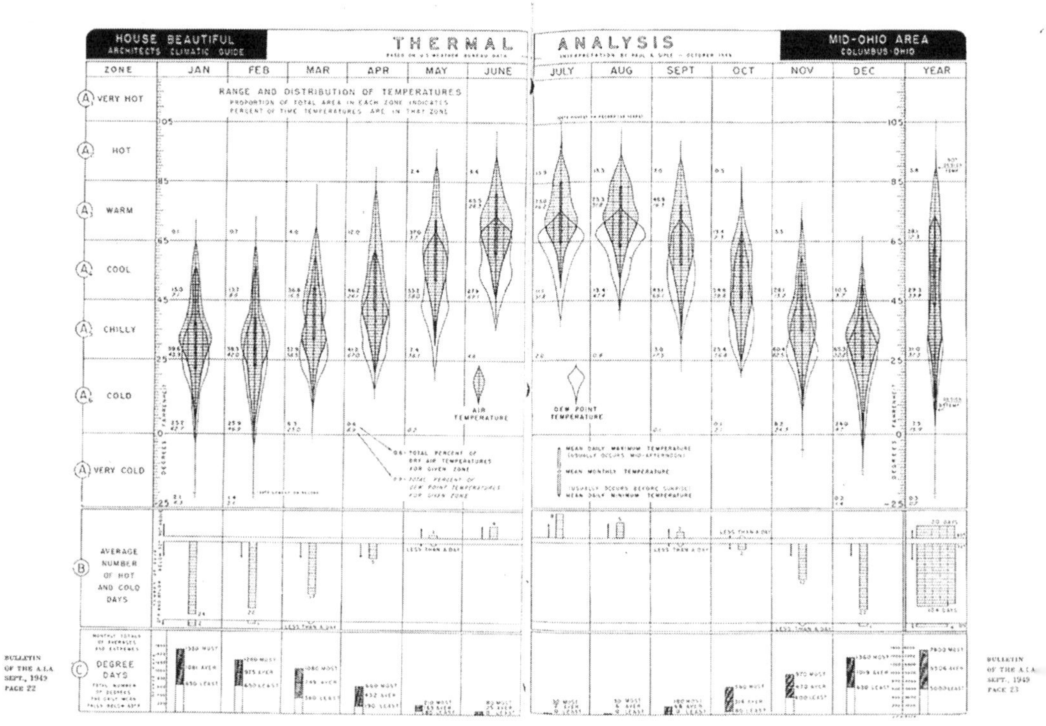

Figure 5.10
"Thermal Analysis" for the Mid-Ohio area in the *House Beautiful Climate Control Project*. Source: American Institute of Architects, *Regional Climate Analyses and Design Data: The House Beautiful Climate Control Project*, 1949.

For the British colonial context, gathering and analyzing comprehensive climatic data of such vast territories and varied geographies was far more difficult, if not impossible. J. K. Page, one of the building scientists working with Atkinson at the CLU, went as far as claiming that the Unit was "handicapped by the lack of climatological information for overseas territories."[96] Page was reacting to the responses to the circular and Atkinson's note. Most of the colonies replied that they did not have the meteorological data Atkinson requested and they had neither "the staff nor the instruments to supply the data required."[97]

Despite the lack of comprehensive climatological data and knowledge about thermal comfort in the tropics, Atkinson was able to provide overviews of the principles of climatic design in the tropics in his two articles. In his 1950 article, he sketches out three basic tropical climates "from the standpoint of building design" – very hot and dry, hot and humid, and cooler upland climate. He then provides three air temperature ranges in relation to thermal comfort for a "lightly-clad" man resting indoors – below 78 degrees Fahrenheit as too cold, between 78 and 84 degrees Fahrenheit as the comfort zone, and above 84 degrees Fahrenheit as too warm. Although Atkinson draws from the latest physiological research and specifically cites C. E. A. Winslow and L. P. Herrington's *Temperature and Human Life* and Thomas Bedford's *Basic Principles of Ventilation and Heating*, there is nothing in these books that suggests these exact air temperature ranges for thermal comfort. In fact Winslow and Herrington noted that there was no agreement on the optimum temperature for comfort because the different studies carried out yielded different findings and they felt that "[t]he diversity of findings is altogether understandable when the complexity of the factors involved is kept in mind."[98] In his book, Bedford likewise notes that the "diversity of opinion as to what constitutes [comfort] ... is sometimes very wide."[99] Winston and Herrington, however, tried to reconcile the conflicting results from various studies by understanding them in relation to the physiological mechanisms of heat exchange. They claimed that a "normally clothed subject" at rest experiences comfort at an air temperature of 78 degrees Fahrenheit.[100] While 78 degrees Fahrenheit was also the lower limit of Atkinson's comfort zone, nothing in both books suggests that thermal comfort is still attainable at 84 degrees Fahrenheit. Not only is it unclear how Atkinson derived the air temperature range for his thermal comfort zone, it is also well established that air temperature on its own is an insufficient indicator of thermal comfort because other environmental conditions, such as relative humidity and air movement, also affect thermal comfort. Despite these uncertainties and insufficiencies, Atkinson's formulation of climatic types and thermal comfort zones allowed him to put forth practical general suggestions for architects to "design for comfort" in the different types of tropical climate.

The 1953 article is a further elaboration of the 1950 article. In it Atkinson provides a more elaborate schema of tropical climate. Instead of three tropical climatic types listed in the 1950 article, Atkinson put forth four tropical climatic types and includes sub-types within the hot and humid, and hot and dry categories. He also organized the climatic types and their characteristics in a table form, making the classification more legible. For each climatic type, Atkinson provides design recommendations that are more detailed than his 1950 article. For example, he notes that providing "free air movement" is the main design consideration for buildings in the hot and humid tropics. He thus recommends orientating the building to the prevailing wind directions, having "one room thick so as to ensure through ventilation" and avoiding "dead air pockets on plan, as well as in section." The model climatically responsive building in the hot and humid tropics should be like the "standard Stevenson screen – 'a well ventilated wooden box with a double top and double-louvred sides, the whole painted white' used by meteorologists to house thermometers for measuring shade temperatures."[101] Not only is this climatic classification more elaborate, and the recommendations more detailed than in his 1953 article, they also take on greater clarity and certainty.

Much of this clarity and certainty can be attributed to the psychometric graph at the beginning of the article (Figure 5.11). In the graph, Atkinson plots the climatic data of three localities – Freetown in Sierra Leone, Kano in Nigeria and Nairobi in Kenya – which represent the three principal tropical climatic types of warm and humid, hot and dry, and upland respectively. Juxtaposed onto the graph is a zone that represents that of the thermal comfort zone. The thermal comfort zone is based on the findings of studies done by the American Society of Heating and Ventilating Engineers on summer conditions in the United States.[102] While Atkinson acknowledges that "in warmer climates, other zones may give a better indication of comfort" and cites researches conducted in tropical Queensland and Malaya that show higher air temperature and relative humidity levels for comfort, he chooses not to incorporate them in his graph.[103] The selective exclusion of

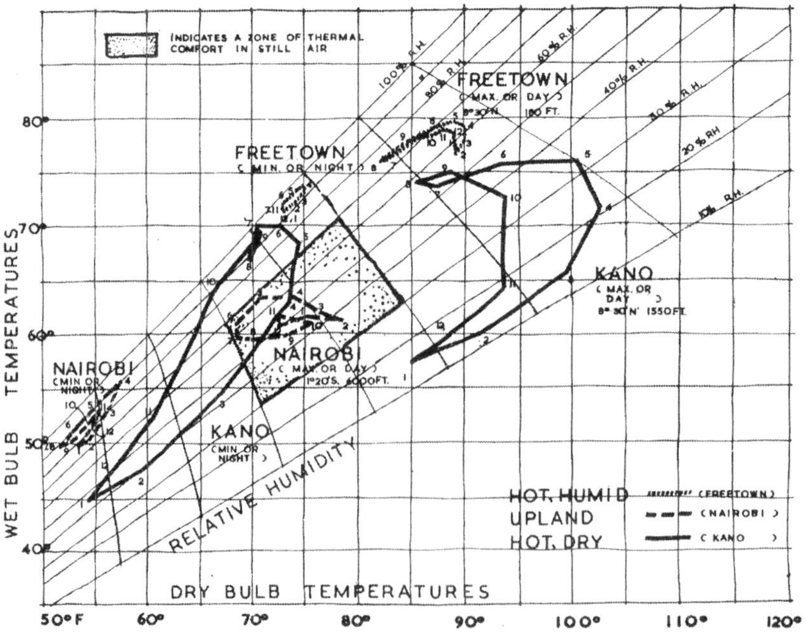

Figure 5.11
Psychometric chart of thermal comfort by George Atkinson. Courtesy of George Atkinson.

certain research findings permits the graph to present greater clarity and certainty in terms of what climatic design could do to help achieve thermal comfort in different types of tropical climate. For example, the graph clearly shows that the mean daytime temperature of Kano, which represents the hot and dry climate, tends to be higher than that within the thermal comfort zone. Thus, Atkinson recommends the use of "heavy-weight (i.e. high thermal capacity) construction ... to give protection from the heat of the day."[104]

On the whole, these overviews of climatic design in Atkinson's articles seem to have achieved a few things. First, the complex tropics become "knowable" through three principal climatic types. Climate was privileged because men and women were deemed primarily as biological entities affected by their physiological mechanism of heat exchange and their sensations of thermal comfort and discomfort. In privileging climate and the physiology of heat exchange, the complex socio-political conditions of the tropics, especially the highly politicized problems regarding anti-colonial struggles, emerging nationalism and problems of development, could be overlooked as part of the technical focus on climate and thermal comfort. Knowing the climate almost stood in for knowledge about the locality through the reduction, simplification and standardization of a complex life-world into a set of climatic parameters. Second, knowing locality through climate might peculiarly mean that socio-politically diverse entities such as Freetown and Singapore could be conveniently grouped together because they both share the characteristics of hot and humid tropical climate. Not only could they be grouped together, but architectural responses to these socially, culturally and politically different sites could also be conceived in a similar manner, primarily in terms of the provision of thermal comfort. Third, by representing different localities according to climatic types and providing recommended architectural responses through immutable mobiles like tables, graphs and diagrams, climatic design gathered distant and foreign places in one place, compressed their realms of reality into a flattened form that allowed them to be presented at once, and facilitated "action at a distance on unfamiliar events, places and people" at the center of calculation.[105]

Action at a distance is manifested in at least two main forms. For British architects based in the metropole working on projects in the tropics, overviews of climatic design at the center of calculation allowed them to produce tropical architecture without even needing to travel to the colonies. In other words, the technoscientific clarity and certainty of climatic design facilitated the export of British architectural expertise to the tropical colonies. Given this, it is no wonder that the special issue of *Architectural Review* focusing on Commonwealth architecture in the tropical Commonwealth featured mainly tropical architecture "*designed in England* by English architects (as in the case of many of those in West Africa) or designed by architects of English origin, largely trained in England or America, who practice locally".[106] The second manifestation of action at a distance was less direct but perhaps more pervasive. Overviews of climatic design provided clear design recommendations that allowed TBD and the Colonial Office to set building standards and establish new design norms that subsequently became known as modern tropical architecture to regulate architectural production in the colonies. The standards and norms of modern tropical architecture included specifications of planning standards, building materials and construction methods. The technoscientific certainty and clarity that climatic design provided were especially important at a time when societies in many tropical territories were in flux, experiencing rapid changes and transformations brought about by modernization, economic development and rural–urban migration. These changes included deskilling and the destruction of traditional building practices.[107] A few commentators have argued that these new design and building norms created a dependency on imported construction materials, components and expertise from the metropole in the tropics (Figure 5.12).[108] Seen in such a manner, climatic

HOPE'S Windows
& sunbreakers
CO-OPERATIVE BANK, ACCRA
Architects: James Cubitt, Scott and Partners
Both east and west elevations of this six-storey building are completely covered by aluminium sunbreakers in galvanized steel frames.
Sunbreakers being unnecessary on north and south elevations, only windows with horizontally sliding casements were supplied.
HENRY HOPE & SONS LTD SMETHWICK, BIRMINGHAM, ENGLAND
Represented in West Africa by
NIGERIA: CRITTALL-HOPE TECHNICAL SERVICE, Private Mail Bag 1085, Burma Road, Apapa
GHANA: THE SWISS AFRICAN TRADING CO, P.O. Box 188, Accra and at Kumasi
SIERRA LEONE: PATERSON ZOCHONIS & CO. LTD, Freetown
HOPE'S Resident Representatives available throughout West Africa

Figure 5.12
An Advertisement for Hope's Aluminium Windows and Sunbreakers. Source: *West African Builder & Architect*, 1961.

design could be understood as a power–knowledge configuration in that the accumulation of climatic knowledge of distant places and physiological knowledge of human comfort under different climatic conditions at the center of calculation was also the accrual of power, specifically the power to act on and influence the architectural production of these places from afar.

CONFLICTING INTERESTS AND THE CONTINGENT CENTER

While the creation of dependency by "action at a distance" was evident in how CLU and TBD provided advisory services to "help U.K. industries exporting building materials and components, air conditioning equipment, etc. to the Colonial Territories," the CLU and TBD had also acted in ways that contradicted this tendency.[109] For example, Atkinson wrote a widely circulated note in 1949 advising colonial governments against importing prefabricated buildings manufactured in Britain. In that note, Atkinson states that prefabricated buildings were not suitable for colonies as they were more expensive than buildings constructed locally in the colonies using locally available materials. He also wrote that "many of the so-called 'tropical' houses being developed by manufacturers in Great Britain are based on plans quite unsuitable for life in hot climates" because they did not make provision for "through ventilation." Furthermore, aluminum was extensively used in the prefabricated buildings because many of the manufacturers in the industry were only established in the postwar period to make use of the "available capacity in aircraft and other surplus war production factories."[110] Owing to its thermal conductivity, aluminum was not a material easy to adapt to tropical conditions. In contrast to Britain where prefabricated building systems had been studied extensively to make sure that they conform to certain minimum technical standards, Atkinson noted that there was inadequate research on "the behavior of buildings" and materials like aluminum in the tropical climates of the colonies.[111] In subsequent years, Atkinson reiterated the view that the tropical colonies should not import prefabricated buildings from Britain, in response to queries from the Jamaican government and after his visit to Africa.[112]

Atkinson, however, was forced to revisit his position on the import of prefabricated buildings in the tropics in 1954. That year the Secretary of State for the Colonies Oliver Lyttleton issued a circular to all British colonies encouraging them to "make greater use of the potential of the U.K. pre-fabricated building industry" in solving the "Colonial building problems." Lyttleton noted that the prefabricated building industry had developed tremendously since 1949, when Atkinson's circular discouraging the import of prefabricated building was issued, and the industry had since been able to produce buildings "suitable for colonial needs at a realistic price."[113] In the circular, Lyttleton asked all colonial governments to consider the use of prefabricated buildings and components for all future building projects. He specifically instructed the colonial governments to furnish him with the details of future projects so that the prefabricated building industry could explore participating in such projects. This circular came about because the

Ministry of Work, which was responsible for promoting the prefabricated building industry, especially the expansion of the export of prefabricated buildings "to aid the national balance of payments," approached the Colonial Office for assistance.[114] The Ministry was concerned with the contraction in Britain's export of prefabricated buildings in 1953, especially after it was projected to grow following four years of expansion in export from £80,000 in 1949 to £7 million in 1952. It was particularly disappointed with the minuscule size of export to the colonies given that many British firms had developed prefabricated buildings targeted at the tropical market. For example, Aluminium Union Limited developed the "Kingstrand" range of prefabricated buildings – a range known for its low price, ease of transport and resistance to atmospheric deterioration – for the underdeveloped tropics and "sub-tropics"[115] (Figure 5.13) and Booth & Co.

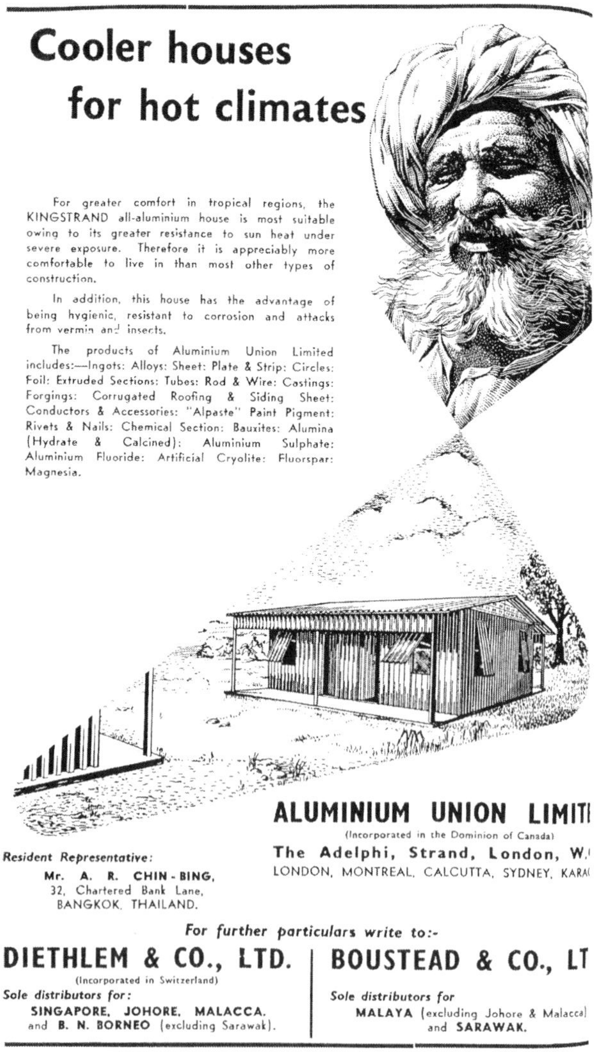

Figure 5.13
An advertisement for the "Kingstrand" range of prefabricated aluminum building that appeared in the *Journal of the Institute of Architects of Malaya* in the early 1950s. Source: *JIAM*.

(England) Ltd. introduced the "Overseer Tropical II" in which "every detail has been designed to suit conditions in hot and humid climates" including "complete natural through ventilation; with additional concealed ceiling fans, well worked-out louvre windows of a proprietary type and folding doors to open the living room on to a verandah."[116]

An article by Atkinson on prefabrication and building in the tropics was attached to Lyttleton's circular. This article unsurprisingly did not mention Atkinson's previous criticisms of prefabricated buildings. Instead, suggestions for manufacturers on how prefabricated houses could be better designed for the tropics, particularly in terms of addressing the climatic conditions and types of housing and schools needed, was provided.[117] Even then, Atkinson cautioned that it was more practical for the tropical colonies to import building components, especially the roof structure, rather than a whole prefabricated building.

Atkinson afterward elaborated on this position in a two-part article for the official journal of the British prefabrication industry. In the later article, he reviews the burgeoning building industry and the rapid modernization in building techniques in the colonies in order to "distinguish those [developments] which are likely to have a permanent influence on building overseas." Atkinson argues that "the simple low-cost house" needed to address the tropical housing problem "will generally have either to be fabricated locally or built conventionally." He implies that the import of fabricated buildings – which tend to be complicated and expensive – to the colonies was only the right practice in "specially favourable circumstances." It was often only used as a temporary stop-gap measure to address shortages when the local building industry did not have the capacity – mainly due to unskilled labor, inadequate facilities and insufficient capital – to meet the demands for modern buildings.[118] Instead of importing prefabricated buildings, Atkinson suggests that the capacity of the local building industry be strengthened. He notes that in many colonies, there were already some plants manufacturing modern building components like concrete blocks, concrete tiles and asbestos cement, which contributed appreciably to the lowering of building costs (Figure 5.14). Atkinson argues that, instead of prefabricated buildings or building components, colonies really needed "a variety of types of plant and materials handling equipment" so that their local building industry could produce more modern buildings more efficiently and economically to address their housing problems.[119] He concludes by recommending that the British industry research and develop such equipment for export to the tropics.

In the same article, Atkinson also discusses "improved earth building" as an example of research and experiment in traditional local building material. He notes that earth construction was a part of local building tradition in many tropical colonies but it suffers from low structural strength and poor durability. To improve the strength and weather resistance of earth construction, experiments with additives such as clay and Portland cement were undertaken successfully, creating cement earth blocks in colonies like Uganda and the Gold Coast. This discussion is really an extension of that in many *Colonial Building Notes* articles that document

Figure 5.14
A 1950s photograph showing female construction workers operating a machine making concrete blocks. Courtesy of the REL.

the numerous experiments with various soil–cement mixtures – such as "landcrete", "swishcrete" and rammed earth – for building in Africa and the West Indies (Figure 5.15). These soil–cement construction methods were cheaper than masonry and concrete construction and they were deemed as suitable for remote localities where labor was comparatively cheap and imported materials were difficult and expensive to obtain.[120] Experimenting with locally available building materials was something CLU had been encouraging and supporting since it was established in 1949. In fact, the development of local materials in the tropics was one of the four foci Atkinson identified for the CLU in 1949.[121]

While the network built by Atkinson and CLU helped turn the metropole into a center of calculation and facilitated action at a distance, especially with regards to the advisory service provided by CLU to British architects who were designing buildings in the tropics, the network was not monolithic. Atkinson's acceptance of the need to export British architectural and building science expertise to the tropics and his reservations on, if not rejection of, the need to export British prefabricated buildings to the tropics reveal diverging tendencies and conflicting interests within the network. In his network-building work of translating interests and enrolling allies, Atkinson himself might have better understood the interests of the tropical colonies and saw that the strengthening of local building capacity was the most economical and sensible way of addressing the colonies' building and development needs. Instead of having the center of calculation dominate other sites in the network by supporting the British prefabrication industry and helping Britain's national balance of payments, Atkinson sought to strengthen the authority and legitimacy of the center of calculation by providing advice that took into

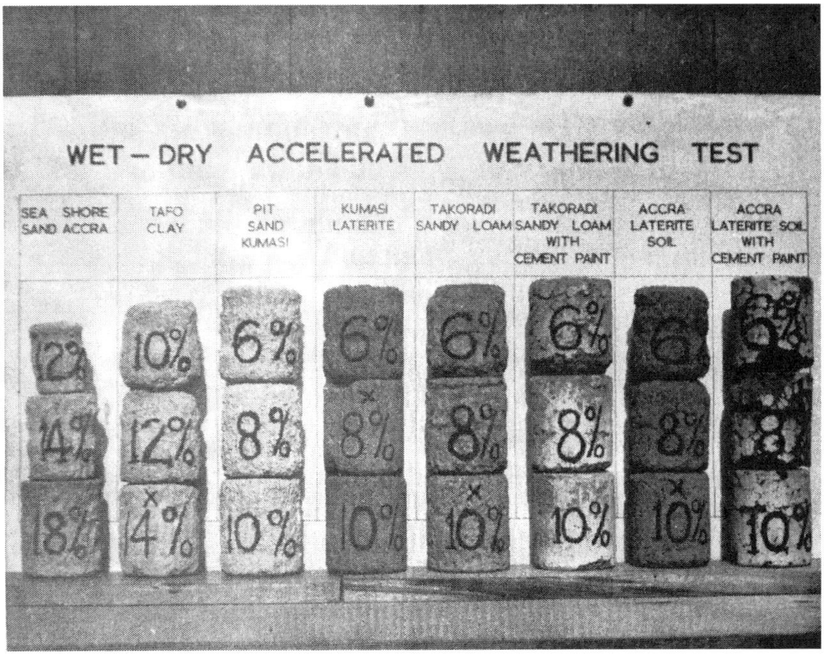

Figure 5.15
A photograph showing the outcomes of the weathering tests of different types of cement–soil mixtures. Source: *Colonial Building Notes*, 1953.

consideration the interests of the periphery. As the center of calculation occupied by CLU and later TBD was not permanent, it had to be constructed through network building and its power was contingent on how well different interests were translated as much as how much knowledge was accumulated.

This was especially so for a center like the CLU that had few research staff members and was not able to conduct much research on tropical building problems. For many years, CLU served primarily as a place for collating and coordinating research findings on tropical building problems. Atkinson and other staff members played advisory roles to the Colonial Office and the colonies, and they sought to shape the production of tropical architecture by regulating the flow of information. But as Atkinson readily admitted, "most of the research work on hot climate building design must, of course, be conducted in the tropics," because "if we want quantitative information which can be applied to low-cost tropical building, it will be necessary to carry out experiments with full scale buildings."[122] In the case of climatic design, Atkinson's discourse was, as he admitted, indebted to the work of researchers based in the tropics or subtropics. Among them, Atkinson cited the "valuable research" carried out by J. W. Drysdale at the Australian Commonwealth Experimental Building Station and A. J. A. Roux at the South African National Building Research Institute.[123]

This chapter started by studying the formation of TBD at the BRS to understand the much-neglected technoscientific dimensions of tropical architecture. At the start, I argued that the TBD was conceived and constructed as the metropolitan center of a network of colonial building stations. I then attended to the building of the technoscientific network by Atkinson and TBD. Drawing from the ANT, the global was not seen as opposing the local. Rather, the local was made "global" through network building and a series of translations that rendered the local mobile and could thus circulate to other sites and situations without distortion. Using ANT, I also proposed another way to conceptualize power in relation to (post)colonial architecture. Using the specific case of climatic design and thermal comfort, I showed that through network building and the accumulation of technoscientific knowledge, the metropole also accrued power and became a center of calculation. However, I also argued that the network was a provisional and contingent entity that consisted of heterogeneous sociotechnical components. Thus, just as the technoscientific network could facilitate the accumulation of knowledge and power at certain centers of calculation, it could also operate in manners that served the interest of the periphery, as Atkinson's critical view of the export of prefabricated structures to the tropics demonstrated.

NOTES

1 Vikramaditya Prakash, *Chandigarh's Le Corbusier: The Struggle for Modernity in Postcolonial India* (Seattle: University of Washington Press, 2002); Elisabetta Andreoli and Adrian Forty, *Brazil's Modern Architecture* (London: Phaidon, 2004).

2 C. Greig Crysler, *Writing Spaces: Discourses of Architecture, Urbanism, and the Built Environment, 1960–2000* (New York: Routledge, 2003).

3 See, for example, Łukasz Stanek, "Miastoprojekt Goes Abroad: The Transfer of Architectural Labour from Socialist Poland to Iraq (1958–1989)," *JoA* 17, no. 3 (2012); Łukasz Stanek, "Introduction: The 'Second World's' Architecture and Planning in the 'Third World'," *JoA* 17, no. 3 (2012); Duanfang Lu, "Introduction: Architecture, Modernity and Identity in the Third World," in *Third World Modernism: Architecture, Development and Identity*, ed. Duanfang Lu (London: Routledge, 2010). See also articles in the themed issue of *JoA* 17, no. 3 on "Cold War Transfer: Architecture and Planning from Socialist Countries in the 'Third World'" edited by Łukasz Stanek and Tom Avermaete.

4 Stanek, "Introduction," 299.

5 See The Natal Regional Research Committee and The University of Natal, *Symposium on Design for Tropical Living* (Durban: The University of Natal, 1957); PRO DSIR4/3647, *Council of Scientific and Industrial Research: Establishment of a Building Research Station in India*.

6 It was initially based at the Thomason College of Engineering at Roorkee. See PRO DSIR4/3647, *Council of Scientific and Industrial Research*.

7 PRO CO927/34/4, *Housing Research Centre, West Africa*; PRO DSIR4/3475, *Establishment of a Building Research Station in West Africa*; PRO DSIR4/3476, *Establishment of a Building Research Station in West Africa*.

8 PRO CO927/35/2, *Trinidad: Proposed Establishment of Building Research Station*; NAS HDB1278 SIT612/48, *Singapore Colonial Development and Welfare Fund Committee*. In Malaya, the proposal was partially realized in the form of a Design and Research Branch within the Public Works Department. See PRO DSIR4/3361, *Tropical Building Division*.

9 PRO CO927/35/7, *Appointment of Colonial Liaison Officer to DSIR Building Research Station*.

10 Maxwell Fry and Jane Drew, *Tropical Architecture in the Humid Zone* (London: Batsford, 1956), 255.

11 UN Department of Social Affairs, *Survey of Problems of Low Cost Rural Housing in Tropical Areas: A Preliminary Report with Special Reference to Caribbean Areas* (New York: UN Department of Social Affairs, 1950), 11, 14.

12 UN Tropical Housing Mission, *Low Cost Housing in South and Southeast Asia: Report of Mission of Experts* (New York: UN Department of Social Affairs, 1951), 31.

13 N. Sutterheim, "Introduction," in *Symposium on Design for Tropical Living*, ed. The Natal Regional Research Committee and The University of Natal (Durban: The University of Natal, 1957).

14 See, for example, Miles Danby, *Grammar of Architectural Design, with Special Reference to the Tropics* (London and New York: Oxford University Press, 1963); David Oakley, *Tropical Houses: A Guide to Their Design* (London: Batsford, 1961); Fry and Drew, *Tropical Architecture in the Humid Zone*; Georg Lippsmeier, Walter Kluska, and Carol Gray Edrich, *Tropenbau/Building in the Tropics* (Munich: Callwey, 1969); Robin M. Campbell, *Designing for Comfort in Tropical Climate* (Melbourne: Department of Architecture, University of Melbourne, 1965); Victor Olgyay and Aladar Olgyay, *Design with Climate: Bioclimatic Approach to Architectural Regionalism* (Princeton: Princeton University Press, 1963).

15 Mark Swenarton, *Building the New Jerusalem: Architecture, Housing and Politics, 1900–1930* (Garston, Watford: IHS BRE Press, 2008); F. M. Lea, *Science and Building: A History of the Building Research Station* (London: HMSO, 1971).

16 An Australian G. B. Gresford wrote a proposal for the Australian building research station in consultation with BRS officials in 1943. Around the same time, E. W. Dohse of South Africa wrote a report on the work of BRS after visiting it. S. Paraswathamy, a member of India's Building Research Unit, wrote to BRS in June 1947 for advice on the organization of building research in India. See PRO DSIR4/3647, *Council of Scientific and Industrial Research*.

17 R. W. Nurse and A. Pott were sent to West Africa between 9 December 1946 and 26 January 1947 to find out about the specific building research needs of West Africa and to propose the scope and nature of work of the building research station there. See PRO CO927/34/4, *Housing Research Centre, West Africa*.

18 Swenarton, *Building the New Jerusalem*, 169.

19 UN Department of Social Affairs, *Survey of Problems of Low Cost Housing Rural Housing in Tropical Areas*, 14.

20 Swenarton, *Building the New Jerusalem*; "The Building Research Station: Its Origin, Work and Scope," *JRIBA* 43 (1936); PRO AT67/63, *A Short History of Building Research in the United Kingdom from 1917 to 1946 – in Particular That of the Building Research Station*; BRS, *The Building Research Station: Its History, Organization and Work* (Garston, Watford: BRS, 1954); Lea, *Science and Building*.

21 David J. Hess, *Science Studies: An Advanced Introduction* (New York: New York University Press, 1997).

22 Such a standpoint epistemology seeks to negotiate between the dichotomy of objectivism and relativism. It objects to the reductive idea of objectivity-as-transcendence, or the "god trick of seeing everything from nowhere." Donna Haraway, "Situated Knowledges: The Science Question in Feminism and the Privilege of Partial Perspective," *Feminist Studies* 14, no. 3 (1988): 581.

23 Warwick Anderson, "Introduction: Postcolonial Technoscience," *Social Studies of Science* 32, nos. 5/6, Special Issue: Postcolonial Technoscience (2002); Michael A. Osborne, "Introduction: The Social History of Science, Technoscience and Imperialism," *Science, Technology & Society* 4, no. 2 (1999); Gyan Prakash, *Another Reason: Science and the Imagination of Modern India* (Princeton: Princeton University Press, 1999).

24 "Housing Research in the Colonies: Report by the Housing Research Group" enclosed in Colonial Office dispatch dated 4 December 1945. PRO CO927/6/7, *Housing Research in the Colonies: Proposal to Establish a Housing Research Centre in West Africa*.

25 The colonial housing problem was already framed in "General Aspects of the Housing Problem in the Colonial Empire" (Papers on Colonial Affairs, No. 1), December 1943. The Group was asked to advise on how colonial housing research should be organized. See PRO CO1005/1, *Colonial Housing Research Group: Minutes of Meeting*.

26 D. B. Blacklock, *An Empire Problem: The House and Village in the Tropics* (London: Hodder & Stoughton Ltd., 1932).

27 Anthony Clayton, "Browne, Sir Granville St John Orde (1883–1947)," in *Oxford Dictionary of National Biography*, ed. by H. C. G. Matthew and Brian Harrison (Oxford: Oxford University Press, 2004), online edition, accessed 5 January 2016, http://www.oxforddnb.com/view/article/40958. An example of the type of detailed report Browne published on the colonial labor problem is G. St. J. Orde Browne, *Labour Conditions in Ceylon, Mauritius, and Malaya* (London: HMSO, 1943).

28 PRO CO927/6/7, *Housing Research in the Colonies*.

29 Chitty was a pioneer British modernist architect, whose firm designed the Royal College at Nairobi, and who was one of the earliest advocates of architectural regionalism. See Anthony M. Chitty, "The Need for Regionalism in Architecture: A Ghana Aesthetic?," *The Builder* CXCV (5 September 1958).

30 Anthony M. Chitty, "Housing in the West Indies: A Note on the Bulletin 'Housing in the West Indies' recently published by the Comptroller for Development and Welfare in the West Indies," *RIBAJ* (October 1958).

31 PRO CO927/7/1, *Proposals for Building Research Programme in the British West Indies and British Guiana*. Joan Burnett, an Assistant Architect with the West Indies Development and Welfare team, was appointed as the Building Research Officer in late 1945. See also PRO CO927/35/2, *Trinidad*.

32 Colonial Office official J. G. Hibbert in a letter dated 19 December 1947. PRO CO927/6/7, *Housing Research in the Colonies*.

33 UN Department of Social Affairs, *Survey of Problems of Low Cost Housing Rural Housing in Tropical Areas*, 11.

34 Ibid.

35 Frederick Cooper, "Modernizing Bureaucrats, Backward Africans, and the Development Concept," in *International Development and the Social Sciences: Essays on the History and Politics of Knowledge*, ed. Frederick Cooper and Randall M. Packard (Berkeley: University of California Press, 1997).

36 For a history of British Colonial Development, see Michael A. Havinden and David Meredith, *Colonialism and Development: Britain and Its Tropical Colonies, 1850–1960* (London: Routledge, 1993).

37 Frederick Cooper and Randall M. Packard, "Introduction," in *International Development and the Social Sciences: Essays on the History and Politics of Knowledge*, ed. Frederick Cooper and Randall M. Packard (Berkeley: University of California Press, 1997).

38 Cited in Havinden and Meredith, *Colonialism and Development*, 198.

39 Cited in Development and Welfare Organization in the West Indies, *Housing in the West Indies* (Bridgetown, Barbados: Advocate Co. Printers, 1945), 1.

40 CO927/7/1, *Proposals for Building Research Programme in the British West Indies and British Guiana*; Frank Stockdale, Robert Gardner-Medwin, and Leo de Syllas, "Recent Planning Developments in the Colonies," *RIBAJ* 55 (1948). Gardner-Medwin was to become an expert on housing in the tropics and the Roscoe Professor of Architecture at Liverpool University. Norman Kingham, "Obituary: Professor Robert Gardner-Medwin," *Independent*, July 8 1995.

41 Besides Evans, Blacklock and Browne, the Group consisted of Mary Blacklock of Liverpool School of Tropical Medicine; R. H. Burt of Colonial Office; C. Y. Carstairs, secretary of Colonial Research Committee; S. E. Chandler and S. J. Johnstone of the Imperial Institute; R. W. Foxlee, deputy chief engineer to the Crown Agents for the colonies; and W. H. Kauntze, deputy medical advisor, Colonial Office. For the work of the Crown Agents, see "Work of the Crown Agents," *The Crown Colonist*, Preliminary Number (1931). For the imperial institute's involvement in colonial research, see Michael Worboys, "The Imperial Institute: The State and the Development of the Natural Resources of the Colonial Empire, 1887–1923," in *Imperialism and the Natural World*, ed. John M. Mackenzie (Manchester: Manchester University Press, 1990). For British imperial research on tropical medicine, see Douglas Melvin Haynes, "The Social Production of Metropolitan Expertise in Tropical Diseases: The Imperial State, Colonial Service and Tropical Diseases Research Fund," *Science, Technology & Society* 4, no. 2 (1999).

42 Swenarton, *Building the New Jerusalem*.

43 Michael Worboys, "The Discovery of Colonial Malnutrition between the Wars," in *Imperial Medicine and Indigenous Societies*, ed. David Arnold (Manchester: Manchester University Press, 1988).

44 Arturo Escobar also makes a similar argument about the development discourses and practices in the mid-twentieth century. See Arturo Escobar, *Encountering Development: The Making and Unmaking of the Third World* (Princeton: Princeton University Press, 1995).

45 PRO CO927/6/7, *Housing Research in the Colonies*.

46 Haynes, "The Social Production of Metropolitan Expertise in Tropical Diseases."

47 This insistence on the division of labor between "pure science" research in the metropole and the "applied science" research in the colony was also evident in the tensed relationship between the two agencies created to advance and apply science in British India – the Indian Advisory Committee of the Royal Society based in the metropole and the Board of Scientific Advice of the Government of India. See Roy MacLeod, "Scientific Advice for British India: Imperial Perceptions and Administrative Goals, 1898–1923," *Modern Asian Studies* 9, no. 3 (1975). Such a division between the center and the periphery was never really stable, however much the imperialist would like to maintain it, because it was subjected to contestations and internal contradictions. See David Wade Chambers and Richard Gillespie, "Locality in the History of Science: Colonial Science, Technoscience, and Indigenous Knowledge," *Osiris* 15 (2000).

48 PRO CO927/6/7, *Housing Research in the Colonies*.

49 This economic relation is best expressed by Leo Amery, the British secretary of state for the colonies in the 1920s. He said: "One of the most striking features of modern industrial development is the marriage of tropical production to the industrial production of the temperate zone. They are essentially complementary regions, and owing to their character and the character of their inhabitants they are likely to remain so.' Quoted in Havinden and Meredith, *Colonialism and Development*, 169.

50 See, for example, Roy MacLeod, "Introduction to Special Issue on Nature and Empire: Science and the Colonial Enterprise," *Osiris* 15 (2000); Paolo Palladino and Michael Worboys, "Critiques and Contentions: Science and Imperialism," *Isis* 84, no. 1 (1993).

51 Havinden and Meredith, *Colonialism and Development*.

52 Sir Charles Joseph Jeffries, ed., *A Review of Colonial Research, 1940–1960* (London: HMSO, 1964).

53 Sabine Clarke, "A Technocratic Imperial State? The Colonial Office and Scientific Research, 1940–1960," *Twentieth Century British History* 18, no. 4 (2007).

54 Cooper and Packard, "Introduction."

55 Escobar, *Encountering Development*, 10. See also Wolfgang Sachs, ed. *The Development Dictionary: A Guide to Knowledge as Power* (London: Zed Books, 1992).
56 PRO CO927/35/5, *Proposed Colonial Housing Bureau: Appointment of Colonial Liaison Officer to DSIR*.
57 Lea, *Science and Building*, 163.
58 Secretary of State for Colonies' circular, "Cost of Buildings in the Colonies," dated 27 July 1948. PRO CO927/35/5, *Proposed Colonial Housing Bureau*. See also PRO CO927/35/7, *Appointment of Colonial Liaison Officer DSIR Building Research Station*.
59 George Anthony Atkinson, "Tropical Architecture and Building Standards," in *Conference on Tropical Architecture 1953: A Report of the Proceedings of the Conference Held at University College, London, March 1953*, ed. Arthur Foyle (London: University College London, 1953).
60 Lea, *Science and Building*, 2.
61 "The Building Research Station," 790.
62 Bruno Latour, *Science in Action: How to Follow Scientists and Engineers through Society* (Cambridge, MA: Harvard University Press, 1987), 215–57.
63 John Law and John Hassard, eds., *Actor Network Theory and After* (Malden: Blackwell, 1999).
64 PRO CO927/35/7, *Appointment of Colonial Liaison Officer DSIR Building Research Station*.
65 See, for example, Atkinson's visit to Singapore. George Anthony Atkinson, "The Work of the Colonial Liaison Building Officer and Building in the Tropics," *QJIAM* 2, no. 1 (1952).
66 PRO DSIR4/3361, *Tropical Building Division*.
67 Ibid.
68 He was included in the list of lecturers and critics of the 1954 and 1955 Prospectuses for Department of Tropical Architecture at Architectural Association.
69 D. C. Robinson, "Towards a Tropical Architecture: The Work of Architects Co-Partnership in Nigeria," *Architectural Design* April (1959).
70 PRO CO927/35/7, *Appointment of Colonial Liaison Officer DSIR Building Research Station*; PRO CO927/131/6, *Appointment of Colonial Liaison Officer to DSIR Building Research Station*.
71 For some useful clarifications about human and non-human actors, see Bruno Latour, "On Recalling ANT," in *Actor Network Theory and After*, ed. John Law and John Hassard (Malden: Blackwell, 1999).
72 Latour, *Science in Action*, 108.
73 George Anthony Atkinson, "British Architects in the Tropics," *Architectural Association Journal* 69 (1953).
74 Atkinson, "The Work of the Colonial Liaison Building Officer and Building in the Tropics," 36.
75 George Anthony Atkinson, "Building Techniques Overseas – II," *Prefabrication* 1, no. 10 (1954).
76 Henry J. Cowan, "The Architectural Science Laboratory," *RIBAJ* 66, no. 12 (1959). Cowan claims that he is the first professor of building science in his autobiography. See Henry J. Cowan, *A Contradiction in Terms: The Autobiography of Henry J. Cowan* (Sydney: Hermitage Press, 1993).
77 The RIBA Joint Committee on the Orientation of Buildings, *The Orientation of Buildings, Being the Report with Appendices of the RIBA Joint Committee on the Orientation of Buildings* (London: RIBA, 1933).
78 George Anthony Atkinson, "Construction and Erection of the Heliodon," *CBN* 26, (1955): 12.

79 George Anthony Atkinson, "Tropical Building Section, Building Research Station: A Brief Account of its Work", January 1961, in PRO DSIR4/3361, *Tropical Building Division*.
80 Ibid.
81 Ibid.
82 Lea, *Science and Building*. Sutterheim, "Introduction."
83 Sutterheim, "Introduction."
84 John Law, "Technology and Heterogeneous Engineering: The Case of Portuguese Expansion," in *The Social Construction of Technological Systems: New Directions in the Sociology and History of Technology*, ed. Wiebe E. Bijker, Thomas P. Hughes and T. J. Pinch (Cambridge, MA: MIT Press, 1987), 114.
85 Latour, *Science in Action*, 180.
86 Alan Lester, "Imperial Circuits and Networks: Geographies of the British Empire," *History Compass* 4, no. 1 (2006): 131.
87 George Atkinson, "Colonial Housing & Building Research: Report on the Colonial Liaison Office at the Building Research Station," April 1949 in PRO CO927/35/7, *Appointment of Colonial Liaison Officer to DSIR Building Research Station*.
88 The two articles are George Anthony Atkinson, "Building in the Tropics," *JRIBA* 57 (1950); George Anthony Atkinson "Warm Climates and Building Design," *CBN* 12 (1953). The 1950 article was regarded as a "comprehensive summary of the problems involved in the design of a house for a hot, humid climate." See UN Department of Social Affairs, *Survey of Problems of Low Cost Housing Rural Housing in Tropical Areas*.
89 See Olgyay and Olgyay, *Design with Climate*; Jeffrey Ellis Aronin, *Climate and Architecture* (New York: Reinhold, 1953); J. W. Drysdale, *Climate and House Design: With Reference to Australian Climate* (Sydney: Commonwealth Experimental Building Station, 1947).
90 See, for example, David Arnold, *The Problem of Nature: Environment, Culture and European Expansion* (Oxford: Blackwell, 1996); Felix Driver and Brenda S. A. Yeoh, "Constructing the Tropics: Introduction," *Singapore Journal of Tropical Geography* 21, no. 1 (2000).
91 Atkinson noted that C. G. Webb's work in Singapore provided evidence that people acclimatized to the hot and humid tropics had a "relatively high temperature of maximum comfort." Atkinson, "Warm Climates and Building Design," 3. Webb subsequently developed the Singapore Index and the Equatorial Index for Thermal Comfort. See C. G. Webb, "An Analysis of Some Observations of Thermal Comfort in an Equatorial Climate," *British Journal of Industrial Medicine* 16 (1959). For a summary of mid-twentieth century research on thermal comfort, see Thomas Bedford, "The Society's Lecture 1961: Researches on Thermal Comfort," *Ergonomics* 4, no. 4 (1961).
92 Atkinson, "Building in the Tropics," 317.
93 George Atkinson, "The Role of Meteorology and Climatology in Tropical Building and Housing: A Preliminary Note", June 1954, in PRO CO937/365, *The Role of Meteorology and Climatology in Tropical Building and Housing*.
94 Ibid.
95 Walter A. Taylor, "Regional Climate Analyses and Design Data," in *The House Beautiful Climate Control Project: Regional Climate Analyses and Design Data*, ed. American Institute of Architects (Washington, D.C.: American Institute of Architects, 1949–52), 15.
96 PRO CO937/365, *The Role of Meteorology and Climatology in Tropical Building and Housing*.
97 Ibid.
98 C.-E. A Winslow and L. P. Herrington, *Temperature and Human Life* (Princeton: Princeton University Press, 1949), 180.

99 Thomas Bedford, *Basic Principles of Ventilation and Heating* (London: H. K. Lewis & Co. Ltd., 1948), 86.
100 Winslow and Herrington, *Temperature and Human Life*, 190.
101 Atkinson, "Warm Climates and Building Design," 3–4.
102 For a more detailed discussion of this, see Jiat-Hwee Chang, "Thermal Comfort and Climatic Design in the Tropics: A Historical Critique," *JoA* (forthcoming)
103 Atkinson specifically refers to the research carried out by J. W. Drysdale in subtropical Queensland in Australia and C. G. Webb in Malaya.
104 Atkinson, "Warm Climates and Building Design."
105 Latour, *Science in Action*; Latour, "Visualisation and Cognition: Drawing Things Together," in *Knowledge and Society: Studies in the Sociology of Culture Past and Present*, ed. Henrika Kuklick and Elizabeth Long (Greenwich: JAI Press, 1986).
106 Editors, "Editorial: Commonwealth 2," *Architectural Review* 127 (1960) (my emphasis).
107 These changes are discussed by many architects and planners working in the tropical colonies in the mid-twentieth century. See Fry and Drew, *Tropical Architecture in the Humid Zone*, 24–25; C. Y. Carstairs, "The Social and Economic Background," in *Conference on Tropical Architecture 1953: A Report of the Proceedings of the Conference Held at University College, London, March 1953*, ed. Arthur Foyle (London: University College London, 1953); Otto Koenigsberger, "Tropical Planning Problems," in *Conference on Tropical Architecture 1953: A Report of the Proceedings of the Conference Held at University College, London, March 1953*, ed. Arthur Foyle (London: University College London, 1953).
108 Shanti Jayewardene, "Reflections on Design in the Context of Development," *Mimar*, no. 27 (1988).
109 Letter dated 7 January 1955 in PRO CO937/365, *The Role of Meteorology and Climatology in Tropical Building and Housing*.
110 "Homes across the Sea," *Prefabrication* 1, no. 1 (1953): 12.
111 ANMKL 1957/0575459, *Prefabrication and Colonial Building*.
112 PRO CO927/131/7, *Building Research: Aluminium Buildings*.
113 Colonial Office circular dated 14 May 1954 in CO859/310, *Export Houses: Prefabrication and Building in the Tropics*. Lyttelton also issued a similar message in Oliver Lyttelton, "Message from the Secretary of State for the Colonies," *Prefabrication* 1, no. 9 (1954).
114 "Homes across the Sea," 12.
115 "Aluminium Aids Prefabrication," *Prefabrication* 1, no. 2 (1953).
116 "Prefabs at the British Industries Fair," *Prefabrication* 1, no. 8 (1954): 21.
117 The included article is George Anthony Atkinson, "Export Houses: Prefabrication and Building in the Tropics," *The Housing Centre Review* 3 (1953).
118 George Anthony Atkinson, "Building Techniques Overseas," *Prefabrication* 1, no. 9 (1954): 7, 11.
119 Atkinson, "Building Techniques Overseas – II," 12.
120 George Anthony Atkinson, "West Indian Schools Built in Soil-Cement Blockwork," *CBN* 5 (1951); George Anthony Atkinson, "Stabilised Earth Walls – Construction," *CBN* 8 (1952); George Anthony Atkinson, "Stabilised Earth Walls – Surface Finishes," *CBN* 14 (1953); A. E. S. Alcock, "'Swishcrete': Notes on Stabilised Cement-Earth Building in the Gold Coast," *CBN* 16 (1953).
121 George Atkinson, "Colonial Housing & Building Research: Report on the Colonial Liaison Office at the Building Research Station," April 1949 in PRO CO927/35/7, *Appointment of Colonial Liaison Officer to DSIR Building Research Station*.
122 Atkinson, "Building in the Tropics," 317.
123 PRO CO927/35/7, *Appointment of Colonial Liaison Officer to DSIR Building Research Station*.

Chapter 6: Teaching Climatic Design

Postcolonial Architectural Education, Scientific Humanism and Tropical Development

When the Department of Architecture and Building at the Singapore Polytechnic (SP) was founded in 1959, one of its stated objectives was to develop "within itself a core of a school of tropical architecture in which instruction [was] based on the requirements of tropical countries."[1] One of the first lectures that D. J. Vickery, the first head of the Department, gave was on "Climate and Architecture."[2] In late 1959, when Kee Yeap took over as the first local head of the Department, his ambition was to establish SP as the "centre for post-graduate work in designing buildings for the tropics."[3] Under his headship, the curriculum at SP continued to be "keyed to instruction, practice and theory of Architecture for the tropical regions, and of building constructional techniques applicable to the country."[4] From the very beginning, the teaching of building science was an integral part of the focus on tropical architecture.[5] Indeed, the very first visiting professor appointed with the assistance of the Colombo Plan to the Department was a building scientist.[6]

The pedagogical emphasis on tropical architecture at the Department was also reflected in Kee's own private practice, which aimed at producing tropical architecture that suited Singapore's climate and Singaporeans' way of life. Kee felt that the emphasis on tropical architecture meant a change of socio-cultural reference. He noted:

> At present we have houses here which are only nostalgic replicas of English ones. We should not look towards temperate climate architecture but to places like Brazil, Africa and other tropical areas where the climate and way of living are similar.[7]

A similar message was conveyed in a speech by Loke Wan Tho, the tycoon patron of SP's Architecture Society who opened the "International Exhibition of Students' work from Tropical Schools of Architecture" organized by the SP's students in August 1962. He noted that "[t]here was a time, not so very distant, when architects in the tropics imported their ideas direct from England and designed us lovely glass houses in which to live and to roast." Loke then urged his audience to change their frame of reference. He suggested,

> It is to the young people who have to live their lives in the tropics, and who are now training to be future architects that we must look for the sort of designs and use of materials which are best suited for Singapore's special conditions.[8]

Both Kee and Loke's discussions of tropical architecture have to be situated in the socio-political context of Singapore during the late 1950s and early 1960s. Malaysia had gained its independence in 1957 and Singapore attained self-governance in 1959, thus that period in Singapore's history was characterized by decolonization and the struggle for not just political but also cultural independence from the British. Many years later, Tay Kheng Soon, prominent Singaporean architect and one of the first batch of architectural students to graduate from SP, would, as we saw in the introductory chapter, recall that tropical architecture represented a "quest for a contemporary architectural aesthetic of tropicality in our terms and none other" and it was a "part of the context of freeing oneself from the political and taste-dictates of our masters."[9]

While tropical architecture was seen by those associated with the Department at the SP as a part of the struggle for independence, tropical architecture was already institutionalized and firmly established in the metropole in the early 1950s, as we have seen in Chapter 5. Tropical architecture was not only practiced by numerous expatriate and local architects in the West Indies, Africa and Asia, underpinned by the technoscientific knowledge that the network of research stations centered around the Tropical Building Division, BRS, produced, it was also taught and researched in many new schools and departments of architecture in the new Commonwealth by the early 1960s, as Robert Gardner-Medwin's 1963 survey showed.[10] In fact, during the late 1950s, there was even the RIBA's Special Overseas Scheme "which encourage[d] the study of architecture in relation to the humid tropical climate."[11] Likewise, the emphasis on building science and the attempt to develop postgraduate work at SP followed similar metropolitan tendencies in architectural education, as we shall see. Complementing the previous chapter's study of building research stations and the technoscientific research on tropical building problems in mid-twentieth century, this chapter explores the role of architecture schools and their teaching of climatic design in the institutionalization of tropical architecture in the mid-twentieth century.

The discussion that follows focuses specifically on the case of the Department of Tropical Studies (DTS) at the Architectural Association (AA) that existed from 1954 to 1972. When it was founded in 1954, the DTS was known as the Department of Tropical Architecture, and according to Patrick Wakely who studied and taught at the Department, it was also known as the AA School of Tropical Architecture. Its name was changed to the DTS in 1961 and since then, the Department was better known as either the DTS or "the Tropical Department."[12] The DTS was the pioneer institution that developed a curriculum to teach tropical architecture; it was also an influential model much emulated in the developing world. Given the prominence of the DTS, particularly the fame of its founder and head Otto Koenigsberger, its history has been recounted in a few publications.[13] This chapter, however, differs from these accounts in important ways. I argue that the curriculum of teaching tropical architecture developed at the DTS was a new model that responded to and exemplified two broad forces of change. The first is the shifting geopolitical relations between the metropole and the colonies in the mid-twentieth century. The shifting geopolitical relations were most evident in the implementation of the colonial development and welfare regime in the British colonies from the 1940s onwards, and the subsequent decolonization and the transition from the British Empire to the new Commonwealth. In connection to architecture, the former led to the ascendency of technical education in the colonies and the establishment of many new schools and departments of architecture. The latter contributed to the formation of the Commonwealth Association of Architects (CAA) and the attendant notion of Commonwealth architecture.

The second force of change was the rise of building science in architectural education. By the rise of building science, I am not just referring to how building science became institutionalized as an integral subfield in architectural education and the application of technoscience to architectural subjects in the 1950s. The rise of building science and the concomitant ascent of architectural research meant an important shift in the manner in which architectural problems were framed and solved: every problem began to be approached anew based on fundamental technoscientific principles, as if there was no precedent. I argue that this new approach to framing architectural problems was central to how tropical architecture was taught at the DTS and, subsequently, other schools of architecture, i.e. through climatic design, or the elevation of climate as the prime determinant of architectural form. I also show that behind the rise of building science and the new approach to framing architectural problems was the ideology of scientific humanism.

In this chapter, I also discuss the DTS together with the RIBA, particularly how the RIBA responded to the shifting geopolitical relations between the metropole and the colonies. Unlike the DTS, which was attuned to the needs of the tropics in architectural education and was willing to adjust its pedagogy and even institutional organization to address those needs, the RIBA and its Board of Architectural Education (BAE) was more concerned with protecting the interests of British architects. It was initially not responsive to the geopolitical shifts and was unwilling to accommodate "tropical architecture" in its recommended syllabus or to recognize the new schools of architecture in the colonies. Later the RIBA recognized the new geopolitical reality and relented. It established the CAA as a purportedly more egalitarian organization to maintain its ties with the "allied societies" in the former/decolonizing colonies and it also incorporated tropical architecture into its recommended syllabus and its official discourse of Commonwealth architecture. Despite the changes, the RIBA still sought to maintain its control in the CAA. In view of the differences between the CAA and the DTS, I end the chapter with a discussion of their contrasting impacts and legacies.

THE NEW MODEL OF ARCHITECTURAL EDUCATION

The Department of Tropical Studies was first founded at the AA because of the recommendations of the 1953 Conference on Tropical Architecture held at University College London. The conference originated in a request from Adedokun Adeyemi to Koenigsberger to organize a short course on designing and building in the tropics. Adeyemi, a Nigerian student studying at Manchester School of Architecture, felt his architectural training did not equip him to deal with the "tropical problems" back home.[14] Instead of a short course, Adeyemi's request led to a major conference that involved many prominent British architects, educators and researchers, such as William Holford, Patrick Abercombie, Percy Johnson-Marshall, and Robert Gardner-Medwin, as speakers. The Colonial Office also encouraged various colonial governments to sponsor the architects in their public authorities to attend the conference.[15] More so than the work by Atkinson and the Tropical Building Division at the Building Research Station that we discussed in Chapter 5, the conference and the establishment of the DTS at the AA afterwards were often regarded as the key events in the founding and institutionalization of modern tropical architecture.

The founding of the DTS not only marked the institutionalization of modern tropical architecture, it also heralded a new form of architectural education that was significant in that it addressed, if not preempted, the contexts of colonial and post-colonial development, and the shift from colonial to commonwealth relations. Underlying the establishment of the DTS was, in the words of William Holford in his foreword to the Prospectus for the DTS in 1955, that "architects must be trained *for* the tropics as well as *in* the tropics" (Figure 6.1).[16] There was a relatively new sense of the purpose and intention of architectural education in the British Empire, which was inextricably linked to the mid-twentieth-century colonial and international development regimes. Before the DTS, architectural training *for* the tropics, i.e. a training that attends specifically to the local conditions of the tropics and the problems peculiar to it, was not provided in any architecture schools, even at a place such as the Liverpool School of Architecture, one of the main training grounds of architects for the British Empire, or accounted for in the syllabi of the RIBA standard examinations.[17] Architectural training *in* the tropics, like most other professional and technical education, was, outside of British India, simply non-existent in the British Empire during the pre-World War II period.

In the prewar years, colonial administrators claimed that the non-industrial economies of the colonies had little demand for native technicians and professionals, thus the colonial state did not provide for technical or professional education – such as architectural education. Since the Europeans filled the main professional and technical positions in the colonies, the colonial economies required only native technical subordinates to assist in the maintenance of colonial technological infrastructures – the roads, railways, ports, postal and telegraph services – or to serve the agricultural and mining industries. As such, an Empire-wide survey of technical education conducted by the Colonial Office in 1937 found

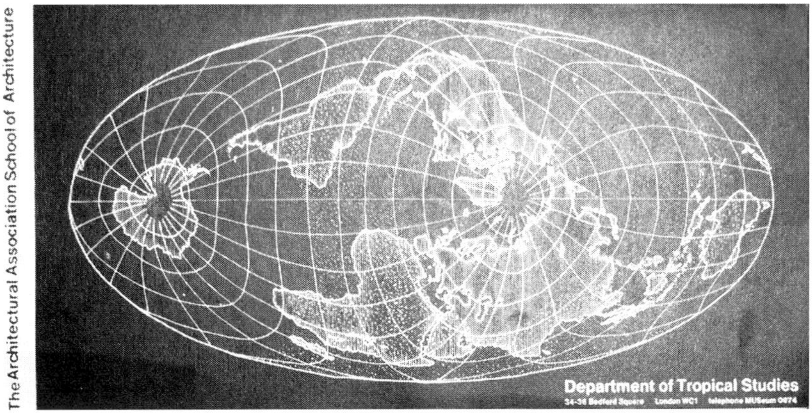

Figure 6.1
Foregrounding the tropics: a postcard from the Department of Tropical Studies, a successor to the Department of Tropical Architecture, c. 1960s. Courtesy of Professor Patrick Wakely.

that there were only small trade schools or technical schools in some colonies for training technical subordinates.[18] While there were a few universities or university colleges in select British colonies, they mainly provided general education in the arts and sciences as their primary function was training teachers for colonial educational systems.[19] Medical training was the only exception to this emphasis on general education because, as we saw in earlier chapters, tropical medicine was seen as essential to colonial economic development since the turn of the twentieth century. Under such a colonial educational policy, architectural training of the indigenous population in the British Empire was largely restricted to the training of draughtsmen and tracers, typically not in schools but under *ad hoc* arrangements.

It was only in the post-World War II period that technical and professional education was developed and new universities, university colleges and technical colleges in different parts of the British Empire were established for technical and professional education. By 1954, a new university was established in Malaya and six university colleges were established in the West Indies, Gold Coast, Nigeria, East Africa, Khartoum, and the Federation of Rhodesia and Nyasaland with the help of the Inter-University Council.[20] Under the Advisory Committee on Colonial Colleges of Arts, Science and Technology, Technical Colleges were also established in Kumasi, Nairobi and different parts of Nigeria. The Kuala Lumpur Technical College was expanded and a polytechnic was proposed for Singapore.[21] These changes took place as part of the new colonial development regime put forward in relation to the CDWA discussed earlier. Expanding the provision of education was deemed necessary for both colonial economic development, in terms of expanding the economic base and diversifying into new industries, and social welfare. It was in such a context that degree and diploma courses in architecture were introduced at the University of Hong Kong in 1950, the Nigeria College of Arts, Science and Technology in 1952, and later at other places such as the Royal Technical College of East Africa, the College of Science and Technology at Kumasi, the SP, and the Kuala Lumpur Technical College. Besides establishing architectural education in the colonies, students from the colonies were also sent to schools of architecture in the metropole, particularly for advanced training at postgraduate level, sometimes sponsored by scholarships granted by the CDWA and other development schemes. The establishment of the DTS of course originated from the request of one such student from the colonies studying in the metropole during the 1950s.

The DTS was therefore inextricably bound up with the context of post-World War II colonial development. It was conceived to cater to three main types of students – British architectural students who hoped to work in the tropics, architectural students from the tropics, and architects from the tropics who wanted advanced training.[22] Funds from Britain's development programs were used to subsidize students to study at the DTS and its various successors.[23] Furthermore, the DTS, as a part of the AA, also helped with the establishment of a School of Architecture in the tropics, i.e. the School of Architecture, Planning and Building at the Kwame Nkrumah University of Science and Technology, Kumasi, Ghana. The DTS and the AA helped the Kumasi School to recruit teaching staff from its network and establish their curriculum.[24] Students from Kumasi were also brought to Britain for a year of academic immersion.[25] This arrangement was along the line of the "special relationship" between the University of London and the various University Colleges in the colonies arranged by the Inter-University Council for Higher Education Overseas, in which the metropolitan university took on an advisory role to help the colonial institutions to guarantee their academic standards, establish their reputations and build up their experience.[26]

The DTS's activities were not just restricted to its involvement in the British (post)colonial development regime. Since the 1950s, while teaching at the DTS, Koenigsberger was also closely involved in the UN technical assistance program and served as expert advisor on housing and urban planning problems in various post-colonial states, such as Pakistan, Nigeria and Singapore.[27] The terms of his employment were in fact arranged such that he would spend half a year teaching at the DTS and the other half of the year carrying out his advisory activities. The curriculum at the DTS was very much shaped by Koenigsberger's involvement with the UN's development work, just as Koenigsberger's UN work was shaped by the teaching and research he did at the DTS. The design projects that Koenigsberger assigned to his students at the DTS frequently stemmed from the problems he encountered in his advisory work with the UN.[28] Conversely, Koenigsberger prepared a manual on tropical housing for the UN based very much on his teaching materials at the DTS.[29] The close connection between the DTS and the international regime of development was even more evident in the changes in name and institutional structure of the DTS – it was renamed as Department of Development and Tropical Studies (DDTS) in 1969, and in 1971 it joined the University College London as the Development Planning Unit (DPU).[30]

The new model of architectural education represented by the DTS and its association with new colonial development policy also reflected a new emerging relationship between the metropole and the decolonized or decolonizing colonies, or the "First World" and the "Third World." The 1965 Prospectus of the DTS notes, "[t]here is a great London tradition in tropical studies of all kinds,"[31] and "[t]he Department has become a meeting place for architects from tropical countries and over the years has achieved prominence as a centre for the exchange of information and experience between practising architects and research workers."[32] It suggests that the DTS was a metropolitan nodal point of colonial research in tropical architecture not unlike the positions occupied by the Imperial Institute and Kew Gardens in the previous colonial scientific research models in geology and agriculture. The Prospectus, however, adds that "London is far from the tropics and education and research within the newly-emerging countries themselves now must command support."[33] It then discusses the AA–Kumasi connection, which appears to suggest that the DTS was a metropolitan center with a difference, one that did not adhere to the previous hierarchical colonial model of imposing the metropolitan economic and cultural priorities on the periphery. In the initial notes outlining his ideas for the teaching of tropical architecture at the DTS, Koenigsberger stressed: "Not to be a missionary of Western superiority is one of the most difficult tasks the architect in the tropics has to learn."[34] Elsewhere, in an article he wrote for one of the two special issues of the *Architectural Design* journal produced after the 1953 Conference, Koenigsberger emphasizes that the metropole–tropics relationship was not a one-way flow. He discussed how cultural contacts with the tropics benefited the British architects and he also sketched out the need for British architects in the tropics to help build up the capacity of the construction industry there through the training of draftsmen, architectural assistants, surveyors, clerks of works and local builders.[35]

The curriculum of the DTS was designed to serve three functions: to study the problems of building in developing countries of the tropics, to run special courses for architects and planners from these countries, and to prepare British professionals for work overseas.[36] The last objective, in particular, could be seen as answering the Colonial Liaison Officer George Atkinson's 1953 famous rally call for British architects to seize the opportunities offered by £33-million-worth of CDWA-funded government building projects in the British tropical/colonial territories. In this rallying call issued just before the establishment of the DTS, Atkinson notes that British historic interest in the tropical colonies was entering a new phase:

> It is a phase in which it is in the mutual interest of the tropical peoples and ourselves to co-operate because we need what the other has to offer. We need Malaya's rubber and tin; Gold Coast's cocoa; Ceylon's tea; the sugar of the Caribbean and Mauritius. They need our machinery, manufactures and technical advice … The building needs of the tropics are great … and we, from experience, can contribute much … But always, we must remember that our clients are more and more the people of the tropics, not Europeans; that we have to work there as equals, only privileged because of our special knowledge.[37]

Atkinson seemed to suggest that in this new phase of mutual interest, the privileges and entitlements associated with the formerly dominant colonists were no longer available to British architects. In order for them to work in the tropics, they have to acquire the "special knowledge" of designing and building in the tropics. One of the DTS's objectives appeared to dovetail nicely with the need to equip British architects with the requisite "special knowledge" or expertise to work in the tropics.

A 1970 reflection of the functions of the DTS in the early days, however, suggests it was not interested in consolidating the influence of British architects in the tropics. The author of the reflection – most likely Koenigsberger – noted that the two functions of running courses for architects and planners from the tropics, and training British architects to work in the tropics, were expected to "disappear after a short time, largely as a result of the activities of the Department itself." The author expected schools of architecture and planning rapidly to emerge in the tropics and train architects and planners in these developing countries. According to the author, these tropical schools were "expected to reduce and eventually eliminate the need for European architects and planners to migrate to the tropics."[38] In other words, the DTS was only envisioned to play a transitional role in educating architects for the tropics. Its success was apparently to be measured by the rate at which it was able to render its own educational functions obsolete by helping architects, planners and schools in the tropics become independent. Unlike the previous hierarchical colonial model of imposing metropolitan economic and political priorities on the periphery, the DTS was conscious of the supporting role it played in addressing the problems of architectural research and especially education in the tropics. It is not unreasonable to surmise from the above that the DTS was created as a benign, empathic and even benevolent conduit of knowledge transfer – through not just one-way diffusion but also two-way exchanges – between the metropole and the tropics.

The DTS's role as a generous conduit of knowledge transfer is perhaps evident in its relationship with Kumasi and the pedagogy of the teaching staff there. Many of these teaching staff, such as Patrick Wakely, Kamil Khan Mumtaz, Martin Evans, and T. G. Ingersoll, were appointed through the DTS–AA connections.[39] These teaching staff members observed that the Kumasi school's curriculum was based on the RIBA syllabus, which they felt were "tragic-comic in their irrelevance."[40] They also lamented that the African student "consciously cut off his origins and was embarrassed by Africa."[41] In response they introduced "live projects" into the design course in which the students were asked to deal with actual cases in order for them to address the reality of designing and building in Ghana. These staff members also sought to redress the students' self-denial and "reawaken" the students' awareness of their own heritage by mounting a "visual survey of Africa" in an avowedly non-Eurocentric manner.[42] Students were also encouraged to study and understand traditional buildings and their building techniques, and "social order" – in terms of hierarchy, family structure, religions and community traditions – and how that affected settlement pattern (Figure 6.2). The DTS's recognition of local conditions, traditions, histories and needs in the colonies/tropics, and the enlightened approach to put these considerations above institutional self-interest and address them in an empathetic and benevolent

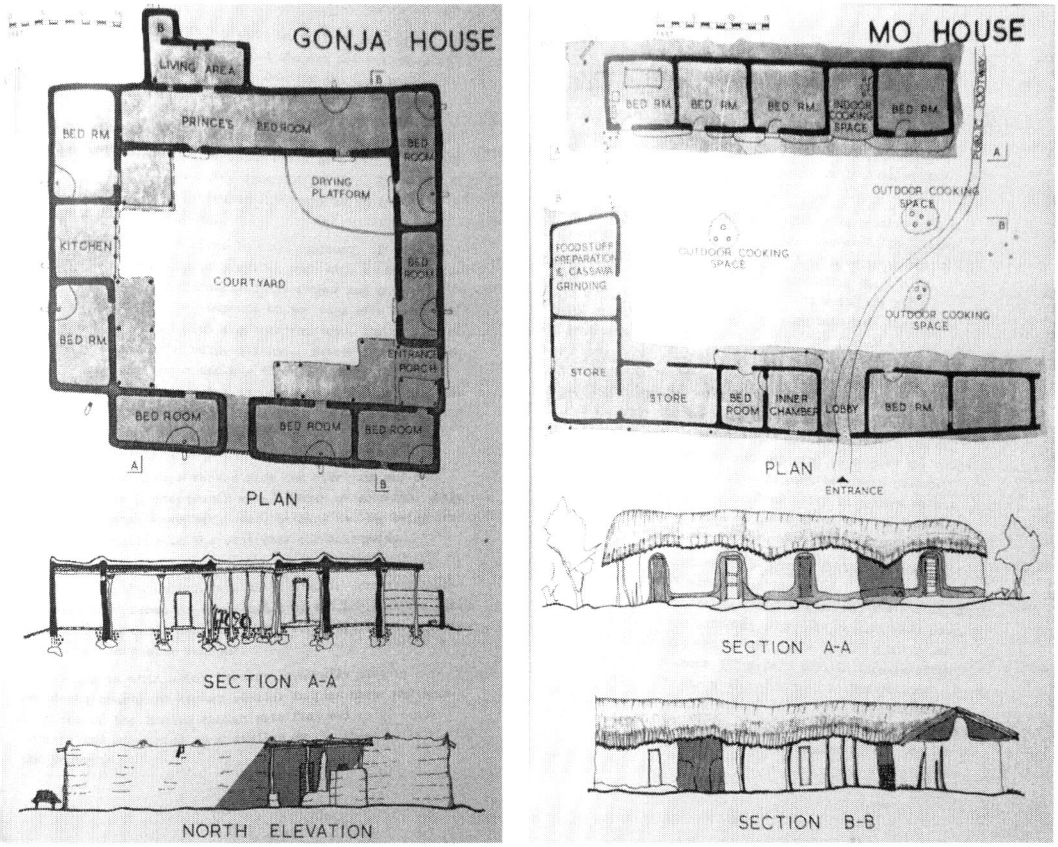

igure 6.2
rawing of two traditional dwellings by Wakely's students in *"Bui Resettlement Area Survey, 1965" by Kumasi students under the upervision of P. I. Wakely and K. K. Mumtaz*. Courtesy of Professor Patrick Wakely.

manner, was, however, the exception at that time. It forms a rather striking contrast to how the RIBA and its Board of Architectural Education (BAE) dealt with the shifting geopolitical relationships between the metropole and the tropics, as we shall see in the next section.

DECOLONIZATION, THE RIBA AND COMMONWEALTH ARCHITECTURE

Since the early twentieth century, the RIBA had served as a "parent organization" of a network of allied societies in the British Empire, regulating the entry into the profession through the systemic control of architecture training in the name of maintaining professional standards.[43] The means of control included the establishment of a standardized examination system with a common syllabus, the accreditation of schools of architecture and the exemption of graduates of recognized schools from the examinations. Until the 1960s, with the exception of Sir Jamsethji Jijibhai School of Art in Bombay, all the overseas schools recognized by the RIBA were in the dominions of Canada, Australia, New Zealand and South Africa. In 1930, the RIBA introduced the "devolution scheme" in which the RIBA passed on some of its gatekeeper's authority to its allied societies in the dominions.[44] The "devolution scheme" took place after the Balfour Declaration of 1926 in which Britain officially recognized the political autonomy of dominions, and the relationship between Britain and these dominions was rearticulated as the voluntary associations of independent states within a Commonwealth of Nations.[45] If the formation of what was known as the old Commonwealth contributed to the changes in the relationship between the RIBA and its allied societies in the dominions, what changes would decolonization and the formation of the new Commonwealth in the mid-twentieth century bring about?

When new architecture schools were first established in British colonies such as Hong Kong, Nigeria and Kenya in the 1950s, they all applied to be recognized by the RIBA. In their applications for recognition and exemption, the schools had to submit their syllabi for the RIBA BAE to review and approve. These schools in general proposed syllabi that deviated from the standard RIBA syllabus because they had to address social, cultural, economic and climatic conditions of the countries/colonies in which they were based, which differed quite significantly from those in Britain. For example, in a 1953 submission by the architecture department in the Nigeria College of Arts, Science and Technology at Ibadan, J. O. Rowell, the Acting Head, notes that "with the needs and means so very different from those in United Kingdom, an entirely new syllabus has been drawn up" for his Department to take into account local crafts, customs and climate. In the syllabus, subjects such as "Nigeria" and special technical topics like "Solar heat and its effects on human comfort" were proposed.[46] Views sympathetic to these requests were expressed by BAE members who had previous experience of working in the tropics, such as Robert Gardner-Medwin and Anthony M. Chitty, whom we have discussed in Chapter 5. Their views were, however, the minority in the BAE. After all, they belonged to what Holford characterized as Britain's "more progressive and interesting" architects who were first sent abroad by the Colonial Office in the early 1940s, and their views were not yet in the ascendant in the early 1950s.[47] As such, the submissions of new syllabi for approval by the new schools of architecture in the tropics were repeatedly rejected by the BAE.

Not only was the BAE unwilling to extend the RIBA recognition to these schools, it was initially also against modifying the RIBA Intermediate and Final Examinations for candidates in the colonies to account for the local differences. It was only after the repeated protests of Chitty and Gardner-Medwin that the BAE grudgingly permitted the RIBA examination questions to be drafted and marked by the local examiners in the colonies with the caveat that the papers were to be sent to London for checking by the RIBA examiners.[48] Officers of the BAE reasoned that because qualification for the RIBA associateship meant statutory registration, which would allow the qualified person to practice in Britain, they were unwilling to compromise on the established standard.[49] In other words, the disqualification of the relevance of local knowledge was not only linked to the arrogance derived from the sense of metropolitan/Western superiority, it was also about the protection of the British architects' domain of practice.

The BAE's refusal to recognize the schools of architecture in the colonies subsequently became a political problem in the late 1950s. The BAE was told by the Colonial Office that in the case of the School of Architecture at Hong Kong University, the denial of recognition up until 1957, seven years after its establishment, had caused "a great deal of distress" with the Hong Kong colonial government.[50] Likewise, the Advisory Committee on Colonial Colleges of Arts, Science and Technology also appealed to the RIBA in 1955 to recognize the Schools of Architecture in the African colleges.[51] By 1956, there were six Schools of Architecture in the British colonies and protectorates. With plans in place for two more schools, the BAE's refusal to recognize the colonial schools became a serious problem for the Colonial Office, particularly to its policy of establishing more institutions of higher education in the colonies to drive colonial socio-economic development. Officials from the Colonial Office told the BAE that there were ample precedents for a modified course that deviated from the metropolitan norms, citing for example the University of London's courses in medicine, botany and geology, which all had special curricula adapted to Nigerian conditions.[52] Under immense political pressure, the BAE finally relented in around 1956 despite claiming that "the standard of architecture could not be judged on a basis of furthering Commonwealth relations."[53] It accepted that these new colonial schools of architecture could include "courses being related to the scope and nature of the architectural practice of the country [or colony] concerned" as long as these were in addition to the RIBA's standard requirements.[54]

The recognition of the need for regional diversity in the curriculum of new schools of architecture in the new Commonwealth by the BAE in 1956 was followed by a shift in the RIBA's stance towards the "allied societies" in the following year. In January 1957, the RIBA Council agreed to promote a Commonwealth organization of architects based on "a common, high standard of education and professionalism, with an associated freedom to move throughout the Commonwealth for practice."[55] The RIBA Council was asked to work out an examination system for the Commonwealth organization that was to be based on "a framework both elastic and compact, a system wherein all countries could subscribe to a common standard of professional proficiency, with local knowledge, variation and experience added at a later stage."[56] An Overseas Examination Committee was formed to work out such an examination system. The committee submitted a report authored by Chitty and William Allen, a Canadian architect and a BRS building scientist who was to become the principal of the AA in 1960, in January 1959. In the report, Chitty and Allen are keen to dispel any concerns that the new organization was "the old 'empire' setup" in a new guise.[57] They noted that while it was natural for the allied societies to look to the "mother country" and the RIBA, which had the largest group of architects, for initial guidance in leading the Commonwealth organization, they foresaw that the RIBA was to gradually become "one among equals."[58]

In order to establish uniformity in education standards and a common examination system for the Commonwealth, Chitty and Allen proposed that architectural training be divided into two main components – the "universal subjects" that were to be "treated uniformly regardless of geographical region and local history" and subjects that would be influenced by local specificities.[59] In their proposal, universal subjects were those technoscientific (including the social sciences) ones such as structures, acoustic, light, heat, preparatory mathematics, science, sociology and economics, while subjects influenced by local conditions were building construction and materials, history, and professional practice and law. This was a two-part system with the universal subjects constituting the larger constant and the local subjects as the smaller variables. A good educational standard for the Commonwealth architects was seen as one that took into account local variations without "substantially affecting the basic education."[60] This two-part system would then serve to facilitate the movement of architects within the Commonwealth: a qualified architect from one country or territory in the Commonwealth could move to and practice in another by simply taking an examination that dealt with the local variations.

When the proposal for Commonwealth education standard was presented in 1957, it raised vehement objections from the overseas allied societies, especially those in the Dominions. An Australian representative saw the proposal as an unwelcome intrusion that potentially had "as its nub the control of Australian Examinations and Australian Schools from overseas," thus undermining the autonomy of the Royal Australian Institute of Architects.[61] Despite the reassurances offered by Chitty and Allen, the critics saw the proposed Commonwealth education standard as an attempt by the RIBA to maintain its role as the chief arbiter of professional standards and extend its influence in the new Commonwealth. The purportedly objective and universal basis for professional standards was seen by its critics as nothing more than a form of legitimation for the RIBA members to continue to practice in the new Commonwealth after the colonial territories became independent.

Some members of the RIBA were mindful of these criticisms and were aware of the consequences if the RIBA refused to compromise. For example, Michael Pattrick, a member of the BAE and the principal of AA in the 1950s, wrote:

> I am sure a universal examination is quite impossible. The only solution to the Commonwealth recognition problem is an active and lively accrediting board composed of Commonwealth and UK members so that *recognition can be given to the Commonwealth schools as soon as possible and before they refuse to recognise the RIBA* ...[62]

The fear that the RIBA, in particular, and the British, in general, might lose influence in the rapidly decolonizing world was again reiterated at the 1961 RIBA Conference of the Head of Overseas Schools of Architecture. An officer with the Department of Technical Cooperation, which took over the former functions of the Colonial Office in relation to matters concerning colonial and international development, noted: "The big issue, of course, was and is the survival of the RIBA – and the British – connection with architectural education throughout the Commonwealth." [63] He recommended that the RIBA be flexible when it came to accessing and recognizing overseas Schools of Architecture. That suggestion was accepted by the RIBA, and in the 1961 conference report, Maxwell Fry, the conference's chairman, notes:

> As the new universities rapidly emerging will be wholly independent, and therefore settle their own entry standards and curricula ... it may soon be unrealistic for the RIBA to "require" a given standard ... Flexibility is desirable when interpreting the RIBA syllabus in order to meet local conditions (which result from difference of race, climate and history) ...[64]

If the earlier decision by the RIBA to rigidly demand that their syllabus and examination standards be adhered to arose from a hierarchical and discriminatory Eurocentric worldview with a concern to protect the British architects' domain at home from the intrusion of foreign-trained "sub-professional" architects, the latest decision to flexibly accommodate local conditions and variations in a supposedly egalitarian Commonwealth likewise arose from a similar fear of losing not only their "freedom" to practice, but also their relevance, in their former stomping grounds once these colonies become independent. The idea of a Commonwealth organization of architects led to the establishment of the Commonwealth Association of Architects (CAA) in 1964 following the recommendation of the 1963 Conference of Commonwealth and Overseas Architectural Societies, the "most representative conference ever held" with the participation of thirty-four representatives from twenty-two architectural societies (Figure 6.3).[65]

igure 6.3 onference of ommonwealth and verseas Architectural ocieties, RIBA, London, 1–25 July 1963. Among ne attendees are Lim hong Keat (from ngapore), second row, ird person from right; nd Oluwole Olumuyiwa rom Nigeria), second w, second person from ght. Reprinted with the nd permission of the niversity of Liverpool orary.

The emergence of this Commonwealth organization was accompanied by the discourse on the idea of Commonwealth architecture. Two special issues of the *Architectural Review*, issued in October 1959 and July 1960, focused on that. The first issue examined the architecture in the old Commonwealth, i.e. the dominions, and the second issue looked at the "remaining Commonwealth territories, all of which lie, in a general climatic sense if not wholly in the strict geographical sense, within the tropics"[66] (Figure 6.4). As Mark Crinson notes, "'Tropical architecture' … was the architectural modality that often came into contemporary view when the two terms, commonwealth and architecture, were spoken of together;"[67] the idea of Commonwealth architecture helped to further popularize the notion of tropical architecture institutionalized earlier.

Figure 6.4
Cover of the special issue of *Architectural Review* c the tropical Commonwealth.

CLIMATE AND FUNDAMENTAL PRINCIPLES

Koenigsberger first designed the course and prepared the syllabus for the DTS in 1953 after the conference on tropical architecture, but he was not able to run the DTS because of his prior commitments. Instead, Maxwell Fry was asked to direct the DTS based on the curriculum drawn up by Koenigsberger. In 1956, Fry decided not to continue and the position of Director of the course was advertised by the Council of the AA. Koenigsberger successfully applied for the position and took over the position in October 1957.[68] In his application materials, he sketched out his ideas for the teaching of tropical architecture. He started by noting that the course should focus on the "special problems which arise in the tropics," problems caused by the different climatic, social and economic conditions. Koenigsberger then emphasized the importance of grasping "fundamental principles" instead of relying on "[r]eady made recipes," a point he would reiterate repeatedly in subsequent years. What were these fundamental principles and why were they regarded as such? Koenigsberger noted that as the DTS focused on problems in the tropics caused by the different climatic, social and economic conditions, "understanding these conditions and their effects on design must form the main objective of the course."[69] Yet, among these multifarious conditions, Koenigsberger appeared to single out and privilege the understanding of climate.

There were various plausible explanations for this. Perhaps it was Koenigsberger's own training as a modernist and his experience of working in India from 1938 to 1951, where he was already advocating the study of local climatic conditions.[70] The needs of the general population and the availability of local materials were also regarded as important. In the 1940s, Koenigsberger was already designing innovative climate-responsive modernist buildings in Bangalore and Bombay.[71] The specific institutional context of the DTS would also account for Koenigsberger's approach. The DTS was based in London, far from the tropics despite its vaunted tradition in tropical studies. London was therefore not the ideal location for students to acquire first-hand knowledge of the social, cultural and material conditions of building in the tropics. Despite the DTS seeing itself as an empathetic center of knowledge transfer, the curriculum at the DTS needed to rely on ways of knowing the tropics that were not different from those at the centers of calculation we discussed in Chapter 5. The concept of climate was a useful entry point to know the diverse sites in the tropics because, in the words of Koenigsberger, climate allowed students to "predict population density, materials and construction systems."[72] Privileging the concept of climate in his pedagogy also enabled Koenigsberger to deal with the practical problem of having to teach students of different nationalities at the DTS. In a 1960s lecture delivered at the University of Liverpool, Koenigsberger noted that the DTS had thirty-six students from twenty-nine different countries and he "could not give 29 different cooking recipes."[73] Instead of dealing with different national contexts for building and proposing unique solutions for each, Koenigsberger chose to deal with commonalities, especially if they were predicated on something that might transcend political divisions. In an introductory lecture on climatic design, he argued: "For the architect, climatic zones are more important than national boundaries ... Bombay and Lagos have more in common than Bombay and Delhi, Lagos and Kano."[74]

Besides transcending divisions, the privileging of climatic conditions in the understanding of problems of building in the tropics also had another advantage in the institutional context of the DTS. This perceived advantage fitted into one of the recurring themes in Koenigsberger's lectures – knowing through defamiliarization. For example, in a grant proposal co-written with Allen for the establishment of a Department of Development Studies at the AA, Koenigsberger notes

> Undergraduate education should take place in a student's home territory. Postgraduate education gains from a change of scene. It is difficult for students to understand the environment in which they have grown up. They belong to it, they are involved in it, and they take it for granted. New thinking is possible only when they move away from home and are confronted with the problems of other societies. They see more when they are forced to look back at their own from the vantage point of an international gathering.[75]

Koenigsberger suggests that exploring a problem at an international center like the DTS at London with students from other countries would allow a comparative understanding of a problem, avoiding the parochialism of attending to a problem from a local perspective. By foregrounding climatic conditions and exploring commonalities beyond the nation, students were likewise able to gain a broader understanding of the nature of the problem. This is a specific form of defamiliarization, achieved through a return to fundamental principles based on technoscientific research, as we shall see below.

Given the centrality of climate in the fundamental principles, Koenigsberger argued that the DTS's "foremost task is to teach architects to produce 'climate-conscious' buildings."[76] What Koenigsberger proposed was essentially to teach tropical architecture through what later came to be known as "climatic design," i.e. the fundamental (re)framing of the problems of building in the tropics by elevating climatic conditions as the central consideration and dealing with these considerations using building science. He wrote:

> The student must learn to understand the concept of climate, how it is influenced by geography, geology, and man-made features and how it effects [*sic*] human health, comfort and efficiency. He must learn how to survey, analyse and classify climatic conditions with reference to general environmental control, indoor comfort, design traditions, and the behaviour and deterioration of materials.[77]

Koenigsberger's bundling of climate with health, comfort and efficiency obviously has a history, especially in the tropics, as we have seen in the earlier chapters of this book. But Koenigsberger justified his privileging of climate in a technoscientific and historical manner that was fairly novel, a reworking of older climatic determinist theories in the mid-twentieth century. His justification rested on a physiological basis. Koenigsberger noted in a co-authored housing manual:

> The study of design in relation to climate must begin with the question "How does climate affect the human body?" This question is answered best by reference to an observation of the great French physiologist Claude Bernard, who found that *happy and healthy human life is possible only as long as the temperature inside the human body is kept constant within fairly narrow limits.*[78]

While a human being is a homotherm, i.e. he or she can maintain a relatively constant body temperature even though environmental temperature fluctuates, Koenigsberger noted that constant body temperature might be achieved only with much external assistance – through clothing and housing – and at the price of inactivity and discomfort, especially when the environmental conditions are not ideal.[79] Moreover, feelings of discomfort increase fatigue, decrease work efficiency, and purportedly even affect health and happiness.

Koenigsberger's discussion of climate went beyond the unit of an individual human to encompass aggregates of many humans, including those of nations and civilizations. Drawing on the early twentieth century climatic determinist work of American geographer Ellsworth Huntington and Sydney F. Markham, Koenigsberger argued that climate affected the energy of nations and even shaped the development of civilization (Figures 6.5 and 6.6).[80] He claimed that although human beings first emerged in "zones of favourable climate," that is the tropics,

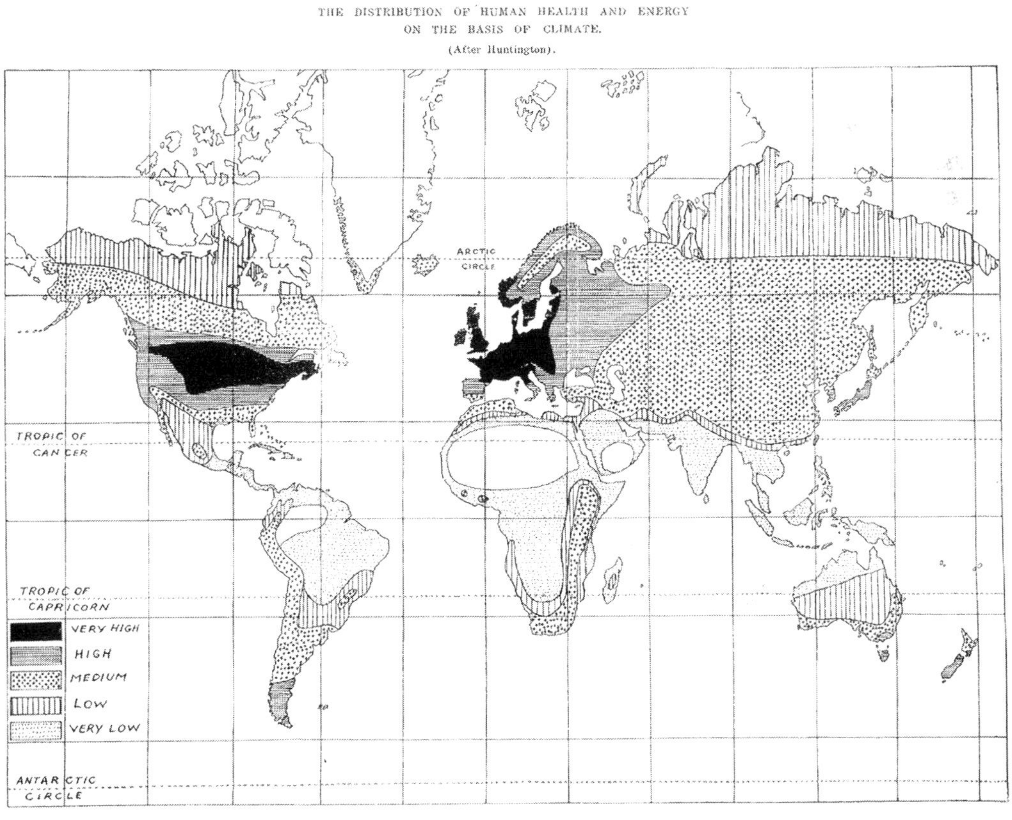

Figure 6.5
Professor Kenneth Black's mapping of "The Distribution of Human Health and Energy on the Basis of Climate," based on a similar map by Ellsworth Huntington.
Source: *TMMJ*, 1932.

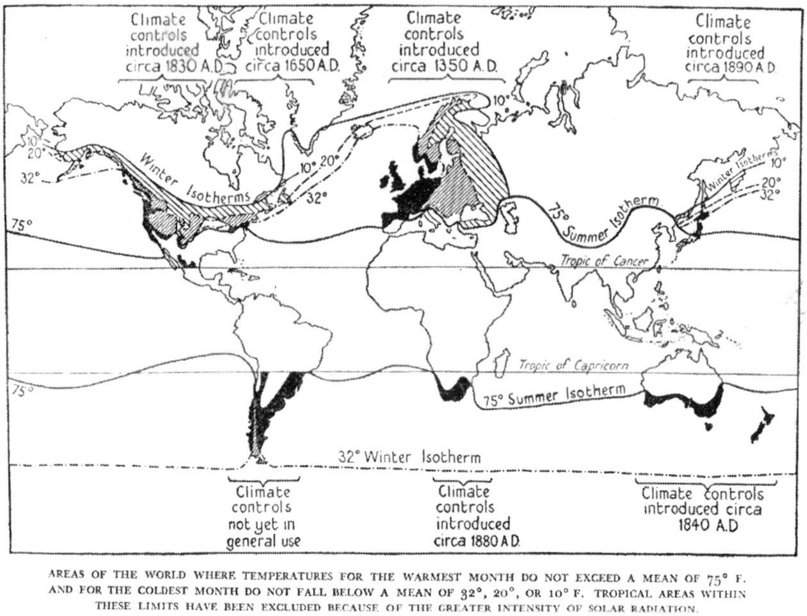

Figure 6.6 Markham's map annotated as "Areas of the world where temperatures for the warmest month do not exceed a mean of 75°F. and for the coldest month do not fall below a mean of 32°, 20°, or 10°F. Tropical areas within these limits have been excluded because of the greater intensity of solar radiation." Note how Markham added further indications to show the introduction of climate controls. Source: Markham, *Climate and the Energy of Nations*, 1947 [1942].

civilizations developed in regions with "ideal climate." By ideal climate, Koenigsberger was referring to the temperate climate because "since man mastered fire, we can heat and dry, but not cool" and, thus, those who lived in temperate climate were more likely to attain comfort, be more energetic and productive at work. However, this old and familiar climatic determinist account was modified by another view on the emergence of various technologies of environmental control in Europe, such as the invention of the grate in the thirteenth century and the Dutch stove in the fifteenth century, and how these technologies allowed indoor work during the cold months, which in turn set the stage for the advancement of Northern civilization. Koenigsberger argued that the "beginning of architects' mastery over the cold climate" marked the "beginning of European political predominance, power and colonization."[81]

Koenigsberger's historical analysis linking the physiological with the civilizational, the individual with the collective, was adopted from Markham's account in his *Climate and the Energy of Nations*.[82] Although Markham's book is conceptually similar to that of Huntington in that they both shared common assumptions about climatic determinism and their mappings of the nations with the highest energy level and civilizational attainments overlapped, their methods and emphases differed. In Markham's sweeping account of the history of world civilizations, climatic condition was attributed much causal power though it was not as overwhelmingly deterministic of civilizational outcomes as in Huntington's account. Markham left more room for human agency and technological innovations – including architectural ones – to modify and even control climatic conditions, particularly indoor climatic conditions. For example, he argued that

Roman civilization was assisted by their invention of the hypocaust system of heating, and sought to show that "[i]t was the chimney, the grate and the use of coal, combined with new developments in architecture, which changed the whole history of mankind" from around the 1300s onward.[83] The new developments in architecture that Markham referred to were "the rediscovery of brick-making and window glass-making" that helped to produce the "sealed house." Not only did that combination contribute to the emergence of the Renaissance, Markham claimed that it laid the foundation for the invention of the stove in the fifteenth century that provided warm indoor temperature that approximated the ideal range most conducive for "mental work." Markham heralded this as the arrival of a "new indoor civilization" in Northern Europe that became the basis for industrial revolution. As this new indoor civilization was also made possible by the extensive use of coal as a fuel source, Markham christened this the "coal civilization." Further technological innovations in the coal civilization – such as gas heating and lighting, steam heating and hot water system – during the nineteenth century further enabled Europeans to control the indoor climatic conditions that would climax in European imperialism.

Markham's historical account provided Koenigsberger with a number of compelling reasons for teaching climatic design. First of all, Koenigsberger could use Markham's central thesis that "one of the basic reasons for the rise of a nation in modern times is its control over climatic conditions: that the nation which has led the world, leads the world, and will lead the world, is that nation that lives in a climate, indoor and outdoor, nearest the ideal"[84] to justify the teaching of climatic design and the privileging of climatic conditions as the prime determinant of architectural form. The conjoining of climate control with the fate of a nation might have proven to be especially seductive at a time of decolonization and the prevailing concern with national development. Equally significant was the conceptual space that Markham's account opened up for architectural intervention in modifying the indoor climatic conditions and transforming the fate of nations. It allowed Koenigsberger to claim that the "historical role of architecture [was as] controller of climatic environment and thereby influences the fate of nations."[85] Coupling the agency given to architecture, and thus architects, with the political economic imbalances created by Western imperial dominance and their mastery of climatic conditions meant that Koenigsberger could arrive at the rather simplistic conclusion that glossed over the intricacies of colonial/Western dominance: "If this historical analysis is correct, it is time for architects to learn to master hot climates to restore the 'balance of power.'"[86]

PEDAGOGY AND CURRICULUM

The centrality given to climatic conditions in the tropics and climatic design by Koenigsberger was reflected in the pedagogy at the DTS and the design of the curriculum. The DTS, however, did not remain stationary and unaltered pedagogically in its close to two decades of association with the AA. Not only did the name of the department change twice, as we have noted earlier, its pedagogical emphases also shifted. "It started with the study of designing and building in the tropics, branched out to cover housing and urban and regional planning, and has lately taken on the study of general problems connected with development," Koenigsberger and Allen noted in the late 1960s.[87] Despite these changes, the climatic design components of the curriculum remained fairly central up until the late 1960s, just before it became the DDTS in 1969. Even when the Department became the DDTS and, subsequently, joined University College London as the DPU, climatic design was still regarded as foundational knowledge though the time committed to teaching it was shortened.

In the curriculum that was taught from 1956, when Koenigsberger joined as Director, to 1961, when the Department of Tropical Architecture became the DTS, topics related to climatic design were taught for the first term while the second term of the two-term-course was spent on the student's thesis project. In the first term, the thirteen weekly topics included "Types of tropical climate," "Measurement of climatic factors, study of indoor climate and its effect on comfort and efficiency," "The effects of climate on design and construction," and "Special types of tropical buildings." In each week, lectures and studios were organized around each of these topics. Many of these lectures were given by a carefully assembled group of visiting lecturers that included technical experts such as J. K. Page, G. P. Crowden, and G. A. Atkinson; and prominent British architects who had experience of building in the tropics, such as Percy Johnson Marshall, Maxwell Fry, Jane Drew, Denys Lasdun, and Richard Llewelyn-Davies. [88]

When the Department of Tropical Architecture was renamed as the DTS, Koenigsberger noted that the change meant a "new outlook" that emphasized the "wider role of [the] architect in a developing country." It was also conceived as a response to the need of the architect in a developing country to work in a team that would include, for example, economists and social scientists, if he or she was to successfully transfer the plan into "bricks and mortar." To reflect his new outlook, "less drawings, more reports" were expected from the students, especially reports that addressed the architectural and urban problems in the students' countries.[89] The lectures were similarly restructured. In the 1964–65 iteration of this curriculum that was reflected in the prospectus, the climatic design topics came under the broad theme of "man"[90] (Figure 6.7). "Man" was followed by the broader theme of "people," which covered the "basic problems of housing." This structure of starting with individual "man" and following that with "people" or the aggregate of many men and women reflected Koenigsberger and Markham's reasoning that expanded from the physiology of "man" to the fate of the nation. In this new outlook, technical building science topics such as "Climate and man," "Man and total comfort," "Radiation," "Light," "Periodic heat flow," "Air flow," and "Noise control" still took up seven weeks. The only changes in the first term were the addition of two weeks on each of the new themes of sociology and economics.[91] Finally, when the DTS was transformed into the DDTS, the course structure became more flexible, where "students make up their own courses of studies from a system of Course Units"[92] (Figure 6.8). Students were offered five options of specialization –

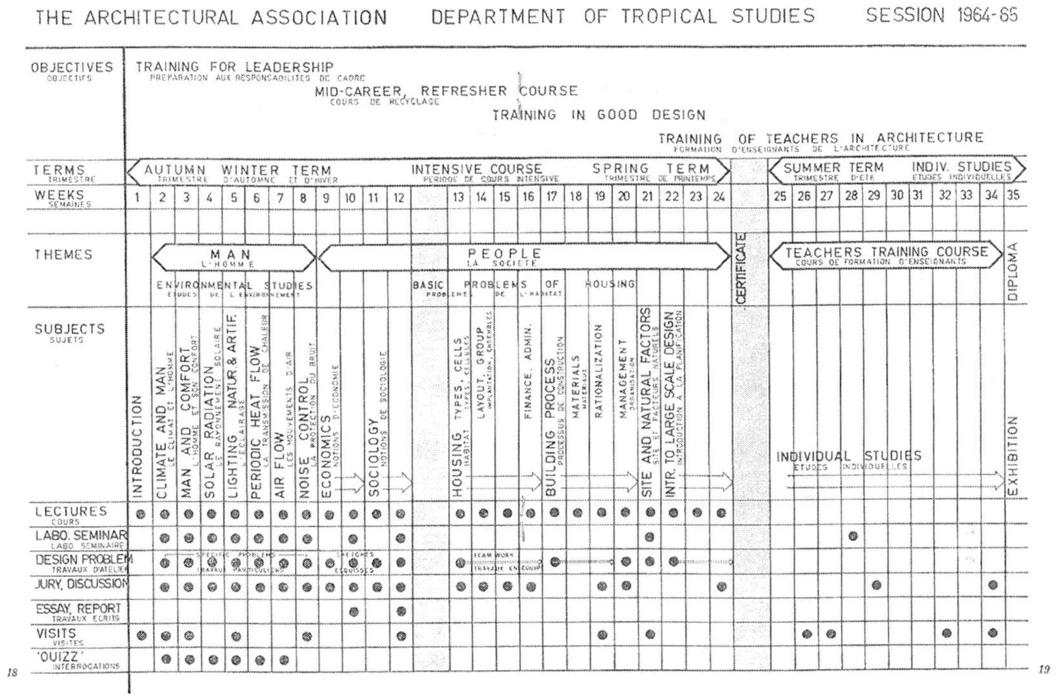
THE ARCHITECTURAL ASSOCIATION
DEPARTMENT OF TROPICAL STUDIES
SESSION 1964-65
OBJECTIVES
OBJECTIFS
TRAINING FOR LEADERSHIP
PREPARATION AUX RESPONSABILITES DE CADRE
MID-CAREER, REFRESHER COURSE
COURS DE RECYCLAGE
TRAINING IN GOOD DESIGN
TRAINING OF TEACHERS IN ARCHITECTURE
FORMATION D'ENSEIGNANTS DE L'ARCHITECTURE
TERMS
TRIMESTRE
AUTUMN WINTER TERM
TRIMESTRE D'AUTOMNE ET D'HIVER
INTENSIVE COURSE
PERIODE DE COURS INTENSIVE
SPRING TERM
TRIMESTRE DE PRINTEMPS
SUMMER TERM
TRIMESTRE D'ETE
INDIV. STUDIES
ETUDES INDIVIDUELLES
WEEKS
SEMAINES
1 2 3 4 5 6 7 8 9 10 11 12 13 14 15 16 17 18 19 20 21 22 23 24 25 26 27 28 29 30 31 32 33 34 35
THEMES
MAN
L'HOMME
PEOPLE
LA SOCIETE
CERTIFICATE
TEACHERS TRAINING COURSE
COURS DE FORMATION D'ENSEIGNANTS
DIPLOMA
ENVIRONMENTAL STUDIES
ETUDES DE L'ENVIRONNEMENT
BASIC PROBLEMS OF HOUSING
PROBLEMES DE L'HABITAT
SUBJECTS
SUJETS
INTRODUCTION
CLIMATE AND MAN
MAN AND COMFORT
SOLAR RADIATION
LIGHTING NATUR.& ARTIF.
PERIODIC HEAT FLOW
AIR FLOW
NOISE CONTROL
ECONOMICS
SOCIOLOGY
HOUSING TYPES, CELLS
LAYOUT, GROUP
FINANCE, ADMIN.
BUILDING PROCESS
MATERIALS
RATIONALIZATION
MANAGEMENT
SITE AND NATURAL FACTORS
INTR. TO LARGE SCALE DESIGN
INDIVIDUAL STUDIES
ETUDES INDIVIDUELLES
EXHIBITION
LECTURES
COURS
LABO. SEMINAR
LABO. SEMINAIRE
DESIGN PROBLEM
TRAVAUX D'ATELIER
JURY, DISCUSSION
ESSAY, REPORT
TRAVAUX ECRITS
VISITS
VISITES
'QUIZZ'
INTERROGATIONS
18
19

Figure 6.7
A table showing the 1964–65 curriculum of the Department of Tropical Studies, AA. Courtesy of AAA.

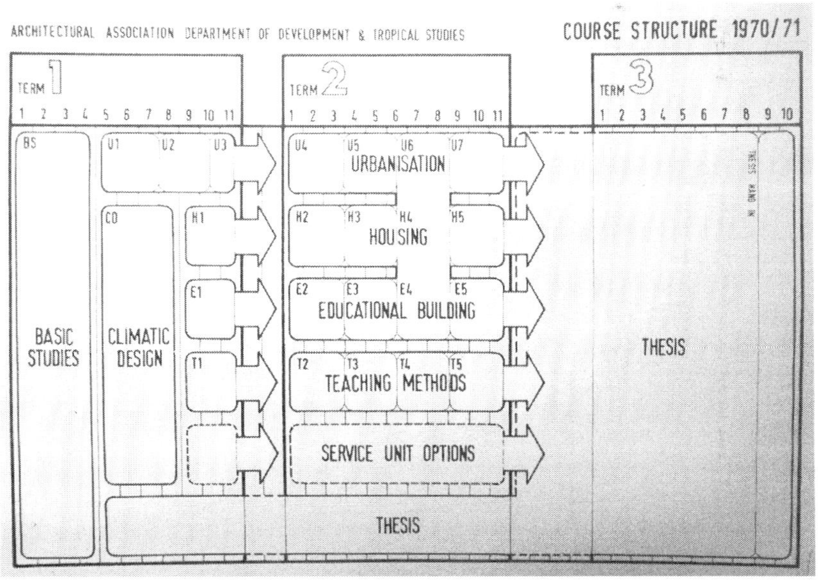

Figure 6.8
A table showing the 1970–71 curriculum of the Department of Development and Tropical Studies, AA. Courtesy of Professor Patrick Wakely.

housing, urbanization, education building, teaching methods, and service unit options. Each of these specializations had its own lectures and seminars, but students in all specializations except urbanization went through a common first term that helped them acquire the "mastery of one skill – climatic design."[93]

The lectures in the climatic design-centric curricula were supported by a set of corresponding design exercises. In the mid-1960s, the first few design exercises were on basic climatological studies in which the students were asked to "compile, digest, and illustrate all the significant factors" of a particular climate, calculate and plot the sun path diagram of a given latitude, and "determine the required shading periods" of an opening and design an effective sun-shading device.[94] Overseas students were even instructed to bring detailed climatic data from their home countries before they arrived in Britain to provide the required data for these design exercises. In these exercises, students were to represent climate visually through a series of diagrams, graphs, tables and charts that capture climatic data – such as air temperature, relative humidity, rainfall, prevailing wind directions, wind velocities, etc. – in "a form applicable to architectural decisions" and with the identification of "critical data for climate concious [*sic*] designing"[95] (Figure 6.9). At the DTS and other institutions that taught climatic design, climatic data were represented in standardized formats that

Figure 6.9
A graphical representation of climatic data of Dar-Es-Salaam for a project by Patrick Wakely in 1963, when he was a student at the DTS. Courtesy of Professor Patrick Wakely.

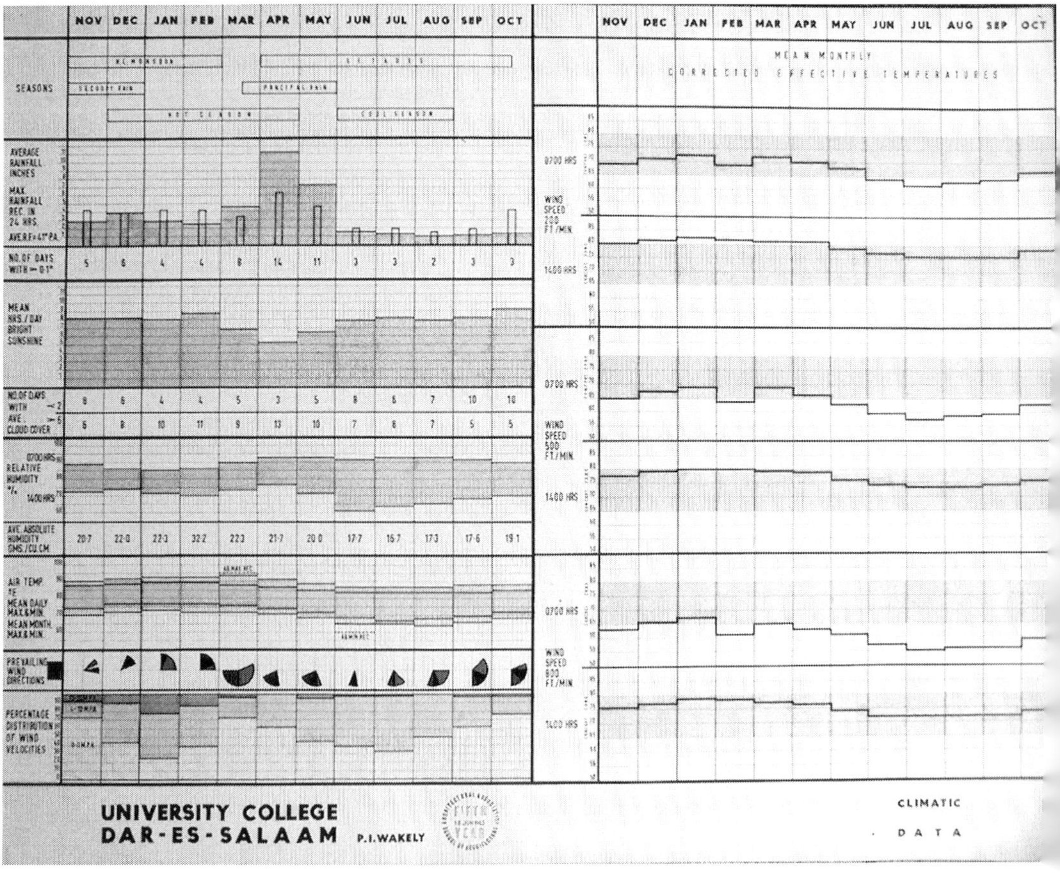

included, among other things, a time series graph that plots temperature, relative humidity or rainfall variations over time, and an equidistant sun path diagram that plots how the position of the sun in terms of solar azimuth and altitude varies over time for different latitudes. These standardized formats allowed different climates of diverse localities in the tropics to be compared and classified into climatic types. The students were also taught how to measure indoor environmental conditions and the various indices of thermal comfort – such as those by Bedford, Olgyay and Webb. From the comparison of tropical climatic data with the requirements of thermal comfort, the students would have quantitative evidence that heat was a major design problem in the tropics. They would then be taught how to calculate heat gain – particularly heat gain through solar radiation – and heat load of a building. Following that, they were taught to use solar charts and protractors to design effective sun-shading devices to protect a building's openings so as to minimize solar heat gain. The students were also taught quantitative assessment methods of day-lighting and the physics of air flow, particularly how these might affect the design of a building.

After going through these various lectures and exercises, the students were asked to put the technical knowledge they had acquired into practice through a design exercise of larger scale and greater complexity. One such example was the 1963 exercise in which the students were asked to adapt the CLASP (Consortium of Local Authority School's Programmes) school building erected at the Milan Triennial in 1960, which received much publicity and plaudits, for the "three contrasting climatic, technological and economic situations" of Delhi, Lagos and Baghdad.[96] CLASP was a construction system that used light steel structures and prefabricated components, designed for building schools cheaply and at great speed in postwar Britain, especially on sites that had subsidence problems. CLASP was, however, not just a constructional system; it also represented a particular postwar approach to research, design and construction of building. Specifically, it exemplified the Development Group method, in which a multidisciplinary team consisting of architects, educationists, engineers and builders applied the technoscientific methods of operational research to study, design, construct and test prototypes in tight feedback loops.[97] Like many other modernist architects in Britain during that time, Allen and Koenigsberger were admirers of the Development Group method, particularly its "translation of industrial techniques for the fulfillment of a wider social need," and wanted to tailor it for the building needs of developing countries.[98] It is therefore not surprising that Koenigsberger set up a design exercise that asked the students to adapt the CLASP school building for the tropics. The students were asked to "acquire an understanding of the effects of climate and technological background on system building methods" and consider how those aspects would influence "the questions of mass manufacture of components, transport and erection"[99] (Figure 6.10).

In the context of the longer genealogy of tropical architecture, it is striking that the DTS taught tropical architecture in a manner that was rather distinctive. Tropical architecture was taught by not relying on, or at least not explicitly

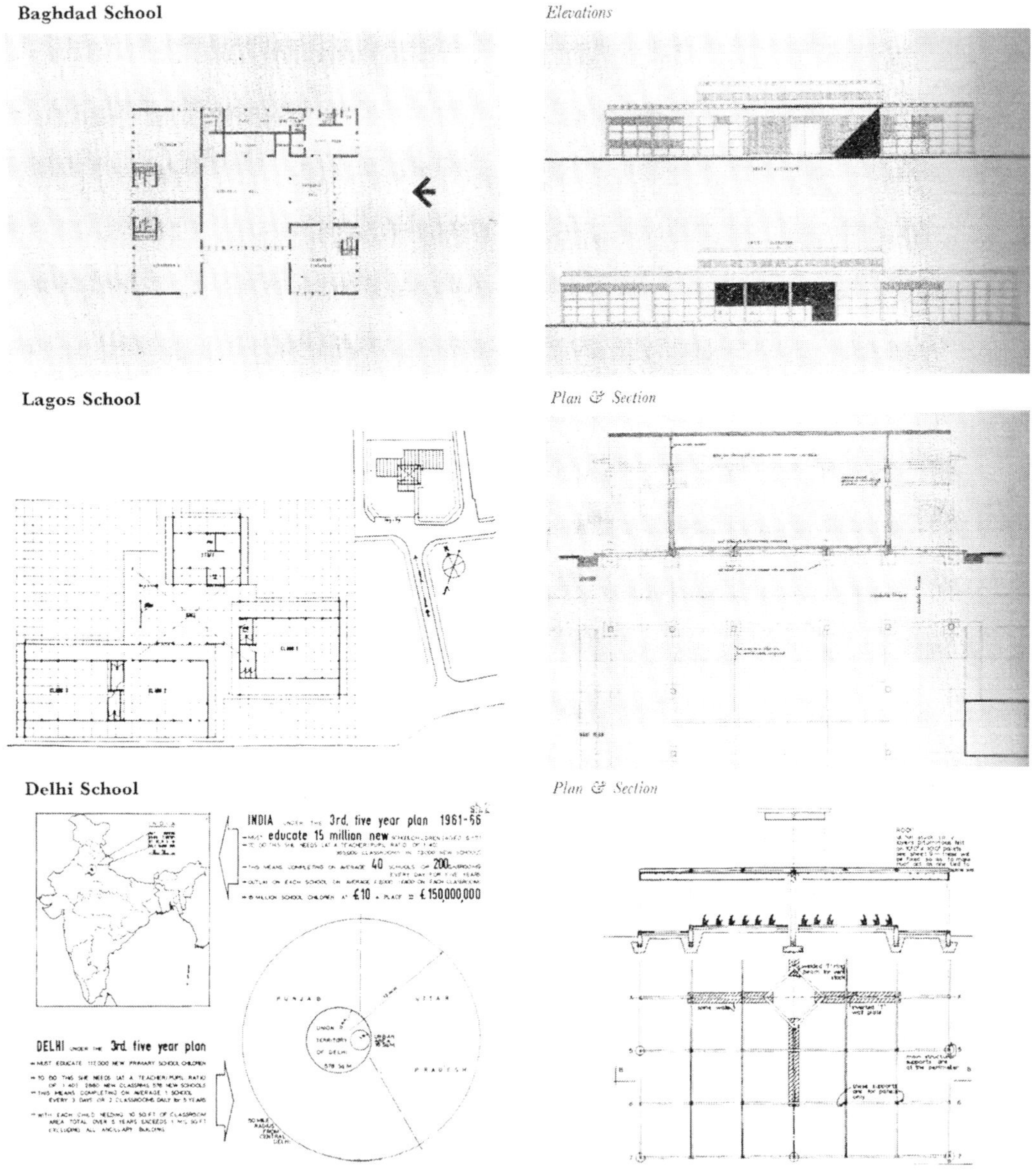

recognizing and acknowledging, prior colonial precedents but through climatic design. As we have seen, climatic design basically reframed the problem of building in the tropics by starting with the fundamental principles of human physiology – particularly how the tropical heat affects human comfort. That was also extrapolated to account for how the heat and humidity of tropical climate, if not properly controlled, might impede national development. Having reframed the problem, climatic design also prescribed its own solution to the problem through the application of technoscientific methods, such as building science experiments

Figure 6.10
The plans and sections of the schools located in the different climatic conditions of Baghdad, Lagos and Delhi. Source: *Architectural Association Journal* 78, 1965. Reprinted with the kind permission of Architectural Association.

and calculations. Technoscientific methods appeared to be especially valued because they yield precise quantitative answers. Koenigsberger once argued in a co-authored paper on roofs in the hot-humid tropics that phrases like " 'protection from solar heat' and 'suitability for tropical climates' are imprecise terms" because they could not provide unambiguous specifications of the climatic performance in a simple and accurate manner. But Koenigsberger also noted that,

> As a matter of fact, physicists, architects and engineers who have specialized in tropical architecture *can* calculate and measure the protection a roof provides against heat and state the results of their calculations in precise form.[100]

In the next section, I argue that the teaching of tropical architecture through climatic design at the DTS, and the attendant reframing of the problem through fundamental principles and the prescription of the solution through technoscientific methods, have to be seen in relation to, not just the cult of expertise in international development that we saw in Chapter 5, but also the rise of building science and architectural research in Britain during the 1950s and 1960s.

THE RISE OF BUILDING SCIENCE AND ARCHITECTURAL RESEARCH

In William Allen's inaugural lecture as the Principal of the AA in 1962, he hailed the DTS as a "delightful and flourishing" center of postgraduate teaching and research and he wanted to use the DTS as an organizational and pedagogical model for setting up similar postgraduate research departments at the AA.[101] Allen's praise of the DTS is unsurprising given his background in building science at the BRS. He was one of the key architectural figures involved in building research and proponents of building science appointed in the 1950s and 1960s to lead British architectural schools. The others included Leslie Martin, who was appointed as the Head of School of Architecture at Cambridge University in 1956, and Richard Llewelyn-Davies, the former director of the Division of Architectural Studies at the Nuffield Foundation, who took over as the Head of the Bartlett School of Architecture in 1960.[102] Besides these new Heads, Departments of Building Science and Professorial Chairs were also created in at least seven British Universities – London, Sheffield, Liverpool, Newcastle, Cardiff, Edinburgh and Strathclyde. Among these Professorial Chairs were Professor A. W. Henry appointed at the University of Liverpool in 1957, Professor J. K. Page appointed at the University of Sheffield in 1961, Professor Thomas A. Markus appointed at the University of Strathclyde in 1966, and Professor C. Barrie Wilson appointed at the University of Edinburgh in 1968.[103] All these signaled the institutionalization of building science as a subfield integral to architectural education and the architectural profession in Britain.

The landmark event marking the institutionalization of building science was, however, the 1958 Oxford Conference on Architectural Education. The conference put forth a set of far-reaching recommendations on architectural education that was endorsed by the RIBA Council and implemented in the subsequent years. Central to the recommendations was the establishment of architectural education within Universities and the elevation of architecture to a proper university discipline. In turning architecture into a proper university discipline, postgraduate work and scientific research were to become an integral part of architectural education in order to develop specialized knowledge and advance "theory."[104] Building science was envisioned as part of the specialized knowledge and "theory" within this scheme of things.

When building science was first introduced in the early twentieth century, it referred primarily to the early research done by the BRS in the scientific study of building materials to determine their structural, thermal, acoustical and chemical properties, and how these studies could be applied in building construction to address the housing shortages in post-World War I Britain.[105] The scope of building research later expanded into other domains, such as building economics, user requirements and, especially relevant for this study, environmental physics, which entailed daylighting, artificial lighting, heating, cooling and ventilation. Despite the work of the BRS, building science was slow to establish itself as an integral part of architectural education and the profession.[106] It was only from 1939 onwards with the establishment of the Architectural Science Group (ASG) between the RIBA and BRS that building science gradually became more integral to the architectural profession and education.[107] Formed to "study and report on scientific developments that [were] applicable to building and on the use of [the] scientific method in building," the group also set up an Education Committee to study and make recommendations regarding "the extent to which science may be given a suitable place in [the architect's] education."[108] The Committee produced three reports, which recommended that science should be given a more prominent place in architectural education. The committee argued that architects with better grounding in science and technology would lead the building industry to improve their "outworn traditional methods" by applying the scientific ideas and technical progress gained from building research. The committee specifically emphasized the importance of teaching fundamental sciences and the underlying scientific principles so that students would acquire a "general scientific outlook and mode of thought" that would serve as a basis for both future specialization and research.[109] To achieve these objectives, the Committee recommended that the schools of architecture reform their curricula and increase the proportion of building science courses.

The ASG Education Committee's recommendations were, however, entirely rejected by the RIBA Special Committee on Architectural Education, of which it was a subsidiary. The 1946 Report of the Special Committee explicitly stated that "[a]rchitecture itself is an art or it is nothing."[110] Among other things, the Report implied that, if implemented, the technocentric recommendations would "inculcate a narrow conception of architecture … stultify artistic imagination and transform potential architects into indifferent technicians."[111] In contrast to the 1946 Report, the recommendations of the 1958 Oxford Conference represented a radically different view of architectural education and fully embraced the importance of building science. One of the key underlying assumptions of the recommendations of the 1958 Conference was the relationship between architectural design, knowledge and research. Quoting directly from Llewelyn-Davies's paper "Deeper Knowledge: Better Design" presented at the conference, Martin noted in his report that:

> Knowledge is the raw material for design ... It is not a substitute for architectural imagination: but it is necessary for the effective exercise of imagination and skill in design. Inadequate knowledge handicaps and trammels the architect, limits the achievements of even the most creative and depresses the general level of design.[112]

The position that more knowledge contributes to better design could be read as a direct rebuttal of the fear expressed in the 1946 Report that too much technoscientific knowledge would stultify the architect's imagination. Martin further emphasized that the accretion of knowledge had to be "guided and developed by principles: that is, by theory," which was in turn advanced by research.[113]

To better understand Martin's point about the relationship between design, knowledge and research, it might be useful for us to delve deeper into Llewelyn-Davies's paper and the ways it echoed and built upon what John Desmond Bernal, prominent scientist and pioneer in social studies of science who was central to the rise of architectural research and building science, had said.[114] Llewelyn-Davies's paper claimed that the architecture profession's years of operating in isolation from life in general and socio-technological transformations in particular had led to the profession's "poverty of knowledge." In order for architecture to reintegrate with life, he urged architects to "expand and consolidate [the profession's] knowledge."[115] Llewelyn-Davies identified two main areas of knowledge – the *means* of buildings and the *needs* of buildings. Referring mainly to the BRS's building research, CLASP and the Nuffield Foundation's architectural studies of hospital design, which he led, Llewelyn-Davies showed how new knowledge in *means* and *needs* of building had been created through research. He argued that this new knowledge did not merely bring about incremental changes; rather, this knowledge which emerged from research that asked fundamental questions would effectively revolutionize the ways buildings were designed and produced. For example, he prophesized that prefabricated schools pioneered by the Ministry of Education's school building program and CLASP meant that "production engineering" and prefabrication in the factory would "slowly but steadily displac[e] sitework."[116]

Llewelyn-Davies's observations bear quite a few similarities to those sketched out by Bernal in a paper read at the RIBA in 1946. Bernal started his paper by stating that his previous ideas, as sketched out in a 1937 article, about the relationship between science and architecture were inadequate.[117] Bernal noted: "All those are what may be called direct applications of science to subjects involved in architecture, but they are not, in my opinion now, really science in the scientific aspect of architecture itself."[118] Instead, Bernal argued that his war experience had taught him that the science in the scientific aspect of architecture was to address the problem through a scientific approach in an "integral way" and ask fundamental questions. He gave an example from the enormous postwar rebuilding and rehousing program in Britain. One of the problems that preoccupied him as the Chairman of the Scientific Committee of the Ministry of Works and which he felt could not be resolved without using the new scientific approach was the architectural one of how to build with minimum cost and maximum speed while satisfying "human requirements and human utilities." By "human requirements and human utilities," Bernal was referring to some of the most fundamental requirements of housing which were unknown scientifically. He noted, for example, that answers to apparently simple questions such as "what the house is used for" and "elementary physiological matters" that would help to ascertain "the amount of air, the amount of heat, and so forth, that are needed to provide a satisfactory, optimum, healthy atmosphere"[119] remained to be researched and known scientifically. Bernal then noted that: "When the requirements are known, we begin to see that they involve problems of a technical kind which are not necessarily problems which are solved by traditional methods."[120] In other words, framing the housing problems scientifically in terms of fundamental requirements meant also rearticulating them as technical problems that would lead to radical solutions.

Common to Bernal and Llewelyn-Davies were their belief in the use of scientific method and the attendant implications that, as Andrew Saint put it, "all problems and propositions ... had to be examined from first principles,"[121] and their faith in technoscience in solving social problems and transforming the world. Mark Crinson and Jules Lubbock also compared research, as the practice of "go[ing] back to first principles and consider[ing] every problem anew as if there had been no inherited body of knowledge and practice," with the Bauhaus notion of *Vorkurs*.[122] *Vorkurs* was first conceived by Johannes Itten to liberate his students from their cultural preconceptions, but it was later modified by Gropius to become a model for the design process in which everything has to be considered afresh, "applying the openness of innocence in conjunction with the infallibility of science."[123]

Crinson and Lubbock noted that building science and research were introduced through the 1958 Conference as a part of the "official system." The key protagonists involved in introducing the changes had all worked for public offices as technocratic mandarins before joining the universities as professorial chairs. The architectural educational reforms in introducing the scientific methods to deal with social problems could thus be read in conjunction with the larger social reforms introduced by the postwar British welfare state. Saint traced the origin of this set of beliefs to the widespread advocacy of the emancipatory potential of science in British society in the 1930s led by a group of Cambridge-trained scientists – mostly socialists and humanists – that included Bernal. At the heart of this advocacy was "scientific humanism" that sought for "a better understanding of science, wider application of its methods and a just use of its social powers" that its advocates felt would lead to the betterment of humanity and the creation of a more equitable and happier society.[124] Implicit in this was of course a certain degree of technological romanticism, a (blind) faith in the omnipotence of technoscience. By extension, one could also argue that the teaching of climatic design and the advocacy of tropical architecture by Koenigsberger and other staff members at the DTS were also shaped by scientific humanism, extending it beyond the limits of British society to the societies in the developing world.

THE LEGACIES

What was the impact of the new pedagogy of teaching climatic design established at the DTS given its relatively short existence? The case of the DTS's impact might be better appreciated if we discuss it in conjunction with the other key institutions covered in this chapter – the RIBA and the CAA. As we have seen earlier, the RIBA was instrumental in setting up the CAA. Although the main objectives of the CAA were outwardly articulated as "mutual support in professional matters and the sustaining of professional codes," the RIBA and the British architects involved had vested interests in maintaining the old imperial pecking order and ensuring the "free and vigorous movement of architects" of the old Empire in the new Commonwealth.[125] However, as Atkinson suggested earlier, in the decolonizing world, British architects had to justify their architectural commissions in the tropics with their "special knowledge" or expertise. One can argue that the special issue of the *Architectural Review* on the architecture of the Commonwealth territories in the tropics was publicizing the expertise of British architects by featuring predominantly buildings designed by British architects.[126] For example, of the twenty-one buildings featured in the sections on Singapore and Malaya, only three were designed by local architects. Justifying his selection, Julius Posener, the author of the section on Malaya, remarked that it was "largely true that the local British architect cares more about tropical architecture ... than his Asian colleague."[127] Both Posener and Lincoln Page, who wrote the section on Singapore, were dismissive of local Asian architects. Posener claimed that they were "full of zest, ready at any moment to fire all their guns at once; and they are not necessarily their own guns either."[128] Page thought that they "seem not to have comprehended the fundamentals" of climatic design and only indulged in "irritating architectural mannerisms" and applied "the outward forms and elements of the modern movement indiscriminately."[129]

The British architects' claim of expertise and the attendant legitimacy to design and build in the tropics did not go unchallenged. Dissent was in fact raised against the British expatriate architects in a high-profile manner at the Conference of Commonwealth and Overseas Architectural Societies, held in July 1963, before the formal establishment of the CAA in 1964. Oluwole Olumuyiwa, Nigeria's delegate to the conference and a future President of the CAA, delivered a sensational speech. "Please stop visiting architects from using my people as guinea-pigs," he pleaded,

> We want visiting architects to practise with Nigerian firms for a period and then, if they want to set up in practice, to take an exam conducted by the Nigerian

> Institute of Architects. Often they design houses suited only to temperate climates. Some of the worst examples are in the main cities, like Lagos. They seem to forget that we have driving rains and storms. Often they don't even know the direction the storm is bound to come from. Some think air-conditioning is the answer to everything. They forget that in our country electrical breakdowns are not uncommon and that when this happens the buildings they have designed turn into ovens.[130]

The claims and counterclaims on the relative expertise of the British/expatriate architects vis-à-vis the local architects to design climatically responsive tropical architecture were just one aspect of the debate on the movement of architects in the Commonwealth. As Robert Matthew, the first president of the CAA, noted at the second CAA conference at New Delhi, "mutual recognition of qualifications" was still needed, "without which there are formidable barriers to international movement."[131] To have mutual recognition of qualifications, members of the CAA had to return to the controversial discussion of what constituted an acceptable common standard for schools. As we saw earlier, the initial attempt at stipulating a common standard for schools in the member countries of the CAA was seen as an attempt by the RIBA to continue to exert its former power and undermine the autonomy of the national architectural institutes. It was vehemently opposed by members of the national architectural institutes, which led to the CAA's "general acceptance of the principle that qualifications and education ... must inevitably rest on national needs and national qualifications."[132]

Yet that acceptance of national priorities was always moderated by the desire of the CAA to provide "some kind of machinery for recording the standard reached and a service from which understandings and agreements for reciprocity can develop." In developing this machinery, the RIBA qualification was still seen as a yardstick since it was "a kind of sterling currency of architectural qualification, of wide acceptance and great benefit to many countries." In other words, while the CAA would purportedly "leave member societies and their Governments with unimpaired authority and independence", the original intent of having the RIBA as the chief arbiter of professional standard in the CAA and using that accredited standard to facilitate the movement of mainly British architects in the Commonwealth did not go away.[133] It was with that intent that the Commonwealth Board of Architectural Education (CBAE) was established in 1966 to visit schools and accredit them.[134] After that, the CBAE published a "founder list" of fifty-four accredited schools – primarily those in Britain and the old Commonwealth of Australia, New Zealand, Canada and South Africa with the University of Hong Kong as the only exception – that was meant to be recognized in all countries within the Commonwealth.[135] The list was, however, not endorsed by the delegates at the Third CAA Conference held at Lagos in 1969. There were doubts over the usefulness, if not validity, of the list because it was later clarified that CBAE standards could vary from country to country with the final decision on the recognition left to individual national institutes. Furthermore, a school recognized by the CAA would not gain automatic recognition by the RIBA.[136]

A few national institutes also disagreed with the "founder list." Singapore Institute of Architects (SIA), for example, viewed the list as "largely a carry-over of the RIBA overseas scheme and system of recognition."[137] SIA also criticized the CBAE for the lack of transparency in its method of accreditation. Instead of addressing the urgent needs of improving the standard of the schools in the developing countries, SIA felt that the CBAE was primarily interested in the inter-recognition of schools to facilitate the movement of architects. The general dissatisfaction of the national institutes in Asia with the CAA and the CBAE led them to form their own organization, the ARCASIA (Architects Regional Council for Asia), in 1970 to promote regional collaboration. The idea was first germinated at the 1967 CAA Conference at Delhi and it was further developed at the three Asian Regional Conferences of CAA held at Singapore and Kuala Lumpur in 1967, at Colombo in 1968 and at Hong Kong in 1969.[138] The thinking behind the establishment of the ARCASIA and the rejection of the CBAE's founder list of recognized schools was perhaps best articulated in a speech by Lim Chong Keat, a Malaysian architect who was instrumental in setting up ARCASIA. He noted:

> Although I am sure that there has been no organised plot to re-colonise Commonwealth countries, the legacy and certain aspects of technical aid between developed and under-developed countries tend to create a phenomenon that is not very different in effect ... In the very establishment of universities and schools of architecture, the British pattern has largely been applicable together with the pomp and ceremony, complete with mortar-boards ... In drawing up curriculum and in the recruitment of staff, more reliance on overseas reference than on local sources for opinion such as from the professional institute, tends to apply. The views expressed are not based on prejudice but rather arise out of the realisation that unless we make a deliberate corrective adjustment, we will continue to be subservient to an external academic empire.[139]

Such attempts to "make a deliberate corrective adjustment" that challenged the "external academic empire" based on the dominance of the architects from the old Commonwealth – especially the British – and the standard they established on the old RIBA scheme might have accounted for CAA's diminished influence subsequently. In 1971, the chair of CBAE appeared to backtrack by acknowledging that standards would vary from country to country and schemes of regional standards and machinery for accreditation should be developed.[140] As the CAA secretariat moved out of the RIBA premises at Portland Place in the 1970s, the CAA finally appeared to be genuinely no longer the "old empire setup" in a new guise. Members outside the old Commonwealth were given key appointments in the CAA. For example, Jai Bhalla and Oluwole Olumuyiwa were appointed the CAA's President and Lim Chong Keat became the chair of the CBAE.[141]

As we have noted in Chapter 5, networks are contingent and heterogeneous entities. Just as they could facilitate domination from certain centers of calculation, they could also ferment resistances and challenges. In the case of the CAA, we saw that the RIBA sought to use the international organization as a way to maintain the influence of metropolitan architects in a decolonized world. But we also saw that the national associations resisted and were able to form a new network of alliances through the CAA, with the ARCASIA a case in point. Tropical architecture was at the center of this contest between hegemony and counter-hegemony. In the metropole, tropical architecture was constructed as a regional variation of the metropolitan standards that were still in the domain of metropolitan expertise. However, as we saw earlier, for many local architects in the former colonies, tropical architecture and the teaching of climatic design in the tropics were seen as an inextricable part of their quest for political independence and cultural emancipation from colonial dominance and neocolonial hegemony.

Compared to the RIBA and its involvement in the Commonwealth, the DTS and its relationship to the tropics presented a study in contrast. Unlike the RIBA, which sought to reconstruct and reinforce the old imperial network through the CAA when the geopolitical tectonic plates were pulling it apart, the DTS was not interested in buttressing some preconceived network. Perhaps due to its small size and a relative lack of historical baggage, the DTS was a much more flexible institution that adapted its network to the movements of the geopolitical tectonic plates. As we have seen earlier, it was renamed and reorganized twice in its less than two decades of existence in the AA tradition of "steady headship but frequent rejuvenation."[142] Furthermore, in contrast to the RIBA's attempt to consolidate its influence and extend its control in the architectural education of the Commonwealth countries, the DTS saw itself as playing a supplementary and transitional role in educating architects for the tropics. When the DDTS left its association with the AA and joined the University College London as DPU, Koenigsberger continued to insist that "the job of the DPU is to do itself out of a job."[143] However, instead of shrinking, the demand for advanced training at the DTS and other European institutions by the architects and planners from the tropics continued to grow. In fact, several schools of architecture and planning in Europe began launching new courses in the 1960s to train European architects and planners for working in the developing world.[144] When Koenigsberger and his colleagues were confronted with the fact that two of the original three functions of the DTS – to provide advanced training for architects and planners from the tropics, and to prepare British architects and planners to work in the tropics – did not diminish, let alone disappear as intended, they launched three new initiatives in the late 1960s and early 1970s. Two of them were related to "do[ing] itself out of a job."

The first new initiative was a formal course option on "teaching methods." This came about because many schools in the tropics modelled their curricula and pedagogies on the schools in Europe and North America without adequate consideration of the compatibility of these models with the architectural and planning needs of a developing country. The course contents were later applied in the training of teaching staff at the new Faculty of Architecture in the University of Costa Rica in 1970, and the course later became a diploma course in "Design and Planning Education for Developing Countries." The second initiative was the establishment of an "Extension Service" in 1972 to run short courses in universities and other training institutions in the developing world. Like the teaching methods option, the intention was to question the curricula and pedagogies of existing institutions in the developing countries and to propose alternative contents and methods.[145]

Related to the above two initiatives was an earlier initiative that better illustrates the differences between the respective approaches of the DTS and the RIBA to raising the standard of architectural education in the tropics. This was the "Long Range Teaching Group" initiative. According to Martin Evans and Cho Padamsee, two of Koenigsberger's colleagues, the decision to start the Group came from their awareness of the "dangers and limitations of a specialised course in a metropolitan centre."[146] According to Evans, the training of teachers would have the "multiplier effect" in the dissemination of climatic design. The Long Range Teaching Group or "travelling circus" consisted of a mobile and flexible team of teaching staff that went around different parts of the developing/tropical world to conduct short intensive training courses for teachers of architecture in these locations. Padamsee, who was involved in the Group, noted that the traveling circus was "capable of being formed and disbanded at will" and they were "available to the developing countries on request." It was regarded as "a more economical and intensive use of existing teaching skills and experience."[147] These traveling circuses made use of specially designed "mobile kits of teaching aids" to teach in various localities. The teaching aids consisted of "an arsenal of mechanical teaching aids; video tapes, films, slides, programmed texts, etc."[148] They even left behind comprehensive course materials so that the dependency of the teachers in the developing countries on the visiting team would be minimized.[149] While the RIBA sought to establish a common standard for inter-recognition in the CAA so as to extend the metropolitan power and facilitate the mobility of primarily British architects, the DTS sought to elevate standards of architectural education in the developing world and empower the "periphery."

Despite its relative short existence of less than two decades, the DTS has introduced and widely disseminated to the developing world a new model of architectural education based on climatic design. Although its model of architectural education could be understood as a response to the shifting geopolitical relations in the context of decolonization and the emergence of building science in architectural education, it was more than a product of the larger context. The responses of the RIBA to similar forces of change show that a metropolitan institution could have responded very differently. Although the RIBA was obviously a very different kind of institution from the DTS, their contrasting responses showed that the DTS has taken on a much more empathetic approach to understanding the educational and professional needs of the developing

Figure 6.11
Book covers of the Malay, Spanish and Arabic versions (from left to right) of the *Manual of Tropical Housing and Building*. Source: Renate Koenigsberger.

countries in the tropics. Unlike the RIBA, which had a vested interest in maintaining the old discriminatory imperial pecking order and disregarded the needs of the newly independent countries in the tropics, the DTS was attentive to their needs and made important intellectual and pedagogical contributions to building and planning in the developing world. In the field of climatic design, the focus of this chapter, the contributions of the DTS lasted well beyond its short existence. Besides the aforementioned influence on the curricula of the different architecture schools in the tropics through its various activities, the key legacy of the DTS today is probably in the form of its publications. The teaching materials used at the DTS were edited and published as *Manual of Tropical Housing and Building* (1974), which was reprinted many times and translated into a number of different languages (Figure 6.11).[150] Former teaching staff of the DTS, such as Martin Evans and Steven Szokolay, also wrote textbooks on climatic design and its affiliated fields.[151] Although the field of climatic design would expand to engage more explicitly with a broader set of issues, such as energy (particularly in the aftermath of the oil crisis of the 1970s) and sustainability (following the Brundtland Report and the 1992 Earth Summit at Rio de Janeiro), the Manual by the DTS staff remains a foundational text.[152]

NOTES

1 Singapore Polytechnic, *Report of the Singapore Polytechnic, Session 1958/59* (Singapore: Government Printer, 1960), 4.
2 "Architect Talk," *ST*, 5 August 1959.
3 "Poly Building Chief Tightens Syllabus," *SFP*, 18 December 1959.
4 Singapore Polytechnic, *Annual Report 1959/60* (Singapore: Government Printer, 1961), 4.
5 D. W. Notley, "Some Work of the School of Architecture, University of Singapore," *SIAJ* 59 (1973).

6 He was Professor T. D. Terazaki from Japan. Besides being an expert in shell structure, Terazaki also lectured on environmental design. T. D. Terazaki, "Environmental Design: Live Cool!," *Dimension: Journal of the Singapore Polytechnic Architectural Society* (1963); "Japanese Expert for Poly Arrives," *ST*, 25 February 1961.

7 Harry Chia, "A Malayan Style of Architecture Is at Last on the Way," *SFP*, 23 June 1960.

8 Cited in "Dato Loke: We Must Look to Local Architects," *ST*, 21 August 1962.

9 Kheng Soon Tay, "Neo-Tropicality or Neo-Colonialism?," *Singapore Architect* 211 (2001): 21.

10 Report on Survey of Teaching Methods, Research, Post-Graduate Work and Practical Training in Overseas School, RIBAA CCCP 1, Commonwealth Conference Committee Papers, Box 1.

11 Singapore Polytechnic, *Report of the Singapore Polytechnic, Session 1958/59*; *Report of the Singapore Polytechnic, Session 1959/60* (Singapore: Government Printer, 1961).

12 Wakely noted that the use of School in this context was "in the widest intellectual sense to denote an intellectual movement with the context of the Modern Movement in Architecture." He attributed its use to Maxwell Fry and Jane Drew. Patrick Wakely, e-mail message to author, 7 August 2015.

13 See, for example, Patrick I. Wakely, "The Development of a School: An Account of the Department of Development and Tropical Studies of the Architectural Association," *HI* 7, nos. 5–6 (1983).

14 Ibid.

15 For example, Malaya town planner Thomas Concannon and Singapore PWD architect Kenneth Brundle were subsidized by their respective colonial governments to attend the conference. See CUL RCS/RCMS104, *Malayan Town Planning Papers*.

16 William Holford, "Foreword," in *Prospectus*, ed. Architectural Association Department of Tropical Architecture (London: AA, 1955).

17 Mark Crinson, *Modern Architecture and the End of Empire* (Aldershot: Ashgate, 2003), 26–51.

18 See, for example, PRO CO323/1420/1, *Technical Education in the Colonies: Replies to Circular Despatch of 10 April 1937, 1937–1938 Part 1*; PRO CO323/1420/2, *Technical Education in the Colonies: Replies to Circular Despatch of 10 April 1937, 1937–1938 Part 2*; Colonial Office, *A Survey of Vocational Technical Education in the Colonial Empire* (London: HMSO, 1940).

19 See, for example, the case of Raffles College in Singapore, PRO CO273/651/9, *Raffles College: Report of the Commission on Higher Education in Malaya, 1939*; W. H. McLean, H. J. Channon and H. North-Hunt, *Higher Education in Malaya: Report of the Commission Appointed by the Secretary of State for the Colonies* (London: HMSO, 1939).

20 Inter-University Council, *Inter-University Council for Higher Education Overseas, 1946–1954* (London: HMSO, 1955).

21 PRO CO859/448, *Technical Education in the Colonies: Survey by Dr F. J. Harlow, Assistant Educational Adviser on Technical Education, 1953*.

22 Note attached to Koenigsberger's letter dated 30 August 1956 to H. J. W. Alexander, secretary of the AA, AAA 2006:S28, *O. Koenigsberger*.

23 "[F]unds have recently been allocated to allow up to eight students, at up to £1,000 each, to attend a new course on educational building to be held by the Department of Tropical Studies at the Architectural Association School of Architecture, London. In addition four students – from Ceylon, Ghana, Nigeria and Thailand – have just completed the tropical studies course at the Architectural Association with the help of UK funds." See W. M. Woodhouse's memorandum on "Overseas Aid: Britain's Contribution", presented at the Conference of Commonwealth and Overseas

Architectural Societies, RIBA, London, 21–25 July 1963. See RIBAA CCCP 1, *Commonwealth Conference Committee Papers, Box 1*.

24 Michael Lloyd, "Design Education in the Third World," *HI* 7, nos. 5–6 (1983).

25 William Allen's note on "A link between the AA and Ghana" in RIBAA CCCP 1, *Commonwealth Conference Committee Papers, Box 1*.

26 Inter-University Council, *Inter-University Council for Higher Education Overseas, 1946–1954*, 5–6.

27 "Biographical Notes on O.H. Koenigsberger," *HI* 7, nos. 5–6 (1983). Koenigsberger was closely involved with the centre for Housing, Building and Planning of the UN ECOSOC (Economic and Social Council) in the 1960s. Patrick Wakely, e-mail message to author, 7 August 2015.

28 "Department of Tropical Studies: A Cross Section of Recent Work," *Architectural Association Journal* 78 (1963): 308–09.

29 Otto H. Koenigsberger, Carl T. Mahoney and Martin Evans, *Climate and House Design* (New York: United Nations, 1971).

30 Wakely, "The Development of a School."

31 Architectural Association Department of Tropical Studies, *Prospectus* (London, 1965), 25.

32 Ibid., 29.

33 Ibid., 25.

34 Note attached to Koenigsberger's letter dated 30 August 1956 to H. J. W. Alexander, secretary of the AA, AAA 2006:S28, *O. Koenigsberger*.

35 Otto H. Koenigsberger, "The Role of the British Architect in the Tropics," *Architectural Design* 24: Special Issue on Tropical Architecture by British Architects, Part 2 (1954).

36 "Introduction," in *Proceedings of Educational Workshop "Planning and Building for Development" July 1st to 3rd, 1970* (London: Department of Development and Tropical Studies, Architectural Association, 1970), 1.

37 Atkinson's paper read at the Architectural Association in London, 29 April 1953; published in George Anthony Atkinson, "British Architects in the Tropics," *Architectural Association Journal* 69 (1953): 8–9.

38 The reflection was published in the proceedings of an educational workshop held at AA DTA. Koenigsberger chaired 5 of the 11 sessions of the Workshop so he should at least be the co-author of the introduction. "Introduction," 1.

39 Besides those appointed through the AA DTS connection, there were also teaching staff members from Germany, Poland, Yugoslavia, and Hungary, appointed through other global networks. S. B. Amissah and Charles K. Polónyi, *Housing and Urbanization: Report on the Postgraduate Urban Planning Course (1967–68, Term 1–2)* (Kumasi: Faculty of Architecture, Kwame Nkrumah University of Science and Technology, 1968); Martin Evans, "Education for Responsive Climatic Design: The Evolution of Postgraduate Courses for the Third World: The Influence of the Institutional Framework on Climatic Design," *HI* 7, nos. 5–6 (1983); Łukasz Stanek, "Architects from Socialist Countries in Ghana (1957–67): Modern Architecture and Mondialisation," *JSAH* 74, no. 4 (2015): 422.

40 Lloyd, "Design Education in the Third World," 368. See also Hannah Le Roux, "Modern Architecture in Post-Colonial Ghana and Nigeria," *Architectural History* 47 (2004): 385–89.

41 Lloyd, "Design Education in the Third World," 368.

42 Ibid., 370.

43 Crinson, *Modern Architecture and the End of Empire*, 43–46.

44 Minutes of 9 July 1953 meeting, RIBAA BAEMOB '52–'60, *Board of Architectural Education: Minutes of Officers of the Board (January 1952 to April 1960)*.

45 John Darwin, "A Third British Empire? The Dominion Idea in Imperial Politics," in *The Oxford History of British Empire, Vol. IV: The Twentieth Century*, ed. Judith M. Brown and Roger Louis (Oxford: Oxford University Press, 1999).
46 Minutes of 15 January 1954 meeting, RIBAA BAEMOB '52–'60, *BAE: Minutes of Officers of the Board (Jan 52 to Apr 60)*.
47 William Holford's comments in Atkinson, "British Architects in the Tropics," 18. The number of British architects sent to work in the tropical colonies started small in the early 1940s but the trend accelerated from 1945, when the budget for CDWA was increased. Within two years of May 1945, a total of forty-five architects and planners were sent by the Colonial Office to work in various British colonial territories, leading Gardner-Medwin to comment that "architects, and even planners, have now penetrated the uttermost parts of the Commonwealth." Frank Stockdale, Robert Gardner-Medwin, and Leo de Syllas, "Recent Planning Developments in the Colonies," *JRIBA* 55 (1948): 141.
48 Reports of the Officers of the Board, dated 12 October 1956 and 26 October 1956, RIBAA, *Board of Architectural Education Minutes (February 1955 to February 1958)*.
49 Minutes of 15 January 1954 meeting, RIBAA BAEMOB '52–'60, *BAE: Minutes of Officers of the Board (Jan 52 to Apr 60)*. See also the comments made by Everard J. Haynes in "Discussion," in *Conference on Tropical Architecture 1953: A Report of the Proceedings of the Conference Held at University College, London, March 1953*, ed. Arthur Foyle (London: University College London, 1953), 112.
50 Minutes of 16 July 1957 meeting, *BAE: Minutes of Officers of the Board (Jan 52 to Apr 60)*.
51 Ibid.
52 Memorandum prepared by A. M. Chitty, dated 23 May 1956, ibid.
53 Minutes of 16 July 1957 meeting, ibid.
54 Letter from M. Everend Haynes, secretary to BAE, to H. M. Collins, chairman of the Advisory Committee on Colonial Colleges of Art, dated March 1956 in R. Gardner-Medwin and J. A. L. Matheson, *Report to the Council of Kumasi College of Technology, Gold Coast, on Professional Education in Subjects Allied to Building* (undated). The report is part of ULLSCA D688/2/1, *Overseas Work, Robert Gardner-Medwin's Papers*.
55 Cited in William Allen and A. M. Chitty, "Report of the Overseas Examination Committee," 1959 in RIBAA BAEM '58–'60, *Board of Architectural Education Minutes (May 1958 to June 1960)*. For a slightly different account of the work of CAA, written from the metropolitan point of view, relying primarily on the papers of Robert Matthew, CAA's first president, see Miles Glendinning, *Modern Architect: The Life and Times of Robert Matthew* (London: RIBA Publishing, 2008), 377–404.
56 Editor, "The Great World of Portland Place," *The Builder* CXCIV (1958).
57 The words of a critic from the dominions, RIBAA CCCP 1, *Commonwealth Conference Committee Papers, Box 1*.
58 Allen and Chitty, "Report of the Overseas Examination Committee."
59 Ibid.
60 Ibid.
61 Letter dated 3 July 1957 in minutes of 30 July 1957 meeting, RIBAA BAEMOB '52–'60, *BAE: Minutes of Officers of the Board (Jan 52 to Apr 60)*.
62 Letter from Michael Pattrick to the Board of Architectural Education, dated 9 July 1957, ibid. (my emphasis).
63 H. M. Collins in PRO OD17/108, *RIBA: Conference of Heads of Overseas Schools of Architectural Education*.
64 Ibid.
65 RIBAA CCCP 1, *Commonwealth Conference Committee Papers, Box 1*.
66 Editors, "Editorial: Commonwealth 2," *Architectural Review* 127 (1960): 4–5.
67 Crinson, *Modern Architecture and the End of Empire*, 128.

68 Before Koenigsberger took over, J. McKay Spence was the interim Director. Before Koenigsberger took over, students at the DTS were dissatisfied with the lack of commitment of the lecturers. I am grateful to Rachel Lee for sharing her notes on this with me.
69 Note attached to Koenigsberger's letter dated 30 August 1956 to H. J. W. Alexander, secretary of the AA in AAA 2006:S28, *O. Koenigsberger*.
70 Koenigsberger's curriculum at the Technische Hochschule Berlin, where he studied architecture, did not have many courses in building science. Besides the usual courses on acoustics, building materials, and heating and ventilation, there is one titled *Bauwissenschaftliche Technologie*, loosely translated as building science and technology that Koenigsberger took in his third year. I am again grateful to Rachel Lee for this information.
71 Rachel Lee, "Constructing a Shared Vision: Otto Koenigsberger and Tata & Sons," *ABE* 2 (2012); Rachel Lee, "Negotiating Modernities: Otto Koenigsberger's Works and Network in Exile (1933–1951)," *ABE* 5 (2014).
72 Otto Koenigsberger, "Introductory Lecture to Climatic Design Series," May 6, 1968, in Renate Koenigsberger Private Collection.
73 Otto Koenigsberger, "Liverpool Lecture: Design with Climate," undated (around 1961), in Renate Koenigsberger Private Collection.
74 Koenigsberger, "Introductory Lecture to Climatic Design Series."
75 William Allen and Otto Koenigsberger, "Proposal to the Ford Foundation for the Establishment of a Department of Development Studies at the Architectural Association, London," 5, undated (probably 1966), in Renate Koenigsberger Private Collection.
76 Koenigsberger, "Liverpool Lecture."
77 Note attached to Koenigsberger's letter dated 30 August 1956 to H. J. W. Alexander, secretary of the AA in AAA 2006:S28, *O. Koenigsberger*.
78 Koenigsberger, Mahoney, and Evans, *Climate and House Design*, 15 (my emphasis). This view is very similar to that expressed in G. P. Crowden, "Indoor Climate and Thermal Comfort in the Tropics," in *Conference on Tropical Architecture 1953: A Report of the Proceedings of the Conference Held at University College, London, March 1953*, ed. Arthur Foyle (London: University College London, 1953).
79 Koenigsberger, "Introductory Lecture to Climatic Design Series"; Otto Koenigsberger, "Lecture on the Importance of Climate," November 8, 1964, in Renate Koenigsberger Private Collection.
80 Both Ellsworth Huntington and S. F. Markham's books were featured in the reading list that Koenigsberger issued to students. See Otto Koenigsberger, "Week 2 Lecture on Climate and Man," 1965, in Renate Koenigsberger Private Collection. For a discussion of Ellsworth Huntington's work, see Marsha E. Ackermann, *Cool Comfort: America's Romance with Air-Conditioning* (Washington, D.C.: Smithsonian Institution Press, 2002), 8–26; S. F. Markham, *Climate and the Energy of Nations* (London: Oxford University Press, 1947 (1942)).
81 Otto Koenigsberger, "Lecture on Climate and History," October 12, 1967, in Renate Koenigsberger Private Collection.
82 Koenigsberger's history was very much a summary of Chapters V, VI and VII of Markham, *Climate and the Energy of Nations*, 38–105.
83 Ibid., 79–80.
84 Ibid., 20.
85 Koenigsberger, "Introductory Lecture to Climatic Design Series."
86 Koenigsberger, "Lecture on the Importance of Climate."
87 Allen and Koenigsberger, "Proposal to the Ford Foundation for the Establishment of a Department of Development Studies at the Architectural Association, London," 7.

88 Page was building physicists at BRS and later Chair of Building Science at University of Sheffield, Crowden was Professor of Applied Physiology at the London School of Hygiene and Tropical Medicine. AAA 2006:S28, *O. Koenigsberger*; AAA 1991:31, *Information and Curriculum Notes, 1950–6*; AAA 2007:50, *AA Tropical Studies Leaflet* (n.d.).

89 Otto Koenigsberger, "Speech for the Opening of the Exhibition of Department of Development and Tropical Studies," July 7, 1968, in Renate Koenigsberger Private Collection.

90 Department of Tropical Studies, *Prospectus*.

91 However, in the detailed curriculum notes from the 1965–66 session, which were likely to be a more accurate depiction of what was taught, only one week each was dedicated to "Sociology" and "Economics." The other two weeks were spent on "Landscape" and "National Planning."

92 Otto Koenigsberger, "Second Term Opening Lecture," January 5, 1970, in Renate Koenigsberger Private Collection.

93 Otto Koenigsberger, "Speech for the Opening of the Exhibition of Department of Development and Tropical Studies," July 4, 1969, in Renate Koenigsberger Private Collection.

94 "Department of Tropical Studies," 303.

95 AAA 2003:29C, *Department of Tropical Studies: Session 1965–66*.

96 "Department of Tropical Studies," 304.

97 See Andrew Saint, *Towards a Social Architecture: The Role of School-Building in Post-War England* (New Haven: Yale University Press, 1987), 157–83.

98 Allen and Koenigsberger, "Proposal to the Ford Foundation for the Establishment of a Department of Development Studies at the Architectural Association, London," 12–13.

99 "Department of Tropical Studies," 304 and 306.

100 Otto H. Koenigsberger and Robert Lynn, *Roofs in the Warm Humid Tropics* (London: Lund Humphries for the Architectural Association, 1965).

101 William Allen, "The Training and Education of Architects," *Architectural Association Journal* 77 (1962): 230.

102 Mark Crinson and Jules Lubbock, *Architecture – Art or Profession? Three Hundred Years of Architectural Education in Britain* (Manchester: Manchester University Press, 1994), 148.

103 Ibid., 126; J. K. Page, *Science and Architectural Education: Inaugural Lecture Delivered 1st March 1961* (Sheffield: The University of Sheffield, 1961); Henry J. Cowan, "Architecture as the Art of the Possible," *Architectural Science Review* 37, no. 1 (1993); "Building Science at Liverpool: Prof. A. W. Henry," *Nature* 179 (1957); Glendinning, *Modern Architect*, 308. I am grateful to Professor Thomas Markus for pointing out the two professors in the Scottish Universities to me. Thomas Markus, e-mail message to author, September 7, 2015. I am also grateful to Ola Uduku for finding out the year of appointment of C. B. Wilson.

104 Leslie Martin, "RIBA Conference on Architectural Education: Report by the Chairman," *AJ* 127 (1958).

105 See, for example, the monthly *Building Science Abstracts* issued by BRS from 1926 to 1976 and F. L. Brady, *An Introduction to Building Science* (London: Edward Arnold & Co., 1927).

106 Although the RIBA traced its scientific lineage to its association with Michael Faraday in the early nineteenth century and the existence of the Science Standing Committee from 1886 to 1938, building science remained largely marginal to the profession and its education up until the 1940s. Angela Mace, *The Royal Institute of British Architects: A Guide to Its Archive and History* (London: Mansell Publishing Limited, 1986), 190.

107 See PRO DSIR4/1557, *Architectural Science Boards: Lectures, Committee Meetings*; PRO DSIR4/1548, *Architectural Science Group Education Sub–Committee; Meetings, Agenda, Minutes, Etc, 1939–1940*; Dex Harrison, ed., *Building Science: Papers Prepared for the Architectural Science Board of the RIBA* (London: George Allen & Unwin, 1948).

108 Cited in Educational Committee of the Architecture Science Group, "The Place of Science in Architectural Education: The First Report of the Education Committee of the Architectural Science Group of the RIBA Research Board," *JRIBA* 48, no. 8 (1941): 133.

109 Ibid., 134, 38.

110 RIBA, *Report of the Special Committee on Architectural Education* (London: RIBA, 1946), 9.

111 Ibid., 8.

112 Cited in Martin, "RIBA Conference on Architectural Education," 281. The proceedings of the 1958 Conference were not published. In fact, the organizers wanted so much to keep the discussions at the conference confidential that they did not even leave a copy of the proceedings in the RIBA Library at that time. Only two copies of the proceedings were available – one kept in the office of the secretary of the RIBA Board of Architectural Education, the other kept by Martin. See minutes of meeting dated 20 May 1958 in RIBAA BAEM '58–'60, *BAE Minutes (May 58 to Jun 60)*. The proceedings could not be found in the RIBA's archives. For this discussion, I rely on a published version of Llewelyn-Davies's paper of the same title, Richard Llewelyn-Davies, "Deeper Knowledge: Better Design," *AJ* 125 (1957).

113 Martin, "RIBA Conference on Architectural Education," 775.

114 The paper formed the basis for Llewelyn-Davies's educational policies at Bartlett when he became its head in 1960, as indicated in his inaugural lecture, Richard Llewelyn-Davies, "The Education of an Architect," *JRIBA* 68 (1961). The inaugural lectures by Allen as the Principal at the AA and J. K. Page as the Chair in Building Science at University of Sheffield also shared many of the key arguments made in this paper by Llewelyn-Davies, see Allen, "The Training and Education of Architects"; Page, *Science and Architectural Education*. For the influence of Bernal on architectural research and building science, see Chris Whittaker, "Building Tomorrow," in *J. D. Bernal: A Life in Science and Politics*, ed. Brenda Swann and Francis Aprahamian (London: Verso, 1999); Saint, *Towards a Social Architecture*, 7–11.

115 Llewelyn-Davies, "Deeper Knowledge: Better Design," 770.

116 Ibid.

117 See J. D. Bernal, "Architecture and Science," *JRIBA* 44, no. 16 (1937).

118 Bernal, "Science in Architecture," *JRIBA* 53, no. 5 (1946): 155.

119 Ibid., 156–57.

120 Ibid., 157.

121 Saint, *Towards a Social Architecture*, 7.

122 Crinson and Lubbock, *Architecture – Art or Profession?*, 153.

123 Ibid., 115.

124 Saint, *Towards a Social Architecture*, 7. For scientific humanism, see also M. C. Otto, "Scientific Humanism," *The Antioch Review* 3, no. 4 (1943). Roy Porter noted that the term "scientific humanism" was coined by Georges Sarton, the Harvard-based philosopher and historian of science in the 1930s. Sarton saw science as the answer to problems plaguing the West at that time. Roy Porter, "The Two Cultures Revisited," *Boundary 2*, 23, no. 2 (1996): 6.

125 Robert Matthew, "Foreword," in *Handbook of Commonwealth Architects*, ed. CAA (London: CAA & The Builder, 1965).

126 Editors, "Editorial: Commonwealth 2."

127 Julius Posener, "Malaya," *Architectural Review* 128 (1960): 60. Julius Posener was a British-German architectural historian. He returned to Berlin in 1961 as chair of architectural history at Hochschule der Künste in Berlin after a brief spell teaching at the Technical College, Kuala Lumpur. Paul Goldberger, "Julius Posener, 91, an Architect and Critic of Modern Movement," *New York Times*, January 31, 1996. Incidentally, Posener was also a friend of Koenigsberger. They both studied at the Technische Hochschule Berlin. I am grateful to Rachel Lee for this piece of information.
128 Posener, "Malaya," 60.
129 Lincoln Page, "Singapore," *Architectural Review* 128 (1960).
130 Gerard Kemp, "Guinea Pigs? Not Us, Says Architect," *Daily Mail*, 27 July 1963. See RIBAA CCCP 1, *Commonwealth Conference Committee Papers, Box 1*.
131 *Conference Report, New Delhi March 1967* (London: Commonwealth Associations of Architects, 1967), 11.
132 "Education Survey: A Brief Survey of Architectural Education and Training in Member Countries," in *Handbook of Commonwealth Architects*, ed. CAA (London: CAA & The Builder, 1965), 65.
133 Ibid.
134 *Conference Report, Malta June 1965* (London: Commonwealth Associations of Architects, 1965), 4.
135 "Report of the First Meeting of the Commonwealth Board of Architectural Education (by Courtesy of the RIBA Journal 1966)," *SIAJ* 8 (1967).
136 "Third Commonwealth Association of Architects Conference Report," *SIAJ* 34 (1969): 23.
137 Cited in "CAA, CBAE, ARCASIA: Background and Objectives," *SIAJ* 43 (1970): 5.
138 "Report of the First Asian Regional Conference," *SIAJ* 20 (1968); "CBAE & ARCASIA Meetings in Singapore," *SIAJ* 43 (1970). My account of ARCASIA here stems from the SIA's perspective and it differs from that given in Glendinning, *Modern Architect*, 385.
139 Chong Keat Lim, "The Role of the Professional Institute in the Development of Architectural Education," *SIAJ* 83 (1977): 6–7.
140 L. H. Wilson, "Objectives and Standards of Recognition of Schools," in *CAA 1976 Handbook*, ed. CAA (London: CAA, 1976 (1971)).
141 Peter Johnson and Susan Clarke, *Architectural Education in the Commonwealth: A Survey of Schools* (Department of Architecture, University of Sydney and CBAE, CAA, 1979). See also the website of CAA, accessed 12 December 2014, http://comarchitect.org/governance-and-management/.
142 Koenigsberger, "Speech for the Opening of the Exhibition of Department of Development and Tropical Studies."
143 Patrick Wakely, "Fifty Years of Urban Development: Notes on the History of the Development Planning Unit," in *Sixty Years of Urban Development: A Short History of the Development Planning Unit*, ed. Patrick Wakely and Caren Levy (London: DPU, 2014 (2004)).
144 "Proceedings of Educational Workshop 'Planning and Building of Development' July 1st to 3rd, 1970."
145 Wakely, "The Development of a School," 342–45.
146 Martin Evans, "Education for Responsive Climatic Design," 347–48.
147 "Proceedings of Educational Workshop 'Planning and Building for Development' July 1st to 3rd, 1970" (London, Department of Development and Tropical Studies, Architectural Association, 1970), 51–52.
148 Ibid., 3.
149 Evans, "Education for Responsive Climatic Design."
150 Otto H. Koenigsberger et al., *Manual of Tropical Housing and Building* (London: Longman, 1974).

151 Martin Evans, *Housing, Climate and Comfort* (London: The Architectural Press, 1980); Andris Auliciems and Steven V. Szokolay, *Thermal Comfort: PLEA Notes*, 2nd ed. (Brisbane: PLEA and Department of Architecture, University of Queensland, 2007).
152 For an important text that represents the expansion of climatic design to address energy issues, see Thomas A. Markus and Edwin N. Morris, *Buildings, Climate, and Energy* (London: Pitman Pub., 1980).

Conclusion

Tropical Architecture Today

In the preceding pages, we have explored the genealogy of tropical architecture from the early nineteenth century till the early 1970s. From the nodal point of Singapore, we have traced how various tropical building types and knowledges circulated in the British colonial and postcolonial networks during this period. After a forty-year interval, tropical architecture today is obviously not the same. But as we have argued earlier, the genealogical approach taken in this book is also a history of the present that helps us understand the current situation by historicizing how we arrive at the present. In other words, although the various manifestations of tropical architecture today appear different from the past, they carry historically sedimented meanings and power configurations. In fact, one can also extrapolate this line of thinking to suggest that the historically sedimented meanings and power configurations in the present will continue to shape the pathways to the future. To explore these connections between past and present, and speculative linkages between present and future, let us revisit the key themes of this genealogy.

NATURE, TROPICALITY AND ANTHROPOCENE

At the beginning of the book, we started with the taxonomic peculiarity of tropical architecture – although implicit in any construction of tropical architecture is its unspoken opposite of temperate architecture, temperate architecture does not exist in our lexicon. While nature, or more specifically climate, was privileged as the prime determinant of architectural form in the tropics, culture was assumed to be the more significant factor in determining the architectural form of the temperate world. We attributed this peculiarity to tropicality and the long history of Western construction of the tropics, especially its persistent perceptions of the tropical nature as an environmental alterity as opposed to the normalcy of the temperate world. The environmental alterity of the tropics was deeply entangled and even conflated with social, economic, cultural and political alterities in colonial and postcolonial discourses. Indeed, in the different chapters of this book, we saw that tropical climate was variously constructed as unhealthy, uncomfortable, unproductive and/or underdeveloped. As James Rodger Fleming and Vladimir Jankovic have argued, "[c]limate is a discursive vehicle capable of naturalizing matters of social concern into matters of natural fact."[1] Despite the entanglements between the climatic and the socio-cultural, tropical climate was also conceived as an external and unchanging entity out there. The conceptual separation and distinction of climate from society is useful for two related reasons – one, for society to have recourse to climate in order to explain social phenomena; two, for society to see climate as a problem that can be controlled and tamed. In other words, the tropical climate was considered as both authority and enemy, explanation and problem.

These colonial perceptions of the tropics lingered on in the post-colonial period. The hot and humid tropical climate continued to be seen as a negative external entity that affected the comfort of the inhabitants in the tropics and hindered the socio-economic development of post-colonial nations, and therefore had to be controlled. In place of passive cooling strategies deployed in the climatic design approach that was prevalent in the mid-twentieth century, mechanical cooling through air-conditioning was subsequently adopted in many parts of the tropics and became increasingly widespread.[2] This shift from climate responsive architecture to architecture of climate control has been lamented by some as the demise of the energy-conserving approach of passive cooling and the rise of the energy profligate approach of active cooling. Architectural historians and theorists such as Kenneth Frampton and his fellow advocates of critical regionalism have also interpreted the shift as one from an architecture based on "rooted culture" to one "indicative of domination by universal technique."[3] But rather than being seen as diametrically opposite approaches, they can be understood as being premised on similar conception of climate as an external entity even if their ways of addressing climate might differ.

Recently, the ontological distinctions between climate and society or nature and human culture have been challenged by the Anthropocene thesis. In response to the current planetary crisis of anthropogenic climate change, the Stratigraphy Commission of the Geological Society of London proposed in 2008 that we have entered the Anthropocene epoch, when the human being is a geological agent that has irretrievably transformed nature and left inerasable traces on the earth.[4] If we are to follow scholars in the humanities and the social sciences who have drawn from the Anthropocene thesis and taken its implications seriously, how should we reconceptualize the relation between climate and architecture? Given that anthropogenic climate change has brought about greater frequencies of extreme weather events, we can no longer see climate as having stable and predictable patterns, as previously assumed. Neither can we assume that the relationship between climate and architecture is unidirectional, with architecture responding to climate or climate shaping architecture. Instead we should see the relationship between climate and architecture as a dynamic interaction, with architecture affecting and even producing, rather than just responding to, climate.

Even a building that relies on low-energy passive cooling in the tropics is affecting the climate in at least two spatial and temporal scales. At the local scale and with a short time-lag, it is changing the microclimatic conditions around the site through, for example, contributing to the urban heat island effect. And the building is also producing carbon emissions that exacerbate global climate change in the longer term and at a planetary scale. If climate is inseparable from architecture, there can be no recourse to climate to determine the form of a building. Neither is it possible to return to some past archetypes of climatic design, whether they are vernacular architecture or the various types of colonial architecture we saw in this book.

TECHNOSCIENTIFIC CONSTRUCTIONS AND NETWORK BUILDING

In this book, we have also emphasized that the constructions of tropical nature and climate were mediated by modern technoscience. For example, systematic knowledge of climate, the prerequisite for "tropical architecture," was only established in the eighteenth century with the emergence of modern meteorology. Building on meteorological knowledge of tropical climate, other technoscientific knowledges, such as tropical medicine and sanitation, building science and physiology subsequently constructed the tropics as the pestilential, uncomfortable and even undeveloped other. Although these constructions of the tropics changed over time with shifting social, cultural and political understandings of the tropics, these constructions were not just influenced by the shifting socio-cultural contours. Central to these changing constructions of the tropics were renewals and modifications in scientific paradigms as the technoscience that mediated the constructions of the tropics was premised on knowledge from various paradigms in the medical and physical sciences. Furthermore, all technoscientific constructions depended on specific sociotechnical practices with their attendant methods, techniques and infrastructure. I have endeavored to show in this book that in addition to understanding the shifting socio-cultural contours, one also needs to comprehend these sociotechnical practices in order to understand how the tropical climate was constructed.

Furthermore, as we have seen, these technoscientific constructions also involved different technoscientific experts from various colonial and post-colonial institutions working within colonial and transnational networks. Many of them were not just involved in the technoscientific constructions of the tropics as the pestilential, uncomfortable and even undeveloped other. Their negative constructions of the tropics frequently came with recommendations for remedying these deficiencies through various technical means that directly or indirectly shaped the production of tropical architecture. For example, we saw in Chapters 2 and 3 that the Royal Commission for the Sanitary State of the Army in India (RCSSAI) and the Barrack and Hospital Improvement Commission (BHIC) addressed the insanitary conditions of the military barracks and hospitals in the British Empire by first dividing the Empire into three climatic zones – home (or temperate), Mediterranean (sub-tropical) and tropical stations. They then proposed space standards, environmental technologies and type plans that embodied the key design and planning considerations for each of the climatic zones. I have argued that these recommendations operated through immutable mobiles and other technologies of distance so they could circulate from one point to another within the network without distortion. We have also explored other technologies of distance that were deployed to guarantee consistent architectural outcomes in the different parts of the colonial and post-colonial networks. These included less prescriptive approaches that sought to ensure that the outcomes meet certain performance criteria rather than directly regulating the means of achieving these outcomes. The building bylaw that regulated the percentage of open space in a building discussed in Chapter 4 and the thermal comfort standard that stipulated the ideal indoor climatic conditions in Chapters 5 and 6 were two such examples.

The promotion of specific technoscientific approaches in the framing of building problems and the design of buildings in the tropics discussed in the second part of the book was another approach used to guarantee consistent results. With regard to these technoscientific approaches, we explored the dissemination of tropical building science research and climatic design pedagogy in Chapters 5 and 6 respectively. Institutions, specifically building research stations and schools of architecture, played important roles in promoting these technoscientific approaches through their institutional networks. Earlier in the book, we also explored the important roles played by other institutions, such as the Royal Engineers and the Improvement Trusts, in facilitating the circulations of technoscientific knowledge and practices that shaped the designs of tropical barracks and housing respectively. It was within these institutional contexts that we situated the metropolitan and local technoscientific experts, such as the military engineer Henry E. McCallum, the architect P. Hubert Keys, the town planner Edwin P. Richards, the building scientist George Atkinson, the architect/educator Otto Koenigsberger.

After the end of this genealogy in the early 1970s, similar technoscientific institutions and networks continued to establish standards and norms that were central to how buildings were designed and built in the tropics. The air-conditioned buildings that became widespread in the tropics were initially based on the thermal comfort standard developed by the American Society of Heating, Refrigerating and Air-conditioning Engineers (ASHRAE) along with Danish building scientist Ole Fanger. The emergence of sustainable architecture in the past two decades or so in the tropics was likewise dependent on new transnational networks of sustainability experts, consultancy firms and, among other things, new adaptive thermal comfort standards and new green building rating tools. Not unlike the old technoscientific networks, these new networks have their own methods and techniques, and technologies and gadgets to produce new sociotechnical norms and architectural forms. The techniques and technologies might have changed but the intricacies of network building discussed in this book are still relevant for understanding the newer networks.

The intricacies of network building are critical for comprehending the relational dynamics between the global and the local, episteme and mētis, particularly how abstract global knowledge was the result of the translation, extension and consolidation of embodied local knowledge. Although the networks that we have studied in this book were predominantly centered on the metropole because of colonial and post-colonial hegemonies, they were different from the static and hierarchical center–periphery conceptual model. The networks we studied were provisional and required constant maintenance. In these networks, a dominating center of calculation can fall into oblivion and become irrelevant just as a point in the previously dominated periphery can rise and become a new center. Indeed, we briefly examined an illustration of this decline and emergence although it was strictly speaking not a technoscientific network. We saw in Chapter 6 how the Commonwealth Association of Architects originally dominated by the Royal Institute of British Architects (RIBA) was challenged by the rise of the Architects Regional Council Asia (ARCASIA), a smaller competing regional network in the 1960s. Later in the 1980s, ARCASIA worked with the Aga Khan Award for Architecture (AKAA) to construct a transnational network that led to the resurgence of tropical architecture in Southeast Asia after almost two decades of post-colonial decline.[5]

POWER AND GOVERNMENTALITY

If the recourse to external and immutable nature has helped to render tropical architecture as seemingly apolitical, our interrogation of external and immutable nature through tropicality, technoscience and the Anthropocene suggests that tropical architecture is political through and through and its production was inextricably linked to colonial and postcolonial power relations. In examining the politics and the underlying power relations of tropical architecture, this genealogy built on but sought to go beyond the focus on visible politics and overt forms of power in the existing scholarship on colonial architectural and urban history. Rather than relying on formal analysis and focusing on power concentrated in highly visible and monumental public buildings, the preceding pages have focused on two more diffused and pervasive but less visible forms of power.

The first form of power pertains to technoscience. We have seen that different forms of technoscientific knowledge could be accumulated and consolidated at certain nodes that we called centers of calculations through network building. We argued that this accumulation and consolidation of knowledge was also an accrual of power because technoscientific knowledge enabled the experts at these centers to know and act on distant places in the network. We have examined cases of the metropole being the center of calculation with metropolitan experts, such as military engineers and building scientists, acting on and affecting the design of military barracks and hospitals, and climatic design in the tropics. Technoscientific knowledge is not just a neutral and objective knowledge describing natural phenomena out there. It is also a situated knowledge affected by its conditions and contexts of production, and technoscientific knowledge has social, cultural and political consequences. We have seen that colonial architecture in the tropics was inextricably linked to various colonial tropical technosciences, such as tropical medicine, sanitation and engineering. These colonial technosciences were in turn indissolubly shaped by the imperatives of colonial governance and socio-economic development. Thus, the colonial technoscience of building in the tropics prioritized solving certain building problems over others. It also framed building problems in manners that privileged particular types of solutions according to their political expediencies. We saw illustrations of these in the organization of building science research, in how the mid-twentieth-century housing problem was framed to ignore the structural socio-economic problems and how climatic design facilitated the export of metropolitan expertise and building components.

The second form of power analyzed in this book draws on Foucauldian analytics of power. In the first part of the book, we deployed Foucauldian governmentality to discuss different colonial building types. Conceptualized as a triangle of sovereignty–discipline–government, governmentality did at least two things for us analytically. First, through its inclusion of multiple modalities of power – specifically sovereign, disciplinary and biopolitical power – it expanded our analytical repertoire for understanding power relations in architecture. For example, we were able to discuss sanitary reforms and the design of tropicalized military barracks, hospitals and housing in relation to the colonial state's attempts at investing biopolitical power and instilling disciplinary power in the different segments of the colonial population. This went beyond the usual analysis of colonial power relations and architecture through the lens of sovereign power, i.e. the visible politics of representation and spectacular display or the punitive politics of violence and coercion. Rather than restricting the study of colonial power-relations to monumental edifices and other sites where sovereign power concentrates, this book is able to explore common building types and sites permeated with diffuse biopolitical and disciplinary power.

Second, by emphasizing the how of government and grouping multiple agencies, different techniques and various forms of knowledge in a strategic bricolage of governing, governmentality provided us with a new framework of understanding colonial power relations and architecture. This is a framework that can incorporate forces which, although central to our understanding of tropical architecture, were as disparate as environmental conditions, statistics and bodily sensations. Environmental technologies of colonial architecture that modified the climate, and ensured physical bodily comfort and health of the inhabitants, were considered together with an array of technical apparatuses such as maps and statistics in constituting the rationalities, means and outcomes of government. Therefore, the panopticon, which was the diagram of disciplinary power, was also a panthermicon because a regulated thermal environment was just as important as concealed vision in the reform of the prisoner.[6]

We have, however, also noted that governmentality was developed to understand the liberal modes of government in Europe and therefore cannot be applied in its entirety to the colonial contexts of illiberal and coercive rule. We have therefore been also attentive to how governmentality was dislocated and modified in colonial contexts, particularly the ways governmentality was translated in racialized, deficient, excessive and fragmented manners in the colonial tropics. These permutations of governmentality displayed different configurations of the multiple modalities of power that were distinct from the metropolitan examples. Spatially, they created a colonial architecture and urban landscape that was fragmented with uneven distribution of resources between the colonial and colonized populations. For the colonized population, it was a largely a landscape of biopolitical neglect by the colonial state, where the colonized population lived their bare lives, with small pockets of spaces for biopolitical relief where some provisions for health and welfare were provided. In stark contrast, the colonial population lived good biopolitical lives primarily in enclaves or spaces of exception.

Similar forms of power continued to permeate the discourse and practice of architecture in the tropics from the 1970s to today. As mentioned earlier, the technoscientific network based on metropolitan organizations such as ASHRAE established the thermal comfort standard used for air-conditioned buildings internationally, including the countries in the tropics. The thermal comfort standard was more than a technoscientific standard; it was a comfort regime that framed comfort narrowly based on a few environmental parameters that ignored socio-cultural differences and ruled out socio-cultural adaptations in maintaining comfort. By creating a thermal comfort standard that could only be met with mechanical cooling in the tropics, and through the spread of air-conditioning and its convergence with new design norms and building systems, the thermal comfort standard changed the comfort expectations of many inhabitants of the tropics and contributed to their air-conditioning dependency.[7] In recent years, climate change and sustainability have encouraged the building industry to explore low carbon and more energy-efficient ways of providing thermal comfort, but the path-dependency created by the sociotechnical assemblages of air-conditioning in the built environment has made the transition incredibly challenging.[8]

In our age of neoliberal capitalism and splintering urbanism, the discourses and practices of tropical architecture have been bifurcated into two main categories, each with its own biopolitical power regime, in response to the following polarizing socio-political and urban developments. On the one hand, there is a recent emergence of premium socio-ecological enclaves complete with luxurious tropical houses.[9] These gated enclaves are not unlike the spaces of exception of the cantonment discussed in Chapter 2 in that special rights and benefits were conferred on the privileged residents of these spaces to attract the investments of highly mobile transnational elites.[10] These elites and their families live their well-endowed biopolitical lives in palatial tropical houses that have infinity pools, jacuzzis, open air gazebos and lushly landscaped gardens. Furthermore, these enclaves came with round-the-clock security, and exclusive amenities such as golf courses and marinas. Some of these enclaves were even planned with resilient design in mind with built-in protection from sea-water level rises and extreme weather events.

On the other hand, in what Mike Davis called our "planet of slums," a large number of urban poor live their bare lives in sub-housing conditions in squatter settlements and slums around the world, particularly in the rapid growing megacities in the southern tropical region.[11] Not only do they not even have an adequate basic shelter and security of tenure, they also do not have access to basic services like clean water supply, electricity, or a proper toilet and sewerage system.[12] Furthermore, many of the slums and squatter settlements were located on sites especially vulnerable to the threat of extreme weather events. However, the mainstream socio-political responses to such conditions today are no longer primarily about slum and squatter settlement clearance, and moving these residents into subsidized public housing. Instead, responses today typically involve recognizing self-help housing as a solution rather than a problem and finding means to facilitate it. These means of further facilitating self-help housing include granting the residents of these squatter settlements and slums security of tenure and providing them with technical and financial assistance to improve and upgrade their housing and community. In most cases, architects act as facilitators, assisting the residents to help themselves. Central to such a form of assistance is a Foucauldian technique of government that we have witnessed partly in Chapter 4 – that of identifying the targets to be governed, i.e. the residents who are also the urban poor, directing their conduct by purportedly empowering and optimizing their capacities for improvement, and thereby turning them into self-reliant subjects.

Having revisited and expanded on the key themes of this genealogy that we have started with, one can say that colonial socio-cultural and technoscientific constructions of the tropics and tropical architecture lingered on and continued to shape the discourses and practices of tropical architecture today. On top of the cultural and epistemic power highlighted by postcolonial criticism, we have also witnessed the significance of colonial technoscientific constructions and techniques of government in shaping our understanding of tropical architecture in the post-colonial era. But we are now at an important historical juncture, when the advent of the Anthropocene epoch means that we no longer have recourse to nature. Without recourse to nature, tropical architecture of the future will have to wrestle with the issues connected to tropicality, technoscience and governmentality laid out in this genealogy.

NOTES

1 James Rodger Fleming and Vladimir Jankovic, "Revisiting Klima," *Osiris* 26, no. 1 (2011): 10.

2 For the history of air-conditioning and architecture in Singapore, see Jiat-Hwee Chang and Tim Winter, "Thermal Modernity and Architecture," *JoA* 20, no. 1 (2015).

3 Kenneth Frampton, "Towards a Critical Regionalism: Six Points for an Architecture of Resistance," in *The Anti-Aesthetic: Essays on Postmodern Culture*, ed. Hal Foster (New York: New Press, 1998 [1983]), 27.

4 Etienne Turpin, "Introduction: Who Does the Earth Think It Is, Now?," in *Architecture in the Anthropocene: Encounters among Design, Deep Time, Science and Philosophy*,

ed. Etienne Turpin (Ann Arbor, MI: Open Humanities Press, 2013); Dipesh Chakrabarty, "The Climate of History: Four Theses," *Critical Inquiry* 35, no. 2 (2008): 201.

5 See Jiat-Hwee Chang, "'Natural' Traditions: Constructing Tropical Architecture in Transnational Malaysia and Singapore," *Explorations* 7, no. 1 (2007); Jiat-Hwee Chang, "Tropical Variants of Sustainable Architecture: A Postcolonial Perspective," in *Handbook of Architectural Theory*, ed. Greig Crysler, Stephen Cairns and Hilde Heynen (London: Sage, 2012).

6 For panthermicon, see Luis Fernández-Galiano, *Fire and Memory: On Architecture and Energy*, trans. Gina Cariño (Cambridge, MA: MIT Press, 2000), 226–33.

7 Tim Winter, "An Uncomfortable Truth: Air-Conditioning and Sustainability in Asia," *Environment and Planning A* 45 (2013); Elizabeth Shove, *Comfort, Cleanliness and Convenience: The Social Organization of Normality* (Oxford: Berg, 2003); Chang and Winter, "Thermal Modernity and Architecture."

8 Stan Cox, *Losing Our Cool: Uncomfortable Truths About Our Air-Conditioned World (and Finding New Ways to Get Through the Summer)* (New York: The New Press, 2010).

9 Stephen Graham and Simon Marvin, *Splintering Urbanism: Networked Infrastructures, Technological Mobilities and the Urban Condition* (London: Routledge, 2001); Mike Hodson and Simon Marvin, "Urbanism in the Anthropocene: Ecological Urbanism or Premium Ecological Enclaves," *City* 14, no. 3 (2010).

10 An example of such a development is Sentosa Cove. See John M. Glionna, "Singapore, a New Home for Riches," *Los Angeles Times*, 11 November 2006; Edward Taylor and Cris Prystay, "Swiss Fight against Tax Cheats Aids Singapore's Banking Quest," *Wall Street Journal*, 6 February 2006; Wayne Arnold, "In Singapore, a Local Switzerland for Asia's Wealthy," *International Herald Tribune*, 24 April 2007.

11 Mike Davis, *Planet of Slums* (London: Verso, 2006).

12 UN-HABITAT, *State of Asian Cities 2010/11* (Fukuoka: UN-HABITAT, 2010); UN-HABITAT, *State of the World's Cities 2010/2011: Bridging the Urban Divide* (London: Earthscan, 2010).

Bibliography

UNPUBLISHED SOURCES

Arkib Negara Malaysia, Kuala Lumpur (ANMKL) National Archives of Malaysia, Kuala Lumpur

ANMKL 1957/0575459. *Prefabrication and Colonial Building.*

Architectural Association Archives (AAA)

AAA 1991:31. *Information and Curriculum Notes, 1950–6.*
AAA 2003:29C. *Department of Tropical Studies: Session 1965–66.*
AAA 2006:S28. *O. Koenigsberger.*
AAA 2007:50. *AA Tropical Studies Leaflet, Undated.*

Archives of the London School of Hygiene and Tropical Medicine (ALSHTM)

ALSHTM, Ross/140/01/08.

National Archives of Singapore (NAS)

NAS HDB1003 SIT148/25. *Housing Scheme at Henderson Road.*
NAS HDB1061 SIT70/41. *Weisburg Building Policy Report.*
NAS HDB1079 SIT29/8/27. *Victoria Street Nos. 256, 258, 260, 262 & 264.*
NAS HDB1079 SIT242/35. *Steel Windows for Tiong Bahru.*
NAS HDB1079 SIT582/25. *Improvement Trust Housing off Lavender Street.*
NAS HDB1080 SIT28/26. *Amended Layout of Lavender Street Housing Scheme.*
NAS HDB1080 SIT744/50. *History and Development of Tiong Bahru Estate.*
NAS HDB1278 SIT612/48. *Singapore Colonial Development and Welfare Fund Committee.*

Patrick Wakely Private Collection (now with AAA)

Public Record Office, National Archives of United Kingdom (PRO NAUK)

PRO AT67/63. *A Short History of Building Research in the United Kingdom from 1917 to 1946 – in Particular That of the Building Research Station.*
PRO CO273/19. *Colonial Hospitals and Lunatic Asylums.*
——. *Colonial Office Report on Hospitals and Lunatic Asylums.*
PRO CO273/310. *Sanitary Condition of Singapore.*

PRO CO273/396. *Report by Committee on Medical Service and Hospitals.*
PRO CO273/502. *Address by His Excellency the Governor to the Members of the Legislative Council at a Meeting Held on the 25th Day of October.*
PRO CO273/529. *Replacement of Opium Revenue.*
PRO CO273/538/3. *Committee of Imperial Defence Minutes.* .
——. *Report of the Gillman Commission.*
PRO CO273/539/1. *Town Planning in Malaya.*
PRO CO273/541/1. *Position of Major P. H. Keys, Government Architect: Petition by Several Architects in Singapore.*
PRO CO273/541/14. *Military Contribution Committee.*
PRO CO273/546/6. *Military Contribution.*
PRO CO273/651/9. *Raffles College: Report of the Commission on Higher Education in Malaya, 1939.*
PRO CO323/1420/1. *Technical Education in the Colonies: Replies to Circular Despatch of 10 April 1937, 1937–1938 Part 1.*
PRO CO323/1420/2. *Technical Education in the Colonies: Replies to Circular Despatch of 10 April 1937, 1937–1938 Part 2.*
PRO CO859/310. *Export Houses: Prefabrication and Building in the Tropics.*
PRO CO859/448. *Technical Education in the Colonies: Survey by Dr F J Harlow, Assistant Educational Adviser on Technical Education, 1953.*
PRO CO885/4. *Further Correspondence Respecting Colonial Defences.*
PRO CO927/6/7. *Housing Research in the Colonies: Proposal to Establish a Housing Research Centre in West Africa.*
PRO CO927/7/1. *Proposals for Building Research Programme in the British West Indies and British Guiana.*
PRO CO927/34/4. *Housing Research Centre, West Africa.*
PRO CO927/35/2. *Trinidad: Proposed Establishment of Building Research Station.*
PRO CO927/35/5. *Proposed Colonial Housing Bureau: Appointment of Colonial Liaison Officer to DSIR.*
PRO CO927/35/7. *Appointment of Colonial Liaison Officer to DSIR Building Research Station.*
PRO CO927/131/6. *Appointment of Colonial Liaison Officer to DSIR Building Research Station.*
PRO CO927/131/7. *Building Research: Aluminium Buildings.*
PRO CO937/365. *The Role of Meteorology and Climatology in Tropical Building and Housing.*
PRO CO1005/1. *Colonial Housing Research Group: Minutes of Meeting.*
PRO DSIR4/1548. *Architectural Science Group Education Sub-Committee; Meetings, Agenda, Minutes, etc, 1939–1940.*
PRO DSIR4/1557. *Architectural Science Boards: Lectures, Committee Meetings.*
PRO DSIR4/3361. *Tropical Building Division.*
PRO DSIR4/3475. *Establishment of a Building Research Station in West Africa.*
PRO DSIR4/3476. *Establishment of a Building Research Station in West Africa.*
PRO DSIR4/3647. *Council of Scientific and Industrial Research: Establishment of a Building Research Station in India.*
PRO MR1/1138. *Drawings of the Proposed Singapore General Hospital.*
PRO OD17/108. *RIBA: Conference of Heads of Overseas Schools of Architectural Education.*
PRO WO33/56. *Correspondence Relating to the Provision of Barrack Accommodation at the Straits Settlements, 1896.*
——. *Correspondence Relating to Water Supply at Tanglin Barracks in the Straits Settlements, 1896.*

Royal Institute of British Architects Archives (RIBAA)

RIBAA. *Board of Architectural Education Minutes (February 1955 to February 1958).*

RIBAA BAEM '58–'60. *Board of Architectural Education Minutes (May 1958 to June 1960).*

RIBAA BAEMOB '52–'60. *Board of Architectural Education: Minutes of Officers of the Board (January 1952 to April 1960).*

RIBAA CCCP 1. *Commonwealth Conference Committee Papers, Box 1.*

RIBAA CRCP1. *Commonwealth Relations Committee Papers, Box 1.*

Renate Koenigsberger Private Collection (now with AAA)

Allen, William, and Otto Koenigsberger. "Proposal to the Ford Foundation for the Establishment of a Department of Development Studies at the Architectural Association, London," undated (probably 1966), Renate Koenigsberger Private Collection.

Koenigsberger, Otto. "Introductory Lecture to Climatic Design Series," May 6, 1968. Renate Koenigsberger Private Collection.

——. "Lecture on Climate and History," October 12, 1967. Renate Koenigsberger Private Collection.

——. "Lecture on the Importance of Climate," November 8, 1964. Renate Koenigsberger Private Collection.

——. "Liverpool Lecture: Design with Climate," undated (around 1961). Renate Koenigsberger Private Collection.

——. "Second Term Opening Lecture," January 5, 1970. Renate Koenigsberger Private Collection.

——. "Speech for the Opening of the Exhibition of Department of Development and Tropical Studies," July 7, 1968. Renate Koenigsberger Private Collection.

——. "Speech for the Opening of the Exhibition of Department of Development and Tropical Studies," July 4, 1969. Renate Koenigsberger Private Collection.

——. "Week 2 Lecture on Climate and Man," 1965. Renate Koenigsberger Private Collection.

Royal Commonwealth Society Library Collections, Cambridge University Library (RCS CUL)

RCS/RCMS104, CUL. *Malayan Town Planning Papers.*

University Library of Liverpool Special Collection and Archives (ULLSCA)

ULLSCA D688/2/1. *Overseas Work, Robert Gardner-Medwin's Papers.*

SECONDARY SOURCES

Newspapers

The Straits Times (ST)

The Singapore Free Press (SFP)

The Singapore Free Press and Mercantile Advertiser (SFPMA)

Books, book chapters, journal articles and others

Abdullah, Munshi, and A. H. Hill. "The Hikayat Abdullah." *JMBRAS* 42, no. 1 (215) (1969): 85–106.

Abercrombie, Patrick. "Town Planning Literature: A Brief Summary of Its Present Extent." *TPR* 6, no. 2 (1915): 77–100.

Ackermann, Marsha E. *Cool Comfort: America's Romance with Air-Conditioning*. Washington, D.C.: Smithsonian Institution Press, 2002.
Adams, Annmarie. *Medicine by Design: The Architect and the Modern Hospital 1893–1943*. Minneapolis: University of Minnesota Press, 2008.
——. "Modernism and Medicine: The Hospitals of Stevens and Lee, 1916–1932." *JSAH* 58, no. 1 (1999): 42–61.
Agamben, Giorgio. *Homo Sacer: Sovereign Power and Bare Life*. Translated by Daniel Heller-Roazen. Stanford: Stanford University Press, 1998.
Alatas, Hussein Syed. *The Myth of the Lazy Native: A Study of the Image of the Malays, Filipinos and Javanese from the 16th to the 20th Century and Its Function in the Ideology of Colonial Capitalism*. London: F. Cass, 1977.
Alcock, A. E. S. "'Swishcrete': Notes on Stabilised Cement-Earth Building in the Gold Coast." *CBN* 16 (1953): 1–13.
Alder, Ken. *Engineering the Revolution: Arms and Enlightenment in France, 1763–1815*. Princeton, NJ: Princeton University Press, 1997.
Allan, George. "The Genesis of British Urban Redevelopment with Special Reference to Glasgow." *The Economic History Review* 18, no. 3 (1965): 598–613.
Allen, William. "The Training and Education of Architects." *Architectural Association Journal* 77 (1962): 223–31.
AlSayyad, Nezar, ed. *Forms of Dominance: On the Architecture and Urbanism of the Colonial Enterprise*. Aldershot: Avebury, 1992.
"Aluminium Aids Prefabrication." *Prefabrication* 1, no. 2 (1953): 11–14.
Amissah, S. B., and Charles K. Polónyi. *Housing and Urbanization: Report on the Postgraduate Urban Planning Course (1967–68, Term 1–2)*. Kumasi: Faculty of Architecture, Kwame Nkrumah University of Science and Technology, 1968.
Anderson, Warwick. *Colonial Pathologies: American Tropical Medicine, Race, and Hygiene in the Philippines*. Durham, NC: Duke University Press, 2006.
——, "Introduction: Postcolonial Technoscience." *Social Studies of Science* 32, nos. 5/6, Special Issue: Postcolonial Technoscience (2002): 643–58.
Andreoli, Elisabetta, and Adrian Forty. *Brazil's Modern Architecture*. London: Phaidon, 2004.
Architectural Association, Department of Tropical Studies. *Prospectus*. London, 1965.
Arnold, David. *Colonizing the Body: State Medicine and Epidemic Disease in Nineteenth-Century India*. Berkeley: University of California Press, 1993.
——, ed. *Imperial Medicine and Indigenous Societies*. Manchester: Manchester University Press, 1988.
——. *The Problem of Nature: Environment, Culture and European Expansion*. Oxford: Blackwell, 1996.
Arnold, Wayne. "In Singapore, a Local Switzerland for Asia's Wealthy." *International Herald Tribune*, 24 April 2007.
Aronin, Jeffrey Ellis. *Climate and Architecture*. New York: Reinhold, 1953.
Atkinson, George Anthony. "British Architects in the Tropics." *Architectural Association Journal* 69 (1953): 7–21.
——. "Building in the Tropics." *JRIBA* 57 (1950): 313–19.
——. "Building Techniques Overseas." *Prefabrication* 1, no. 9 (1954): 7–13.
——. "Building Techniques Overseas – II." *Prefabrication* 1, no. 10 (1954): 7–12.
——. "Construction and Erection of the Heliodon." *CBN* 26 (1955): 12.
——. "Raymond Unwin: Founding Father of BRS." *RIBAJ* 78 (1971): 446–48.
——. "Stabilised Earth Walls – Construction." *CBN* 8 (1952): 1–10.
——. "Stabilised Earth Walls – Surface Finishes." *CBN* 14 (1953): 1–8.
——. "Tropical Architecture and Building Standards." In *Conference on Tropical Architecture 1953: A Report of the Proceedings of the Conference Held at University College, London, March 1953*, edited by Arthur Foyle, 41–59. London: University College London, 1953.

——. "Warm Climates and Building Design." *CBN* 12, no. April (1953): 1–15.
——. "West Indian Schools Built in Soil-Cement Blockwork." *CBN* 5 (1951): 1–8.
——. "The Work of the Colonial Liaison Building Officer and Building in the Tropics." *QJIAM* 2, no. 1 (1952): 35–43.
Atkinson, William. *The Orientation of Buildings or Planning for Sunlight*. New York: John Wiley & Sons, 1912.
Auliciems, Andris, and Steven V. Szokolay. *Thermal Comfort. PLEA Notes*. 2nd ed. Brisbane: PLEA and Department of Architecture, University of Queensland, 2007.
Avermaete, Tom, Serhat Karakayali, and Marion von Osten, eds. *Colonial Modern: Aesthetics of the Past – Rebellions for the Future*. London: Black Dog Publishing, 2010.
Bailey, Harry P. "Toward a Unified Concept of the Temperate Climate." *Geographical Review* 54 (1964): 516–45.
Balfour, T. Graham. "The Opening Address of Dr. T. Graham Balfour, F.R.S., &C, Honorary Physician to Her Majesty the Queen, President of the Royal Statistical Society. Session 1889–90. Delivered 19th November, 1889." *Journal of the Royal Statistical Society* 52, no. 4 (1889): 517–34.
Banham, Reyner. *The Architecture of the Well-Tempered Environment*. 2nd ed. London: Architectural Press, 1984.
Barber, Daniel A. "Tomorrow's House: Architecture and the Future of Energy in the 1940s." *Technology and Culture* 55, no. 1 (2014): 1–39.
Bay, Joo-Hwa, and Boon-Lay Ong. "Social and Environmental Dimensions in Tropical Sustainable Architecture: Introductory Comments." In *Tropical Sustainable Architecture: Social and Environmental Dimensions*, edited by Joo-Hwa Bay and Boon-Lay Ong, 1–14. Oxford: Architectural Press, 2006.
——, eds. *Tropical Sustainable Architecture: Social and Environmental Dimensions*. Oxford: Architectural Press, 2006.
Bedford, Thomas. *Basic Principles of Ventilation and Heating*. London: H. K. Lewis & Co. Ltd., 1948.
——. "The Society's Lecture 1961: Researches on Thermal Comfort." *Ergonomics* 4, no. 4 (1961): 289–309.
Ben-Joseph, Eran. *The Code of the City: Standards and the Hidden Language of Place Making*. Cambridge, MA: MIT Press, 2005.
"A Beneficial Epidemic." *Eastern Daily Mail and Straits Morning Advertiser*, 3 May 1906.
Bennett, Tony. "The Exhibitionary Complex." In *Representing the Nation: A Reader*, edited by Jessica Evans and David Boswell, 332–59. London; New York: Routledge, 1999.
Bernal, J. D. "Architecture and Science." *JRIBA* 44, no. 16 (1937): 805–12.
——. "Science in Architecture." *RIBAJ* 53, no. 5 (1946): 155–59.
Best, Geoffrey. "The Scottish Victorian City." *Victorian Studies* 11, no. 3 (1968): 329–58.
"Biographical Notes on O.H. Koenigsberger." *HI* 7, no. 5–6 (1983): 7–16.
BHIC. *Suggestions in Regard to Sanitary Works Required for Improving Indian Stations*. London: George Edward Eyre and William Spottiswoode, 1864.
Blacklock, D. B. *An Empire Problem: The House and Village in the Tropics*. London: Hodder & Stoughton Ltd., 1932.
Blagden, W. M. "Temporary Electric Light and Power at Changi." *REJ* 43, no. 3 (1929): 408–18.
Bogle, J. M. Linton. "Town Planning in India." *JTPI* 15, no. 5 (1929): 157–60.
Bozdoğan, Sibel. *Modernism and Nation Building: Turkish Architectural Culture in the Early Republic*. Seattle: University of Washington Press, 2001.
——. "The Aga Khan Award for Architecture: A Philosophy of Reconciliation." *JAE* 45, no. 3 (1992): 182–188.
Brady, F. L. *An Introduction to Building Science*. London: Edward Arnold & Co., 1927.

Brandreth, Captain H. R. "Memorandum Relative to a System of Barracks for West Indies Recommended by Colonel Sir C. F. Smith, C.B., R.E., and Approved by the Master-General and Board of Ordnance." *PCRE* II (1844 [1838]): 238–45.
Brockway, Lucile H. *Science and Colonial Expansion: The Role of the British Royal Botanic Gardens*. New Haven: Yale University Press, 2002 [1979].
Brooke, Gilbert E. "Medical Work and Institutions." In *One Hundred Years of Singapore*, edited by Walter Makepeace, Gilbert E. Brooke and Roland St. J. Braddell, 487–519. Singapore: Oxford University Press, 1991 [1921].
Brown, W. Baker. *History of the Corps of Royal Engineers, Volume IV*. Chatham: The Institution of the Royal Engineers, 1952.
Browne, G. St. J. Orde. *Labour Conditions in Ceylon, Mauritius, and Malaya*. London: HMSO, 1943.
BRS. *The Building Research Station: Its History, Organization and Work*. Garston, Watford: BRS, 1954.
Bruegmann, Robert. "Architecture of the Hospital: 1770–1870." PhD diss., University of Pennsylvania, 1976.
——. "Review of Michel Foucault, et al., *Les Machines à guerir (aux origines de l'hôpital moderne)*, Paris: Institut de l'environment, 1976." *JSAH* 38, no. 2 (1979): 210–11.
Brundle, K. A. "Economy in Architecture." *QJIAM* 4, no. 4 (1955): 3.
——. "P.W.D. Housing: Some Comparative Notes & Diagrams on the Planning of Pre-War and Post-War Quarters Built by the Public Works Department, Singapore." *QJIAM* 1, no. 2 (1951): 17–35.
Buckley, Charles Burton. *An Anecdotal History of Old Times in Singapore*. 2 vols., Singapore: Fraser & Neave, 1902.
——. *Anecdotal History of Old Times in Singapore: From the Foundation of the Settlement under the Honourable the East India Company on February 6th, 1819 to the Transfer to the Colonial Office as Part of the Colonial Possessions of the Crown on April 1st, 1867*. New ed. Singapore: Malayan Branch of the Royal Asiatic Society, Oxford University Press, 1923.
"The Building Research Station: Its Origin, Work and Scope." *RIBAJ* 43 (1936): 789–802.
"Building Science at Liverpool: Prof. A. W. Henry." *Nature* 179 (1957): 564–65.
Burdett, Henry C. *Hospitals and Asylums of the World: Their Origin, History, Construction, Administration, Management, and Legislation*. Vol. IV, London: J & A Churchill, 1893.
Burroughs, Peter. "The Human Cost of Imperial Defence in the Early Victorian Age." *Victorian Studies* 24, no. 1 (1980): 7–32.
C.R.E. "Sun-Screens in Sky-Lit Buildings." *REJ* 28, no. 2 (1918): 70–2.
"CAA, CBAE, ARCASIA: Background and Objectives." *SIAJ* 43 (1970): 4–8.
"The Calcutta Improvement Trust." *Garden Cities & Town Planning, incorporating the Housing Reformer* 6, no. 5 (1921): 113.
Cameron, John. *Our Tropical Possessions in Malayan India*. London: Smith, Elder and Co., 1865.
Campbell, Robin M. *Designing for Comfort in Tropical Climate*. Melbourne: Department of Architecture, University of Melbourne, 1965.
Cannadine, David. *Ornamentalism: How the British Saw Their Empire*. Oxford: Oxford University Press, 2007.
Carstairs, C. Y. "The Social and Economic Background." In *Conference on Tropical Architecture 1953: A Report of the Proceedings of the Conference Held at University College, London, March 1953*, edited by Arthur Foyle, 1–8. London: University College London, 1953.
"CBAE & ARCASIA Meetings in Singapore." *SIAJ* 43 (1970): 2–3.
Çelik, Zeynep. "New Approaches to the 'Non-Western' City." *JSAH* 58, no. 3 (1999): 374–81.

Chakrabarty, Dipesh. "The Climate of History: Four Theses." *Critical Inquiry* 35, no. 2 (2008): 197–222.
——. *Provincializing Europe: Postcolonial Thought and Historical Difference*. Princeton: Princeton University Press, 2000.
Chamberlain, Joseph. "Circular from the Secretary of State for the Colonies: Investigation of Malaria and the Training of Medical Officers in the Treatment and Prevention of Tropical Diseases." In *PLCSS 1904*, C69–C79. Singapore: Straits Settlements Government Printing Office, 1905.
Chambers, David Wade, and Richard Gillespie. "Locality in the History of Science: Colonial Science, Technoscience, and Indigenous Knowledge." *Osiris* 15 (2000): 221–40.
Chan, Soo Khian, and Kheng Soon Tay. "Who Is Afraid of the Neo-Tropical?". *Singapore Architect* 212 (2001): 23–25.
Chang, Jiat-Hwee."Multiple Power in Colonial Spaces." *ABE* 5 (2014).
——. "Thermal Comfort and Climatic Design in the Tropics: A Historical Critique." *JoA* (forthcoming).
——. "Tropical Variants of Sustainable Architecture: A Postcolonial Perspective." In *Handbook of Architectural Theory*, edited by Greig Crysler, Stephen Cairns and Hilde Heynen, 602–17. London: Sage, 2012.
——. "Deviating Discourse: Tay Kheng Soon and the Architecture of Postcolonial Development in Tropical Asia." *JAE* 63, no. 3 (2010): 153–58.
——. "An Other Modern Architecture: Postcolonial Spectacles, Cambodian Nationalism and Khmer Traditions." *Singapore Architect* 250 (2009): 146–53.
——. " 'Natural' Traditions: Constructing Tropical Architecture in Transnational Malaysia and Singapore." *Explorations* 7, no. 1 (2007): 1–22.
Chang, Jiat-Hwee, and William S. W. Lim. "Non West Modernist Past: Rethinking Modernisms and Modernities Beyond the West." In *Non West Modernist Past: On Architecture and Modernities*, edited by William S. W. Lim and Jiat-Hwee Chang, 7–24. Singapore: World Scientific, 2011.
Chang, Jiat-Hwee, and Tim Winter. "Thermal Modernity and Architecture." *JoA* 20, no. 1 (2015): 92–121.
Chatterjee, Partha. *The Nation and Its Fragments: Colonial and Postcolonial Histories*. Princeton: Princeton University Press, 1993.
——. *Nationalist Thought and the Colonial World: A Derivative Discourse*. Minneapolis: University of Minnesota Press, 2001 [1986].
Chattopadhyay, Swati. "Blurring Boundaries: The Limits of 'White Town' in Colonial Calcutta." *JSAH* 59, no. 2 (2000): 154–79.
——. *Representing Calcutta: Modernity, Nationalism, and the Colonial Uncanny*. London: Routledge, 2005.
Chitty, Anthony M. "The Need for Regionalism in Architecture: A Ghana Aesthetic?". *The Builder* CXCV (1958): 400.
Chopra, Preeti. *A Joint Enterprise: Indian Elites and the Making of British Bombay*. Minneapolis: University of Minnesota Press, 2011.
Clarke, Sabine. "A Technocratic Imperial State? The Colonial Office and Scientific Research, 1940–1960." *Twentieth Century British History* 18, no. 4 (2007): 453–80.
Clauson, J. E. "Recent Researches on Malaria." *PPCRE* XII (1887).
Clayton, Anthony. "Browne, Sir Granville St John Orde (1883–1947)." In *Oxford Dictionary of National Biography*, edited by H. C. G. Matthew and Brian Harrison. Oxford: Oxford University Press, 2004. Online edition, accessed 5 January 2016, http://www.oxforddnb.com/view/article/40958.
Collier, Stephen J., and Andrew Lakoff. "On Regimes of Living." In *Global Assemblages: Technology, Politics, and Ethics as Anthropological Problems*, edited by Aihwa Ong and Stephen J. Collier, 22–39. Malden: Blackwell, 2005.

Collier, Stephen J., and Aihwa Ong. "Global Assemblages, Anthropological Problems." In *Global Assemblages: Technology, Politics, and Ethics as Anthropological Problems*, edited by Aihwa Ong and Stephen J. Collier, 3–21. Malden: Blackwell Publishing, 2005.

Collyer, W. H. "Appendix B, Improvement Trust for Singapore: Report for 1924 by Deputy Chairman." In *ARSM 1924*, 1–12. Singapore: The Straits Times Press, 1925.

——. "Appendix B, Singapore Improvement Trust." In *ARSM 1925*, 1–35. Singapore: The Straits Times Press, 1926.

Colonial Office. *A Survey of Vocational Technical Education in the Colonial Empire*. London: HMSO, 1940.

The Commissioners. *General Report of the Commission Appointed for Improving the Sanitary Condition of Barracks and Hospitals*. London: George Edward Eyre and William Spottiswoode, 1861.

——. *Report of the BHIC on the Sanitary Condition and Improvement of the Mediterranean Stations*. London: George Edward Eyre and William Spottiswoode, 1863.

——. *Report of the Commissioners Appointed to Inquire into the Regulations Affecting the Sanitary Condition of the Army, the Organization of Military Hospitals, and the Treatment of the Sick and Wounded; with Evidence and Appendix*. London: George Edward Eyre and William Spottiswoode, 1858.

——. *Report of the RCSSAI. Vol. 1: Précis of Evidence, Minutes of Evidence, Addenda*. London: George Edward Eyre and William Spottiswoode, 1863.

Conference Report, Malta June 1965. London: CAA, 1965.

Conference Report, New Delhi March 1967. London: CAA, 1967.

Cooper, Frederick."Modernizing Bureaucrats, Backward Africans, and the Development Concept." In *International Development and the Social Sciences: Essays on the History and Politics of Knowledge*, edited by Frederick Cooper and Randall M. Packard, 64–91. Berkeley: University of California Press, 1997.

Cooper, Frederick, and Randall M. Packard. "Introduction." In *International Development and the Social Sciences: Essays on the History and Politics of Knowledge*, edited by Frederick Cooper and Randall M. Packard, 1–44. Berkeley: University of California Press, 1997.

"Correspondence on the Subject of Hospital Accommodation in Singapore." In *PLCSS 1875*, ccclxx–ccclxxi. Singapore: Straits Settlements Government Printing Office, 1876.

"Correspondence Regarding the Insanitary Site of Tan Tock Seng's Hospital." In *PLCSS 1899*, C453-78. Singapore: Straits Settlements Government Printing Office, 1900.

Cowan, Henry J. "The Architectural Science Laboratory." *RIBAJ* 66, no. 12 (1959): 422–23.

——. "Architecture as the Art of the Possible." *Architectural Science Review* 37, no. 1 (1993): 1–7.

——. *A Contradiction in Terms: The Autobiography of Henry J. Cowan*. Sydney: Hermitage Press, 1993.

Cox, Stan. *Losing Our Cool: Uncomfortable Truths About Our Air-Conditioned World (and Finding New Ways to Get through the Summer)*. New York: The New Press, 2010.

Crinson, Mark. *Modern Architecture and the End of Empire*. Aldershot: Ashgate, 2003.

——. "The Powers That Be: Architectural Potency and Spatialized Power." *ABE* 4 (2013).

Crinson, Mark, and Jules Lubbock. *Architecture – Art or Profession? Three Hundred Years of Architectural Education in Britain*. Manchester: Manchester University Press, 1994.

Crowden, G. P. "Indoor Climate and Thermal Comfort in the Tropics." In *Conference on Tropical Architecture 1953: A Report of the Proceedings of the Conference Held at University College, London, March 1953*, edited by Arthur Foyle, 27–35. London: University College London, 1953.

Crowley, John E. *The Invention of Comfort: Sensibility and Design in Early Modern Britain and Early America*. Baltimore: Johns Hopkins University Press, 2001.

Crysler, C. Greig. *Writing Spaces: Discourses of Architecture, Urbanism, and the Built Environment, 1960–2000*. New York: Routledge, 2003.
Cuff, Dana. *Architecture: The Story of Practice*. Cambridge, MA: MIT Press, 1991.
Curtin, Philip D. *Death by Migration: Europe's Encounter with the Tropical World in the Nineteenth Century*. Cambridge: Cambridge University Press, 1989.
Danby, Miles. *Grammar of Architectural Design, with Special Reference to the Tropics*. London and New York: Oxford University Press, 1963.
Darwin, John. "A Third British Empire? The Dominion Idea in Imperial Politics." In *The Oxford History of British Empire, Vol. IV: The Twentieth Century*, edited by Judith M. Brown and Roger Louis, 64–87. Oxford: Oxford University Press, 1999.
Datta, Partho. "How Modern Planning Came to Calcutta." *PP* 28, no. 1 (2013): 139–47.
Davis, Howard. *The Culture of Building*. Oxford: Oxford University Press, 1999.
Davis, Mike. *Planet of Slums*. London: Verso, 2006.
Dean, Mitchell. *Governmentality: Power and Rule in Modern Society*. London: Sage, 1999.
Defence Department. *Barrack Synopsis (India)*. London: HMSO, 1939.
Demeritt, David. "Scientific Forest Conservation and the Statistical Picturing of Nature's Limits in the Progressive-Era United States." *Environment and Planning D: Society and Space* 19 (2001): 431–59.
"Department of Tropical Studies: A Cross Section of Recent Work." *Architectural Association Journal* 78 (1963): 302–11.
Development and Welfare Organization in the West Indies. *Housing in the West Indies*. Bridgetown, Barbados: Advocate Co. Printers, 1945.
Dickson, Frederick. "Minute by the Colonial Secretary." In *PLCSS 1891*, C9–C16. Singapore: Straits Settlements Government Printing Office, 1892.
"Discussion." In *Conference on Tropical Architecture 1953: A Report of the Proceedings of the Conference Held at University College, London, March 1953*, edited by Arthur Foyle, 113–16. London: University College London, 1953.
Doggett, Marjorie. *Characters of Light*. 2nd ed. Singapore: Times Books International, 1985 [1957].
Douet, James. *British Barracks 1600–1914: Their Architecture and Role in Society*. London: Stationary Office, 1998.
Drayton, Richard. *Nature's Government: Science, Imperial Britain, and the "Improvement" of the World*. New Haven: Yale University Press, 2000.
Dreyfus, Hubert L., and Paul Rabinow. *Michel Foucault: Beyond Structuralism and Hermeneutics*. 2nd ed. Chicago: University of Chicago Press, 1983.
Driver, Felix. "Imagining the Tropics: Views and Visions of the Tropical World"." *Singapore Journal of Tropical Geography* 25, no. 1 (2004): 1–17.
——. "Moral Geographies: Social Science and the Urban Environment in Mid-Nineteenth Century England." *Transactions of the Institute of British Geographers* 13, no. 3 (1988): 275–87.
——. *Power and Pauperism: The Workhouse System 1834–1884*. Cambridge: Cambridge University Press, 1993.
Driver, Felix, and Brenda S. A. Yeoh. "Constructing the Tropics: Introduction." *Singapore Journal of Tropical Geography* 21, no. 1 (2000): 1–5.
Drysdale, J. W. *Climate and House Design: With Reference to Australian Climate*. Sydney: Commonwealth Experimental Building Station, 1947.
Duncan, James S. *In the Shadows of the Tropics: Climate, Race and Biopower in Nineteenth Century Ceylon*. Aldershot: Ashgate, 2007.
Dutta, Arindam. "Review of Mark Crinson, *Modern Architecture and the End of Empire* (Aldershot: Ashgate, 2003)." *JSAH* 67, no. 2 (2008): 292–93.
Editor. "The Great World of Portland Place." *The Builder* CXCIV (1958): 569.
Editors. "Editorial: Commonwealth 2." *Architectural Review* 127 (1960): 4–5.

"Education Survey: A Brief Survey of Architectural Education and Training in Member Countries." In *Handbook of Commonwealth Architects*, edited by CAA, 65–68. London: CAA & The Builder, 1965.
Educational Committee of the Architecture Science Group. "The Place of Science in Architectural Education: The First Report of the Education Committee of the Architectural Science Group of the RIBA Research Board." *JRIBA* 48, no. 8 (1941): 133–44.
Edwards, A. Trystan. "Sunlight in Streets." *TPR* 8, no. 2 (1920): 93–98.
——. "Sunlight in Streets II." *TPR* 9, no. 1 (1921): 27–36.
Edwards, Jay D. "The Complex Origins of the American Domestic Piazza-Veranda-Gallery." *Material Culture* 21, no. 2 (1989): 2–58.
——. "The Origins of Creole Architecture." *Winterthur Portfolio* 29, no. 2/3 (1994): 155–89.
Escobar, Arturo. *Encountering Development: The Making and Unmaking of the Third World*. Princeton: Princeton University Press, 1995.
Evans, Martin. "Education for Responsive Climatic Design: The Evolution of Postgraduate Courses for the Third World: The Influence of the Institutional Framework on Climatic Design." *HI* 7, nos. 5–6 (1983): 347–55.
——. *Housing, Climate and Comfort*. London: The Architectural Press, 1980.
Evans, Robin. "Rookeries and Moral Dwellings: English Housing Reform and the Moralities of Private Space." In *Translations from Drawing to Building and Other Essays*, 93–118. London: AA, 1997.
"Extension to Ipoh Grand Stand for the Perak Turf Club." *JIAM* 1, no. 4 (1931): 13–14.
Fair, Alistair. "'A Laboratory of Heating and Ventilation': The Johns Hopkins Hospital as Experimental Architecture, 1870–90." *JoA* 19, no. 3 (2014): 357–81.
Feldman, Theodore S. "Late Enlightenment Meteorology." In *The Quantifying Spirit in the Eighteenth Century*, edited by Tore Frängsmyr, J. L. Heilbron and Robin E. Rider, 143–78. Berkeley: University of California Press, 1990.
Ferguson, James. "Anthropology and Its Evil Twin: 'Development' in the Constitution of a Discipline." In *International Development and the Social Sciences: Essays on the History and Politics of Knowledge*, edited by Frederick Cooper and Randall M. Packard, 150–75. Berkeley: University of California Press, 1997.
Fernández-Galiano, Luis. *Fire and Memory: On Architecture and Energy*. Translated by Gina Cariño. Cambridge, MA: MIT Press, 2000.
Fife. "The Thickness and Materials of Walls and Roofs of Buildings, Considered in Respect of Coolness in Tropical Climates." *PCRE , New Series* XIII (1864): 24–26.
Fleming, James Rodger, and Vladimir Jankovic. "Revisiting Klima." *Osiris* 26, no. 1 (2011): 1–15.
Fletcher, Bannister. *Light and Air: A Text-Book for Architects and Surveyors*. London: B. T. Batsford, 1895.
Forty, Adrian. "The Modern Hospital in England and France: The Social and Medical Uses of Architecture." In *Buildings and Society: Essays on the Social Development of the Built Environment*, edited by Anthony D. King, 61–93. London: Routledge & Kegan Paul, 1980.
Foucault, Michel. *Discipline and Punish: The Birth of the Prison*. Translated by Alan Sheridan. 2nd ed. New York: Vintage Books, 1995 [1977].
——. "The Eye of the Power." In *Power/Knowledge: Selected Interviews and Other Writings*, edited by Colin Gordon. New York: Pantheon, 1980.
——. "Governmentality." In *The Foucault Effect: Studies in Governmentality*, edited by Michel Foucault, Graham Burchell, Colin Gordon and Peter Miller, 87–104. Chicago: University of Chicago Press, 1991.
——. *The History of Sexuality: An Introduction, Volume 1*. Translated by Robert Hurley. New York: Vintage, 1990 [1978].

——. "Nietzsche, Genealogy, History." In *The Essential Foucault: Selections from the Essential Works of Foucault 1954–1984*, edited by Paul Rabinow and Nikolas S. Rose. New York: The New Press, 2005 [1971].
——. "The Politics of Health in the Eighteenth Century." In *Power/Knowledge: Selected Interviews and Other Writings*, edited by Colin Gordon, 166–82. New York: Pantheon, 1980.
——. *Society Must Be Defended: Lectures at the Collège de France, 1975–76*. Translated by David Macey. New York: Picador, 2003.
——. "Two Lectures." Translated by Alessandro Fortana and Pasquale Pasquino. In *Power/ Knowledge: Selected Interviews and Other Writings, 1972–1977*, edited by Colin Gordon, 78–108. New York: Pantheon Books, 1980.
Foucault, Michel, Graham Burchell, Colin Gordon, and Peter Miller, eds. *The Foucault Effect: Studies in Governmentality*. Chicago: University of Chicago Press, 1991.
Foucault, Michel, Michel Senellart, François Ewald, and Alessandro Fontana. *Security, Territory, Population: Lectures at the Collège De France, 1977–78*. Basingstoke: Palgrave Macmillan, 2007.
Frampton, Kenneth. "Towards a Critical Regionalism: Six Points for an Architecture of Resistance." In *The Anti-Aesthetic: Essays on Postmodern Culture*, edited by Hal Foster, 16–30. New York: New Press, 1998 [1983].
Fraser, J. M. *The Work of the Singapore Improvement Trust 1927–1947*. Singapore: Singapore Improvement Trust, 1948.
Fraser, James M., and Lincoln Page. "Singapore Improvement Trust, 1950 Programme: Two Blocks of Flats and Shops in Tiong Bahru Road, Singapore." *QJIAM* 1, no. 2 (1951): 37–42.
The Friends of Singapore, ed. *The House in Coleman Street*. Singapore: The Friends of Singapore, 1958.
Fry, Maxwell, and Jane Drew. *Tropical Architecture in the Humid Zone*. London: Batsford, 1956.
Fuller, Mia. *Moderns Abroad: Architecture, Cities, and Italian Imperialism*. London: Routledge, 2010.
Furnivall, J. S. *Colonial Policy and Practice*. New York: New York University Press, 1956.
Gandy, Matthew. "Planning, Anti-Planning and the Infrastructure Crisis Facing Metropolitan Lagos." *Urban Studies* 43 (2006): 371–96.
George, Cherian. *Singapore, the Air-Conditioned Nation: Essays on the Politics of Comfort and Control, 1990–2000*. Singapore: Landmark Books, 2000.
Ghosh, Birendra Nath, and Jahar Lal Das. *A Treatise on Hygiene and Public Health, with Special Reference to the Tropics*. 2nd ed. Calcutta: Hilton and Co, 1914.
Gilbert, Pamela K. *Mapping the Victorian Social Body*. Albany: State University of New York, 2004.
Glacken, Clarence J. *Traces on the Rhodian Shore: Nature and Culture in Western Thought from Ancient Times to the End of the Eighteenth Century*. Berkeley: University of California Press, 1967.
Glendinning, Miles. *Modern Architect: The Life and Times of Robert Matthew*. London: RIBA Publishing, 2008.
Glionna, John M. "Singapore, a New Home for Riches." *Los Angeles Times*, 11 November 2006.
Glover, William. *Making Lahore Modern: Constructing and Imagining a Colonial City*. Minneapolis: University of Minnesota Press, 2008.
Goad, Philip. *Architecture Bali: Architectures of Welcome*. Sydney: Pesaro Publishing, 2000.
Godlewska, Anne, and Neil Smith. *Geography and Empire*. Cambridge, MA: Blackwell, 1994.

Goldberger, Paul. "Julius Posener, 91, an Architect and Critic of Modern Movement." *New York Times*, January 31, 1996.
Gordon, A. "The Old Order Changeth." *JSSAI* 3, no. 6 (1930): 1–2.
Goto-Shibata, Harumi. "Empire on the Cheap: The Control of Opium Smoking in the Straits Settlements, 1925–1939." *Modern Asian Studies* 40, no. 1 (2006): 59–80.
Graham, Stephen, and Simon Marvin. *Splintering Urbanism: Networked Infrastructures, Technological Mobilities and the Urban Condition*. London: Routledge, 2001.
Guillemard, Laurence. "Singapore in 1926: Sir Laurence Guillemard's Speech at the Straits Settlements (Singapore) Association Dinner." *British Malaya* 1, no. 8 (1926): 224–28.
Gullick, J. M. "The Builders." *JMBRAS* 85, no. 2 (2012): 79–98.
Gupta, Raj Bahadur. *Labour and Housing in India*. Calcutta: Longmans Green & Co., 1930.
H., E. O. "Opium Control in Malaya." *Far Eastern Survey* 7, no. 2 (1937): 21–22.
Hack, Karl, and Kevin Blackburn. *Did Singapore Have to Fall? Churchill and the Impregnable Fortress*. London: Routledge, 2004.
Hacking, Ian. "How Should We Do the History of Statistics?" In *The Foucault Effect: Studies in Governmentality*, edited by Michel Foucault, Graham Burchell, Colin Gordon and Peter Miller, 181–96. Chicago: University of Chicago Press, 1991.
Hall-Jones, John, and Christopher Hooi. *An Early Surveyor in Singapore: John Turnbull Thomson in Singapore 1841–1853*. Singapore: National Museum of Singapore, 1979.
Hancock, T. H. H. *Coleman of Singapore*. Singapore: Antiques of the Orient, 1985 (1955).
——. *Coleman's Singapore*. Singapore: The Malaysian Branch of the Royal Asiatic Society, 1986 (1955).
——. "George Doumgold Coleman, Architect & Planning Advisor to Sir Stamford Raffles, Designer of the Armenian Church, Singapore." *QJIAM* 1, no. 3 (1951): 57–70.
Hancock, T. H. H., and C. A. Gibson-Hill. *Architecture in Singapore*. Singapore: Singapore Art Institute & Institute of Architects of Malaya, 1954.
Haraway, Donna. "Situated Knowledges: The Science Question in Feminism and the Privilege of Partial Perspective." *Feminist Studies* 14, no. 3 (1988): 575–99.
Harris, Eileen. *British Architectural Books and Writers, 1556–1785*. Cambridge: Cambridge University Press, 1990.
Harris, Richard, and Robert Lewis. "A Happy Confluence of Planning and Statistics: Bombay and Calcutta in the 1901 Census." *PP* 28, no. 1 (2013): 113–16.
——. "Introduction." *PP* 28, no. 1 (2013): 113–16.
Harrison, Dex, ed. *Building Science: Papers Prepared for the Architectural Science Board of the RIBA*. London: George Allen & Unwin, 1948.
Harrison, Mark. *Climates and Constitutions: Health, Race, Environment and British Imperialism in India 1600–1850*. Oxford: Oxford University Press, 1999.
——. *Public Health in British India: Anglo-Indian Preventive Medicine 1859–1914*. Cambridge: Cambridge University Press, 1994.
Harvey, E. H. "R.E. Works Abroad." *REJ* 11, no. 2 (1927): 93–94.
Hattendorf, John B. *The Two Beginnings: A History of St. George's Church Tanglin*. Singapore: St. George's Church, 1984.
Havinden, Michael A., and David Meredith. *Colonialism and Development: Britain and Its Tropical Colonies, 1850–1960*. London: Routledge, 1993.
Haynes, Douglas Melvin. "The Social Production of Metropolitan Expertise in Tropical Diseases: The Imperial State, Colonial Service and Tropical Diseases Research Fund." *Science, Technology & Society* 4, no. 2 (1999): 205–38.
"A Healthier Singapore." *The Malayan Architect* 5, no. 5 (1933): 107–13.
Hemming, E. H. "Progress in Barrack Design." *PPCRE* XXVI (1900): 41–68.
Herbert, Gilbert. *Pioneers of Prefabrication: The British Contribution in the Nineteenth Century*. Baltimore: Johns Hopkins University Press, 1978.

Herschel, John F. "Instructions for Making and Registering Meteorological Observations at Various Stations in Southern Africa, and Other Countries in the South Seas, as also at Sea." *PCRE* II (1844): 214–31.
Hess, David J. *Science Studies: An Advanced Introduction*. New York: New York University Press, 1997.
Hilton, R. N. "The Basic Malay House." *JMBRAS* 29, no. 3 (175) (1956): 134–55.
Hindmarsh, E. H. "Air in the Tropics – Particularly Malaya." *JIAM* 4, no. 4 (1933): 19–21.
Hobsbawm, Eric. *The Age of Extremes: A History of the World, 1914–1991*. New York: Vintage, 1994.
Hodge, Joseph M. "Science, Development, and Empire: The Colonial Advisory Council on Agriculture and Animal Health, 1929–43." *The Journal of Imperial and Commonwealth History* 30, no. 1 (2002): 1–20.
Hodson, Mike, and Simon Marvin. "Urbanism in the Anthropocene: Ecological Urbanism or Premium Ecological Enclaves." *City* 14, no. 3 (2010): 298–313.
Holford, William. "Foreword." In *Prospectus*, edited by Architectural Association Department of Tropical Architecture. London, 1955.
Hollis, H. P. "Glaisher, James (1809–1903)." In *Oxford Dictionary of National Biography*, edited by H. C. G. Matthew and Brian Harrison. Oxford: Oxford University Press, 2004. Online edition, accessed 5 January 2016, http://www.oxforddnb.com/view/article/33419.
Home. "On Engineering Operations on the Gold Coast During the Recent Expedition." *PCRE, New Series* XXIII (1876): 85–119.
Home, Robert K. *Of Planting and Planning: The Making of British Colonial Cities*. London: Spon, 1997.
"Homes across the Sea." *Prefabrication* 1, no. 1 (1953): 12–13.
Hoops, A. L. *Annual Straits Settlements Medical Report for 1921*. Singapore: Government Printing Office, 1922.
Hosagrahar, Jyoti. *Indigenous Modernities: Negotiating Architecture and Urbanism*. London; New York: Routledge, 2005.
——. "South Asia: Looking Back, Moving Ahead – History and Modernization." *JSAH* 61, no. 3 (2002): 355–69.
"Hospital Construction – Wards." *The Builder* 16, no. 816 (1858): 641–43.
"Housing the Army – St. George's Barracks – the Tower." *The Builder* 16, no. 788 (1858): 169–71.
Hulme, Mike. *Why We Disagree About Climate Change: Understanding Controversy, Inaction and Opportunity*. Cambridge: Cambridge University Press, 2009.
Huxley, Margo. "Geographies of Governmentality." In *Space, Knowledge and Power: Foucault and Geography*, edited by Jeremy W. Crampton and Stuart Elden, 185–204. Aldershot: Ashgate, 2007.
Imran bin Tajudeen. "Beyond Racialized Representations: Architectural Linguae Francae and Urban Histories in the Kampung Houses and Shophouses of Melaka and Singapore." In *Colonial Frames, Nationalist Histories: Imperial Legacies, Architecture and Modernity*, edited by Mrinalini Rajagopalan and Madhuri Desai, 213–52. Burlington: Ashgate, 2012.
——. "Kampung/Compound Houses." *Singapura Stories* website. Accessed 31 October 2015, http://singapurastories.com/2012/06/1267/.
Imrie, Rob. "The Interrelationships between Building Regulations and Architects' Practices." *Environment and Planning B: Planning and Design* 34 (2007): 925–43.
Imrie, Rob, and Emma Street. *Architectural Design and Regulation*. Oxford: Wiley-Blackwell, 2011.
Inter-University Council. *Inter-University Council for Higher Education Overseas, 1946–1954*. London: HMSO, 1955.

"Introduction." In *Proceedings of Educational Workshop "Planning and Building for Development" July 1st to 3rd, 1970*, 1–3. London: Department of Development and Tropical Studies, Architectural Association, 1970.
J.F.F. "Changi Cantonment 1933–1937." *REJ* 51 (1937): 355–62.
Jacobs, Jane M. *Edge of Empire: Postcolonialism and the City*. London: Routledge, 1996.
Jayewardene-Pillai, Shanti. *Imperial Conversations: Indo-Britons and the Architecture of South India*. New Delhi: Yoda Press, 2007.
Jayewardene, Shanti. "Reflections on Design in the Context of Development." *Mimar*, no. 27 (1988): 70–75.
Jebb, Joshua. "On the Construction and Ventilation of Prisons." *PCRE* XVII (1845): 10–32.
Jeffreys, Julius. *The British Army in India: Its Preservation by an Appropriate Clothing, Housing, Locating, Recreative Employment, and Hopeful Encouragement of the Troops*. London: Longman, 1858.
Jeffries, Sir Charles Joseph, ed. *A Review of Colonial Research, 1940–1960*. London: HMSO, 1964.
Jenkins, Peter, and Waveney Jenkins. *The Planter's Bungalow: A Journey Down the Malay Peninsula*. Singapore: Editions Didier Millet, 2007.
Johnson, Peter, and Susan Clarke. *Architectural Education in the Commonwealth: A Survey of Schools*. Department of Architecture, University of Sydney and CBAE, CAA, 1979.
Joyce, Patrick. *The Rule of Freedom: Liberalism and the Modern City*. London: Verso, 2003.
Kaye, Barrington. *The Development of the Architectural Profession in Britain: A Sociological Study*. London: Allen & Unwin, 1962.
Kemp, Gerard. "Guinea Pigs? Not Us, Says Architect." *Daily Mail*, 27 July 1963.
Kennedy, Dane. "The Perils of the Midday Sun: Climatic Anxieties in the Colonial Tropics." In *Imperialism and the Natural World*, edited by John M. Mackenzie, 118–40. Manchester and New York: Manchester University Press, 1990.
Keys, Major P. H. "Memorandum on the New Post Office and New General Hospital, Singapore." In *PLCSS 1922*, C215-29. Singapore: Government Printing Office, 1923.
Kidambi, Prashant. "Housing the Poor in a Colonial City: The Bombay Improvement Trust, 1898–1918." *Studies in History* 17, no. 1 (2001): 57–79.
——. "Planning, the Information Order, and the Bombay Census of 1901." *PP* 28, no. 1 (2013): 117–23.
King, Anthony D. *The Bungalow: The Production of a Global Culture*. 2nd ed. New York: Oxford University Press, 1995 [1984].
——. *Colonial Urban Development: Culture, Social Power, and Environment*. London: Routledge & Kegan Paul, 1976.
——. "Hospital Planning: Revised Thoughts on the Origin of the Pavilion Principle in England." *Medical History* 10, no. 6 (1966): 360–73.
Kingham, Norman. "Obituary: Professor Robert Gardner-Medwin." *Independent*, July 8 1995.
Koenigsberger, Otto. "The Role of the British Architect in the Tropics." *Architectural Design* 24: Special Issue on Tropical Architecture by British Architects, Part 2 (1954): 1.
——. "Tropical Planning Problems." In *Conference on Tropical Architecture 1953: A Report of the Proceedings of the Conference Held at University College, London, March 1953*, edited by Arthur Foyle, 13–22. London: University College London, 1953.
Koenigsberger, Otto H., Carl T. Mahoney, and Martin Evans. *Climate and House Design*. New York: United Nations, 1971.
Koenigsberger, Otto H., T. G. Ingersoll, Alan Mayhew, and S. V. Szokolay. *Manual of Tropical Housing and Building*. London: Longman, 1974.
Koenigsberger, Otto H., and Robert Lynn. *Roofs in the Warm Humid Tropics*. London: Lund Humphries for the Architectural Association, 1965.
Lagae, Johan, and Kim De Raedt. "Editorial." *ABE* 4 (2013).

Lanchester, H. V. "Calcutta Improvement Trust: Précis of Mr. E. P. Richards' Report on the City of Calcutta, Part I." *TPR* 5, no. 2 (1914): 115–30.

——. "Calcutta Improvement Trust: Précis of Mr. E. P. Richards' Report on the City of Calcutta, Part II." *TPR* 5, no. 3 (1914): 214–24.

——. "Notes on the Calcutta Report of Mr E. P. Richards, Summarised in Nos. 2 and 3 of Vol. V." *TPR* 6, no. 1 (1915): 27–30.

Larson, Magali Sarfatti. *Behind the Postmodern Facade: Architectural Change in Late Twentieth-Century America*. Berkeley: University of California Press, 1993.

Latour, Bruno. "Give Me a Laboratory and I Will Raise the World." In *Science Observed: Perspectives on the Social Study of Science*, edited by Karin D. Knorr-Cetina and Michael Mulkay, 141–69. London: Sage, 1983.

——. "On Recalling ANT." In *Actor Network Theory and After*, edited by John Law and John Hassard, 15–25. Malden: Blackwell, 1999.

——. *Science in Action: How to Follow Scientists and Engineers through Society*. Cambridge, MA: Harvard University Press, 1987.

——. "Visualisation and Cognition: Drawing Things Together." In *Knowledge and Society: Studies in the Sociology of Culture Past and Present*, edited by Henrika Kuklick and Elizabeth Long, 1–40. Greenwich: JAI Press, 1986.

——. *We Have Never Been Modern*. Cambridge, MA: Harvard University Press, 1993.

Lauber, Wolfgang, Peter Cheret, Klaus Ferstl, and Eckhart Ribbeck. *Tropical Architecture: Sustainable and Humane Building in Africa, Latin America, and South-East Asia*. New York: Prestel, 2005.

Law, John. "Technology and Heterogeneous Engineering: The Case of Portuguese Expansion." In *The Social Construction of Technological Systems: New Directions in the Sociology and History of Technology*, edited by Wiebe E. Bijker, Thomas P. Hughes and T. J. Pinch, 111–34. Cambridge, MA: MIT Press, 1987.

Law, John, and John Hassard, eds. *Actor Network Theory and After*. Malden: Blackwell, 1999.

Le Roux, Hannah. "Modern Architecture in Post-Colonial Ghana and Nigeria." *Architectural History* 47 (2004): 361–92.

——. "The Networks of Tropical Architecture." *JoA* 8 (2003): 337–54.

Lea, F. M. *Science and Building: A History of the Building Research Station*. London: HMSO, 1971.

Lee, Kip Lin. *The Singapore House, 1819–1942*. Singapore: Times Editions, Preservation of Monuments Board, 1988.

Lee, Kuan Yew, "Message." In *Homes for the People*, edited by Housing Development Board, 1. Singapore: HDB, 1965.

Lee, Rachel. "Constructing a Shared Vision: Otto Koenigsberger and Tata & Sons." *ABE* 2 (2012). [http://abe.revues.org/356, DOI : 10.4000/abe.356, last accessed 5 January 2016].

——. "Negotiating Modernities: Otto Koenigsberger's Works and Network in Exile (1933–1951)." *ABE* 5 (2014). [http://abe.revues.org/696, last accessed 5 January 2016].

Lee, Yong Kiat. *The Medical History of Early Singapore*. Tokyo: Southeast Asian Medical Information Center, 1978.

——. "Singapore's Pauper and Tan Tock Seng Hospital (1819–1873): Part 2." *JMBRAS* 49, no. 1 (1976): 113–33.

——. "Singapore's Pauper and Tan Tock Seng Hospital (1819–1873): Part 4, the Government Takes Over." *JMBRAS* 50, no. 2 (1977): 111–35.

Legg, Stephen. *Spaces of Colonialism: Delhi's Urban Governmentalities*. Malden: Blackwell, 2007.

Lester, Alan. "Imperial Circuits and Networks: Geographies of the British Empire." *History Compass* 4, no. 1 (2006): 124–41.

Li, Tania Murray. "Beyond 'the State' and Failed Schemes." *American Anthropologist* 107, no. 3 (2005): 383–94.
Lim, Ah Poh. "Changes in Landuse in the Former British Military Areas in Singapore." BA (Hons) Thesis, National University of Singapore, 1974.
Lim, Chong Keat. "The Role of the Professional Institute in the Development of Architectural Education." *SIAJ* 83 (1977): 6–8.
Lim, Jee Yuan. *The Malay House: Rediscovering Malaysia's Indigenous Shelter System*. Pulau Pinang: Institut Masyarakat, 1987.
Lim, Jon Sun Hock. "Colonial Architecture and Architects of Georgetown (Penang) and Singapore, between 1786 and 1942." PhD thesis, National University of Singapore, 1990.
——. *The Penang House and the Straits Architect 1887–1941*. Penang: Areca Books, 2015.
Lim, William S. W., and Jiat-Hwee Chang, eds. *Non West Modernist Past: On Architecture and Modernities*. Singapore: World Scientific, 2011.
Lippsmeier, Georg, Walter Kluska, and Carol Gray Edrich. *Tropenbau/Building in the Tropics*. Munich: Callwey, 1969.
Llewelyn-Davies, Richard. "Deeper Knowledge: Better Design." *AJ* 125 (1957): 769–72.
——. "The Education of an Architect." *JRIBA* 68 (1961): 118–20.
Lloyd, Michael. "Design Education in the Third World." *HI* 7, no. 5–6 (1983): 367–75.
Loops, A. L. *Annual Straits Settlements Medical Report for 1925*. Singapore: Government Printing Office, 1926.
Low, Whye Mun. "A History of Tanglin Barracks: The Early Years." *Pointer* 25, no. 4 (1999). Accessed 5 January 2016, http://www.mindef.gov.sg/safti/pointer/back/journals/1999/Vol25_4/10.htm.
Lu, Duanfang. "Introduction: Architecture, Modernity and Identity in the Third World." In *Third World Modernism: Architecture, Development and Identity*, edited by Duanfang Lu, 1–28. London: Routledge, 2010.
——, ed. *Third World Modernism: Architecture, Development and Identity*. London: Routledge, 2010.
Lyttelton, Oliver. "Message from the Secretary of State for the Colonies." *Prefabrication* 1, no. 9 (1954): 6.
Mace, Angela. *The Royal Institute of British Architects: A Guide to Its Archive and History*. London: Mansell Publishing Limited, 1986.
MacGregor, R. B. "A Historical Review of the General Hospital, Singapore." *TMMJ* 8 (1933): 1–12.
MacLeod, Roy. "Introduction to Special Issue on Nature and Empire: Science and the Colonial Enterprise." *Osiris* 15 (2000): 1–13.
——. "Scientific Advice for British India: Imperial Perceptions and Administrative Goals, 1898–1923." *Modern Asian Studies* 9, no. 3 (1975): 343–84.
Mahbubani, Gretchen. *Pastel Portraits*. Singapore: Singapore Coordinating Committee, 1984.
Makepeace, Walter. "The Military Contribution." In *One Hundred Years of Singapore*, edited by Walter Makepeace, Gilbert E. Brooke and Roland St. J. Braddell, 399–402. Singapore: Oxford University Press, 1991 [1921].
Malan, L. N. "Singapore: The Founding of the New Defences." *REJ* 52, no. 2 (1938): 213–35.
Manderson, Lenore. *Sickness and the State: Health and Illness in Colonial Malaya, 1870–1940*. Cambridge: Cambridge University Press, 1996.
Markham, S. F. *Climate and the Energy of Nations*. London: Oxford University Press, 1947 [1942].
Markus, Thomas A. *Buildings and Power: Freedom and Control in the Origin of Modern Building Types*. London: Routledge, 1993.

Markus, Thomas A., and Edwin N. Morris. *Buildings, Climate, and Energy*. London: Pitman Pub., 1980.
Martin, Leslie. "RIBA Conference on Architectural Education: Report by the Chairman." *AJ* 127 (1958): 772–76.
Matthew, Robert. "Foreword." In *Handbook of Commonwealth Architects*, edited by CAA, 5. London: CAA & The Builder, 1965.
Mbembe, Achille. "Necropolitics." *Public Culture* 15, no. 1 (2004): 11–40.
McCallum, H. E. "Report on Blasting Operations at Mount Siloso, Singapore." *PPCRE* IV (1881): 53–57.
McFarlane, Colin. "Governing the Contaminated City: Infrastructure and Sanitation in Colonial and Post-Colonial Bombay." *International Journal of Urban and Regional Research* 32, no. 2 (2008): 415–35.
McLean, W. H., H. J. Channon and H. North-Hunt. *Higher Education in Malaya: Report of the Commission Appointed by the Secretary of State for the Colonies*. London: HMSO, 1939.
McNair, John Frederick Adolphus. *Prisoners Their Own Warders*. Westminster: A. Constable, 1899.
Melosi, Martin V. *The Sanitary City: Urban Infrastructure in America from Colonial Times to the Present*. Baltimore, MD: Johns Hopkins University Press, 2000.
Metcalf, Thomas R. *An Imperial Vision: Indian Architecture and Britain's Raj*. New Delhi: Oxford University Press, 2002 [1989].
Mitchell, Timothy. *Colonising Egypt*. Berkeley: University of California Press, 1991.
Mintz, Sidney W. *Sweetness and Power: The Place of Sugar in Modern History*. New York: Penguin, 1986.
Monmonier, Mark. "Telegraphy, Iconography, and the Weather Map: Cartographic Weather Reports by the United States Weather Bureau, 1870–1935." *Imago Mundi* 40 (1988): 15–31.
Moore, E. C. S. "Sanitary Engineering Notes." *PPCRE* XVII (1892): 1–238.
"Murdering the Soldier – Portman-Street Barracks – the Commissioners' Report." *The Builder* 16, no. 787 (1858): 149–51.
Murfett, Malcolm H., John N. Miksic, Brian P. Farrell, and Ming Shun Chiang. *Between Two Oceans: A Military History of Singapore from First Settlement to Final British Withdrawal*. Singapore: Marshall Cavendish Academic, 2005.
Nalbantoğlu, Gülsüm Baydar "Toward Postcolonial Openings: Rereading Sir Banister Fletcher's 'History of Architecture'." *Assemblage* 35 (1998): 6–17.
Naraindas, Harish. "Poisons, Putrescence and the Weather: A Genealogy of the Advent of Tropical Medicine." *Contributions to Indian Sociology* 30, no. 1 (1996): 1–35.
The Natal Regional Research Committee and The University of Natal. *Symposium on Design for Tropical Living*. Durban: The University of Natal, 1957.
Nelson. "Engineer Details: For the Most Part Collected at Bermuda between April, 1829, and May, 1833." *PCRE* IV (1840): 136–97.
"The New Capitol Theatre Building." *JSSAI* 2, no. 4 (1930): 10–12.
"The New China Building." *JSSAI* 1, no. 2 (1930): 10–12.
"The New K. P. M. Building." *JSSAI* 4, no. 4 (1931): 8–9.
"New Ward for Tan Tock Seng's Hospital." In *PLCSS 1900*, C166–C70. Singapore: Straits Settlements Government Printing Office, 1901.
Nightingale, Florence. "Answers to Written Questions Addressed to Miss Nightingale by the Commissioners." In *Report of the Commissioners Appointed to Inquire into the Regulations Affecting the Sanitary Condition of the Army, the Organization of Military Hospitals, and the Treatment of the Sick and Wounded; with Evidence and Appendix*, edited by The Commissioners. London: George Edward Eyre and William Spottiswoode, 1858.

——. *Observations on the Evidence Contained in the Stational Reports Submitted to Her by the RCSSAI*. London: Edward Stanford, 1863.

Nilsson, Sten. *European Architecture in India 1750–1850*. Translated by Agnes George and Eleonore Zettersten. London: Faber and Faber, 1968.

Notley, D. W. "Some Work of the School of Architecture, University of Singapore." *SIAJ* 59 (1973): 5–7.

Oakley, David. *Tropical Houses: A Guide to Their Design*. London: Batsford, 1961.

Olgyay, Victor, and Aladar Olgyay. *Design with Climate: Bioclimatic Approach to Architectural Regionalism*. Princeton: Princeton University Press, 1963.

Ong, Aihwa. *Neoliberalism as Exception: Mutations in Citizenship and Sovereignty*. Durham, NC: Duke University Press, 2006.

Osborne, Michael A. "Introduction: The Social History of Science, Technoscience and Imperialism." *Science, Technology & Society* 4, no. 2 (1999): 161–70.

Otter, Chris. *The Victorian Eye: A Political History of Light and Vision in Britain, 1800–1910*. Chicago: University of Chicago Press, 2008.

Otto, M. C. "Scientific Humanism." *The Antioch Review* 3, no. 4 (1943): 530–45.

Page, J. K. *Science and Architectural Education: Inaugural Lecture Delivered 1st March 1961*. Sheffield: The University of Sheffield, 1961.

Page, Lincoln. "Singapore." *Architectural Review* 128 (1960): 65–70.

Pain, William. *The Builder's Pocket-Treasure; or, Palladio Delineated and Explained*. London: W. Owen, 1763.

Palladino, Paolo, and Michael Worboys. "Critiques and Contentions: Science and Imperialism." *Isis* 84, no. 1 (1993): 91–102.

Pan, Xingnong, ed. *Xinjiapo Zhinan* (*Singapore Directory*). Singapore: Nanyang Chubanshe (Nanyang Publisher), 1932.

Parkes, Fanny. *Begums, Thugs and Englishmen: The Journals of Fanny Parkes*. Delhi: Penguin Books India, 2002 (1850).

Parkinson, C. Northcote. "Foreword." In *The House in Coleman Street*, edited by The Friends of Singapore, 3. Singapore: The Friends of Singapore, 1958.

——. "The Homes of Malaya." *The Malayan Historical Journal* 2, no. 2 (1955): 123–30.

"Perak Turf Club Extensions Competition." *JSSAI* 1, no. 6 (1930): 10–13.

Pieris, Anoma. *Hidden Hands and Divided Landscapes: A Penal History of Singapore's Plural Society*. Honolulu: University of Hawaii Press, 2009.

——. *Imagining Modernity: The Architecture of Valentine Gunasekara*. Colombo: Stamford Lake & Social Scientists' Association, 2007.

PLCSS 1922. Singapore: Government Printing Office, 1923.

Polanyi, Michael. *Personal Knowledge: Towards a Post-Critical Philosophy*. Chicago: University of Chicago Press, 1958.

Porter, Roy. "The Two Cultures Revisited." *Boundary 2*, 23, no. 2 (1996): 1–17.

Porter, Theodore M. *Trust in Numbers: The Pursuit of Objectivity in Science and Public Life*. Princeton: Princeton University Press, 1995.

Posener, Julius. "Malaya." *Architectural Review* 128 (1960): 59–64.

Potter, Simon J. "Webs, Networks, and Systems: Globalization and the Mass Media in the Nineteenth- and Twentieth-Century British Empire." *Journal of British Studies* 46, no. 3 (2007): 621–46.

Powell, Robert, ed. *Architecture and Identity: Proceedings of the Regional Seminar in the Series Exploring Architecture in Islamic Cultures*. Singapore: Concept Media, 1983.

——. *Ken Yeang: Rethinking the Environmental Filter*. Singapore: Landmark Books, 1989.

——, ed. *Regionalism in Architecture: Proceedings of the Regional Seminar in the Series Exploring Architecture in Islamic Cultures*. Singapore: Concept Media, 1985.

Powell, Robert, and Kheng Soon Tay. *Line, Edge and Shade: The Search for a Design Language in Tropical Asia*. Singapore: Page One Pub., 1997.

Prakash, Gyan. *Another Reason: Science and the Imagination of Modern India*. Princeton: Princeton University Press, 1999.
Prakash, Vikramaditya. *Chandigarh's Le Corbusier: The Struggle for Modernity in Postcolonial India*. Seattle: University of Washington Press, 2002.
Prashad, Vijay. "The Technology of Sanitation in Colonial Delhi." *Modern Asian Studies* 35, no. 1 (2001): 113–55.
Pratt, Mary Louise. *Imperial Eyes: Travel Writing and Transculturation*. London: Routledge, 1992.
"Prefabs at the British Industries Fair." *Prefabrication* 1, no. 8 (1954): 21–26.
Probert, Henry. *The History of Changi*. Singapore: Changi University Press, 2006 [1965].
"Proceedings of Educational Workshop 'Planning and Building for Development' July 1st to 3rd, 1970." London: Department of Development and Tropical Studies, Architectural Association, 1970.
Purcell, Victor. *The Chinese in Modern Malaya*. Singapore: Eastern Universities Press, 1960.
Rabinow, Paul. *French Modern: Norms and Forms of the Social Environment*. Chicago: University of Chicago Press, 1989.
Rabinow, Paul, and Nikolas S. Rose. "Introduction." In *The Essential Foucault: Selections from Essential Works of Foucault, 1954–1984*, edited by Paul Rabinow and Nikolas S. Rose, vii–xxxv. New York: New Press, 2003.
Redfield, Peter. *Space in the Tropics: From Convicts to Rockets in French Guiana*. Berkeley: University of California Press, 2000.
Reiff, Daniel Drake. *Houses from Books: Treatises, Pattern Books, and Catalogs in American Architecture 1738–1950*. University Park, PA: Penn State University Press, 2000.
"Report of the First Asian Regional Conference." *SIAJ* 20 (1968): 6.
"Report of the First Meeting of the Commonwealth Board of Architectural Education (by Courtesy of the RIBA Journal 1966)." *SIAJ* 8 (1967): 10–11.
Report of the Housing Committee Singapore, 1947. Singapore: Government Printing Office, 1947.
Richards, E. P. "Appendix E, Improvement Trust for Singapore: Report for 1921 by Deputy Chairman." In *ARSM 1921*, 92–100. Singapore: The Straits Times Press, 1922.
——. "Appendix H, Improvement Trust for Singapore: Report by Deputy Chairman, May to December 1920." In *ARSM 1920*, 125–27. Singapore: The Straits Times Press, 1921.
RIBA. *Report of the Special Committee on Architectural Education*. London: RIBA, 1946.
The RIBA Joint Committee on the Orientation of Buildings. *The Orientation of Buildings, Being the Report with Appendices of the RIBA Joint Committee on the Orientation of Buildings*. London: RIBA, 1933.
Robinson, D. C. "Towards a Tropical Architecture: The Work of Architects Co-Partnership in Nigeria." *Architectural Design*, April (1959): 128–40.
Rose, Nikolas S. *Powers of Freedom: Reframing Political Thought*. Cambridge: Cambridge University Press, 1999.
Ross, Ronald. *Report of the Malaria Expedition to West Coast of Africa 1899*. Liverpool: Liverpool School of Tropical Medicine, 1900.
——. *Report on the Prevention of Malaria in Mauritius*. London: J & A Churchill, 1908.
Sachs, Wolfgang, ed. *The Development Dictionary: A Guide to Knowledge as Power*. London: Zed Books, 1992.
Said, Edward W. *Culture and Imperialism*. New York: Vintage Books, 1994 [1993].
——. *Orientalism*. New York: Vintage Books, 1994 [1978].
Saint, Andrew. *Architect and Engineer: A Study in Sibling Rivalry*. New Haven: Yale University Press, 2007.
——. *Towards a Social Architecture: The Role of School-Building in Post-War England*. New Haven: Yale University Press, 1987.

Savage, Victor R. *Western Impressions of Nature and Landscape in Southeast Asia*. Singapore: Singapore University Press, 1984.

Sayers, F. R. *Annual Straits Settlements Medical Report for 1926*. Singapore: Government Printing Office, 1927.

Scott-Moncrieff, G. K. "The Design of Soldiers' Barracks." *PPCRE* XXI (1895): 125–36.

Scott, David. "Colonial Governmentality." In *Anthropologies of Modernity*, edited by Jonathan Xavier Inda, 23–49. Malden: Blackwell, 2005 [1999].

Scott, James C. *Seeing Like a State: How Certain Schemes to Improve the Human Condition Have Failed*. New Haven: Yale University Press, 1998.

Scriver, Peter. "Empire-Building and Thinking in the Public Works Department of British India." In *Colonial Modernities: Building, Dwelling and Architecture in British India and Ceylon*, edited by Peter Scriver and Vikramaditya Prakash, 69–92. London and New York: Routledge, 2007.

——. *Rationalization, Standardization, and Control in Design: A Cognitive Historical Study of Architectural Design and Planning in the Public Works Department of British India, 1855–1901*. Delft: Publikatieburo Bouwkunde, Technische Universiteit Delft, 1994.

Scull, Andrew. "A Convenient Place to Get Rid of Inconvenient People: The Victorian Lunatic Asylum." In *Buildings and Society: Essays on the Social Development of the Built Environment*, edited by Anthony D. King, 37–60. London: Routledge & Kegan Paul, 1980.

Seow, Eu-jin. "Architectural Development in Singapore." PhD thesis, University of Melbourne, 1973.

Shove, Elizabeth. *Comfort, Cleanliness and Convenience: The Social Organization of Normality*. Oxford: Berg, 2003.

Siah, U Chin. "The Chinese in Singapore No. II: General Sketch of the Numbers, Tribes, and Avocations of the Chinese in Singapore." *JIAES* 2, no. 1 (1848): 283–90.

Simpson, W. J. *The Principles of Hygiene as Applied to Tropical and Sub-Tropical Climates*. London: John Bale, Sons & Danielsson, 1908.

——. *Report on Sanitary Matters in Various West African Colonies and the Outbreak of Plague in the Gold Coast, Presented to Parliament by Command of His Majesty*. London: HMSO, 1909.

——. *The Sanitary Conditions of Singapore*. London: Waterlow, 1907.

Singapore Housing Commission. *Proceedings and Report of the Commission Appointed to Inquire into the Cause of the Present Housing Difficulties in Singapore and the Steps Which Should Be Taken to Remedy Such Difficulties*. Vol. 1, Singapore: Government Printing Office, 1918.

Singapore Polytechnic. *Annual Report 1959/60*. Singapore: Government Printer, 1961.

——. *Report of the Singapore Polytechnic, Session 1958/59*. Singapore: Government Printer, 1960.

——. *Report of the Singapore Polytechnic, Session 1959/60*. Singapore: Government Printer, 1961.

Smith, Bernard. *European Vision and the South Pacific*. 2nd ed. New Haven: Yale University Press, 1985.

Smith, Cecil C. "Military Contribution." In *PLCSS 1891*, C3–C8. Singapore: Straits Settlements Government Printing Office, 1892.

Smith, T. Roger. "On Buildings for Europeans Occupation in Tropical Climates, Especially India." In *Papers Read at the Royal Institute of British Architects 1867–68*, 197–208, 1868.

Smyth, Captain. "On the Construction of Barracks for Tropical Climates." *PCRE* II (1844 [1838]): 232–37.

Sopandi, Setiadi, and Avianti Armand. *Tropicality Revisited*. Frankfurt: The German Architecture Museum, 2015.

Stanek, Łukasz. "Introduction: The 'Second World's' Architecture and Planning in the 'Third World'." *JoA* 17, no. 3 (2012): 299–307.
——. "Miastoprojekt Goes Abroad: The Transfer of Architectural Labour from Socialist Poland to Iraq (1958–1989)." *JoA* 17, no. 3 (2012): 361–86.
——. "Architects from Socialist Countries in Ghana (1957–67): Modern Architecture and Mondialisation." *JSAH* 74, no. 4 (2015): 416–42.
Stepan, Nancy Leys. *Picturing Tropical Nature*. Ithaca, NY: Cornell University Press, 2001.
Stockdale, Frank, Robert Gardner-Medwin, and Leo de Syllas. "Recent Planning Developments in the Colonies." *JRIBA* 55 (1948): 140–48.
Stockley, E. N. "Barracks." In *The Encyclopedia Britannica: A Dictionary of the Arts, Sciences, Literature and General Information, Vol. 3*, 427–31. Cambridge: Cambridge University Press, 1910.
Stoler, Ann Laura. *Race and the Education of Desire: Foucault's History of Sexuality and the Colonial Order of Things*. Durham, NC: Duke University Press, 1995.
Sudjic, Dejan. "Is That Room Service? Where Am I?" *Observer*, 20 August 2000.
Sutphen, Mary. "Not What, but Where: Bubonic Plague and the Reception of Germ Theories in Hong Kong and Calcutta, 1894–1897." *Journal of the History of Medicine* 52 (1997): 81–113.
Sutterheim, N. "Introduction." In *Symposium on Design for Tropical Living*, edited by The Natal Regional Research Committee and The University of Natal, v–vii. Durban: The University of Natal, 1957.
Swenarton, Mark. *Building the New Jerusalem: Architecture, Housing and Politics, 1900–1930*. Garston, Watford: IHS BRE Press, 2008.
Tan, Han Hoe. "A Study of the Singapore Slum Problem, 1907–41: With Special Reference to the Singapore Improvement Trust." Unpublished Academic Exercise, University of Malaya, 1959.
Tay, Kheng Soon. "Neo-Tropicality or Neo-Colonialism?". *Singapore Architect* 211 (2001): 21.
Taylor, Edward, and Cris Prystay. "Swiss Fight against Tax Cheats Aids Singapore's Banking Quest." *Wall Street Journal*, 6 February 2006.
Taylor, Jeremy. *The Architect and the Pavilion Hospital: Dialogue and Design Creativity in England, 1850–1914*. London: Leicester University Press, 1996.
Taylor, Walter A. "Regional Climate Analyses and Design Data." In *The House Beautiful Climate Control Project: Regional Climate Analyses and Design Data*, edited by American Institute of Architects, 15–16. Washington, D.C.: American Institute of Architects, 1949–52.
Terazaki, T. D. "Environmental Design: Live Cool!". *Dimension: Journal of the Singapore Polytechnic Architectural Society* (1963): i–xxi.
"Third Commonwealth Association of Architects Conference Report." *SIAJ* 34 (1969): 21–23.
Thompson, F. Longstreth. "Suggested Regulations Regarding Density, Proportion of Curtilage to Be Built Upon, and Height of Buildings." *JTPI* 9, no. 8 (1923): 129–42.
Thompson, John D. and Grace Goldin. *The Hospital: A Social and Architectural History*. New Haven: Yale University Press, 1975.
Thomson, John Turnbull. "Account of the Horsburgh Light-House." *JIAES* 4, no. 1 (1852): 376–498.
Tulloch, A. M. "On the Mortality among Her Majesty's Troops Serving in the Colonies During the Years 1844 and 1845." *Journal of the Statistical Society of London* 10, no. 3 (1847): 252–59.
——. "On the Sickness and Mortality among the Troops in the West Indies I." *Journal of the Statistical Society of London* 1, no. 3 (1838): 129–42.

——. "On the Sickness and Mortality among the Troops in the West Indies II." *Journal of the Statistical Society of London* 1, no. 4 (1838): 216–30.

——. "On the Sickness and Mortality among the Troops in the West Indies III." *Journal of the Statistical Society of London* 1, no. 7 (1838): 428–44.

Turnbull, C. M. "McNair, (John) Frederick Adolphus." In *Oxford Dictionary of National Biography*, edited by H. C. G. Matthew and Brian Harrison. Oxford: Oxford University Press, 2005. Online edition, Jan 2008. Accessed 5 January 2016, http://www.oxforddnb.com/view/article/34804.

——. *The Straits Settlements 1826–67: Indian Presidency to Crown Colony*. London: The Athlone Press, 1972.

Turnbull, William. "Practical Essay on the Strength of Cast Iron Beams, Girders, and Columns; in Which the Principles of Calculation Are Exhibited in a Plain and Popular Manner." *PCRE* VI (1843): 77–142.

Turpin, Etienne. "Introduction: Who Does the Earth Think It Is, Now?". In *Architecture in the Anthropocene: Encounters among Design, Deep Time, Science and Philosophy*, edited by Etienne Turpin, 3–10. Ann Arbor, MI: Open Humanities Press, 2013.

Tzonis, Alexander, and Liane Lefaivre. "The Suppression and Rethinking of Regionalism and Tropicalism after 1945." In *Tropical Architecture: Critical Regionalism in the Age of Globalization*, edited by Alexander Tzonis, Bruno Stagno and Liane Lefaivre, 14–49. Chichester: Wiley-Academic, 2001.

Tzonis, Alexander, Liane Lefaivre, and Bruno Stagno, eds. *Tropical Architecture: Critical Regionalism in the Age of Globalization*. Chichester: Wiley-Academic, 2001.

UN Department of Social Affairs. *Survey of Problems of Low Cost Rural Housing in Tropical Areas: A Preliminary Report with Special Reference to Caribbean Areas*. New York: UN Department of Social Affairs, 1950.

UN Tropical Housing Mission. *Low Cost Housing in South and Southeast Asia: Report of Mission of Experts*. New York: UN Department of Social Affairs, 1951.

UN-HABITAT. *State of Asian Cities 2010/11*. Fukuoka: UN-HABITAT, 2010.

——. *State of the World's Cities 2010/2011: Bridging the Urban Divide*. London: Earthscan, 2010.

Unwin, Raymond. *Town Planning in Practice: An Introduction to the Art of Designing City*. New York: Benjamin Blom, 1971 [1909].

Upton, Dell. "Defining the Profession." In *Architecture School: Three Centuries of Educating Architects in North America*, edited by Joan Ockman, 36–65. Washington, D.C. and Cambridge, MA: ACSA & MIT Press, 2012.

——. *Holy Things and Profane: Anglican Parish Churches in Colonial Virginia*. New York; Cambridge, MA: Architectural History Foundation, MIT Press, 1986.

——. "Pattern Books and Professionalism: Aspects of the Transformation of Domestic Architecture in America, 1800–1860." *Winterthur Portfolio* 19, no. 2/3 (1984): 107–50.

URA. *Living the Next Lap: Towards a Tropical City of Excellence*. Singapore: URA, 1991.

van Burgst, Baron H. G. Nahuijs. "A Dutch Account of Singapore." In *Travellers' Singapore: An Anthology*, edited by John Bastin, 13–18. Kuala Lumpur: Oxford University Press, 1994 (1823).

Victoir, Laura. "Hygienic Colonial Residences in Hanoi." In *Harbin to Hanoi: Colonial Built Environment in Asia, 1840 to 1940*, edited by Laura Victoir and Victor Zatsepine, 231–50. Hong Kong: Hong Kong University Press, 2013.

Wakely, Patrick. "Fifty Years of Urban Development: Notes on the History of the Development Planning Unit." In *Sixty Years of Urban Development: A Short History of the Development Planning Unit*, edited by Patrick Wakely and Caren Levy. London: DPU, 2014 (2004).

——. "The Development of a School: An Account of the Department of Development and Tropical Studies of the Architectural Association." *HI* 7, nos. 5–6 (1983): 337–46.

Wallenstein, Sven-Olov. *Biopolitics and the Emergence of Modern Architecture*. New York: Princeton Architectural Press and Buell Center/FORuM Project, 2009.
War Office. *Barrack Synopsis, 1911 Edition*. London: HMSO, 1911.
——. *Barrack Synopsis, 1923 Edition*. London: HMSO, 1923.
——. *Barrack Synopsis, 1931 Edition*. London: HMSO, 1931.
——. *Barrack Synopsis, 1948 Edition*. London: HMSO, 1948.
Ward, B. R. "The School of Estimating and Construction at the S.M.E.". *REJ* 7, no. 1 (1908): 32–42.
——. *The School of Military Engineering, 1812–1909*. Chatham: The Royal Engineers Institute, 1909.
Warren, James Francis. *Rickshaw Coolie: A People's History of Singapore, 1880–1940*. Singapore: Oxford University Press, 1986.
Watson, Chas. M. "Barrack Policy." *REJ* 6, no. 6 (1907): 344–51.
Watson, Malcolm. *Rural Sanitation in the Tropics: Being Notes and Observations in the Malay Archipelago, Panama and Other Lands*. London: J. Murray, 1915.
——. "Twenty-Five Years of Malaria Control in the Malay Peninsula." *British Malaya* 1, no. 9 (1927): 245–50.
Watson, Malcolm, and Mary Sutphen. "Simpson, Sir William John Ritchie." In *Oxford Dictionary of National Biography*, edited by H. C. G. Matthew and Brian Harrison. Oxford: Oxford University Press, 2004. Online edition, Jan 2008, accessed 5 January 2016, http://www.oxforddnb.com/view/article/36106.
Webb, C. G. "An Analysis of Some Observations of Thermal Comfort in an Equatorial Climate." *British Journal of Industrial Medicine* 16 (1959): 297–310.
Webster, J. S. "Hospital Construction." In *Transactions of the Fifth Biennial Congress of the Far Eastern Association of Tropical Medicine Held at Singapore 1923*, edited by A. L. Hoops and J. W. Scharff, 845–63. London: John Bale and Sons and Danielsson, 1924.
Weiler, John. "Army Architects: The Royal Engineers and the Development of Building Technology in the Nineteenth Century." PhD Thesis, University of York, 1987.
Whittaker, Chris. "Building Tomorrow." In *J. D. Bernal: A Life in Science and Politics*, edited by Brenda Swann and Francis Aprahamian, 268–94. London: Verso, 1999.
Williams, Raymond. "Ideas of Nature." In *Problems in Materialism and Culture: Selected Essays*, 67–85. London: Verso, 1980.
Williamson, Thomas. *The East India Vade Mecum*. Vols. 1 and 2, London: Black, Parry, 1810.
Wilson, L. H. "Objectives and Standards of Recognition of Schools." In *CAA 1976 Handbook*, edited by CAA, 61–63. London: CAA, 1976 (1971).
Wilton-Ely, John. "The Rise of the Professional Architect in England." In *The Architect: Chapters in the History of the Profession*, edited by Spiro Kostof, 180–208. New York: Oxford University Press, 1977.
Winslow, C.-E. A., and L. P. Herrington. *Temperature and Human Life*. Princeton: Princeton University Press, 1949.
Winter, Tim. "An Uncomfortable Truth: Air-Conditioning and Sustainability in Asia." *Environment and Planning A* 45 (2013): 517–31.
Wong, Yunn Chii, "Public Works Department Singapore in the Inter-War Years (1919–1941): From Monumental to Instrumental Modernism" Unpublished Research Report, National University of Singapore, 2003.
Woodruff, Charles Edward. *The Effects of Tropical Light on White Men*. New York: Rebman Company, 1905.
Worboys, Michael. "The Discovery of Colonial Malnutrition between the Wars." In *Imperial Medicine and Indigenous Societies*, edited by David Arnold, 208–25. Manchester: Manchester University Press, 1988.

——. "The Imperial Institute: The State and the Development of the Natural Resources of the Colonial Empire, 1887–1923." In *Imperialism and the Natural World*, edited by John M. Mackenzie, 164–86. Manchester: Manchester University Press, 1990.
"Work of the Crown Agents." *The Crown Colonist* 1 (1931): 41–45.
Wright, Gwendolyn. *The Politics of Design in French Colonial Urbanism*. Chicago: University of Chicago Press, 1991.
Yeang, Ken. "Green Design in the Hot Humid Tropical Zone." *In Tropical Sustainable Architecture: Social and Environmental Dimensions*, edited by Joo-Hwa Bay and Boon-Lay Ong. Oxford: Architectural Press, 2006.
Yeoh, Brenda S. A. *Contesting Space: Power Relations and the Urban Built Environment in Colonial Singapore*. Kuala Lumpur: Oxford University Press, 1996.
Zuck, David. "Jeffreys, Julius (1800–1877)." In *Oxford Dictionary of National Biography*, edited by H. C. G. Matthew and Brian Harrison. Oxford: Oxford University Press, 2004. Online edition, May 2007, accessed 5 January 2016, http://www.oxforddnb.com/view/article/14706.

Index

Jiat-Hwee Chang is Assistant Professor in the Department of Architecture, School of Design and Environment, National University of Singapore.

Archi*text* Series
Edited by
Thomas A. Markus and Anthony D. King

"In this masterly account of the evolution of tropical architecture, Jiat-Hwee Chang combines the insights of Foucauldian governmentality with in-depth historical research and a keen understanding of colonial exceptionality... he uncovers the colonial lineage of modern architectural forms and offers a radical reinterpretation of the ancestry of architectural tropicality. While centring on Singapore, Chang's theoretically informed and richly empirical study opens up a wider critical perspective on architectural history across the entire region of South and Southeast Asia."
David Arnold, *Professor Emeritus, University of Warwick, UK*

"Meticulous and rigorous, Jiat-Hwee Chang brings us the first major study convincingly to span Victorian and modern colonial architecture. From colonial bungalows, through barracks, hospitals, public housing, court buildings and shophouses, covering technoscientific research and architectural education, and drawing from rich visual and scientific material, the book provocatively re-draws our understanding of tropical architecture. This is a true 'genealogy', a history of an idea as much as an account of its technologies and architectural manifestations."
Mark Crinson, *Professor of Architectural History, Birkbeck College (London), UK*

A Genealogy of Tropical Architecture traces the origins of tropical architecture to nineteenth-century British colonial architectural knowledge and practices. It uncovers how systematic knowledge and practices on building and environmental technologies in the tropics were linked to military technologies, medical theories and sanitary practices, and were manifested in various colonial building types. It also explores the various ways these colonial knowledge and practices shaped postwar technoscientific research and education in climatic design and modern tropical architecture.

Drawing on the interdisciplinary scholarships on post-colonial studies, science studies, and environmental history, Jiat-Hwee Chang argues that tropical architecture was inextricably entangled with the socio-cultural constructions of tropical nature, and the politics of colonial governance and post-colonial development in the British colonial and post-colonial networks.

By bringing to light new historical materials through formidable research and tracing the history of tropical architecture beyond what is widely considered today as its "founding moment" in the mid-twentieth century, this important and original book revises our understanding of the colonial built environment. It also provides a new historical framework that significantly bears upon contemporary concerns with climatic design and sustainable architecture.

This book is an essential resource for understanding tropical architecture and its various contemporary manifestations. Its in-depth discussion and path-breaking insights will be invaluable to specialists, academics, students and practitioners.

ARCHITECTURE / TROPICAL ARCHITECTURE / ARCHITECTURAL HISTORY

Cover image: Drawing of a ventilating helmet designed by Julius Jeffreys (Source: The Commissioners, The Report of the RCSSAI, Vol. 1, 1863)

Routledge
Taylor & Francis Group
www.routledge.com
Routledge titles are available as eBook editions in a range of digital formats

an **informa** business
ISBN 978-0-415-84078-1
9 780415 840781